1980

ASSASSINATION ON EMBASSY ROW

ASSASSINATION
ON
EMBASSY ROW

by JOHN DINGES
and SAUL LANDAU

PANTHEON BOOKS   NEW YORK

Library of Congress Cataloging in Publication Data

Dinges, John, 1941–
Assassination on Embassy Row.

Includes index.
1. Letelier, Orlando—Assassination.   2. Moffitt, Ronni.   3. Assassination—Washington, D.C.
I.   Landau, Saul,   joint author.   II.   Title.
F3101.L47D56   364.1′524′0924   79–3306
ISBN 0–394–50802–5

Manufactured in the United States of America

FIRST EDITION

For Alejandro Avalos Davidson, a teacher,

and Jorge Müller, a film maker,

two Chilean friends who disappeared

Contents

Illustrations

(Between pages 206 and 207)

President Salvador Allende *(John Dinges)*

Orlando Letelier takes the cabinet oath

Popular Unity campaign poster *(Marcelo Montecino)*

The military coup: troops in the street *(John Dinges);*
arrests *(Marcelo Montecino)*

Letelier's arrest *(Isabel Letelier Private Collection)*

The stadium after the coup *(Marcelo Montecino)*

Pinochet and his generals *(Charles Gerretsen—*
Gamma/Liaison)

Sketch of Letelier at Dawson Island, by Miguel Lawner.
The stone he carved at Dawson to "Isa" *(Miguel Sayago).*
The Dawson drinking cup *(Miguel Sayago)*

Orlando Letelier *(Top: Marcelo Montecino; bottom:*
Benjamin Lourie)

Isabel Margarita Morel de Letelier *(Marcelo Montecino)*
Isabel Letelier teaching Spanish to FBI agents. Orlando
and Isabel Letelier. Young Letelier

Letelier with Nixon, Castro, and Kissinger

The Letelier family. Dancing the *cueca (Marcelo*
Montecino)

Ronni Karpen Moffitt *(Bob Connan)*

Ronni and Michael Moffitt *(Bob Connan)*. Michael Moffitt
(Marcelo Montecino)

Acknowledgments

WE CAN THANK BY NAME only some of those whose generous assistance made this book possible. We owe a special debt of gratitude to many Chileans, in Chile and in exile, who believed in our work and helped us at great personal risk.

Scott Armstrong, Richard Barnet, John Marks, Marcus Raskin, and Peter Weiss provided us with wisdom, counsel, and encouragement. Ralph Stavins, who played a lion's role in the independent investigation by the Institute for Policy Studies, helped us to gain perspective for the research needed in many chapters of the book. Isabel Letelier and Michael Moffitt became the heart and soul of both the independent investigation and the political movement that grew up around the case, one that kept it alive. Their courage and determination in the face of murder and state power make them heroes.

Rebecca Switzer, Jeff Stein, Trin Yarborough, and Bob Borosage devoted many hours to reading and editing portions of the manuscript and offered us tough and useful criticisms. Carolina Kenrick offered invaluable support and assistance during the long writing task.

Our editor, Susan Gyarmati, added lucidity and precision and forced us to make sense out of some of the mysteries that continue to surround the crime.

Kiki Anastasakos, Kate Louise Gottfried, Nina Terrell, Eliana Loveluck, Cynthia Arnson, Ann McWilliams, Peter Kornbluh, Jack Kasofsky, Eddie Becker, David Pion, Rhonda Johnson, Marcelo Montecino, Miguel Sayago, Max Weisenfeld, Joanna Schulman, Winslow Peck, Fred Landis, John Alves, Chris Cole, Peter Almquist, and Rodrigo R. took part in a variety of ways in the investigative work that led to this book.

The Institute for Policy Studies served as our base for writing, and its staff provided us with help and inspiration in countless ways.

To all those who helped us we feel grateful. The content and conclusions, however, are ours alone, and we share exclusive and joint responsibility for them and for any errors.

JOHN DINGES
SAUL LANDAU

Washington, D.C.
March 1980

A Note on Sources

CHILEAN AGENT Michael Vernon Townley described the assassination plot in hundreds of hours of interrogations with FBI agents and prosecutors, in testimony before a federal grand jury, in a long first-person account written as a deposition, and in his week-long appearance as a witness in the January 9–February 14, 1979 trial of three Cuban accomplices. We generally accept the credibility of that account. Other documents we obtained and our interviews of hundreds of persons in the United States, South America, and Europe corroborated many points of Townley's story of the plot and revealed a number of discrepancies and self-serving omissions but no major contradictions that would lead us to doubt its overall accuracy.

The narrative of political events in Chile before and after the assassination is based entirely on our own research and personal knowledge. The most difficult part of our work was the account of the United States investigation leading up to the identification of Townley and his decision to reveal the assassination plot. United States government agencies involved in the case have imposed an extraordinary mantle of secrecy over the actions of United States officials before and after the assassination and over the records and files relating to their actions. As of March 8, 1980, we have received not one piece of paper in response to our Freedom of Information Act requests made to the CIA, FBI/Justice Department, and State Department. Some United States documents in the case were withheld from us here even after they had been made public in court proceedings in Chile. Therefore the sources of our "investigation of the investigation" must remain confidential.

In some cases our interpretations and conclusions differ from those of persons who made extraordinary efforts to help us and to puzzle out with us the unanswered questions. We are deeply appreciative of their help and respectful of their differences with us.

Cast of Characters

ALLENDE, SALVADOR   Elected president of Chile September 1970; killed September 1973

BARCELLA, E. LAWRENCE   Assistant U.S. attorney

BOSCH, ORLANDO   Cuban exile terrorist

BUSH, GEORGE   CIA director who received information about Chilean covert action

CALLEJAS, INÉS (MARIANA)   Wife of Michael Townley and DINA agent

CANETE, RICARDO   Former member of the Cuban Nationalist Movement who became an informer for the FBI

CONTRERAS, JUAN MANUEL   Colonel, then general, who founded and headed DINA, Chile's dreaded secret police

CORNICK, L. CARTER   FBI special agent who coordinated the investigation

CUBAN NATIONALIST MOVEMENT (CNM)   Anti-Castro terrorist organization with a fascist ideology

DINA (DEPARTMENT OF NATIONAL INTELLIGENCE)   Chile's secret police

DRISCOLL, ROBERT   Chile desk officer at the State Department who was informed of the presence of DINA agents

ESPINOZA, PEDRO   Colonel in charge of DINA operations

ENYART, KENNETH   An alias used by Michael Townley

FERNÁNDEZ, ARMANDO   Chilean army captain working for DINA

GUANES, BENITO   Colonel, head of Paraguayan secret police

INSTITUTE FOR POLICY STUDIES (IPS)   A Washington research center where Orlando Letelier and Ronni Moffitt worked

LANDAU, GEORGE W.   U.S. Ambassador to Paraguay in 1976, to Chile in 1977

LEIGHTON, BERNARDO   Exiled Chilean Christian Democrat wounded in Rome in 1975

LETELIER, ISABEL MARGARITA   Wife of Orlando Letelier

LETELIER, ORLANDO   Leader of Chilean exile resistance to General Pinochet in the United States, murdered on Embassy Row

MOFFITT, MICHAEL   IPS associate of Orlando Letelier, married to Ronni Moffitt

MOFFITT, RONNI KARPEN   IPS fund raiser, murdered on Embassy Row

MOSQUEIRA, ROLANDO   Army captain assigned to DINA

NOVO, GUILLERMO   Leader of the North Zone of the Cuban Nationalist Movement

NOVO, IGNACIO   Brother of Guillermo and member of CNM

OTERO, ROLANDO   Cuban exile terrorist who infiltrated DINA

PAPPALARDO, CONRADO "TERUCO"   Paraguayan President Stroessner's top aide

PAZ, VIRGILIO   CNM terrorist

PETERSEN SILVA, HANS   Name used by Townley to enter the United States in 1976

PINOCHET, AUGUSTO   Chilean dictator who led the military coup September 11, 1973

PRATS, CARLOS   Pinochet's predecessor as commander of Chile's armed forces; murdered in Buenos Aires in September 1974

PROPPER, EUGENE   Assistant U.S. attorney

RIVERO, FELIPE   Founder of the Cuban Nationalist Movement

RIVEROS, RENÉ   DINA officer

ROMERAL JARA, ALEJANDRO   Name used by Fernández in Paraguay, by Mosqueira in Washington

ROSS, ALVIN   CNM terrorist

SCHERRER, ROBERT   FBI agent; legal attaché in Buenos Aires

SCHNEIDER, RENÉ   Head of the Chilean Army, assassinated in 1970

SUÁREZ, JOSÉ DIONISIO   CNM terrorist

TOWNLEY, JAY VERNON   Businessman, father of Michael Townley

TOWNLEY, MICHAEL VERNON   Born in Waterloo, Iowa; a DINA agent with special skills

WACK, LARRY   FBI special agent

WALTERS, VERNON A.   Deputy director of the CIA informed of Chilean covert action

WILLIAMS ROSE, JUAN   Name used by Townley in Paraguay, by Riveros in Washington

WILSON SILVA, ANDRÉS   Michael Townley's DINA alias

ASSASSINATION
ON EMBASSY ROW

THE ACT

SEPTEMBER 9, 1976. At Kennedy International Airport the arrival of LAN-Chile Airlines flight 142 from Santiago was announced. Minutes later a tall, fair-haired man in his thirties handed his passport to a U.S. Immigration official. It was mid-morning. A taut half-smile masked the traveler's nervousness as he watched the official page through the passport, remove the official entrance form the traveler had filled out on the plane, and glance up from the passport photo to the man before him. Many times in many airports the traveler had seen officials go through the identical motions: verify the likeness of the photo, check the name, stamp the passport.

The official absorbed the facts he needed in a second: name, Hans Petersen Silva (the last name a matronymic, according to Spanish custom); nationality, Chilean; official Chilean passport and official visa indicating Chilean government business. A cut above the average Latin American tourist—probably a government expert, deserving of more than routine courtesy, the official may have thought. He began the routine turning of pages in the foot-thick loose-leaf volume called the "lookout book." The traveler stiffened imperceptibly. His passport wouldn't appear in the book—unless something had gone wrong.

U.S. Immigration checks all arriving passengers' names against the several thousand names listed alphabetically and phonetically in the lookout book. Each listing appears there at the request of a

United States government agency—the Federal Bureau of Investigation, the Drug Enforcement Administration, the Central Intelligence Agency. Alongside the names, coded instructions indicate the action required: F-1, notify interested agency; F-2, search; F-3, bar entry and arrest.

The traveler's legs felt rubbery as it became obvious that the immigration official had matched his name with a listing in the lookout book. "He examined my passport several times, reread the inscription, and finally shrugged his shoulders and returned it to me," he would testify after his discovery. "This left me quite shaken since I thought that the inscription could refer to some other Hans Petersen or could be something referring to the passport I was carrying. From that moment on, I was quite jumpy."

He placed the red passport in an inside pocket and headed toward the customs area. LAN-Chile crew members greeted him as he joined them and passed through customs without inspection. Some of the crew had known him for years. They thought his name was Andrés Wilson. Beyond the luggage checkout barrier he recognized Fernando Cruchaga, a New York–based LAN-Chile official.

They did not acknowledge each another until they had left the customs area. Tradecraft. It had been violated too many times on this mission already. The traveler touched the pocket where he had hidden the flash caps he called "electric matches." He had not tested them, and this made him uneasy at the prospect of having to use them on this trip. Hidden in a medicine bottle in his shaving kit were two grams of lead trinitrite powder—in that quantity it could blow a man's hand off. He had violated his own rules, his professional standards, by smuggling explosives. His superiors had not allowed him sufficient time to do it another way. He despised haste.

Cruchaga embraced him and addressed him as Andrés. With Cruchaga was Enrique Gambra, the New York director of LAN-Chile. The three men spoke Spanish as they walked to an airport restaurant near the LAN offices.

The men had something to eat. Gambra left. Then the traveler gave Cruchaga the name of the man he had expected to meet on arrival. Had the man appeared? "Yes," Cruchaga later testified, "a man approached me because I had my ID from LAN-Chile on my pocket, and he said, 'Is Andrés Wilson on the aircraft?' I said, 'Yes. What's your name?' He mentioned a name that I think was Fáundez, something like that."

Hans Petersen Silva, alias Juan Andrés Wilson, alias Kenneth Enyart, alias Juan Williams Rose, was on a mission to arrange the assassination of Orlando Letelier. The traveler's real name was Michael Vernon Townley. The man he was to meet was Captain Armando Fernández, alias Armando Fáundez Lyon. Both men were experienced operatives from the External Section of DINA, Chile's secret police.

"When I met Captain Fernández. he had various suitcases and several tennis rackets," Townley later wrote. Fernández was accompanied by two women, one his sister, the other an "extremely well dressed and well groomed" companion carrying a fashion magazine. Fernández and Townley politely left the two women with Cruchaga.

Once they were alone, "Captain Fernández gave me one sheet of paper which contained a sketch of Letelier's residence and employment as well as written information setting forth a description of Letelier's automobile and his wife's automobile." The two discussed in whispers and short phrases Letelier's daily movements at work in Washington and in the Maryland suburb where he lived. A group of rabbis passed them in the terminal lobby close to the LAN-Chile lounge. Townley listened to Fernández' report, asked questions, and filed each detail in his mind. He studied the drawing, the license-plate numbers, and the addresses, memorized them, and destroyed the papers. From a secret compartment in his wallet he removed Orlando Letelier's photograph, looked at it, and replaced it. Others might have to refer to it later, though he himself knew it well. The two men talked for more than an hour.

Fernández' mission was now over. For fifteen days he had been in the United States gathering "preoperative intelligence" on the target. Townley's mission, to organize the hit team and ensure the hit, had begun.

After the meeting, Cruchaga ushered Fernández and his fashionable companion, a DINA agent using the alias Liliana Walker, into the LAN-Chile first-class lounge.* Their flight to Chile wouldn't depart until II:00 P.M. The rabbis were still wandering back and forth in the airport lobby.

Townley found Cruchaga again and asked his help in renting a car. DINA had provided him with a false passport and an international driver's license in Petersen's name, but no credit cards. Haste. Cruchaga obliged. As LAN assistant manager he vouched for Petersen's credit, and Townley left a $200 cash deposit with Hertz.

As he waited, Townley's eyes scanned like radar, picking up people and objects. The disconcerting incident at the immigration counter, the official's too-casual attitude, had put his antennae on alert. Two men loitering near the LAN-Chile lounge could have been FBI; he had noticed them several times now. Townley had good reason to feel insecure on this mission. That fiasco in Paraguay haunted him. He hated loose ends, sloppiness, imprecision.

In the car, he took a long look in his rear-view mirror. "After assuring myself that I was not under surveillance, I proceeded through Lincoln Tunnel to New Jersey, where I checked into a motel . . . using the identity of Hans Petersen. I telephonically contacted Virgilio Paz. . . ." He made a dinner date for that evening with Paz and his wife. Then he made a collect call to his sister Linda, who lived in nearby Tarrytown, New York.

Townley met Virgilio and his wife, Idania, at the Bottom of the Barrel Restaurant, a Cuban exile hangout in Union City, New Jersey. The town has a Cuban exile population of some 50,000. Paz and his wife called Townley Andrés Wilson; they beat him at an electronic game; during dinner they discussed family and friends. Paz had recently been Townley's house guest in Santiago.

"During dinner with Paz I conveyed my desire to speak with Guillermo Novo Sampol concerning an unspecified matter. I then returned to my hotel."

. . .

---

*Agustín "Duney" Edwards, one of Chile's most prominent banking and publishing figures, shared the lounge with the two DINA agents and returned to Santiago on the same LAN-Chile flight that night.

HE HAD TO FINISH composing his speech by noon. After dressing hurriedly, he gulped coffee and said goodbye, patting Alfie, the sheepdog with hair over his eyes, who followed him outside to the blue Chevelle.

Orlando Letelier gunned the engine and headed out of Ogden Court, a quiet cul-de-sac in Bethesda, Maryland, and onto River Road, a main artery into Washington, D.C. The Leteliers' neighborhood, populated by professionals and business people living in comfortable split-level homes, evoked stability and shelter.

Letelier was thinking and planning as he turned right onto 46th Street and drove toward Massachusetts Avenue. There were other ways to drive from home to his Dupont Circle office, but since returning to Washington he used the same Massachusetts Avenue route he had taken habitually during his years at the Inter-American Development Bank and the Chilean Embassy. The embassy had been his home for three years, but he wasn't welcome there now. The present occupants represented the military junta that on September 11, 1973, had bombed and machine-gunned their way to power, overthrowing the elected government of Salvador Allende, of which Letelier was a member.

Letelier had chosen Washington as the ideal base from which to fight against the military dictatorship. A week before, an article by him in *The Nation* had argued that the junta's systematic human rights violations were inextricably linked to the United States–sponsored "Chicago School" economic model imposed on Chile by the junta. The article had received favorable comments from Letelier's United States colleagues. He was trying to arrange to have it circulated in Chile, where it could provide ammunition to the regime's opponents. That was one of the items on his day's agenda. Top priority, though, was work on the speech he would deliver at the Madison Square Garden concert on September 10, a commemoration and protest marking the third anniversary of the coup.

He turned left from Q Street into the alley bordering the Institute for Policy Studies. A truck blocked the entrance to his parking space. He looked back across the street toward the sidewalk tables of the Rondo Café. A couple, engrossed in each other, were drinking coffee. Several days before, Juan Gabriel Valdés, Orlando's co-worker at the institute and political colleague, had mentioned seeing a man at the Rondo who "had the DINA look." Perhaps Juan Gabriel was right, Letelier thought. But what could DINA do besides watch? Maybe rob or harass? What would they dare do here in the capital city of their most important international supporters? Letelier had often told his friends that inside the United States he felt safe from DINA, despite the threats. He had dismissed Juan Gabriel's apprehensions. Paranoia was a state of mind he could ill afford. It led to paralysis.

He walked toward his office, passing two white-clad waitresses, their high turbans bobbing, members of the Oriental sect that ran the Golden Temple Restaurant nearby.

It was exactly two years since he was released from concentration camp. He saw his reflection in the mirrorlike window of IPS, tall, erect, meticulously dressed in a beige summer suit. He smiled at the image of the dashing businessman, the diplomat. Bizarre. He had first come to know about IPS when, as ambassador, he had found it a source of solid support for the programs of Chile's Popular Unity government. Now IPS had become his base of operation, since shortly after his release from prison.

IPS had named him director of the Transnational Institute, its international program. He had just returned from his third trip that year to Amsterdam, the European seat of the Transnational Institute, and as usual the trip had afforded him an opportunity to meet with other exile leaders and with European political leaders.

As he walked up the two flights of stairs to his office, he began to rehearse phrases for the anniversary speech. Three years since the coup. Two years since my release.

He had survived a year in one concentration camp after another, the first one on Dawson Island, a cold and barren rock in the stormy Strait of Magellan, only a few hundred miles from Antarctica. There he had lost forty pounds. When he left, the camp commander had warned him that "General Pinochet will not and does not tolerate activities against his government." The military government, the officer declared, could deliver punishment "no matter where the violator lives."

. . .

SEPTEMBER 10, 1976. Just beyond Union City's only Sears Roebuck store, Michael Townley met two Cubans in their late thirties. The Cuatro Estrellas Restaurant served Cuban fare and attracted large numbers of midday shoppers. Guillermo Novo and José Dionisio Suárez knew the waitresses there. They also knew Townley—as Andrés Wilson, agent for DINA. They had worked with him before. As Latin American custom demanded, the men went through the amenities of asking about families and recalling past good times before they got down to the business at hand.

"At this luncheon," Townley later wrote, "I outlined my DINA mission to assassinate Letelier and requested the assistance of the Cuban Nationalist Movement."

Novo and Suárez weren't surprised. Phone calls from Townley from Chile in recent weeks had alerted them that DINA had another job for them. But they had to be convinced. They began to complain about the Pinochet government's shabby treatment of some of their comrades in the anti-Castro Cuban exile movement. But their arguments were half-hearted. They were hero-worshippers, and Pinochet was their hero. He had led the coup that eliminated what they considered a communist regime—precisely what the Cuban Nationalists had been trying so long and unsuccessfully to pull off against the Castro government. After the coup, the Cubans began to call Chile their "darling." But there had been an ugly incident that marred the relationship, and Novo, as head of the North Zone of the Cuban Nationalist Movement, demanded the satisfaction of a full explanation.

The Cubans complained that Chile had given safe haven to two Cuban terrorists, Orlando Bosch and Rolando Otero, both fugitives from the FBI, only to betray them. Otero had been turned over directly to FBI agents aboard a plane headed for Miami—and jail. And Bosch, after spending more than a year in Chile, was informed while outside the country that Chile had issued a warrant for his arrest.

Novo reminded Townley that his own CNM, Bosch's group, Cuban Action (Acción Cubana), and Otero's group, the Cuban National Liberation Front (Frente Nacional de Liberación Cubana— FNLC) had joined together just two months before in a formal alliance, the Commando of United Revolutionary Organizations (Comando de Organizaciones Revolucionarias Unidas—CORU), to coordinate "militant" actions.

How can we help you, Novo objected, when you treat our people badly? Townley explained the Chilean position: Otero had entered Chile under his own name and passport. His whereabouts were known to the FBI and couldn't be hidden after the fact. Novo argued that DINA should have killed Otero rather than turn him over to the FBI. Townley was ingratiating. The Bosch matter, he said, wasn't even handled by DINA. Finally Novo and Suárez agreed to get back to him on the new DINA request. That night they would have their regular Friday meeting of the leaders of the CNM. The matter would be presented to them, then they would come to Town-ley's hotel to hear him make his case. Their manner, however, indicated that they—Novo and Suárez—were interested in the operation and would argue in favor of DINA's request to the larger meeting.

ORLANDO and Isabel Margarita Letelier set off on their drive to New York City. Isabel read and edited the text of Orlando's speech for that evening's Madison Square Garden commemoration of the Chilean coup. "In the name of our dead ones," the speech began.

Orlando and Isabel discussed the program, which would feature Joan Baez, and guessed at how many people would attend. They talked about house and family affairs and recalled good times and bad together in Chile and the United States. They stopped for coffee at Howard Johnson's. Orlando drank coffee and chain-smoked all day; his office always had an electric percolator and instant coffee. Sometimes with the coffee he took a Valium tablet. At age forty-four he felt surges of uncontrollable energy, the kind that allowed him to juggle many different projects within the course of a day and to move back and forth between professional and social activities with ease.

The couple drove north through Maryland and Delaware and into New Jersey in the late morning hours. Shortly after arriving in

New York and checking into the Algonquin Hotel, they received a call from a United Press International reporter, who read Letelier a wire dispatch just received from Chile. The military government, it said, had revoked his Chilean citizenship. He was accused of "carrying out in foreign lands a publicity campaign aimed at bringing about the political, economic and cultural isolation of Chile." His "ignoble and disloyal attitude," the decree continued, "made him deserving of the maximum . . . moral sanction contemplated by our juridical order . . . the loss of the Chilean nationality."

Letelier listened, more shocked and hurt than he would admit. He asked the reporter to read the whole cable. General Pinochet and all his ministers had signed the decree, but no other members of the military junta. "In the concrete case of his activities in Holland," it said, "he [Letelier] has incited port and transportation workers of that country to declare a boycott against goods destined for or originating from Chile and has influenced its government to hinder or prevent the investment of Dutch capital in Chile." The reporter offered one more detail: the decree had been published that day in Chile's Official Gazette, but it was dated three months earlier—June 7, 1976.

Visibly upset, Letelier sat down to rewrite his speech. He paused, looking up at a group of friends who had gathered in the hotel room. "Can you imagine," he asked, "that they have done something only the Nazis have done?" Yet it wasn't really surprise that Letelier was suffering but shock, more intense and painful because, deep down, he had felt it coming. He knew that his public denunciations and lobbying against the junta would provoke, if not this reaction, then something like it. He told friends later that he felt annoyed with himself for letting himself react so emotionally, so personally, to what he realized intellectually was the illegitimate act of an illegitimate government.

That night, as keynote speaker, from the stage of Madison Square Garden's Felt Forum, he condemned again the junta's reign of terror. Some five thousand people filled the hall. "From the very moment that that group of generals, serving the most reactionary economic groups, decided three years ago to declare war against the Chilean people and to occupy our country," he said, "an impressive worldwide movement of solidarity with the Chilean people has emerged. This vast solidarity movement has expressed, from the most diverse ideological and political perspectives, the revulsion of the civilized world against the barbaric and brutal violation of all human rights by the Chilean military junta . . . the most repressive regime the world has known since the destruction of fascism and Nazism in Europe."

In the middle of the speech he proclaimed his defiance. "Today," he said slowly, changing his tone, "Pinochet has signed a decree in which it is said that I am deprived of my nationality. This is an important day for me. A dramatic day in my life in which the action of the fascist generals against me makes me feel more Chilean than ever. Because *we* are the true Chileans, in the tradition of O'Higgins, Balmaceda, Allende, Neruda, Gabriela Mistral, Claudio Arrau, and Víctor Jara; and they—the fascists—are the enemies of Chile, the traitors who are selling our country to foreign interests."

Raising his voice in anger, he continued, "I was born a Chilean, I am a Chilean, and I will die a Chilean. They, the fascists, were born traitors, live as traitors, and will be remembered forever as fascist traitors."

MICHAEL TOWNLEY, a few miles away across the Hudson River in Union City, New Jersey, was aware that Letelier was speaking at Madison Square Garden at that moment. Tradecraft dictated that he stay away. Some of the Chilean immigrants and exiles living in New York might have recognized Townley. Among them was his stepson, Ronnie Ernest. Other agents from the Chilean diplomatic mission to the United Nations could be counted on to cover Letelier's activities that night, Townley knew.

Besides, Townley was waiting for the arrival of the members of the political directorate of the Cuban Nationalist Movement. He was staying in the Chateau Renaissance Motel, just outside Union City, registered under the name Hans Petersen. About midnight, seven men filed into his room. Two of them were Guillermo Novo and José Dionisio Suárez. Later he became vague about the identity of the others. They had drinks; Townley had set up a bar with whiskey and rum. He laid out DINA's plan. The CNM would provide men to assassinate Orlando Letelier in Washington. The leftists would undoubtedly scream DINA, but there would be no proof. In exchange, DINA would continue to provide a safe haven in Chile for fugitive Cuban exiles and would allow them to make use of a DINA farm in the south of Chile; they would be able to train their men there if needed. Instruction from DINA experts would be available from time to time, but Townley could not guarantee that. The CNM would have the distinction within the Cuban exile community of being associated with the Pinochet government.

They bargained; the atmosphere was charged. The Cuban leaders again brought up the Otero and Bosch matters. Townley cajoled them. They said they were not just anybody's gun for hire, but a political movement. Their primary motives for cooperating with DINA were political: their agreement with DINA's project to physically eliminate communists, and their desire to enhance their own political stature within the world anticommunist movement.

Townley later said he did not recall the name of the portly middle-aged physician who spoke up against CNM involvement in the assassination. Townley said the man spoke in a whining fashion and resembled a Chilean television commentator. Guillermo Novo argued in favor of assisting in the DINA mission. Suárez, although still critical of the Chilean government's stance in the Otero and Bosch affairs, indicated his inclination to do the job. He loved action.

"At the termination of the meeting in my motel room," Townley said later, "I was convinced that the CNM would collaborate with DINA in assassinating Letelier. . . . Novo and Suárez, as the principal leaders of the CNM, were in favor . . . and . . . any objection that any other CNM members might have would bear no weight. . . ."

Townley claimed that he did not know exactly why Letelier had been selected as a DINA target, nor did he ask. He had heard that Letelier had plans for organizing a coalition government in exile; but that was not his concern. Townley saw himself as an exemplary soldier, an officer without uniform, without the pomp of official rank. In pay, prestige, and perquisites he considered himself the equivalent of a major. He liked to receive difficult orders and to rely on his imagination and intelligence in carrying them out.

To kill Letelier by an unspecified method with the assistance of the CNM: that was the way Townley described his orders from his DINA superior, Colonel Pedro Espinoza. "Try to make it seem innocuous, but the important point is to get it done." Townley had brought the electric matches and the small quantity of lead trinitrite as gifts for the CNM, to overcome their resentment of the way Otero and Bosch had been handled. Now he felt he had succeeded in patching up a potentially ugly situation. Guillermo Novo appeared to have believed his explanation about Otero, and to care less about the Bosch affair. He would try to make it up to the CNM when he returned to Chile; he thought their arguments had some merit. He felt comfortable with them. They shared the same values, the same vocational skills (although less developed than Townley's), and the same *modus operandi.*

After the meeting, Townley went with Novo and Suárez to the Bottom of the Barrel bar. They didn't discuss the assassination, but he sensed that they were celebrating the conclusion of a deal. At the bar Novo introduced Townley to a comrade, Alvin Ross. Ross, paunchy, muscular, a blackjack dealer at Cuba's Tropicana nightclub before the revolution, had heard of the famous "Mr. Wilson" who was Novo's contact with the Chileans, and held him in awe. Later, Ross would describe his meetings with "Wilson" in a typewritten report to an associate. He said that he and Townley talked about stereos and the problems Ross was having with his set. Townley, Ross wrote, promised to help him fix it if he got a chance.

SEPTEMBER 11–14, 1976. Townley didn't waste time thinking about how he would assassinate Letelier. As a seasoned traveler, he was bent on taking full advantage of his duty time in the New York area. After spending some time with his sister Linda and her family in Tarrytown, he returned his rented car to Kennedy Airport.

As he expected, after the Chateau Renaissance Motel meeting he received formal word from Guillermo Novo that the CNM had decided to assist DINA in murdering Letelier. But, Novo informed him, because of concern about DINA's fidelity to the principles of cooperation with the CNM, Townley would have to accompany Virgilio Paz on the mission. Suárez would also help with the job. Townley's orders from Espinoza were that he should not be in the country when the actual hit was made. But he had no control over that now. In any case, he concluded, his presence would ensure that the job would be completed, and that, Espinoza had said, was "the bottom line."

Arrangements had to be made to accommodate the change in plans. Still concerned about the immigration official's hesitation over his Hans Petersen identity, Townley decided to continue the mission using a set of false United States documents made out in the name of Kenneth Enyart. He called his wife, Inés, collect from a public phone and asked her to send the Kenneth Enyart papers to him with a pilot on the next LAN-Chile flight. Then he contacted DINA directly and, using a simple code, explained that the assassination would be carried out but that it would be necessary for him to participate directly. A DINA official informed him that the changes had been approved by Condor personally. Townley understood.

Townley had time. Suárez and Paz, who had been designated by Novo to go to Washington, were busy for a few days. Townley wrote, "I was informed by Novo that the CNM was engaged in some other operation which required their immediate attention." Townley gave the Cuban exiles a shopping list for building the bomb.

THE MORNING after his Madison Square Garden appearance Letelier had breakfast with Rose Styron of Amnesty International, a human rights organization. "He was very depressed over the decree," she said later. "It obviously meant a lot to him to be a Chilean, more than I ever would have thought. He referred to a letter from his family that he had received a short time before in which he was told that there had been a debate within the military government between 'hards' and 'softs'—whether to kill him or do something less. He told me, 'I suppose this decree means the softs won the debate.' "

Back in Washington a few days later, Letelier told his IPS colleagues Juan Gabriel Valdés and Saul Landau that he was planning to travel to Cuba in a few days. Landau gave Letelier a letter to take to a friend in Havana. Valdés also gave Letelier an envelope, finally making good on a long-overdue promise to a Cuban official for some research on Christian Democratic movements. Letelier placed the envelopes in his briefcase and promised to deliver them. He gathered his Cuba files so that he could review them on the plane, and put them in his briefcase along with the articles he always carried: aspirin, a sleep shade, address book and itinerary.

Cuba was one of the few locations where high officials of the Chilean exile movement could safely meet and plan strategy. A meeting of Letelier's Socialist Party was planned, with Carlos Altamirano, the party's secretary-general, Clodomiro Almeyda, head of the Popular Unity coalition of Chilean leftist parties, and Beatriz Allende, party treasurer. Married to a Cuban government official, she had been living in Cuba since the coup in Chile and the death of her father, Salvador Allende.

MIDNIGHT, SEPTEMBER 15, 1976. Virgilio Paz and Townley drove in Paz's rust-colored Volvo to a house in Union City where Guillermo Novo and Dionisio Suárez awaited them. Novo handed Townley a paper bag. As Paz drove on to the New Jersey Turnpike, Townley checked the contents of the bag: a detonating cord; a small piece of grey puttylike explosive known as plastique, or C-4 compound; a package containing TNT. Earlier in the day, Paz had given him a remote-control detonator that looked familiar; it was one that Townley himself had constructed months before in Santiago by modifying a radio paging device. Paz was carrying a pistol.

The 120-mile New Jersey Turnpike merged into its Delaware equivalent. After a coffee stop the two men continued through the dark morning hours from Delaware into Maryland. At dawn they approached the District of Columbia and headed for Letelier's suburban neighborhood. Before eating or sleeping Townley wanted to check out firsthand the surveillance information given him by Captain Armando Fernández at Kennedy Airport. They drove around, surveying the parallel streets, entrances, and exits, entered Ogden Court, and circled back out, after getting a look at the Letelier house and the two cars in its driveway. After breakfast at a twenty-four-hour diner in Bethesda, they checked into the Rhode Island Avenue Holiday Inn, half a mile from the Institute for Policy Studies, where Letelier worked.

SEPTEMBER 17, 1976. Letelier drove from his Bethesda home to the institute. Waiting at the Roy Rogers Restaurant on River Road, Townley and Paz spotted Letelier's Chevelle and followed it at a distance. Townley commented to Paz that Fernández had mistakenly designated the Chevelle as Isabel's car. Letelier drove faster than the traffic flow that morning, and the men lost him for a few blocks. When they arrived at the IPS building, he had already parked his car in the alley and entered his office.

Townley and Paz lounged at a sidewalk table at the Rondo Café, watching the movement in and out of the institute. Like Fernández, they failed to realize that Letelier's office was not in the main building—but no matter. They left the Rondo and drove to Sears on Wisconsin Avenue, where they bought what appeared to the Sears clerk to be items for baking: aluminum baking pans and cookie sheets. Then they moved on to a different department and bought several rolls of black electrical tape and rubber gloves. While the Volvo's tank was being filled at the Sunoco station farther up Wisconsin Avenue, Townley recalled, Paz phoned Suárez in New Jersey to tell him that "the preparatory surveillance on Letelier had been completed and that all that remained to carry out Letelier's murder was to construct the bomb and to place it on Letelier's automobile."

IN THE EARLY afternoon, Letelier drove to Washington's National Airport, parked his car, and caught a shuttle to New York.

SEPTEMBER 18, 1976. José Dionisio Suárez drove to Washington in his late-model American car. At a McDonald's restaurant on New York Avenue he met the other two men. He lent Townley more than $100 because Townley had already spent more than Fernández had given him for the mission. Paz and Townley checked out of the

Holiday Inn and into the Regency Congress Inn on New York Avenue. Suárez took a room in a different motel nearby and went to sleep for the afternoon. Paz and Townley meanwhile made more purchases at Radio Shack, an electronic appliances chain store: wire cutters, needlenose pliers, a soldering iron, slide switches, and a lever switch.

They had planned to make the bomb at a leisurely pace the next day, a Sunday, to place it that night, and to detonate it Monday morning while Letelier drove to work. Suárez, however, pressured them into changing their plans. He arrived in Washington worried about his livelihood; he had just lost his job at a car dealership and was about to begin a new one back in New Jersey on Monday afternoon. So instead of waiting until morning, Paz and Townley returned to New York Avenue directly from Radio Shack to begin work. The three ate a light supper at the Regency Congress. They joked with a middle-aged, greying waitress who had recently lost sixty pounds on a water diet.

After dinner all three went to Paz and Townley's motel room and began to construct the bomb, using the TNT, the plastique, and the components purchased at Sears and Radio Shack. Suárez provided a blasting cap, and Townley added one of his custom-made electric matches to the bomb as well. Townley shaped the plastique to fit the eight-inch-square baking pan; the fit wasn't quite right.

AT 8:30 P.M. Isabel and Orlando Letelier left their house, where a festive and freewheeling party had just disbanded. It was Chilean Independence Day. Orlando had returned from New York in the afternoon. The guests drank jugs of red wine and ate *empanadas,* the traditional Chilean meat or cheese pastry. Letelier played the guitar and sang, and danced the *cueca*—a Chilean folk dance—with Isabel. The middle finger of his left hand hurt him when he played the guitar, one of the physical legacies of his year at Dawson Island.

The Leteliers arrived at the public Chilean Independence Day celebration, held at the community center of the racially mixed neighborhood where most of Washington's Latin American population lives. They smiled, shook hands, said the proper words. A man walked in—"just off the street," he said—and tried to lure Isabel into an argument by defending Pinochet. Some of the young people shouted that he was a provocateur, but Isabel maintained her composure and prevented the incident from turning ugly. At eleven the couple said their goodbyes and set off for home.

TOWNLEY ADDED the final touches to the bomb as Paz held the parts in place for him. Suárez read and talked. Townley planned to place the bomb under the driver's seat; he molded the plastique to blow the full explosive force directly upward.

At about midnight he felt satisfied with his handiwork. The three left the motel in Paz's Volvo and stopped by the train station; Townley went to the ticket window to find out if there were any trains leaving for the New York area in the early morning hours. There were none.

"During the ride to Letelier's house," he wrote, "I was informed by Paz and Suárez that they expected me to place the device on the car as they wished to have a DINA agent, namely myself, directly tied to the placing of the device."

Townley kept quiet. He carried the bomb under his dark blue sweatshirt and wore corduroy pants. He hadn't planned on getting his pants dirty, but he had weighed the alternatives and decided he would have to tape the bomb himself.

Paz drove into the street parallel to Ogden Court. Townley walked from behind two houses into the turn-around area of the cul-de-sac and surveyed the block. People were entering a neighboring house, "so I turned around, returning to the parallel street, and walked up the hill on this parallel street, until I met Paz and Suárez, at which time we drove around to take up some time and then returned to the entrance of Letelier's street, where I was dropped off at the top of the hill."

On one side of the Leteliers lived an FBI agent; on the other, a Foreign Service officer. As Townley walked down the hill, some dogs barked, then stopped. Television screens glowed greyly through windows.

Letelier's car was parked in the driveway, nose in. Townley

walked directly to the car, lay down on his back on the driver's side, pulled up his blue sweatshirt to expose the bomb, put his tools in accessible positions, and slid under the car. The space was small, Townley large. Moving as little as possible, he attached the bomb to the crossbeam with black electrical tape, occasionally flicking on a pencil flashlight to check its position.

Footsteps. Townley froze, trying to control his breathing. Not more than two inches separated him from the car chassis. The footsteps faded. He began to run tape from the speedometer cable to the explosive. What had seemed like an ample supply of tape now appeared scanty. He didn't want the bomb to slip or fall off.

He heard the sound of an engine: a car was approaching with its radio on. He stopped again, perspiration now pouring down his face and soaking his hands and body. The radio became louder; it was a police band. Townley fought to stay calm. The radio got still louder; now he could see the tires from the corner of his eye. But the car moved on, turned around in the cul-de-sac, and picking up speed, left the block. Townley flicked the flashlight on. The bomb was firmly attached, even though he would have preferred to run more tape around the crossbeam. He began to slide out. But had he taped the slide switch into the "on" position? He might have covered it in the "off" or "safety" position. He slid back under and felt, trying to remember which side was on and which off. He found the nub; it was off. He pushed it until it clicked, then pressed the tape into the groove with his finger to prevent the switch from falling back. But electrical tape is pliant and may not hold the switch, he thought.

Lack of time could lead to mistakes. Paz and Suárez had insisted that he place the bomb personally and that he do it that night. Townley felt a chill enter his sweat-laden body as he walked up the hill out of Ogden Court.

The Cubans picked him up on the deserted corner and headed slowly onto River Road. Townley told them of his uncertainty about the switch being in the correct position.

At the motel, Townley and Suárez rehearsed the script as Paz slept. The hit would be made at the latest on Monday morning. The Cubans would wait for Letelier in front of the Roy Rogers on River Road, follow him as far as the minipark on 46th Street just at the

District of Columbia border, and at that point press the remote-control detonator button. Letelier should be alone, Townley instructed.

Townley took a nap, showered, and changed his clothes. His part of the hit was done, but he felt uneasy. He would wait to be sure that Letelier was dead before leaving the country. Suárez drove him to National Airport to catch the first Eastern Airlines plane to Newark and phoned a CNM member to meet the flight. The airport was quiet. On a Sunday morning few travelers were around. Before boarding Townley phoned his wife and gave her a coded message to pass on to DINA: the bomb was in place.

As he walked into Newark's passenger terminal, Townley saw Alvin Ross waiting for him. They stopped at a Holiday Inn for breakfast. Townley described to Ross in detail every step of the operation; Ross ate, drank coffee, and took in the information. He asked more than once for assurances that the bomb had indeed been placed. Townley didn't know how much Ross had to do with CNM operations, but during breakfast, Townley said later, it became evident that Ross "definitely had specific, detailed knowledge of the plan to assassinate Letelier."

Ross would write later: "During that period from September 11, 1976 [the post midnight meeting with Townley at the Bottom of the Barrel bar] to September 19, 1976, Guillermo told me about the 'plan.' Just to make sure, I told Guillermo, why didn't we make sure this 'fucking guy' has the backing of the Chileans? He agreed, then he— Guillermo—called the Chilean Embassy to double-check, and somebody told him that Mr. Wilson was OK."

After breakfast they went to Ross's apartment, which Townley would later remember as being Guillermo Novo's home, because a few minutes after they arrived, Novo greeted them, then went to bathe and dress. Novo was a "very sharp dresser," Townley recalled.

Ross remembers Townley repairing his stereo as he had promised at their first meeting. When Novo reappeared, Townley recounted the details of the bomb's construction and placement and the plan for its detonation the next morning.

Townley and Novo drove into Manhattan that day and went to the office of Senator James Buckley. A cousin of Guillermo's, Bill

Sampol, worked there. Buckley's office had worked with the CNM on a supposed prisoner exchange between Chile and Cuba. Half an hour later they went back to New Jersey. Townley borrowed Guillermo's car and drove north on Palisades Parkway, across the Tappan Zee Bridge, and into Westchester County, where he spent the afternoon with his sister and her family. They had an early chicken dinner together.

On his way back to New Jersey, he set out on a little detour. He would employ a clever piece of tradecraft to establish that the Chilean official Hans Petersen was outside the United States at the time of the bombing. He drove to Kennedy International Airport and went to the Iberia Airlines counter, where passengers were checking their luggage for the evening flight to Madrid. As an Iberia clerk left his post in one of the lines, Townley walked casually to the counter and dropped his I-94 immigration form into a stack accumulated from passengers checking in for the flight. Two copies of the form are filled out by foreigners arriving in the United States, one to be handed in upon arrival and the second upon departure. Hans Petersen Silva would be recorded as having left the United States for Spain on September 19, 1976. Michael Townley walked out of the terminal and drove back across Manhattan to Union City.

He picked up Guillermo Novo and continued on to Newark Airport. He promised Novo he would touch base there with Felipe Rivero, the founder and leader of the CNM.

LETELIER relaxed on Sunday, one of the few that summer that he had spent at home without feeling compelled to tackle the mountain of work that usually obsessed him. Isabel went out early to spend several hours at her sculpture studio, and from there to the Chile Human Rights Office, which she had founded.

Orlando read, made some phone calls, and lounged in the garden. For a while he remembered to follow Isabel's careful instructions about the time and temperature required for the dinner roast she had put in the oven. Working at a leisurely pace, he began to put thoughts on paper in preparation for a series of meetings on IPS business, and for a pamphlet he was writing with a young economist and IPS colleague, Michael Moffitt. The paper dealt with imbalances in trade and financial relations between the wealthy industrialized nations and the rest of the world and with proposals for the establishment of a "New International Economic Order."

In the evening he granted an interview to *Internews,* a bimonthly news bulletin published on the West Coast. He spoke about the structure of any future coalition between the Popular Unity and the Chilean Christian Democratic Party, and about the strong and weak points of Pinochet's regime. He denied any intention of forming a government in exile, explaining that it would serve little purpose at this time.

Isabel came home, and they had drinks and talked with two dinner guests, Saul Landau and Rebecca Switzer. The partially burned roast fed the first round of jokes; Isabel and Orlando teased each other. The conversation strayed occasionally to institute and political shoptalk. Over dessert and coffee Orlando launched into a long and hilarious account of his last few trips abroad. Everyone felt good as they said their goodbyes outside, breathing the first air of Indian summer.

SEPTEMBER 20, 1976. Townley set out to do chores in Miami. He put the Hans Petersen Silva passport in an envelope together with driver's license and receipts and mailed it to a DINA front address in Chile. In the afternoon he took a limousine to his parents' home in Boca Raton. The radio newscast made no mention of a bombing.

LETELIER INVITED Michael and Ronni Moffitt to a working dinner at Ogden Court that evening. Deadline pressure mounted for completion of the International Economic Order pamphlet. At six o'-clock, Michael tried to start his car outside the institute. Although he had retrieved it from the repair shop that very afternoon, the engine would not turn over. Letelier offered to take them home with him; they could then take his car home overnight—they lived in nearby Potomac, Maryland—and pick him up in the morning on the way to work.

The two couples dined and drank red wine. Ronni Karpen Moffitt's presence relaxed whatever atmosphere she entered. Isabel remembered later that Ronni had a new hairdo that gave her twenty-five years a more mature look. Ronni talked enthusiastically about her promotion to IPS fund raiser and promised to help the human rights defense committee that Isabel had organized. After they left, the Leteliers commented how energizing it felt to be in the presence of a young couple in love, and to know young Americans who supported the Chilean cause as if it were the only reasonable and natural thing to do.

SEPTEMBER 21, 1976. Michael and Ronni Moffitt drove Orlando's car into Ogden Court and parked in front of his house. They had just missed the Leteliers' maid, who left every Tuesday morning at 8:45 to walk to the bus stop. She worked elsewhere on Tuesdays. This morning she had seen a group of four people in a parked car near the house. She thought, by their *presencia,* that those she caught a glimpse of were definitely Latin American, perhaps Chilean. When the Moffitts arrived neither the maid nor the four people in the car were in sight. Orlando was behind schedule; he was on the phone. Ronni and Michael had coffee while Isabel read the paper.

At about 9:15 the Moffitts and Orlando left the house. Rain drizzled from a pale grey sky. Michael took the back seat. The car reached the Roy Rogers Restaurant at about 9:20. Ronni and Orlando, in animated conversation, didn't notice a large grey late-model car pulling into River Road behind them. Michael was trying to read. He cracked his window, wrinkling his nose at the already thick cloud of cigarette smoke emanating from Orlando.

The driver of the grey car following them checked the position of a flat metal device on the seat beside him and plugged it into the car's cigarette lighter outlet. The two cars turned left onto Massachusetts Avenue from 46th Street. Embassy Row stretched ahead.

2

PYRRHIC VICTORY

ON SEPTEMBER 4, 1970, in the Providencia neighborhood of Santiago, thousands of walls and windows displayed posters with Jorge Alessandri's name. The candidate of the right wing had the almost unanimous support of Chile's wealthy and upper-middle classes. The only poor who lived in Providencia, the servants, had no means of hanging banners or posters. But like more than 90 percent of eligible Chileans, they too had voted in the presidential election. And when late evening television reports projected victory by a narrow plurality for the candidate of the leftist Popular Unity coalition, many of the servants clasped each other's hands in silent rejoicing. But their patrons, on hearing the same news, tore down their Alessandri posters, turned off their lights and pulled down their shades, locked and relocked their gates and doors.

The road to Santiago's Pudahuel Airport was jammed with the cars of residents of Providencia and similar neighborhoods, anxious to leave the country on the first available flight. A Popular Unity victory, they assumed, would bring on an orgy of looting and raping, and they, the possessors of Chile's wealth and virtue, would become the sole objects of the masses' wrath and desire.

Teen-agers from wealthy neighborhoods like Providencia brought their cars into the main streets, honking and shouting that the vote was a fraud. Others chanted, "Chile sí, Cuba no." Some of them screamed to passers-by that the election should not be recognized, that the military would stage a coup and save the nation. Others shouted, "Arm yourselves, for the communist hordes will march on Providencia!"

But the "hordes" who had voted for the Popular Unity (UP— Unidad Popular)* had no intention of looting or raping. They celebrated their victory in the streets with chanting, singing, and Chile's abundant working-class drink, *vino tinto*—red wine—shouting the Popular Unity slogan thousands of times: "El pueblo unido jamás será vencido"—the people united will never be vanquished.

Their candidate, Dr. Salvador Allende Gossens, stepped out on a balcony on Plaza Bulnes to celebrate with the crowd a victory that climaxed four decades of struggle by the Chilean working class to win political power through the polls. Allende and the assembled throng believed they had won it. The question would become one of how to keep it.

Allende had prepared for this moment most of his adult life. Only a young medical student in 1932 when a free-wheeling colonel, Marmaduke Grove, proclaimed the first socialist republic (crushed by an armed-forces coup two weeks later), Allende joined with fellow socialists the following year to found the Socialist Party. In 1938 the formation of a Popular Front culminated in the election of Radical Pedro Aguirre Cerda, and Allende served the reform-minded president as minister of health. In 1946 the people of Valparaíso, Chile's second largest city, elected him as their senator to the Chilean Congress. There he remained for twenty-four years. The quintessential socialist, the consummate parliamentarian, Allende became the leader that the various parties and factions of the left could and did trust. But he was more than their perennial presidential candidate:† he was in fact and symbol the left's physician whose confident and

---

* The Popular Unity was a coalition of the predominantly working-class-based Communist and Socialist parties and several smaller groups: the Radical Party, the Movement of United Popular Action (MAPU), the Social Democratic Party, and Independent Popular Action; most of these were remnants or recent splinters of center parties.

†Allende ran in four consecutive presidential elections. The first time, in 1952, he received 5.4 percent of the vote. For his second campaign in 1958, Allende's Socialist Party formed an electoral alliance with the Communists called the FRAP, or Popular Front. Allende lost to conservative Jorge Alessandri by 35,000 out of a total of 1.3 million votes cast. In 1964, the Christian Democratic Party, with conservative backing, elected Eduardo Frei on a platform that included agrarian reform and other populist measures. Frei's campaign relied heavily on

sober treatment promised to bring into being a just society through peaceful and rational processes. At age sixty-two, the stiff-backed physician with the wry wit and the Popular Unity coalition that he had led into the 1970 election thought that at last they would be able to translate their dream, their social vision, into political reality.

The program of the Popular Unity promised "to end the dominion of the imperialists, the monopolists, and the landholding oligarchy and to begin the construction of socialism in Chile." To Chilean workers socialism meant that they would eventually, through their organizations and parties, control the mines and factories, that the profits would find their way into public investment and social services rather than into the pockets of the wealthy.

Allende did not promise the immediate installation of a socialist economy. He outlined a six-year program of gradual social and economic change to lay the foundation of a legal revolution from capitalism to socialism. Allende was not naïve, or sentimental, or easily swayed by heroic proclamations. Important sectors of the left, including members of his own party, eschewed electoral politics or saw it at best as a stage in the conquest of state power; many of them found their inspiration in the Cuban Revolution. But Allende disagreed.

"We are not in Cuba in 1959," he told a French correspondent, Serge La Faurie (*Nouvelle Observateur,* December 14, 1970). "The right has not been crushed here by popular uprising. It has only narrowly been beaten in elections. Its power remains intact. It still has its industries, banks, land, and its allies in the army." Allende saw himself as an actor who played his part in the context of a long historical process, one who had traveled along an electoral path and steadfastly clung to that road. "Our only chance of success," he contended, "is to play to the end the game of legality—using all the weapons that the Constitution gives us: and they are numerous."

At the Letelier's country cottage in the Shenandoah Valley near Washington, Isabel woke her sleeping children at 3:00 A.M. with shouts of "Ganó Allende!" (Allende won!) when she heard the news

anticommunist propaganda and received more than $3 million in CIA funds. In 1970, Allende, the candidate of the Popular Unity, came in first, running against former president and National Party candidate Jorge Alessandri and Christian Democrat Radomiro Tomic.

over a Radio Prague short-wave broadcast. Orlando had stayed in Washington to follow the results by telephone to Chile. He drove out to the country early that morning, honking his horn to announce the victory before his car was in sight of the cottage. He hugged Isabel. "I've decided to resign my post at the IDB—" he began.

"—and we're all going to Chile," Isabel continued.

In the back of his mind, however, Letelier could not shake the nagging sensation that the celebration, while justified, was also premature. He knew that Chile's conservative business establishment would not passively accept the victory of their adversary. He knew they would begin to conspire, to arm, to do everything necessary to preserve their dominance. He knew it as certainly as he knew the time, place, and date. He knew the Chilean upper class intimately because he had been born into it.

In 1932, AT ALMOST THE same time as Allende and his comrades were forming the Chilean Socialist Party, Orlando Letelier del Solar was born in the quiet agricultural market city of Temuco some four hundred miles south of Santiago. That part of Chile has the heaviest concentration of Native Americans, Indians, who are called Mapuches in Chile and are known to anthropologists as Araucanians.

Orlando's father, Don Orlando Letelier, operated a print shop and published a daily newspaper for the city of 30,000 at the time his son was born. Inés del Solar,* his mother, wrote poetry and became active in volunteer social work. The Chilean Leteliers traced their origins to Saint-Malo in France and the emigrations during the Napoleonic era. Don Orlando was a member of the Radical Party,† Chile's first thoroughly middle-class party, which led the struggle for

*A Chilean woman does not lose her surname at marriage. The matronymic—mother's surname—is part of every Chilean's name, according to Spanish custom, although it is common to use only the father's surname. Thus Letelier's full name is Orlando Letelier del Solar. It is also common for a Chilean woman living in the United States to use her husband's last name in order to avoid confusion. Isabel Letelier's real name, therefore, is Isabel Morel.

†The Radical Party was founded in 1858, and developed a platform calling for free, compulsory, lay education and espousal of the separation of church and state.

social reform beginning in the 1930s. He also belonged, like Salvador Allende, to Chile's Masonic order. In the Letelier family of landlords and bankers, who thought of themselves as aristocrats, Don Orlando was something of a black sheep. Besides operating a print shop and engaging in progressive politics, he bred racehorses and frequented the weekly boxing arena. "Audacious and independent" conceded his blue-blooded relatives. Don Orlando tried to tell his young son what made the Mapuche Indians poor and what life was like for the oppressed. The message stuck.

"Corilonco, corilonco!" the Mapuche women shouted when they saw the three-year-old boy with orange hair. The word means "fire" in Araucanian. Orlando Letelier's thick red hair thinned as he grew older, but it gained him the nickname "El Fanta," from a brand of orange soda pop.

When Orlando was three his father and mother moved to Santiago. As Chile's poor suffered through the worldwide depression of the 1930s, Orlando's father continued to explain to his son the causes of the poverty he saw in the city. Orlando, placed in a Montessori school during the nursery and primary years, learned in a freer atmosphere than his cousins and other members of his class. From Montessori to public school seemed a logical step for a boy growing up in a house where Radical Party politics informed discussion. To the surprise of his parents he chose to enlist in the Bernardo O'Higgins Military School at age fourteen. Assuring his father that he did not envision a military career, Orlando explained that military school would give him a sense of personal independence and would allow him to gain discipline with which to face the world. He excelled in school and, to his father's delight, in boxing as well. He was appointed cadet officer, an honor reserved for special students. He also organized a theater group, which performed musicals.

Chile gave birth to a small Nazi movement in the 1930s which survived after World War II, and there were brief intervals of military rule. But Chile, including its middle and upper classes, remained firmly and proudly democratic. Chileans reveled in their country's reputation as "the England of the Andes." Orlando himself had internalized a commitment to democracy along with his ABCs. When in 1946 Gabriel Gonzáles Videla won the presidency in the third straight Radical victory, many Chileans, including Orlando's father, rejoiced that finally the full reforms promised in each campaign would be realized. Instead, Radical "continuism," as it became known, turned to the right. Under pressure from the United States, Videla outlawed the Communist Party, took away from former Communists the right to vote, and banned Communists from holding union positions. The Videla government sent Communist leaders to a concentration camp in Pisagua, a coastal city in the northern Atacama Desert. This was Chile's first concentration camp; it was closed after several years of use, and would be reopened twenty-one years later.

The Chilean cadets always went on summer maneuvers. In Orlando's fourth year at military school he drank from what he thought was a pure mountain stream and ingested amoebas, causing him to suffer a prolonged bout of dysentery. The cure the doctors administered burned holes in his stomach, and after he recovered from dysentery he remained bedridden with bleeding ulcers. He withdrew from military school, no longer able to meet its physical requirements.

He entered the university law school, and in his first year met Isabel Margarita Morel, whose family had left Saint-Malo in 1832, the same year as the Leteliers. Also from a Chilean blue-blooded family, Isabel became Orlando's friend and then his sweetheart. In 1952, the first year of the administration of President Carlos Ibáñez, a retired general, Orlando presented Isabel with an "illusion ring" —a rough equivalent of pinning.

Isabel majored in Spanish literature, while Orlando attended law and economics classes and was apprenticed half a day a week to a practicing lawyer. Both became involved in supporting a student art center, and those being the days of the existentialist craze on campuses throughout the Western world, they decided to throw a Sartre-Camus party to raise money.

Orlando could not help but become involved in campus activity. He had joined the youth arm of the rightist Liberal Party in his first university year as a protest against Radical corruption. The Liberal Party, which would later form an alliance with the Conservative Party, was made up of upper-class urban property owners who espoused the "enlightened capitalism" of nineteenth-century British liberalism that emphasized natural law and free trade. Letelier aspired to leadership and ran for the office of student representative as an independent. "Promises abound! Realities are lacking!" ran one campaign slogan. "Orlando Letelier del Solar has shown his ability. Vote for him." Soon, however, he found the Liberal Party incompatible with his ideals, just as his fellow Liberals judged him out of bounds when he casually admitted to having voted for a leftist student candidate.

He found his friends among the leftists and artists, among them José Tohá, who would later serve as a fellow cabinet minister, and Venezuelan exile Jorge Dager. Both influenced Orlando's thinking as it changed from old-fashioned radicalism, with a brief liberal transition, to Chilean socialism à la Salvador Allende. Isabel, who considered herself a "leftist Christian," confounded Orlando since he thought that "leftist" and "Christian" were a contradiction in terms.

Much of the politics Isabel and Orlando learned was from Venezuelans banished by dictator Pérez Jiménez. "We also learned how sad is the state of an exile," Isabel recalled. In 1952 Orlando's ulcers flared up again, forcing him to bed for four months.

Isabel graduated in 1953. Orlando finished his last year at the university, now involved deeply with radicals, Marxists of various stripes, and innovative artists. Isabel and a friend had organized a marionette theater for children, and when he could, Orlando played the male roles, using his baritone voice to speak the lines of heroes and fools and singing and playing the guitar to accompany the shows. On Sundays the troop would appear at birthday parties and celebrations, packed into Orlando's small pickup truck.

In 1954 Orlando graduated with a degree in law and one in economics. He began to work in the Department of Copper, researching the regulation of mining, sales, marketing, and shipping of copper—Chile's most precious resource, the base of its foreign-exchange earnings.

In 1955 they were married. Orlando became so obsessed with copper that he could recite from memory the price falls and rises over a decade in the metal market. Isabel lost the first baby. In 1957 Orlando, his ulcers apparently healed, fell victim to a typhoid attack just when his first son, Cristián, was about to be born. To get to the hospital Isabel had to secure a safe-conduct pass because students were rioting in the streets and a state of emergency prevailed. After Cristián's birth Orlando stood above the crib. White from illness, he forced a smile. Then he fell unconscious to the hospital floor.

Orlando and Isabel began to work with the team, many of them university friends, that were planning the 1958 election campaign for Salvador Allende Gossens.

Isabel's father, a conservative who nevertheless liked Orlando, adored his grandson. He was present when the baby said his first word: to his horror, it was "Allende."

During the campaign Orlando had left Chile for the first time on a Copper Department mission to Europe, to study the metal markets in Paris and London. On this trip he wrote frequently to Isabel, one of his constant themes his love for Chile, his sense of rootedness there. He returned after two months. The elections were held in September 1958; and the Conservative candidate, Jorge Alessandri, won.

Right after the Chilean election, Venezuelan dictator Pérez Jiménez fell and democratic government succeeded decades of tyranny. Orlando and Isabel's exiled friends returned home, many of them to occupy posts in the new government. They invited Orlando to come to live and work in Venezuela. Allende's defeat, they predicted, would result in persecution for Orlando since he and only a few others in the Copper Department had announced themselves as Socialists and had actively campaigned for Allende. "I'm a professional," Orlando responded to their invitation. "Nothing will happen to me. I'm not a politician." He continued to work at the Copper Department.

In August 1959 Isabel's father, an old and close friend of newly elected President Jorge Alessandri, died. Two weeks later on a Friday, Orlando Letelier found an envelope on his desk. Inside: "Do not report to work on Monday. Your services at the Copper offices are officially terminated." With Isabel's father dead, Alessandri owed nothing to Orlando.

No one in the Copper Department management would speak with Orlando. Events were taking a disconcerting turn for him. He had seen his future in copper, and was passionately absorbed in his work. His family was growing as well. Pancho, his third son in as many years, was only three days old when Orlando received his dismissal notice. Others who had worked for the Allende campaign received similar notices. Upper-class acquaintances told Orlando that he had gotten what he deserved. Orlando recalled a high Alessandri government official saying to him, "Your punishment is an example, for betraying your class."

Former friends became distant enemies. They did not visit Isabel at the hospital when she had given birth after the election. Allende, defeated in his first presidential try, did visit her. They reminisced how she had tripped and fallen at his house while in her late pregnancy, and how he had rushed to help her up, offering on the spot to become the child's godfather. Allende also later publicly denounced the copper minister for firing Orlando. José Tohá wrote an editorial condemning such persecution in the newspaper he now edited, *Última Hora.*

Orlando now looked with more favor at the offers to work in Venezuela. An older friend of the family counseled him: "Look, Orlando, you will not find work in the Copper Department or any other government ministry from the far north to the Polar south of Chile. You are such a talented man. It is a pity you did what you did, but you should go to Venezuela because you can exercise your natural talents better there in any case."

In September 1959 the Leteliers left for Venezuela. In a way leaving also spelled relief. "People who were our best friends, who worked with Orlando in the Copper Department, young couples, people with whom we had shared pregnancies and births, with whom we had partied and played, now crossed to the other side of the street when they saw us," Isabel remembered. "At the farewell parties for Orlando, some of those who attended told Orlando that he should blame himself for getting fired."

Orlando worked for a private investment group in Caracas, doing market studies. Then Felipe Herrera, a former professor of Orlando's in law school, was elected president of the Inter-American Development Bank. He asked Orlando to come and work for him in Washington, D.C. But Letelier received another attractive offer. On May

1, 1960, Orlando and Isabel stood at Salvador Allende's side—in Havana, Cuba. Invited to attend May Day ceremonies, Allende had asked them to accompany him.

Jaime Barrios, an economist whom Orlando knew well from university days, now worked for the Cuban government as did other Latin American technicians and experts who could not find outlets in their own countries for their expertise. Late one night Barrios took the Leteliers to Cuba's Central Bank. In front of the building a toothless militia guard lowered his Czech submachine gun and waved the familiar Barrios and his party through the door. Inside, the Leteliers encountered a short, scruffily bearded man holding a piece of chalk and explaining numbers and equations on a blackboard to another man. The short man stopped his lesson after a few minutes, and Barrios introduced the Leteliers to Major Ernesto "Che" Guevara, president of Cuba's Central Bank.

Orlando spent much of the night talking with Che Guevara, who offered him a position at the Central Bank. Letelier would join Jaime Barrios, Juan Noyola, and a host of other distinguished Latin Americans in helping Cuba overcome its extreme shortage of educated and trained people. For the next five days Orlando and Isabel looked and listened. They both realized that Fidel would soon proclaim the revolution a socialist one, that hard times were to come. Isabel and Orlando talked about how she could teach in Cuba and he could work with his old friends.

They left the island tempted. Felipe Herrera's offer, however, was even more tempting. "The Cuban Revolution is a fact. It will endure, with or without me. What Felipe Herrera is offering," he reasoned with Isabel, "is a chance to build an integrated Latin America." Letelier, once obsessed with making copper the foundation of a healthy Chilean economy, now saw in Herrera's plan for an Inter-American Development Bank a base for economic integration, for a Latin American common market under progressive leadership, a way to end poverty, illiteracy, and misery throughout the continent. They chose Washington over Havana.

The day after their arrival in Washington, Orlando left Isabel and the children at the Presidential Hotel and went to find out the specifics of his bank job. Isabel looked for living quarters, doctors and hospitals, schools for the kids. Letelier took little time to become totally immersed in his new job. With a team of economists and statisticians he set out to compile the first accurate statistical report on Latin America, a prerequisite for a comprehensive development plan. Statistics either did not exist or were unreliable. There were no gross national income figures, and population, employment, health, and education statistics made no sense. Methods of compilation varied from country to country or even within certain nations, often to serve political ends.

Isabel rented a townhouse in Northwest Washington just large enough for the growing family. The Leteliers became members of Washington's international organization community—people who enjoyed certain privileges without being part of the diplomatic corps. They spoke Spanish at home, they socialized with Spanish-speaking friends, and Spanish reigned as the official language at the Inter-American Development Bank. On occasions when it was necessary to dine with non-Spanish-speakers Orlando would quip, "Too bad we have to eat in English tonight." His accent remained thick even as he mastered the subtleties of Americanisms. The physical effort to speak English showed in his neck muscles, in the unusual and forced positions his jaw and mouth had to assume to pronounce the Anglo-Saxon consonants.

Isabel supplemented the family income by teaching Spanish at the State Department's Foreign Service Institute. It was not always an edifying experience. "Native Spanish speakers were supposed to repeat basic sentences, and then American linguists would come in and explain in English. I was a native." Among her students she recalls Nathaniel Davis, who was to become the United States' ambassador to Chile in the period just before, during, and after the coup. She also taught FBI agents and members of the White House staff.

Letelier became a member of the working jet set. Part of his bank job was to go to each Latin American country to help reason, argue, cajole, and persuade local authorities into accepting a unified data-collection system, to impress them with the seriousness of the IDB's mission, to remind them of Bolívar and their history, and finally, to find technicians and bureaucrats with whom he and the bank staff could work.

In 1961 the Leteliers bought a house in Bethesda, Maryland. Their fourth son, Juan Pablo, was born. Isabel maintained her dynamism and her figure. But by 1963, despite two salaries, the Leteliers discovered that like other young couples with children they had gone deeper and deeper into debt. They sold the Bethesda house and again became renters.

"We had a huge house with little furniture, and at night we ate potatoes." Orlando did not care. As 1963 came to an end he became increasingly concerned about the 1964 Chilean election. Once again his friend and mentor, Salvador Allende, would represent the unified left. Letelier quietly collected money and inspired as much enthusiasm as he could among bank staff and officials. He took a few extra trips to Chile. He tried to arrange for Allende to visit the United States in order to muster liberal support, explain his moderate and legal approach to socialism, and gain valuable firsthand knowledge of United States politics. But fear and suspicion of the United States, bred by bitter experience and lack of knowledge, led Socialist Party leaders to decide against Letelier's request. Allende did not visit Washington. The Chilean right, in a tactical move to ensure Allende's defeat, did not run a candidate, and Christian Democrat Eduardo Frei Montalva won the combined votes of the right and center to capture the presidency with 55 percent of the vote. Allende lost with 38.9 percent.

Letelier and his closest friends decided that he should remain at his job in Washington, for Chile still offered little prospect of an outlet for his skills and talents. His socialist politics would continue to work against his obtaining an effective position inside the country. Moreover, Latin Americans in Washington, including Letelier, had not yet lost the high hopes instilled in them by President Kennedy that a new era was opening up for relations between Latin America and its big brother to the north. Even the April 1961 Bay of Pigs invasion of Cuba did not erode their confidence in Kennedy's basic good intentions toward their countries.

"He must have been misinformed by his intelligence sources," Letelier observed to Isabel. "We were all in love with Kennedy at the time," she recalled. "The Alliance for Progress provided Orlando and Felipe Herrera with a sense of optimism that the United States could and would change its ways, its policies, and wake up to the realities of Latin American needs."

But after Kennedy was assassinated the United States government reverted to its traditional role. A military coup, later proved to have had heavy CIA and Pentagon involvement, overthrew the progressive Brazilian president João Goulart in 1964. In 1965 President Lyndon Johnson sent marines to the Dominican Republic to install a president acceptable to the United States. Argentina, Bolivia, and Ecuador fell to the military. The Kennedy years and the reformist ideals of the alliance faded into the middle and late sixties as the United States–Vietnam war grew and enveloped all of Southeast Asia.

Between 1965 and the election of Salvador Allende to Chile's presidency in September 1970, the Leteliers continued to adjust to Washington life. They shared a summer cottage with relatives in the Shenandoah Valley, but Isabel made sure to spend three months each year in Chile with her sons. She hired a tutor for them and personally supervised their curriculum of Chilean history, culture, and Spanish-language literature. All four attended United States schools, spoke unaccented English, and looked and acted like American kids. She made certain that they knew they were Chileans. They resented losing their summer vacations, but nevertheless they learned what she intended.

Orlando's trips to Chile, more frequent but of shorter duration, always involved long meetings with Allende and other Socialist Party leaders, who would often closet themselves with Orlando for several days of strategy sessions.

As the years passed and Letelier rose in the IDB bureaucracy, the early mystique of the bank and its possibilities lost its glow for him. Latin American development would not come to pass in a decade and perhaps not in his lifetime. He concentrated on projects that would lead to real development rather than serve narrow interests. Then he left projects altogether and became Herrera's assistant.

Isabel moved from the State Department to teach Spanish at Georgetown University. She also taught remedial reading to ghetto blacks and circulated petitions in her neighborhood calling for open housing in then segregated Bethesda. She painted and occasionally accompanied Orlando on his missions. She observed that her husband had gained the respect and friendship of colleagues all over the world—socialists, liberals, apolitical technocrats. By 1970 Orlando Letelier had achieved a reputation as an economist, diplomat, problem solver, and dashing figure.

ALLENDE'S AWARENESS of the limits of his plurality-based power led him to seek entente with those political and military sectors that he had known as open to dialogue. As he began day and night discussions with leading Christian Democrats and key members of the armed forces to assure them of his loyalty to the Constitution and to get their pledges of loyalty in return, other groups of men were meeting in Washington, D.C.

When the news of Allende's election reached the White House, "Nixon was beside himself," Nixon's national security adviser Henry Kissinger reports in his memoirs. Kissinger himself met twice within ten days of Allende's election with the 40 Committee, which on his urging adopted a covert policy to bring economic pressure against Chile.* The State Department was directed by the 40 Committee to contact American businesses having interests in Chile to see if they could be induced to take action in accord with the American government's policy of economic pressure on Chile. Kissinger made certain that the CIA station chief in Chile had more than a quarter of a million dollars with which to work for special elections and other maneuvers against Allende. CIA officers

---

*The 40 Committee is a subcabinet-level body belonging to the Executive Branch which must review proposed covert-action projects. Originally fashioned in the early 1950s, the group has existed under a variety of names, but the 40 Committee, since 1969, has been chaired by the president's assistant for national security affairs. High-level representatives from State, Defense, CIA, and the Joint Chiefs of Staff also sit on the committee.

A staff report by the Senate Select Committee to Study Governmental Operations with Respect to Intelligence Activities defined "covert action" as "any clandestine or secret activities designed to influence foreign governments, events, organizations, or persons in support of U.S. foreign policy conducted in such a manner that the involvement of the U.S. Government is not apparent." *Covert Action in Chile, 1963–1973* (Washington, D.C., 1975), vol. 7, p. 4.

received authorization to bribe Chilean congressmen to vote against Allende's confirmation.

Nixon's attitude toward Allende remained intransigent. He made no distinctions between Castro and Allende, between different kinds of Marxists, between socialists and communists. At bottom he saw only one issue, ironically the same that Allende viewed as crucial: who would control the productive wealth of Chile.

Joining the exodus of the wealthy from Chile was a man who wanted desperately to see President Nixon. The archduke of Chile's untitled nobility, Don Agustín " Duney " Edwards ran one of Chile's largest banks and published *El Mercurio,* the country's leading newspaper. Edwards talked to his close friend Donald Kendall, who ran the Pepsi-Cola Company and was an intimate friend of Nixon. Kendall made an appointment for him with Nixon.

On September 15 Kendall brought Edwards to the White House. Edwards had earlier breakfasted with National Security Adviser Kissinger and Attorney General John Mitchell. Now he spoke with the president personally. Nixon already knew about the economic squeeze that was set in motion by Kissinger and the 40 Committee on September 8. Listening to Edwards, Nixon's worst fears became magnified. According to Kissinger, who was present at the meeting, he told CIA Director Richard Helms, in a conversation that lasted less than fifteen minutes, "that he wanted a major effort to see what could be done to prevent Allende's accession to power. If there were one chance in ten of getting rid of Allende we should try it; if Helms needed $10 million he would approve it. . . . Aid programs should be cut; [Chile's] economy should be squeezed until it 'screamed.' "

"If I ever carried the marshal's baton out of the Oval Office," Helms boasted to a Senate committee, "it was that day." His notes, written on a single sheet of paper, read:

One in ten chance perhaps, but save Chile!
worth spending
not concerned risks involved
no involvement of embassy
$10,000,000 available, more if necessary

full-time job—best men we have
game plan
make the economy scream
48 hours for plan of action*

In September and early October of 1970, 40 Committee funds found their way to important Chilean papers and magazines and into the pockets of right-wing members of Congress who would have to confirm Allende's accession to the presidency. On another track CIA officials plotted with certain officers in the Chilean armed forces.

Two days before the congressional vote, a group of men synchronized their wristwatches and scrambled into four automobiles. Their mission: to kidnap General René Schneider, commander in chief of the Chilean Army. Schneider had declared himself loyal and steadfast to the Constitution and had refused the entreaties of several fellow officers to back a coup. Without the head of its highly disciplined command structure, organized by Prussian officers in the nineteenth century, the Chilean Army would be paralyzed. The CIA had provided guns and money to groups planning the kidnapping of Schneider.†

On October 22 General Schneider's chauffer took the usual route from the general's house to the commander's office. The kidnappers had already made two abortive attempts; this time they had vowed not to fail. One car sped ahead of the general's, blocking it; the other blocked it from the rear. The men raced toward Schneider's car, pistols in hand. Schneider drew his own side arm, as did his bodyguard. The kidnappers opened fire, and Schneider fell mortally wounded.

Instead of inspiring a coup or emboldening the Chilean Congress to deny Allende the presidency, the assassination of Schneider pro-

*Hearings before the Senate Select Committee to Study Governmental Operations with Respect to Intelligence Activities, held in 1975 under the chairmanship of Senator Frank Church, provided the principal source of information about United States government intervention in Chile. The findings of what came to be known as the "Church Committee" appeared in the committee staff report *Covert Action in Chile, 1963–1973.*

†The Church Committee later reported a CIA disclaimer which stated that the guns provided by the CIA were not used in the actual murder.

duced the opposite reaction. In a surge of support Congress gave Allende 135 out of 170 votes, and he became president of Chile on November 4, 1970.

ORLANDO AND ISABEL returned to Chile. They began discussions with party and government friends that often lasted all night. They became witnesses to the liberation of the leftist political prisoners, the re-establishment of relations with Cuba, the long-awaited nationalization of the copper mines.*

Allende tried to organize his forces on two fronts: internally, to forge a cabinet that would not frighten the Christian Democrats and yet would not appear to weaken his campaign pledges. He also had to establish close contacts with the armed forces and remain ever alert for developments that might signal a coup. On the foreign front he needed in Washington, more than any other place, a loyal and reliable representative and analyst who commanded respect in economic and diplomatic circles and who could bridge the gap with the Americans without causing suspicion inside the edgy leadership of Chile's left parties.

"Orlando," Allende told him in December 1970, "I need you to return to Washington." He described the already evident effects of the economic squeeze, his suspicions about the role of certain United States companies as well as the CIA. Letelier nodded. He had heard, felt, suspected the same. Both agreed that the pervasive violence had foreign encouragement. Neither knew that Kissinger had requested and the 40 Committee had granted $38,000 for covert support of the neofascist Patria y Libertad, the most prominent terrorist group.†

In February 1971 the Leteliers returned to Washington and

---

*Previous formulas called "Chileanization," arranging for Chile to control 51 percent of its mines, had not proved satisfactory to most of the Chilean copper technicians, since in the formulas the United States companies took an additional percentage for management and other services. By the time Allende moved, not only the left but the Christian Democrats and some of their supporters had called for nationalization.

†Patria y Libertad (PL) means Fatherland and Liberty. Led by attorney Pablo H. Rodríguez Grez, PL was a paramilitary group with fascist leanings.

moved into the Chilean Embassy residence off Sheridan Circle on Massachusetts Avenue. On March 2 a State Department limousine drove Orlando to the White House, where he was greeted by President Nixon. They shook hands. "So nice to meet you, Mr. Ambassador." Letelier handed Nixon the formal letter from Salvador Allende which accredited him as Ambassador Extraordinary and Plenipotentiary to the United States of America. Nixon read a formal speech, and Letelier particularly remembered one part. "I am sure you will agree, Mr. Ambassador," Nixon said, "that no nation can in good conscience ignore the rights of others, or the international norms of behavior essential to peace and mutually fruitful intercourse. For our part this government and this nation stand pledged to mutual respect for independence, diversity, and international rights and obligations."

As Letelier left the White House a band was playing a military march and the Chilean flag was flying alongside the Stars and Stripes. He began to feel uneasy. Official United States hostility to the new Chilean government had been expounded by Henry Kissinger in a widely quoted press briefing of September 15.* Now Nixon appeared overly friendly. In the car, Orlando, puzzled, turned to Isabel and wondered why Nixon had stressed respect for independence. He consulted the copy of the speech that the White House aide had given him: "Mutual respect . . ."

Letelier had worked long hours in his years at the Inter-American Development Bank. As ambassador he worked around the clock. He would rise before seven and review the day's agenda and headlines. At seven-thirty the family would have breakfast in the second-floor den. By nine he would arrive at the Chilean Embassy offices† about a mile away. Between nine and ten he received reports from

---

*In that briefing, Kissinger told a group of Midwestern journalists: "Now, it is fairly easy for one to predict that if Allende wins [the congressional runoff election], there is a good chance that he will establish over a period of years some sort of Communist government. In that case you would have not on an island off the coast, which has not a traditional relationship and an impact on Latin America, but in a major Latin American country you would have a Communist government. . . . So I don't think we should delude ourselves that an Allende takeover in Chile would not present massive problems for us, and for democratic forces and for pro–United States forces in Latin America and indeed to the whole Western Hemisphere."

†Also on Massachusetts Avenue. The Chilean Embassy offices are called the chancery and include the consulate and the military mission.

his staff and prepared for the routine protocol visits with other ambassadors at ten. During these hours, Isabel would take the chauffeured car to do the shopping. The Popular Unity government had cut embassy budgets while urging ambassadors to exert themselves to establish good relations for the new government. She shopped at discount stores and supervised the preparations for lunch. Returning from his round of official visits, Letelier would scan the cable traffic before noon.

He and Isabel had struck a balance. Orlando concentrated on politics and economics, Isabel on culture. Within a month of the Letelier's arrival, an invitation to luncheon at the Chilean Embassy, which usually included guests from the press, the diplomatic corps, or the State Department, was an acknowledged pleasure rather than the dreary obligation to be subjected to Marxist-Leninist propaganda that right-wing innuendo in press and government circles might have suggested.

Bidding a gracious *adiós* to his guests, Letelier would race back to the office to inspect the contents of the daily diplomatic pouch, including the Chilean press. He noted the increasingly anti-Allende tone of *El Mercurio*—"Duney" Edwards' paper. Cables arrived throughout the day. Questions about cotton purchases, credits, oil shipments, and fluctuations in copper prices often required a quick response. With his small political staff he would spend the late afternoon in thorough group discussion and analysis. The policies of private and international banks and the United States government became overwhelmingly the focus of discussion. In addition to this, Letelier supervised consular affairs.

After luncheon Isabel Letelier would prepare the dining room for tea, and meet with student, women's, and church groups whom she had invited to learn about the new Chile, the milk-distribution program for slum children, the construction of polyclinics and schools in the impoverished areas, and the enlistment of volunteer teachers, nurses, and doctors—programs that Allende eloquently described to an interviewer. "I am a doctor," he explained. "Today in Chile there are 600,000 children mentally retarded because they were not adequately nourished during the first eight months of their lives, because they did not receive the necessary proteins. Because of this the daily

half-liter milk plan was developed. . . . The real solution is in changing the existence of their parents, in restructuring the life conditions
of the family."

On March 22, 1971, Henry Kissinger wrested $185,000 from the
40 Committee to be funneled into Christian Democratic campaign
coffers in preparation for the April municipal elections in Chile. The
same day he met with Letelier in the Executive Office building. The
next evening in his memo to the Chilean foreign minister, Letelier
culled the key points from his forty-minute conversation with Kissinger. "I told Mister Kissinger," Letelier wrote, "that the Chilean
government is taking various measures so as to be in compliance with
the UP program and consequently with the establishment of a socialist system." Letelier looked at his notes and continued that Kissinger
"underlined especially that his government does not wish for any
reason to interfere with the actions that the Chilean government
would adopt internally. The United States has enough enemies
abroad already not to want to direct its actions in such a way as to
transform Chile into a new enemy."

Letelier had smiled, listening to Kissinger's welcome declaration.
The pudgy national security adviser had folded his hands on his
table, reminding Letelier of a child in grade school. "I mentioned to
him press references that alluded to a secret White House document
designed to organize coordinated action against Chile within the
inter-American system." Letelier cabled Kissinger's response in quotation marks: "Absolutely absurd and without foundation."

The cable continued, listing the points Kissinger had made. "As
a political scientist he viewed the Chilean case as 'fascinating' and
the way in which President Allende was leading this process as
'worthy of the greatest admiration.' "

Kissinger, observed Letelier, "showed a great interest in learning
any information I had about the upcoming municipal elections, asking especially about the percentage of votes that we expected the
various parties to win, and particularly the parties inside the Popular
Unity. He also asked about the forms into which we had divided the
three areas of property—state, private, and mixed—which I explained to him in some detail."

Letelier had left Kissinger's office feeling satisfied. He did not know that Kissinger and the 40 Committee, since Allende's inauguration, had approved $1.5 million dollars for opposition groups and media in Chile. The radio and print media quickly became saturated with anti-Allende, anti-UP stories; the Christian Democrats and the rightist National Party deluged the Chilean voters with campaign propaganda. On April 4, 1971, in 280 municipal elections the Popular Unity parties won 49.7 percent of the vote, a gain of nearly 14 percent over the presidential elections in September. The early reforms had won over sectors of the working class that had traditionally voted Christian Democrat and part of the cautious middle class.

On December 21, 1970, President Allende had proposed a constitutional amendment to nationalize Chilean copper. He had tried to explain not only to Chileans, who already understood, but to United States and world leaders how precarious Chile's position was because of foreign ownership and investment. In the last sixty years, as Allende told Saul Landau in a filmed interview in February 1971, foreign investors have taken some $10 billion out of Chile. "That is to say that the total value of all the capital accumulated in Chile over the last four hundred years has left its frontiers. We base the right to nationalize our own resources on that fact."

Allende had declared Chile's willingness to pay compensation, but left the form and amount to negotiation. Letelier began to handle much of the tough bargaining because most of the foreign investors affected by nationalization were United States–owned companies. On June 28, 1971, Letelier transmitted a cable outlining a conversation between himself and Gordon Murphy, president of Cerro-Andino Company, a large mineral investor. Much of this cable traffic dealt with complex technical details worked out between Allende negotiators and United States corporate lawyers. After summing up the points raised by Murphy, Letelier concluded that "the Cerro executives appear more interested in signing the contract for the already negotiated deal than in helping increase production." The ITT, Anaconda, and Kennecott discussions were more negative from the beginning and remained that way, or worsened as each month went by.

Letelier understood, as did every United States executive, that the central issue that placed the United States and Chile in an adversary position involved the ownership of property, and that there was only so much room for resolving the conflict without head-on confrontation. However, Orlando Letelier was an optimist who cherished a romantic and poetic love of just victory.

In Chile, in stark contrast to the polite dialogue conducted by embassy officials in Santiago and Washington, the struggle between the Popular Unity and its opposition was fought in the language of class warfare. The struggle involved more than ideological competition. Groups of peasants in Chile's south began to seize parcels of land, claiming an inalienable right to take back property that the bourgeoisie had taken from them unlawfully in the past. Workers took over factories, declaring that the producers had a right to own the means of production.

Each land seizure and factory occupation undermined Allende's credibility, his pledge to proceed according to the legal process. The Christian Democrats and the right, who had remained aloof from support for or participation in the emerging reform program, spoke with one voice: they demanded a crackdown. Sectors of the military threatened to take matters into their own hands. The right wing took advantage of the political climate and carried out a series of bombings and other acts of sabotage. Often they attempted to place the blame for the street violence on the left.

Letelier, in Washington, felt confused for the first time. Carrying out an urgent assignment, he had prepared a loan-guarantee request to the Export-Import Bank for $21 million to finance LAN-Chile's purchase of three Boeing jetliners. He had filed the necessary papers in the early spring only to receive an unusual request from bank officials for more information, more paperwork, complicated economic and commercial data. Friends in the banking community confirmed that the EXIMBANK was under pressure from the White House and the office of the national security adviser to deny the loan financing.

In the world of diplomacy and banking, gentlemen did not tell outright lies. Evasion, omission, subtle and careful phrasing had become over the course of centuries the very fabric of diplomacy even in times of adversary relations. Nixon and Kissinger had told him specifically that they would not take direct measures, that they would not intervene, that they wanted a peaceful and friendly relationship. Yet the economic squeeze was obvious on many fronts, rumors in the daily press and in diplomatic circles spoke of a destabilization effort, and now the EXIMBANK stalling allowed for no interpretation other than that United States policy differed drastically from its leaders' words.

On July 11 the formal nationalization of the copper mines took place as the vast majority of Chileans cheered. As expected, most congressmen, including those from the right, voted for the amendment. But negotiations with the United States–owned copper companies had not gone well. Even Cerro-Andino, the least complicated of the cases, had presented what the Popular Unity negotiators considered unjust claims. Kennecott and Anaconda, the giants, had made compensation claims that outreached what the UP considered just by millions of dollars.

On June 28 Allende had advised Letelier by cable that he had met with U.S. Ambassador Edward Korry to explain that there would still be ample room for negotiations to solve differences after the constitutional reform was enacted. Letelier was instructed to remain flexible and avoid confrontation.

In mid-July, Letelier was recalled to Chile for consultations. Cabinet ministers and Socialist Party leaders brought him up to date. The Chilean left had always seen the United States government as a monolithic imperialist power. Letelier, without engaging in argument, tried to present some of the complexities of United States politics which he had learned to understand during his ten years in Washington.

Lunching with Allende, who listened carefully to his ambassador's assessment of United States motives, he expanded on this theme. He told Allende that the United States political system contained complex pressures and forces that made simple assessment of policy difficult. Certainly, sectors within the banking and business communities were pressuring for tough United States action, and the right wing had made up its mind that Allende and the UP were the same as Castro and Cuban-Soviet communism. But there were reasonable people in the State Department and in other agencies who understood the complexities of Chile and Latin America and the changes taking place in the Third World. These people did not appear anxious to force confrontation or have the CIA play a role that would turn into a scandal. In addition, powerful senators like William Fulbright, chairman of the Senate Foreign Relations Committee, had made positive comments about the democratic socialist experiment in Chile.

The day after his return from Chile, Letelier again met with National Security Adviser Henry Kissinger. On his agenda were the Boeing jet sale, which required EXIMBANK authorization of loan credits, and the high-level meeting with Allende, for which Kissinger was Letelier's first choice. Kissinger greeted Letelier warmly and entertained him with stories about China and the impending dialogue that he had established with Peking. Letelier smiled and offered congratulations on Kissinger's successful diplomacy. Coded "Eyes only," telex number 429, Letelier reported to his foreign minister on the August 5, 1971 meeting:

> I explained to Kissinger the background of the EXIM-BANK request and told him . . . that the alternative for LAN would be to buy Soviet-made planes. . . . I indicated to him that our country wanted to continue using United States technology in this area, and I emphasized finally that the acquisition of Soviet aircraft as a consequence of a delay on the EXIMBANK request—which would really mean a rejection—would have various political ramifications that would inevitably have a negative effect on Chile–United States relations, which my government wanted to keep on a constructive level.

Kissinger knew about the Boeing problem and told Letelier that he understood its political ramifications.

> He added that surely I would agree with him that we did not want to fool ourselves, since both of us knew each side harbored mistrust of the other. He told me that it was

clear that the United States government would not intervene in any way in the internal affairs of Chile, but that at
the same time the White House was under "enormous
pressure" from different sectors in the government, from
private groups, and from Congress to suspend all financial
help to Chile until a clear picture emerges of the indemnifi-
cation process for United States companies nationalized by
Chile.

Kissinger promised Letelier he would personally look into the
EXIMBANK situation because "it was convenient to avoid as long
as possible a specific case that would then lead to a sequence of
negative results." Letelier tried to probe for specific indications of
policy. "At this point in the conversation," cabled Letelier, Kissinger's Latin American aide spoke up to complain about the failure
to resolve the Cerro-Andino case rapidly. Letelier interpreted: "This
remark shows that the White House is deeply involved in the various
aspects of this company's interests."

Letelier judged that Kissinger's remarks and interest in Chile
should be seen as only one facet of worldwide politics. His conclusion
reflected his growing pessimism about improved relations, but also
his view that all was not over. "I don't see a favorable reaction soon
by the Americans on the LAN case, but I also don't want to imply
that they have shut down all avenues." He again assured Santiago
that Chile had complied with all the EXIMBANK requirements, but
that if they did not respond favorably soon, Boeing would surely
cancel the deal.

On August 11, 1971, the Export-Import Bank rejected the loan.
The investment community, taking its lead from the White House,
stopped all investment. Chile's credit rating dropped to zero. United
States aid ended, and all relations except military ones began to break
down from late 1971 on because of the United States executive
branch's response to Allende's programs—including programs it
feared he would initiate later.

Letelier nevertheless attempted to keep as many friendly ties as
possible with the United States government and to publicize the

image that reflected Chilean reality: a constitutional, elected, moderate socialist government that had no quarrel with the people of the United States. Yet despite official denial, actual evidence pointed to a massive covert interference by the United States in his country's affairs.

In December 1971 Orlando and Isabel Letelier received an invitation to a party at the home of syndicated columnist Joseph Alsop. Shortly after dinner, Secretary of State and National Security Adviser Henry Kissinger made his entrance, accompanied by a stunning young woman in hot pants. Taking a moment to chat casually with Letelier in a quiet spot between the dining and living rooms, Kissinger put his hand on Letelier's shoulder and said, almost in a whisper, "I want you please to convey a message to your president that the United States government does not have agents running all over Chile as it is reported in your press. I want you personally to know also that if you fail, it will be due to your own mistakes. You have my word." Letelier assured Kissinger that he would communicate the message to President Allende.

On Tuesday morning, May 9, 1972, Andrés Rojas asked Letelier for a moment in private. Rojas was the youngest official of the embassy staff, and press attaché. "Compañero," he addressed Letelier in a whisper, "my house was robbed last night." Letelier expressed his sympathies. "No, compañero," Rojas said, "you don't understand. The thieves took only documents and papers." Letelier shook his head. This was the fifth burglary that embassy officials had reported to him. In some cases property was missing; in others only papers and documents. None of the officials had possessed anything sensitive or secret.

On Tuesday morning, May 16, Letelier was working on his third cup of coffee with the *New York Times* spread in front of him when his private line rang. A burglary at the embassy. "Don't touch anything," he barked at his assistant. "Phone the State Department and the police."

Letelier arrived within ten minutes. In his third-floor office he found a filing cabinet pried open, drawers jimmied. Files and papers covered the floor. Upstairs, Embassy First Secretary Fernando

Bachelet found a similar scene. The burglars had not removed cash and expensive office equipment but had taken four small radios and one electric razor. Letelier told police that he estimated the total value at around fifty dollars. Letelier received formal apologies and assurances from State and the Metropolitan Police. The police solved none of the break-ins.

Before 1972 ended, Kissinger recommended and received 40 Committee approval for more funds to be spent, including another $1 million to *El Mercurio,* in support of anti–Popular Unity candidates in a by-election, to promote division inside the UP, to sponsor and support anti-Allende business and labor groups, and to provoke violence. Throughout 1972 acts of major and minor violence occurred almost daily in Chile. The Chilean rightist parties organized shopkeepers' strikes and a devastating national truckers' strike that left the Chilean economy paralyzed. Newspapers in Chile and around the world began referring openly to CIA intervention in Chile.

In October of 1972 the 40 Committee earmarked another $1.5 million to defeat the Popular Unity in the congressional elections scheduled for the following March. During the truckers' strike and the shopkeepers' strikes and thereafter, syndicated columnist Jack Anderson received documents which laid bare the ITT intervention.

By late 1972, after two years in office, Allende and his advisers and ministers assessed their situation. Open and violent class warfare, which they were committed to avoid at all cost, had escalated. The right, through economic sabotage and understandings with some elements of the Christian Democratic Party, had blocked political compromise in the legislature and forced a polarization. The ultra-left had responded in kind.

Later Augusto Pinochet, in an interview with a Reuters correspondent, dated the origin of the coup as April 13, 1972. "On April 13, 1972, at the Army Command center, we analyzed the possibilities, and on that day we concluded that the conflict between the executive and the legislative did not allow for a constitutional solution." Pinochet later showed documents to a reporter as evidence that the military had begun to respond to political crises. A memorandum dated August 1972 and another dated July, "already suggested the possibility of taking control of the nation. In 1972 we had begun to prepare units to face extremist groups around the capital."

Even so, the armed forces had not yet united by late 1972. Pro-Allende sectors still existed, and more important, broad pro-Constitution sectors still tipped the balance of power. General Carlos Prats, who succeeded the murdered General Schneider, supported Allende and also stood firm in his conviction that *caudillismo* (the old Latin notion of the infallible military/political leader) had no place in Chilean history, even less so the fascist doctrines espoused by certain sectors of the military.

By December 1972, when President Allende was scheduled to address the United Nations, and Ambassador Letelier accompanied him to New York, there was no doubt in either of their minds that Kissinger had lied—that he was in fact masterminding a covert-action campaign designed to destroy the Allende government.

In his speech on December 4, Allende explained his program, speaking to the nations and peoples of the Third World and to those in the industrialized world who sustained a commitment to fairness and justice. The General Assembly broke into applause when he charged that "we have experienced the effects of large-scale aggression."

Within the limits of nonviolent options, Allende had to select tactics to keep his growing list of adversaries divided and off balance, and at the same time devise a strategy to push forward with his program. To forestall a coup, Allende selectively exercised his presidential prerogative to retire certain suspect generals from active duty; when confronted by right-wing-inspired strikes, he used his charisma to call for massive working-class turnouts to show solidarity with the Popular Unity government. By late 1972, however, the escalating violence and political chaos had weakened Allende's position to the point where he felt required to appoint members of the military to join his cabinet. This move, he believed, would tide him over until the March 1973 congressional elections. If the UP showed its strength at the polls, Allende would then call for a clearly worded plebiscite which, if necessary, would show that the majority of voters supported Allende's use of the presidential powers to overcome the legislative obstacles presented by the newly formed Christian Democratic–National Party coalition.* It would also remind the military that even if the UP parties did not win a majority, more than 50 percent of the Chilean people would rally behind Allende the man, the president, to allow him to carry out his reforms. But first Allende and the UP parties had to face the formidable task of campaigning for the elections in a vicious political atmosphere.

Pollsters and journalistic observers predicted that the orchestrated violence and economic destabilization would cost Allende at least half of the votes that he had received in 1970. The majority of Christian Democrats and the right-wing National Party expected to gain two-thirds of the seats in the Chilean Senate, which would enable them to impeach Allende and call for new elections. They came together and confidently planned the impeachment moves. The ultra-right, which had always seen a coup as the only solution, found many new allies. Former President Eduardo Frei, the leader of the Christian Democratic Party, believed that a coup would oust the Popular Unity with minimal bloodshed. Then, Frei's script read, the military would call for new elections, and he would rise once again from the ashes to lead Chile for six more years.

The congressional election gave the UP 43.4 percent of the vote —7 percent more than in 1970. But the right wing controlled the courts; they retained sufficient strength with the Christian Democrats to block certain Allende initiatives in the legislature. They had effective control of many units of the police and armed forces; they occupied key civil service posts in all branches of the executive; they controlled more than 80 percent of the mass media. Allende had the presidency, and 43.4 percent of the voters. Chile remained divided

*In June 1972 the 40 Committee passed through the CIA some $50,000 to break a proposed agreement between the Popular Unity and the Christian Democratic Party, and to forge instead Christian Democratic unity with the right wing in future elections. The immediate effect of this effort was the legislative impeachment of José Toha as minister of the interior. The UP never attained a congressional majority, and under Chile's parliamentary system a majority coalition, which the Christian Democrats formed with the National Party, could and did literally vote "no confidence"—impeachment—on a series of Allende cabinet appointees. This forced Allende to constantly reshuffle his cabinet, which severely encumbered the routine process of governance.

between center, right, and ultra-right. That division among non-UP forces and a staunch pro-Constitution minority in the military had so far impeded the successful organization of a military move.

AS ALLENDE BEGAN immediately to plan strategies for a plebiscite, the opposition in Congress began to create a new obstacle course for him, designed to force him into moves that would provoke the armed forces to take control. The impeachment tactic became central, and this had an impact on the life of the Leteliers. By constantly impeaching cabinet members, the right forced Allende to reshuffle his ministers. Letelier was called home from Washington in May 1973 to become minister of foreign relations. He returned at the very moment when United States–Chilean discussions had broken down.

Letelier was as ideal a choice for this position as he had been for ambassador to the United States in 1970. He understood the paramount importance and the problems of renegotiating Chile's foreign debt. His diplomatic ability, his military schooling, his universally recognized charm and wit, made him as comfortable with generals as with socialist intellectuals and politicians and allowed him to smooth over some of the rougher edges in the newly formed relationships inside the cabinet.

Letelier's formal appointment as foreign minister coincided with the outbreak of the worst violence and sabotage experienced yet. A copper strike, which had begun in April 1973 over wages and which had brought the right wing into an unusual alliance with the copper workers, forced Chile to suspend its foreign shipments of copper. Two weeks after Chile's main source of foreign revenue was shut off, doctors, teachers, and students struck to protest Allende's handling of the copper strike. The CIA gave financial and organizational support both to the officials of the miners' union and to the sympathy strike. Never before had the right rallied to the cause of striking workers. In fact, much of the Chilean right had opposed trade unionism per se in the past and had led moves to abolish unions and strikes.

On June 21, a sympathy rally ended in a series of shootings, bombings, and street riots. Patria y Libertad heavies played a key role in inciting and committing the acts of violence. Allende called out the police force and closed *El Mercurio,* which by that time had received millions in CIA funds and had played a particularly inflammatory role in the growing violence. The charge against *El Mercurio* was "inciting subversion"; a lower-court judge agreed. The next day the Chilean Appeals Court invalidated the lower court's decision, and *El Mercurio* resumed publication.

Having spent most of the past thirteen years in Washington, Isabel Letelier and her four adolescent sons returned to Chile on June 28, 1973. Class warfare had broken out in all areas of life— except for the trenches. Each routine life transaction became a potentially loaded confrontation between the poor and the wealthy. The civilized forms refined over the centuries to evade mutual recognition of the basic difference of having and not having wealth broke down. The classes expressed open hatred for one other, in groups and as individuals. The resentment felt by the underprivileged for the middle-class and upper-class consumers and the fear and hate of these privileged sectors toward the majority poor found expression in words, gestures, and actual physical confrontations.

On June 29 the act everyone had either awaited or dreaded appeared to be taking place. Tanks, trucks, and troops moved from their bases into downtown Santiago. The soldiers under the command of Colonel Souper showed a ruthless efficiency as they surrounded La Moneda Palace. Allende remained calm. He spoke with General Prats, who reassured him of his loyalty, and together they received loyalty assurances from key generals and admirals in the army, air force, and national police. Prats, with Pinochet right behind him, demanded that the rebellious officers surrender in the name of the Chilean Constitution. Twenty-two persons had died during the day's gunfire.

The troops returned to their barracks. The plotters were removed from their command. But the *tancazo,* as it came to be called, proved to key generals that the Chilean military could move fast, and that removing certain officers would also remove the major military obstacles to a coup. Equally important, the civilian mobilization that the right wing had anticipated had not occurred. Allende's strict adherence to the Constitution had obviously impeded the militant left in its organizational efforts.

On July 26 Orlando, with Isabel and Mrs. Allende, traveled to Cuba to represent Chile at the twentieth anniversary celebration of the beginning of the Cuban Revolution. As the plane landed, Cuban officials delivered the news to the Chilean delegation that Chilean Navy Captain Arturo Araya, President Allende's friend and aide-de-camp, had been murdered by right-wing hoodlums.

In Chile the assassination coincided with the most successful CIA-sponsored act of sabotage: a strike by large numbers of Chilean truck owners, joined a week later, on August 2, by more than 100,000 owners of taxis and buses, paralyzed Chile's economy.

Allende, to counter possible coup moves, named General Carlos Prats González as defense minister and retained him as well as army commander. The armed forces, Prats promised, would maintain law and order. But large parts of the military refused to act now as the instrument of Allende's authority. Despite a long history of repressing workers and strikes, these officers, faced with the insurrection of the bourgeoisie, sided with the rebels and instead condemned the state itself. Letelier, now minister of the interior because of a late July cabinet shuffle, became Prats's friend and working colleague—for a short time.

On August 22 Letelier watched from Prats's window as the wives of certain Chilean officers surrounded Prats's house and berated the slight, proud general, screaming "Maricón!" (homosexual). Prats, his cheeks burning red, stood rigidly throughout the ordeal. He had acquired his military bearing at the same school as the husbands of these jeering women, the same military academy that Letelier had attended. Behind the shouting women stood scores of young men with clubs, chains, and blackjacks. Letelier recognized some by sight, some from photographs. They belonged to the Patria y Libertad goon squads or to the National Party's "Rolando Matus Brigade." Letelier picked up the phone; as minister of the interior, he was responsible for maintaining public order. He gave details of the scene to the director of the Santiago police. As he watched, some of the young men who had come as "protection" for the women began to strike passers-by and smash the windows of parked cars.

Later, Prats sat erect in his living-room chair, his ironed Prussian-style tunic with polished epaulets tailored to fit his middle-aged body. "I never thought," he said to Letelier, "that generals and colonels whom I have known since childhood would hide behind the skirts of their wives. I am sad for Chile because I have seen not only treason but a kind of cowardice that I did not conceive as possible."

The police arrived some two hours after Letelier's call. The captain politely requested the women to leave. The thugs who had accompanied them had already destroyed some of the cars and thrown objects against Prats's house.

In the early hours of the morning of August 23, Letelier left his colleague's house. Prats sat at his desk and began to write his letter of resignation as minister of defense and commander of the army. He no longer commanded the respect of his officers; he was no longer an obstacle to the coup.

On the day that Prats resigned, Allende spoke to the assembled chiefs of the armed forces: Pinochet of the army, Montero of the navy, Leigh of the air force, and Sepúlveda, the head of the Carabineros. He read from a list of two hundred acts of terrorism that had been committed in the country over the past few days. He chided them for their failure to enforce the law and told them: "Gentlemen, this is a civil war. I want you to understand very well that I will not leave La Moneda alive. If you want to overthrow me, I will die at my post as president of Chile. I will never surrender to anyone."

On August 28, 1973, Allende named Orlando Letelier minister of defense. When Letelier took over the defense portfolio he knew that only a massive display of support in a nationwide referendum could hold back a bloody coup. General Augusto Pinochet Ugarte, who replaced General Prats as commander of Chile's army, told Letelier that he agreed with him. Pinochet and Letelier had had several conversations after Letelier's appointment as defense minister, one in the presence of Allende. Pinochet assured both men that he was, like his predecessor, loyal to the Constitution and to President Allende.

Letelier's inauguration as defense minister was a simple ceremony. Other cabinet members posed with him and Allende for a group picture. Letelier took the oath of office on August 28 in a small room in La Moneda Palace. The cabinet, Popular Unity dignitaries, a few generals, the press, and television elbowed each other for space.

Pinochet, present at the ceremony, approached Isabel Letelier and kissed her on both cheeks. "I am very happy to have our Orlando. He was at the military school, you know. We've followed his career." Then he took Isabel by the elbow and said, "I want you to meet my wife. We shall become good friends. We've been so fortunate in having extraordinary defense ministers like José Tohá and Orlando Letelier. And their wives," he smiled, "have been so genteel. We'll see a lot of each other in the future." "You know, Orlando," he told Letelier, "the army had hoped for your appointment. What fortune to have had Tohá and now you in this position."

The new army commander always nodded or spoke in agreement with the new defense minister's ideas and suggestions. Meanwhile, unknown to Letelier, Pinochet authorized scores of military operations against factories, farms, and poor neighborhoods, using the arms-control law as his pretext.

Letelier did know that a coup was coming. But when? How? Would resistance be organized in time? Would units of the armed forces join with the workers for mutual defense? How many of them? Time, time, time, thought Letelier. To answer the escalating violence, to sober those sectors already celebrating a victorious coup, Allende called on the Chilean masses to show their strength and determination. On September 4 in Santiago's main plaza, a million Popular Unity supporters marched in a show of solidarity with the government.

The climate of conspiracy produced deep unrest inside working-class ranks. Factory and neighborhood discussions turned exclusively to defense: how to stop the reactionaries. All positive debate about work and social structure had been crowded out by the crisis.

On September 7, U.S. Ambassador Nathaniel Davis telephoned Letelier to advise him that he had to return to Washington for an urgent meeting with Secretary of State Kissinger. He bade Letelier goodbye and said that he intended to return September 11 or 12 and wished for an appointment on the twelfth to discuss a request for a purchase that the Chilean armed forces wanted to make in the United States. Ambassador Davis returned to Chile, not on the eleventh or twelfth, but on September 10.

Also on September 7, General Prats informed Allende and Letelier that he had received information that the coup date was September 14. If Allende were to remove five or six generals, the coup date would have to be postponed and there would be more time to prepare for defense. Prats assured Allende that Pinochet was personally loyal to the president.

The coup, like the Chilean spring, was in the air. Navy Admiral Montero faced a mutiny of senior officers in Valparaíso, Chile's major port and naval center. Allende instructed Letelier to deal with the problem. Letelier forced the rebellious officers to meet with Montero in his office. Pinochet whispered in Letelier's ear: "Duro con ellos, ministro" (be tough with them, sir). On the same day Pinochet assured Allende that a nationwide referendum would resolve the parliamentary obstacles and clear the path to effective government. But when Letelier tried to get information on army raids against Popular Unity strongholds, Pinochet became either inaccessible or vague. "He gives me the creeps," Letelier complained of Pinochet to Isabel. "He's flattering and servile like the man in the barber shop who runs after you with a whisk broom after you've had your hair cut and doesn't stop sweeping at your back until you've given him a tip. He's constantly trying to help me on with my coat and always trying to carry my briefcase."

On September 7, the Leteliers invited several undersecretaries of defense to their house for a dinner party. Letelier, delayed by Allende at the palace, implored Isabel to play host as well as hostess. She conversed with the colonels and navy captains. During predinner conversation, she overheard a pro-Constitution colonel comment on the turnout three days before, "A million people is impressive, don't you think?" A young navy officer, Captain Laluz, responded, "I believe our last census reported our population at ten million. Surely we could get along with nine."

On the morning of September 10 Letelier received several of Pinochet's orders authorizing military operations. When Letelier confronted him, Pinochet became vague and refused to admit that he had authorized the raids.

Letelier spent most of September 10 with President Allende and the other cabinet ministers and advisers. The meeting began in the Moneda Palace in a room decorated with objects from colonial times.

At the meeting the cabinet ministers reported sabotage, violence, army raids against UP villages and factories. Letelier told about the beginning of internal armed-forces proceedings against Captain Ballas and other officers who had demonstrated outside General Prats's residence. Letelier remained optimistic: "If they don't overthrow us this week, we'll never fall. Everything they have set up is ready to explode now." The ministers planned countermeasures, relying on the mobilization of workers' defense units using supposedly loyal elements inside the armed forces. Pinochet was one of the generals on whom most of the assembled officials counted.

They ate lunch and continued talking. Allende looked at his watch: "It's after three. You, Orlando, go right away to the Defense Ministry and make sure the air force is obeying my order to suspend all raids."

Letelier went to his office. It was his thirteenth day as defense minister. In and around his office men in uniform bowed and greeted him. He had solid information that some of them were plotting, suspected others, and believed that a core of the top brass remained loyal. But he knew he did not have the key to the puzzle.

On the evening of September 10, Letelier gave a televised press conference on the issue of national security and the armed forces. The themes were repeats of Popular Unity policy: respect for the institutional character of the armed forces; improvement of its professional equipment and training; attempts to end its isolation from civilian society; the need to take measures to avoid civil war.

During the months of June, July, and August an average of one terrorist act per hour had occurred in Chile. Right up until September 11 the armed forces continued to raid the work and political centers of UP supporters; raids on right-wing paramilitary targets either never materialized or else warnings were somehow sent to the targeted groups. Allende, however, remained firm. He told his wife, "Tencha," as they dined for the last time at their home, "The Unidad Popular can't respond to terrorism with terrorism, because that would produce only chaos."

Reports came to Allende that the navy had begun its exercises and ships had set sail from Valparaíso. "We can at least be sure,"

Allende commented, "that the coup won't include all of the armed forces."

Letelier arrived at the Allende residence on the night of September 10 after his press conference and rejoined the meeting of ministers and advisers. Augusto Olivares, a friend and adviser, interrupted the strategy session to announce: "Reports of trucks with troops that have left Los Andes base going toward Santiago—" Allende snapped an order: "Orlando, please phone the head of the Santiago Guard and find out what's happening." Letelier phoned General Herman Brady, recently named head of the Second Army Division: "He says he knows nothing." Letelier called back fifteen minutes later to give Brady time to check. At midnight Letelier reported on his second conversation with Brady: "He says there's no information on truck movements—the troops are in barracks and in preparation for the Independence Day parade—and that he's taking charge of the situation."

Shortly after midnight, Socialist Party General Secretary Carlos Altamirano phoned Letelier to report trucks with soldiers having left the Los Andes base. Letelier offered three solutions to deal with the probable coup plotters. Allende liked the one that Prats had recommended: force six or seven generals into retirement before the end of the week. "Tomorrow in my radio speech to the country I'll inform the people of the plan."

At 2:30 A.M. Allende adjourned the meeting. "I spoke with Brady. Go to bed, it's late. Tomorrow will be a long, hard day."

THAT NIGHT Isabel Letelier fell asleep at about 1:30 A.M. At a meeting earlier in the evening she had been nominated for the presidency of her neighborhood Food Distribution Council, along with two other women. But the vote could not be taken because a government official whose presence was required to legitimate the election never arrived. Her chauffeur, a Defense Ministry employee, drove her to a friend's house above a little store. Her friend gave Isabel a small portion of powdered milk for breakfast coffee and also offered some of the scarce commodity to the driver, who looked awkward. Isabel recalled his discomfort at all friendly gestures that evening.

She told him to take the car home with him as he had done for several nights. Orlando would be driven in his own car. Since the beginning of a prolonged transportation strike the chauffeur had no other means to get to his house. The drivers and cars were provided routinely by the armed forces to the defense minister and his family.

Orlando Letelier was a notorious insomniac. For years he had slept less than five hours a night even when exhausted. When he returned home from Allende's house at 3:00 A.M., he said goodnight to his bodyguard, smoked a last cigarette—was it his fourth or fifth pack?—and let the reports from intelligence officers about coup plots run through his mind as he undressed.

Orlando tiptoed into the bedroom. They had just moved into their new seventh-floor apartment, and the makeshift curtains did not altogether shield the windows from the streetlights or from the occasional car headlight. "How was your meeting?" Isabel murmured as he climbed into bed beside her.

"Excellent. Salvador will announce later today that we will have a referendum. I am certain we will win it, and that will reduce the chances of a coup." Isabel came fully awake. "We were waiting for the coup," she later explained. "Each day we kind of expected it, so when Orlando told me that plans had been made for the national vote of confidence we both went to sleep happy."

"That night I had a strange dream," Letelier told one of the authors. "When I finally fell asleep I dreamed that I was dancing all by myself. Generals and admirals watched me dance. I was very graceful. Pinochet smiled at me from his chair when I looked at him, but when I wasn't looking all the generals were whispering."

The ringing of the telephone awakened Isabel Letelier at 6:30 A.M. on September 11, 1973. "It's Salvador," she said. Allende, calm, firm, clear, told Orlando, "The navy has revolted. Six truckloads of navy troops are on the way to Santiago from Valparaíso. The Carabineros are the only units that respond. The other commanders in chief don't answer the phone. Pinochet doesn't answer. Find out what you can."

Orlando asked Isabel to call Admiral Montero and General Prats. He would use the other telephone to call Investigaciones, the political division of the national detective police, and the Ministry of the Interior.

Isabel dialed and waited and waited. No answer at the Prats or Montero houses or offices. Orlando's calls confirmed Allende's reports.

Letelier then phoned his own office. To his surprise Admiral Patricio Carvajal answered. "Your information is wrong, Señor Minister," Carvajal told Letelier. "It's some kind of a raid, nothing more. We're trying to get through to Valparaíso now. I'm looking into it."

Letelier phoned Allende. "Go, Orlando, and take control of the Defense Ministry if you can get there."

Orlando gulped down a cup of coffee. His second son, José Ignacio, came into the kitchen fully dressed. He told his father that he and a group of students planned to take over the school they were locked out of. Letelier smiled for the first time in several days. He had sat down twice in his dentist's chair since September 8, and both times an urgent phone call from Allende had interrupted the dental work. On the first occasion Orlando's fillings had been removed prior to a gum procedure. On the next occasion the dentist had begun a complicated root canal repair when Orlando had to leap from the chair to answer his president's call. His mouth hurt. His head hurt each time hot or cold food, liquid, or air touched the exposed nerves; he had not eaten for more than a day. As he put on his suit jacket while waiting for the elevator, Isabel brought him two aspirins.

Allende had offered to send a car to take Letelier to his office since Letelier's chauffeur was not expected till later. When Orlando reached the street, however, he found his driver but not his bodyguard. Isabel went with him to the car. Letelier inquired about the absence of his bodyguard. Jiménez, the driver, a giant of a young man, appeared vague and confused. He said that the bodyguard's wife was giving birth. Isabel, noticing his odd demeanor, went up to Jiménez; she had to look almost straight up to meet his eyes. His face reddened as she put her arms around him in a maternal gesture and said, "You take care that nothing happens to him."

As the car drove through the Santiago streets Letelier noticed troops in small patrol-size units. They watched his car with interest. There was no traffic other than army trucks and vehicles. Letelier leaped from his car as it pulled up in front of the Defense Ministry. His usual entry door was locked. He went to the front door. Troops in battle dress guarded the door. Letelier approached, and the troops pointed automatic weapons at him. "I'm sorry, I have orders that you cannot enter," a sergeant said. "I give the orders here. Step aside," Letelier responded in a voice that he hoped sounded authoritative, like the voices of the instructors he recalled from his student days in the military academy. "I'm sorry, sir," the soldier answered, "but you are not allowed to enter." A battle-garbed officer approached and said, "If you continue to insist on this point, we will be forced to execute you immediately."

Then a voice from inside the ministry doors said, "Let the minister come inside." The doors opened. Letelier forced his spine erect, stuck his chin forward, and marched inside with his best military bearing. Just inside the door, "I felt a sharp poke in my back and some ten to twelve men moved to surround me, aiming submachine guns at me. They wore combat uniforms and seemed excited. Among them was my 'sick' bodyguard," Letelier said. He was shoved downstairs into the basement. "They took my tie, my belt, my jacket. They searched me, threw me against the wall."

Another officer arrived and told the man in charge of Letelier's groups that a military junta headed by Pinochet had been constituted. At 8:20 A.M. Letelier was told that he was to be moved to a more secure location. He was pushed outside and surrounded by armed troops, as a British photographer snapped a photo.

Letelier did not know or learn anything more. Inside La Moneda, Allende and his intimates tried to make plans. Allende expected that Letelier would keep him informed about troop movements. He asked his aides if they had heard from Letelier. None had. He sent a member of the military escort to the Defense Ministry to find out what had happened to Letelier.

Allende's news all morning went from bad to worse. The air force offered to fly him and his family out of the country if he would quietly resign. He told the air force chief, "The president of Chile doesn't desert in a plane, and [General Von Showen] should know how to act like a soldier just as the president knows how to carry out his sworn duty." Allende was strangely prepared for that phone call. He had often told friends how President Pedro Aguirre Cerda answered a potential coup maker who offered the president an airplane and safe passage. "Look," Aguirre told the air force general, as he sat in his presidential chair and calmly lit a cigarette, "I've been a man of the law all my life. Now I'm President of the Republic. You will have to remove me by force because I will not leave." That one act helped destroy the 1939 attempted coup. Allende had paraphrased Aguirre; ironically, their lives had run parallel—until the day of the coup.

"I've just come from the Defense Ministry," shouted the colonel whom Allende had sent to check on Letelier. "I tried to get in, but they wouldn't let me. The army controls it."

By 8:30 Allende learned that Pinochet was certainly involved. He heard a radio broadcast announcing the formation of a junta by decree. The decree was signed by Air Force General Leigh, by Admiral Toribio Merino, by Carabinero General César Mendoza, and by Pinochet. Allende, his hand on his work table, looked out the window, and said, "Traitors."

Letelier was walked to a car. With three guns pointed at him, he tried to watch the activity in the streets. It was 9:15 A.M. The car headed south to the headquarters of the Tacna Regiment. "Every twenty or twenty-five meters there was a platoon of six or seven soldiers occupying each block." At Tacna the search began again, the stripping. Tacna was only a short distance to the south of the Moneda Palace, and all during the day Letelier heard the firing of artillery, machine guns, automatic rifles. In early afternoon he heard bombs explode and felt the building vibrate.

Allende, with a small group of intimates and his bodyguard, had chosen to remain in La Moneda. Despite their limited arms they had compelled the armed forces to use planes and for the first time bomb the historic presidential palace. At about 3:00 P.M., the burning palace was overrun by soldiers. Allende was killed by a burst of machine-gun fire.

Letelier was moved from one room to another. He was told he could use the telephone, but the phone did not work. Alone at first, he witnessed a steady stream of people arriving at Tacna, their hands raised over their heads. Some of the detained were taken to a court-yard. Letelier heard periodic rifle volleys, short bursts of fire. Among the persons carrying out the arrests and guarding the prisoners, he recognized men dressed in civilian garb whom he knew from his brief time at the Interior Ministry.

Letelier continued to insist on his right to talk to the command-ing officer. His guards smiled, threatened him, cursed him, made excuses and promises. He heard a radio but could not make out the words. He heard his name repeated several times. Night fell. He had no cigarettes and began to feel the symptoms of deprivation. The volleys continued every six or seven minutes. From a small window Letelier could see people lying on the ground in the courtyard. He could not see the firing squad, but he saw soldiers picking up the bodies. The light was dull and yellowish, and Letelier's window was some hundred yards from the scene of the firing squads.

At what he thought was about 4:00 or 4:30 A.M. he heard a voice: "Bring out the minister now. It's the minister's turn." Someone banged on the door of his room: "It's your turn, minister." An officer entered and said, "Move it."

Years later, Letelier told the story of that moment:* "Six persons shoved me between them and we began to walk down the corridor and down a staircase. . . . One of the guards had a small towel and I realized it was meant to be a blindfold. I immediately concluded that, given what I had been seeing from my window, they were taking me to be executed. It's funny when one reads or speaks about what human beings think before being executed. I didn't review my life, the past, my family situation. I thought about very concrete things. I didn't want my knees to buckle. I thought about whether or not I would ask for the blindfold when I reached the courtyard. I counted the number of meters that remained between me and the execution area. It seemed that what was about to happen to me was unreal, yet I had a very real, rational feeling that they were going to execute me. It also seemed strange to me that the ability to feel

*Quotations from Orlando Letelier are taken from a *Playboy* interview by Tad Szulc and from conversations between Letelier and Saul Landau.

horror or fear leaves one's body. Perhaps the level of fear is so high that it raises one above oneself and allows one to observe as if one were somewhere else.

" 'Halt!' " the sergeant shouted. We were on the next to last step leading to the courtyard where the executions were taking place. They began to talk. One thinks of idiotic things at times like these, like how uncomfortable it was going to be standing with one foot on a step and the other on the ground, and so I tried to get them level and one of the guards gave me a hard poke and told me not to move. In the meantime there was a discussion with someone else which lasted for four or five minutes. . . . It was all about who was in charge around here . . . and finally a low-ranking officer shouted from below, 'Take the prisoner up again!' And one of the guards next to me said, 'You lucked out, asshole, they're not going to off you.'

"If you were to ask me why they didn't shoot me and shot others, I wouldn't be able to say there were political reasons. I'd have to say that bureaucratic reasons prevented my execution because a particular captain appeared at that moment. . . . The discussion between the officers was bureaucratic: 'I'm in charge here and you don't have the right to take prisoners down.' "

From his chilly room Letelier peeked into the courtyard to see what was happening. As day began to break, he fell asleep. He knew he was alive, that his suffering had just begun, that terrible things were happening outside. He knew that the life he had lived as student, economist, banker, ambassador, and minister had come to an end, and that the cold that chilled his bones in the tiny room presaged the future.

Nothing about his life until then had been especially romantic, much less heroic. Criminals, terrorists, revolutionaries, perhaps, might find themselves in jail and see their predicament as consistent with the way they had chosen to live their lives. For a person of Letelier's background, prison was a total shock and an anomaly bordering on the absurd.

3

THE YEAR
OF TERROR

AT 3:30 P.M. on September 12, 1973, in his cell at the Tacna Regiment, Orlando Letelier learned that President Allende had died in the battle of La Moneda. He felt an overwhelming anxiety somewhere between intellectual confusion and animal fear—a feeling he shared with millions of other Chileans that day. A few minutes later, Letelier and a fellow prisoner, Enrique Kirberg, rector of the Technical University of Chile, were taken by jeep across Santiago, deserted except for busy military patrols and soldiers setting up bunkers at street corners and public buildings. The junta had decreed a twenty four-hour curfew, and civilians—if they were Popular Unity supporters—waited in their houses hoping to be spared by the military raiding parties. Other civilians had draped their houses with flags.

After more than an hour the prisoners arrived at the Bernardo O'Higgins Military School, Chile's West Point. A plaque over the entrance through which Letelier and Kirberg were led proclaimed the reigning military hierarchy—now usurped by the coup: President, Salvador Allende; Minister of Defense, Orlando Letelier; Commander in Chief of the Army, Augusto Pinochet. Letelier thought wryly that he, the prisoner, outranked every officer at the academy. He turned to the guard and, pointing to the sign, demanded in vain to be taken immediately to the colonel in charge. Letelier's former school had become his prison. About twenty high-level prisoners had been assembled there, including all of Allende's ministers.* In another part of Santiago, the gigantic National Stadium was overflowing with thousands of people rounded up by troops or Patria y Libertad patrols.

In a smaller Santiago stadium, Chilean folksinger Víctor Jara tried to keep up the prisoners' spirits. He kept talking, though the guards forbade it, and when they punched him he began to lead the entire stadium in song. The guards broke his guitar. He went on singing. In full view of thousands of prisoners, the guards broke Jara's hands and wrists and then beat him to death. Other prisoners, in isolated parts of the stadium complex, were forced to lie face down all day, then two, three, four days. No food, no water; they soiled their clothes.

Isabel Letelier telephoned the offices and homes of generals and admirals. At Pinochet's home a servant answered. The general was eating and could not be disturbed. She continued to call, and in the mid-afternoon General Leigh spoke to her: "He is all right. Don't worry, we have taken measures to guarantee his security."

She responded, "But how do I know?"

He became irritable: "I give you my word."

"But General Leigh, my husband's security—"

Leigh hung up.

The Allende government lay in ruins, but remained the repository of constitutional legitimacy. Allende had refused to resign, to turn over the mantle of government voluntarily to the military usurpers. Before he died, he stressed in a radio address the legitimacy, the legality of his government, his right to act as he did, and denounced the treason of those who rose against the lawful government, using aerial bombardment and heavy artillery.

The civilian opposition leaders, like former President Eduardo

---

*The prisoners included: Clodomiro Almeyda, foreign minister; Sergio Bitar, minister of mining; Carlos Briones, minister of the interior (the only prisoner released before the trip to Dawson Island); Edgardo Enríquez, rector of the University of Concepción, minister of education; Fernando Flores, minister of mining; Arturo Girón, minister of health; Aníbal Palma, former minister of education; Osvaldo Puccio and his sixteen-year-old son, Osvaldo Junior; Aniceto Rodríguez, senator; and José Tohá, former minister of the interior.

Frei, who welcomed the coup, had counted on Allende's "reason-ableness," his ability to behave like a parliamentary gentleman. Frei and the others did not envision the holocaust that came. No Christian Democratic–right-wing coalition could move into power after so much blood. No constitution could survive such an assault. No set of institutions could simulate even a façade of prestige.

Allende's resistance destroyed any possibility of rapid transition to traditional government. His "suicide," contrived by the coup makers and announced after his death, removed Allende himself as an obstacle, but damaged further the military's tenuous claim to legitimacy.

The four military commanders that formed the ruling junta formally selected General Augusto Pinochet as president, not of Chile, but of the junta itself. His rule began two days after the coup, on September 13. The junta decreed that all power resided in the new military rulers, even the power to change the Constitution. They announced that their task was to uproot Marxism forever from Chile.

The roots of the leftist coalition were millions of supporters deep (a million of them activists) and many decades long. The process that had produced the Allende victory and propelled it forward through its three years of existence became the foremost challenge for the junta, who realized they would have to instigate a reaction equal to the depth of UP support in order to neutralize the past. The generals decided quickly that repression, in its most physical form, was the required equal reaction. The terror that had existed in underground cells during the Allende period became institutionalized. The ones who had bombed and run, murdered and fled, now became officers in the state's repressive apparatus.

From the north to the south military commanders ruled cities and regions. For the first month, perhaps a million books alleged to contain "Marxist" ideas were piled and burned outside libraries and houses. Curfew began at nightfall, ended with sunrise. Soldiers, policemen, and rightist commandos had a free hand to arrest, kidnap, torture, construct makeshift prison camps, and summarily execute leftists the length of Chile. An army general later admitted that at least 3,000 persons were killed, less than a dozen of them military and police personnel. U.S. Embassy and intelligence estimates at the time, for the same period, put the number dead at around 5,000. But in their public statements, United States officials played down the bloodshed. By conservative calculation, some 50,000 persons were arrested and interrogated as jails, military installations, ships, soccer stadiums, and public auditoriums bulged with an average political-prisoner population of between 15,000 and 20,000.

Exiles from other Latin American dictatorships who had found a haven in Chile during Allende's administration became special targets of military patrols as a wave of xenophobia swept the country. The United Nations High Commission on Refugees set up emergency evacuation centers off limits to the patrols in churches and convents in Santiago. Leftist militants and Popular Unity officials who escaped arrest in the early days of the coup crowded into foreign embassies seeking asylum.* By early 1974 over 10,000 Chileans and foreigners in protective asylum left the country for resettlement as political exiles elsewhere.

Another 50,000 Chileans poured over the borders into neighboring Argentina and Peru and applied for status as political exiles. The numbers seemed incredible. Of Chile's 10 million people, more than 100,000—one in every hundred—became a victim of repression by death, exile, or arrest by the end of the first year of military rule.

The junta's most immediate problem was what to do with the cabinet ministers and other government representatives whom they were holding captive. At the military academy, the temporary jail for officials and dignitaries, confusion reigned.

After three days there the UP dignitaries were visited by the junta's minister of justice, who, Letelier said, "offered us sympathy on the death of the president, saying that human rights would be respected, and that he thought we would be taken out of the coun-

---

*Even higher estimates of deaths, arrests, and exiles are frequently cited by Popular Unity exile organizations. The figures in our text are based on interviews with Chilean armed forces and U.S. Embassy personnel and on estimates by the Chilean human rights organization, the Vicariate of Solidarity (Vicaría de la Solidaridad), which is sponsored by the Catholic Church. See also the study "Five Years of Military Government in Chile (1973–1978)," an unpublished manuscript by Bernarda Elgueta et al. Dependable information is also available from the various reports of Amnesty International and the UN Human Rights Commission's special working group on Chile.

try." Letelier and the group told him that they had committed no crime and did not see why they should be removed from the country. "We want due process," they said.

On the following day, as the prisoners prepared to sit down at the lunch table, "they forced us to return to the rooms where we slept, gather our possessions, and with lots of violence, pushing, and cursing they made us line up in formation and pushed us onto a bus."

Once on the bus the prisoners had to keep their heads down, and their armed guards warned them, "Anyone who raises his head will immediately be shot." Orlando had nothing but the clothes he had worn on the day he left his house. It seemed a long time ago. Four days without shaving or changing clothes made the fastidious man crawl with discomfort. Worse, his four-pack-a-day habit was reduced to zero—cold turkey. The bus took them to the El Bosque Air Force Base near Santiago. Once again all the prisoners had to spread their legs and be searched by the guards. As Letelier and the others boarded a DC-6 he was left only his identification card and, curiously, the document certifying him as ambassador to the United States.

There were almost as many guards as prisoners on the plane. "I knew we were heading south and I tried to conjecture where," Letelier said later. Eight hours later the plane landed in Punta Arenas, the southernmost city in the world. It was night. Blinding floodlights were trained on the prisoners as they were led off the plane two by two. Mug shots were taken. Letelier saw troops with fixed bayonets, armed cars, tanks, and transport trucks. The treatment of the prisoners continued violent and abusive.

Arturo Girón, the minister of health, who had remained in the Moneda Palace with Allende until taken prisoner, was especially victimized; the guards kicked him repeatedly. Letelier drew on his knowledge of the military to try to cope with his fears and the circumstances in which he found himself. "Each soldier is a prisoner in all situations. Each private has a corporal above him, each corporal is observed by a lieutenant, and each one is trying now, because of fear and terror, to show that he's more violent than the others, because he knows that if he doesn't they will apply the sanctions to him: there's a verticality of terror . . . softness, acting human, could lead them to real harm," he reasoned.

Letelier and the others were placed in an armored vehicle; hoods were tied to their necks. "I heard firing," Letelier said. "I thought as we sat huddled together that they would shoot us all and dump our bodies into the Strait of Magellan. . . . It seemed so unreal, so inconceivable, so absurd, so weird. . . . You come to a point where the anguish and the terror disappear because you've become so upset that you overcome the terror, there are no more spaces for terror and a great calm descends on you. . . . There's an urge to say to yourself, well, if they're going to kill me I'm going to die dignified, as a man. These guys are killers, and in some way it's my historic responsibility, my responsibility as a man, to act correctly."

Before the truck left, there was more shooting. "I've been hit," shouted the man next to Letelier. "I was sure I was going to be next," Letelier remembered. A voice shouted, "What's going on?" "I'm wounded." "Shit." "Shut the door. Go." The shots Letelier heard had been fired by nervous guards inside the armored cars. One shot ricocheted off the ceiling and hit Interior Undersecretary Daniel Vergara in the arm. For an hour and ten minutes as the trucks bumped along Letelier felt a steady dripping of warm liquid onto his leg. The hoods stifled and terrorized them; no one was allowed to speak.

They were herded on board a troop transport. Hoods off, huddled next to each other on the floor or on narrow seats, the prisoners felt the movement of the sea; some became sick. Vergara's arm began to swell and become discolored. The Strait of Magellan swirled the ship about, throwing the prisoners against each other.

They landed on an island at about 6 A.M. It was cold; snow patches dotted the rocky landscape. A mountain could be seen in the distance. "We were dressed in summer clothes," Letelier recalled. "We walked up the beach, and they put the oldest men into old American trucks from World War II, and we marched through the snow, wind blowing, stepping on barbed wire and getting cut because this was Dawson Island, a marine base now being converted into a concentration camp. José Tohá had started an agricultural experiment station there." The other prisoners marched about two miles to a group of ramshackle cabins beside a stream. There navy officer

Jorge Feles addressed the group. Letelier remembered that he called them "war prisoners who have the rights and obligations of war prisoners under the Geneva Treaty. . . . They gave us two blankets and we were sent to our barracks with instructions on tomorrow's routine." Letelier had spent nearly a week as a prisoner.

On the morning of September 18 Isabel and Moy Tohá decided they would find out where their husbands had been taken and what the junta was planning. They arrived at the Ministry of Defense and identified themselves to the corporal at the door. "The corporal shouted inside, 'The wives of Minister Letelier and Minister Tohá are here,' " Moy Tohá recalled the scene. "To my astonishment, I saw Pinochet in a corridor. Isabel said under her breath, 'He's going to hug you, He'll hug you.' " Moy put her hands behind her back and forced her fingernails into the flesh of her palms: "And I saw Pinochet approaching, after gesturing to the journalists to withdraw. He grasped me and pressed me to his chest. 'Nothing will happen, nothing will happen,' he said."

Pinochet agreed to receive the women. The next day Isabel Letelier, Moy Tohá, and Irma Almeyda, wife of former Foreign Minister Clodomiro Almeyda, sat in General Pinochet's waiting room. After some twenty minutes the waiting-room door opened and Pinochet stepped into the room. He started to shout, Isabel recalled: "For your information, your husbands are being fed well, well cared for, in a secure place with medical attention."

Pinochet allowed no one else to speak, Moy Tohá recounted. "He stood there in this room with three seated women and shouted at the top of his lungs." "We watched him in astonishment," Isabel said, "because he stuck his tongue out and ranted about Plan Z.* He repeated that our husbands were well and then, sticking his tongue out again, said, 'It would have been quite different for us if the situation had been reversed, because in this case'—and he made a

*Plan Z was the alleged conspiracy by Allende and his cohorts to stage a pro-left coup. Plan Z then served as the pretext for the actual coup, Pinochet and the other conspirators claiming that they had acted when they did and with such force and brutality as the only way to save Chile from a Sovietizing military takeover. No evidence to support charges about Plan Z was ever produced. The military later dropped all references to the plan, which was elaborately described in a CIA financial publication, *Libro Blanco.*

horrible gesture, drawing his hand across his throat and sticking out his tongue." Pinochet then said that he wished to end the encounter. "But our husbands had vanished and we were determined to find out where they were. . . . He went on shouting, but when he saw our determination he allowed us to enter his office. He went on talking, saying of Allende, 'We shall always continue to persecute this traitor, even if he is many feet under the earth.' "

Pinochet finally agreed to allow the women to write to their husbands, to let them exchange messages, to reassure the wives and children that the vanished ministers were indeed alive.

Letelier and the other ministers and dignitaries began to adjust to semipolar life on Dawson Island. The prisoners suffered from hunger, cold, illness, extreme discomfort in every form. Many contracted virulent cases of flu, with high fevers. The men organized themselves as best they could to maximize their chances of survival. They became forced laborers, constructing buildings, latrines, and fences, hauling and breaking rocks. Each day, Letelier said, "the cold wind blew seventy or eighty miles an hour, and the forced labor which began at seven and lasted till seven at night made it difficult for us." He laughed: "Fascism is a terrible thing, but when you combine it with underdevelopment . . ."

When a group of officers came to visit Dawson, Letelier's eyes sparkled with expectation. He recognized Colonel Vicuña, a close friend and bunkmate at cadet school. "Orlando waited until he could sort of ease his way close to Vicuña. We all expected him to find out important information about what would happen to us," said Luis Matte, a fellow prisoner. "When Orlando returned he looked very pale. We asked him what had happened. 'He said terrible things. He said if it were up to him he would kill us all and be rid of a big problem because if he didn't kill us, one day we would leave here, and eventually our children would seek revenge on him and kill him.' "

"We had only lentils to eat, much of which was pebbles. No fruit, no vegetables, no meat. Rarely would we get a hunk of fat, and we needed this because of the climate," Letelier said. After a month, the wives were allowed to send packages of clothes and food, but the junta limited their size and frequency of delivery. One day José Tohá could not get up. He was taken to a hospital in Punta Arenas. Tohá, six feet, six inches tall, weighed 108 pounds by the end of 1973. "Tohá began to go out like a candle," a prisoner recalled. "He was always cheerful and joking, but he was like a rare bird that couldn't survive in a cage." Tohá was removed from the camp and returned to Santiago's Military Hospital. Several months later, on a smuggled radio, the Dawson prisoners heard that the frail Tohá had hanged himself with his belt. A short time before, another VIP prisoner had died in captivity. Air Force General Alberto Bachelet, a staunch Allende supporter, had been imprisoned after the coup and confined in a military prison where he died, allegedly of a heart attack, in March 1974.

In the camp began what Letelier called "a torturous comedy of the absurd." The prisoners had begun to sing while they marched and worked, but "they didn't let us sing just any song, but instead began to force us to sing old Chilean military marches, many of them dating from last century's war against Peru. One famous march written during World War II, the 'Hymn of the Americas,' in which all the names of the countries are recited, we had to sing over and over again. On one occasion an officer overheard us singing and stopped us. 'There's disloyalty here,' he said. 'You have all been singing North America, Mexico and Peru, Cuba and Canada brothers, but the word Cuba is prohibited in the Chilean language.' From then on we sang the song without mentioning Cuba." Five hours by ship south of the last Chilean city, Letelier and the other prisoners felt completely cut off from Chile and from the rest of the world.

The terror felt by the Dawson prisoners, as well as by some of the guards and other low-rank military personnel, had its counterpart at all levels of society. The junta had to find replacements for all elements of Chilean society that had "been influenced by Marxism." That required a new economic order, new laws where old ones conflicted with the new economics, and a new educational system. For their economic model junta intellectuals turned to University of Chicago economists Dr. Milton Friedman and Arnold Harberger.

Internally, Chilean workers saw their economic and social gains reversed. Public services that were cheap or free under Allende became costly. Real wages plummeted as inflation soared. Prices for basic commodities rose on "the free market." In two months the price of bread leaped to twenty-two times the controlled price under Allende. Luxury items reappeared in abundance.

After three months in the Dawson Island concentration camp, Orlando Letelier, six feet tall and broad-shouldered, weighed approximately 125 pounds. "To resist each day" had become his guiding principle. He did not like to receive photos or letters from his family. He observed that other prisoners expressed great emotion when letters arrived from home. Then the joy turned to sorrow, self-pity, psychological breakdown. "My concern centered on my life as a prisoner and on trying each day to dedicate myself to the task of being alive. At night before falling asleep I thought and said aloud, 'Well, I'm alive.' " Yet at times he felt ready to quit, to give up, lapse into despair. "One thinks, How is it possible that the world allows this to happen to me?" he said later. "That this thing, so brutal, so unjust, so immoral, in this century with all the concepts that guide civilized people, could be possible, that this irrationality could be permitted. . . . One tends to think one has been abandoned, that one's friends are not thinking about one, that they're concerned only about themselves. . . ."

The arrival of a guitar gave the prisoners some of their few joyous moments and alleviated somewhat the dreariness of life in Dawson. Letelier persuaded a soldier to buy the guitar for him in Punta Arenas. "Letelier had a rich, strong, deep voice," fellow inmate Luis Matte remembered. "The guards and even the officers liked to listen to him. In that cold and desolate place the sound of the guitar and a voice singing a *cueca* could bring tears to one's eyes."

In late December, the Dawson guards moved the high-level political prisoners across Dawson Island to a new site called Rio Chico. "This was a real concentration camp, one that looked exactly like the pictures of the German models and we began to think we would be there forever. Such desolation . . . in the other camp at least there were some trees." The new seaside camp consisted of four long wooden barracks inside a double row of high barbed-wire fence. Steep hills rose abruptly on two sides, and from four guard towers high-caliber machine guns were trained on the camp day and night. Batteries of artillery lined the tops of the hills, aimed out to sea. The prisoners were told the artillery was to defend the camp from attack by Soviet submarines. The guards warned them that if such an attack occurred, all the prisoners would immediately be executed.

Other high-ranking leaders joined the prisoners in Dawson. About 160 local union leaders and leftist militants rounded up by the military commander of Punta Arenas in Magallanes Province raised the concentration-camp population to nearly two hundred. An army captain looked over the new buildings and remarked to one of the prisoners, "This is just like the film *The Great Escape.*"

In February the Dawson commander ordered Letelier sent by boat to the hospital at Punta Arenas for a medical checkup. Through the grapevine Isabel heard the news and booked passage to Punta Arenas. In the plaza there, she recounted, somebody came up to her, put his hand on her shoulder and said, "Comrade, we congratulate you on your bravery." Confused, she walked on to the town hall. "Repeatedly, people came up to me and said, 'We feel solidarity with you, comrade.' Later I realized that I was wearing the stone which Orlando had carved and sent to me. Such stones come exclusively from Dawson, and the people recognized it."

Isabel requested permission to see her husband from the hospital authorities, who referred her to the military authorities, who in turn sent her back to the hospital. Finally, on her second trip to the military command, a stern, stiff-backed major granted her permission—on condition that the couple speak only about "domestic affairs" and in the presence of an intelligence officer.

In the hospital, the couple touched hands and embraced in front of a gruff young officer who interrupted their conversation several times to rebuke them for "political references." Thirty minutes later, the officer abruptly terminated the interview. He allowed the couple a brief embrace, scrutinizing Isabel's hands to make certain she did not pass Orlando notes or weapons. "I love you," each said to the other.

The pro-Allende Chileans who escaped or were abroad during the coup joined with sympathizers throughout Western Europe and the United States to launch an international campaign focused on the issue of freeing the political prisoners. They enlisted prominent political leaders and cultural emissaries to petition the Pinochet government for their release, while they encouraged journalists and humanitarian groups to monitor the actual condition of the encarcerated. Print and television journalists demanded interviews with the prisoners and the right to film and inspect their living conditions on Dawson Island. The pressure worked. Faced with what seemed like worldwide and escalating criticism on that issue, Pinochet ordered his star prisoners moved from Dawson to Santiago.

On May 8, 1974, the prisoners were awakened at 4:00 A.M. and ordered to have their possessions ready for transport in fifteen minutes. "On the previous nights the camp guards had simulated attacks on the camp, firing toward our barracks," Letelier said. "They forced us to march that morning some ten miles to an airstrip. On the way we had to ford two icy streams and take off our trousers and underpants, and I felt as if my legs would freeze as we formed a human chain passing our clothing across the river. The officers naturally didn't cross the river there, but at another point."

The former ministers were taken to Punta Arenas airport, where they boarded a Chilean Air Force C-130. Letelier recognized the plane. "I recalled talking with the air force attaché in Washington before we purchased it: 'Colonel, this plane is used only for transporting equipment. Does the air force have enough cargo to warrant buying it?' and he answered, 'It can also be used to transport people at any given moment.' "

Hands and feet tied, the prisoners rode on the plane Letelier had thought to be a questionable purchase. Letelier reasoned with himself in his discomfort that if he were to be thrown out of the plane from that height it would make little difference whether his hands and feet were tied or free. The C-130 cabins were not pressurized; the noise caused a temporary loss of hearing. Just before landing at Santiago, the guards untied the prisoners.

Standing on the runway to meet them were men in white coats with Red Cross insignias, hovering about officiously. A Colonel Espinoza gave a short speech to the prisoners, telling them that they would have better conditions. The colonel, who administered one hundred concentration camps throughout Chile, smiled and asked the group if any of them were sick. Letelier spoke up: "I must tell you that you have treated us inhumanly. All of your actions are creating infamy in the eyes of the world."

Colonel Espinoza smiled: "Very well, now you may leave." A man wearing the Red Cross insignia took Letelier's arm and led him behind some buildings. There his arms were pulled behind his back, rope placed around them and tied tight, a hood strapped over his head. The men he had mistaken for Red Cross officials were actually military officers. Pushing and kicking the prisoners, the "officers" threw them onto trucks and sped away.

Letelier found himself in a basement of the Air Force Academy, with the few panes of glass papered over. Upstairs he heard almost continuous screaming and moaning, some of it in women's voices. Through his cell window he saw people facing the corridor wall. Guards would force them to stand hooded for as long as three days until they fell.

"Are you a homosexual?" they asked Orlando. They implied that he was a cuckold. "They tried to destroy us psychologically," Letelier recalled. Some prisoners were placed in isolation for weeks, tied to their beds, hooded. Letelier admitted that after the guards placed a hood on his head, "that was one of the most difficult things for me, not being able to distinguish night from day, not being able to deal as one usually does with the very practical place that time has in one's life.

"They interrogated me as well, especially about the ITT thing.* They said they had proof that I had paid $70,000 to the journalist Jack Anderson so that he would accuse ITT, that I personally gave him the documents, which we had fabricated, and that I personally went to the Press Building in Washington and delivered the check to him."

---

*At a company board meeting in New York September 9, 1970, according to the Church Committee report, Harold Geneen, International Telephone and Telegraph's chief executive officer, told ITT board member John McCone, former CIA director, that he was prepared to offer $1 million of company money "for the purposes of assisting any government plan designed to form a coalition in the Chilean Congress to stop Allende." McCone communicated the offer to National Security Adviser Henry Kissinger and CIA Director Richard Helms in that same week. The CIA later denied that it had accepted the ITT offer, after columnist Jack Anderson published a leaked report of it. The documents themselves surfaced at the Church Committee hearings in 1975.

In the interrogations the questioners would ask, " 'Do you know so and so?' Then they'd change the subject to the Jack Anderson column, and then say 'Do you know that your wife is a whore?' "

Then early one morning, without warning, Letelier and the others from Dawson were awakened by shouts. Guards pushed them onto a truck and took them to a police station. From there "they threw us onto the floor of a bus and they kicked us to make us open our legs, with our hands in back of our heads." The bus arrived at Ritoque, a coastal resort north of Santiago. They were interned in cabins built under Allende to house vacationing workers. Barbed wire and guard towers had converted the resort into a concentration camp.

Letelier began to feel somewhat reassured. He had known the admiral who was in charge of the province of Valparaíso and a colonel connected with the nearby air base as military attachés in Washington. They had dined with him and Isabel at the goodbye supper, spent time socially with the Leteliers. At the farewell dinner both had toasted Letelier and spoken of "the gratitude they felt for the way he had treated them." Admiral Eberhard landed by helicopter in Ritoque. The guards ordered the prisoners to line up in formation. The admiral reviewed them, asking each his number. When he came to Letelier, whom he had previously addressed as Señor or Embajador, the admiral stopped.

"¿Cómo está usted?" he asked. (How are you?)

"Estoy bien," Letelier responded. (All right.)

"Do you need something?"

"No, I don't need anything."

"And how is your wife?" the admiral inquired.

"Not very well. How's yours?" asked Letelier.

"She's well," he said.

An air force colonel came to Letelier's cabin. Letelier recalled how he tried to "throw the blame on something, someone, to avoid being directly connected with the circumstances that had produced these things. I responded very tersely, very tough. He didn't retaliate. He just left."

These visits reinforced Letelier's moral strength. He never doubted that he had right and reason on his side, the Constitution and the law. "A sergeant found time to speak to me," Letelier said. " 'Don Orlando,' he addressed me, using Don, which connotes respect, 'I'm against this thing, against those generals, but I can't do anything. You know I'm married. I have a family and if one . . . imagine. What's happening is that the lieutenant here is a fascist.' "

Then the lieutenant would appear. "Look, Mr. Letelier. You hate me, right? You hate me, but you don't realize that I am a professional. I really must obey orders. They taught me how to fight against enemies. I know it isn't good to do these things to Chileans, but I obey orders . . . from Captain Zamora, who is in charge."

Later Captain Zamora dropped by. "You think I do these things for revenge, from a spirit of vengeance. No. I want you to know I have nothing personal against you, and you would be wrong to think bad of me. Because above all I'm a professional man, and the major gives me orders. I don't do nearly as many negative and bad things as he would like. But if I didn't do them, do you know what would happen? I would end up a prisoner in one of these cells myself."

This is what Letelier later called "the verticality of terror."

The same international pressure that forced Pinochet to close the Dawson Island camps assured better treatment for the VIP prisoners at Ritoque. After July 20, 1974, Letelier and the other prisoners began to receive family visits. The winter rains began, but in Ritoque they had sufficient clothing and protection from the weather. In fact, Ritoque was, after Dawson Island and the Air Force Academy, a kind of prisoners' vacationland. In addition to weekly family visits, the prisoners had recreation time, during which they could talk, play chess, and organize other activities. In early September Isabel visited Orlando and told him that Diego Arias, the governor of Caracas, Venezuela, planned to visit Chile.

Diego Arias loved Orlando Letelier, who was a close friend and the godfather of his only daughter. Letelier's plight represented the deepest kind of obligation for Arias, one of Venezuela's most powerful politicians. He flew to Chile and received an appointment with General Pinochet on September 9, 1974.

"I've come on a personal and humane mission," Arias began. "My government of course approves, but I want you to know that Orlando Letelier is the godfather of my only daughter. I understand that you plan to release some prisoners this month, and I ask you in the name of friendship to include Orlando Letelier."

"You are right," replied Pinochet. "I am planning to free some prisoners, but Letelier is not on the list." Pinochet leaned back in his chair, a smug expression on his face.

Arias searched for a new line of argument: "Mr. President, I want you to recall that Letelier spent little time in Chile during the Allende period, compared with many of the prisoners."

Pinochet countered, "Often, those who spend least time do the most damage."

"But there's an international campaign from all political sectors . . ."

"I've told you," answered Pinochet emphatically, "that he's not on the list. Therefore I've decided that he'll go with you tomorrow."

Arias, stunned, muttered a thank-you.

"But," continued Pinochet, "he will need a passport." Pinochet dialed a number and spoke to his foreign minister. "Please arrange the necessary papers for Orlando Letelier to leave the country tomorrow."

Pinochet dictated two resolutions that day after meeting with Arias. One resolution released Letelier because the state of siege under which he was taken prisoner had ended—no charges were ever brought against him—and the other expelled him from Chile.

On September 9, Letelier found himself once again removed from his cell and transported to an air base. Here one group of guards handed him over to another group, and he heard the chauffeur announce an address, a street and a number Letelier recognized as the Venezuelan Embassy. He was searched several more times. Many guards surrounded him; the officer in charge told Letelier that ninety men had been mobilized to transport him. "Once you are outside, remember," the officer said, "the arm of DINA is long. General Pinochet will not and does not tolerate activities against his government."

Later in the day a Venezuelan Embassy official went to Chile's Foreign Ministry to pick up the papers Pinochet had ordered. He returned empty-handed. Isabel Letelier waited at the embassy. She had hurriedly packed two suitcases for her husband, but now she felt nervous. Arias had Pinochet's promise, but the assured passport was not delivered. At midnight an army vehicle screeched to a halt at the embassy gate. Two expressionless guards gripped Letelier by the arms. Another covered him with an automatic weapon. A fourth man rang the bell. The embassy's minister counselor raced to the door.

The bell ringer pushed a receipt in front of the Venezuelan diplomat and offered him a pen. The receipt read: "I, ———, accept delivery of one man, height 1 meter 85, weight approximately 150 pounds, fair complexion, red hair." The Venezuelan signed the form and handed it to the Chilean, who nodded at the guards. They pushed Letelier toward the Venezuelan like a package, made a military about-face, and marched to their vehicle.

Inside the embassy the Leteliers embraced. Orlando was in a rare mood, joking about his "delivery" and completely at ease. Diego Arias and the ambassador uncorked the finest champagne to celebrate the release. They talked until after 1:00 A.M., then Orlando and Isabel went to bed.

Letelier's plane to Caracas was to leave at 7:30 A.M. He rose after sleeping less than an hour and began to inspect the contents of the suitcases Isabel had packed. "He had a fit," she recalled. " 'Why did you bring this polka-dotted tie? I can't wear it with the pin-striped suit. And this underwear I would never wear.' " Letelier threw the clothes out of the suitcase. " 'This is the sloppiest packing I've ever seen,' he told me."

The fury that had built up inside him burst forth in a tantrum. The inexpressible rage that he had felt for 364 days spewed out of him in the tiny bedroom in the Venezuelan Embassy as he repacked his suitcase. The explosion over and done with, the Leteliers drove in the ambassador's car to the airport to board the plane for Caracas. Not until the plane left the runway did Isabel breathe a sigh of relief, fearing till that point that Pinochet might still change his mind.

THE FIRST HIGH-LEVEL prisoner to be released by the junta, Letelier spoke cautiously to the waiting newspeople at Caracas. Isabel and his sons were still in Chile. Keenly aware that they would face whatever consequences resulted from his press conference, he limited himself to denouncing "the horrible conditions that prevail in the concentration camps" and confirming already published reports of conditions there.

Letelier's release from confinement meant that he could wake, sleep, buy, and eat when and what he wanted. But more important, freedom, he discovered, "meant in a very profound way the recognition of necessity. I didn't understand it in my body when I read Marx, but when I was released and arrived in Caracas I knew only necessity." If duty, luck, or personal preference had helped dictate the paths of his life before prison, his personal fate could no longer be divorced from the overwhelming need to work against the junta, to act without hesitation in the political arena.

Diego Arias tried to persuade Letelier to take a vacation, a Caribbean cruise, to regain his weight and health. Orlando declined to take the vacation but did accept Arias' offer to work as a consultant in the Ministry of Housing, a job that provided him with an office, a secretary, a telephone, and access to important people. From this office at Centro Bolívar, he kept in touch with other exiled politicians and, with Aniceto Rodríguez and other older Socialist Party officials, petitioned, organized, and agitated on behalf of Chilean refugees and political prisoners.

The Letelier who returned from Dawson Island was a changed man, his Venezuelan friends noticed. The impatient, high-strung, supercharged performer in the banking, diplomatic, and cabinet worlds had slowed down. His efforts to free prisoners and secure decent living conditions for refugees were conducted with care and deliberation in comparison with his previous style, although Orlando Letelier still did, and always would, function at a quicker pace and higher energy level than most people. His face showed new lines of worry and age, marks of a pain he himself had undergone and which he still suffered for the other prisoners and for those dead or missing. He felt in a new way for the deprived and hungry throughout the world.

He also felt lonely. Isabel had sent their second son, José, to be with him in Caracas until the entire family could arrange to leave.

Even so, his loneliness led him into a love affair. Caridad* was wealthy, beautiful, and sophisticated.

"She initiated the affair. For a man who has felt extreme deprivation, can you realize what it is like to all of a sudden have everything offered to you?" Letelier later said. "She was like Lady Bountiful, and I felt like an underprivileged child. I knew what I had to do, but the confidence that I had always gathered to take on each task, the quality that comes from self-assurance, had seeped out of me. And while I was secretly wondering at night who I really was, this woman came along and told me I was wonderful." She listened to his every word, sympathized with his plight, offered her resources to the Chilean cause. She gained a man possessed of undisputed radical credentials, yet polished enough to accompany her in her social circles.

Letelier felt torn. His friends advised him to have a good time, to keep it light, to take what life offered. But he knew that Isabel and the three other boys would soon arrive, and he also knew that he owed every ounce of his creative energy to the people he had lived and suffered with at Dawson and Ritoque. They counted on him, and he drew strength from his sense of solidarity with them.

After the Letelier family was reunited in Caracas in December, Isabel recalled, "I felt something, sensed something. He confessed that he had had an affair, but said it was not important. He told me that he hoped I would understand. I told him that I did understand. Then I looked him straight in the eye and said, 'I hope you also could understand such a thing.' And he looked at me in horror and shouted, 'Never!' "

The Leteliers enjoyed a second honeymoon in Venezuela. "He laughed a lot and told me stories. We had a very good time in Caracas. And yet every day he worked, talked with our comrades."

Saul Landau telephoned Orlando shortly after he arrived in Caracas and offered him, on behalf of Marcus Raskin and Richard

*Not her real name.

Barnet, a fellowship at the Institute for Policy Studies in Washington.* Letelier called back in a few days and said he would come to Washington to discuss the details, but in principle it sounded like an offer he would be anxious to accept.

IPS NAMED LETELIER an associate fellow to develop a study of United States–Chilean relations during the Allende years. He also agreed to organize a major intellectual and policy conference on United States–Latin American affairs. In his IPS office only infrequently at first, Letelier spent his early months in Washington rekindling old friendships and connections and meeting new and important people. At the institute he did not talk about his work for Chile, but it was no secret that he kept busy day and night, that Chilean exiles dropped in to see him, that he made speeches throughout the United States and Canada and eventually in Europe and Mexico.

In February 1975 the exiled leaders of the Popular Unity parties converged on Mexico City. The World Peace Council had established an "International Tribunal to Judge the Crimes of the Military Junta" and arranged to hold this public forum in Mexico. The Mexican government agreed, knowing that the meeting would afford the UP leaders an opportunity to come together and discuss their strategies, while delivering a publicity blow to Pinochet.

The meeting brought together for the first time since the coup the major figures of the Popular Unity coalition, some only recently released from junta prisons. While the public sessions of the International Tribunal concentrated on human rights violations inside Chile, the UP leaders huddled in private to hold post-mortems on the Allende years and to plan strategy for a resistance movement.

*The Institute for Policy Studies was founded in 1962 in Washington, D.C., by former Kennedy administration officials Richard Barnet and Marcus Raskin to develop critiques of and alternatives to United States foreign and military policies. The institute became a center for radical thought and civil rights activism in the mid-1960s and by the end of the decade had developed a reputation for its anti–Vietnam War work as well. By this time it had developed a fellowship of more than twelve and focused attention on domestic as well as foreign policy issues. In 1973 IPS founded the Transnational Institute, with offices in Washington and Amsterdam, to investigate causes and remedies of the disparities between rich and poor nations.

. . .

LETELIER, RETURNING from Mexico, felt a surge of optimism and began to think that more than rhetoric could be generated by exile activities. At the same time he was bothered by something that had troubled him during the UP years: the kind of political thinking that he associated with old-fashioned doctrine, the habit of speaking in polemical language, and behavior that was shaped in antiquated molds. His twelve-plus years of living in the United States had inclined him toward a vigorous pragmatism. He wanted political action against the junta, not concentration on ideological purity. For him, each unified activity that isolated Pinochet, that focused attention on his illegitimacy, was a step closer to restoring civilized rule to Chile. Unity now, he believed; ideological argument could come later.

He felt comfortable at a second-level position inside the Socialist Party and the Popular Unity. He did not have the veteran political status of Carlos Altamirano or of Clodomiro Almeyda, and he had always understood that in Chilean Socialist politics years of service weigh heavily in access to party leadership. Letelier had no intention of challenging his senior comrades for party posts. He possessed neither the patience nor the endurance for endless meetings, especially not in the world of exile politics. Despite the skepticism of his older comrades, he felt confident that he could lobby the United States for important and dramatic measures against Pinochet.

Although few of them grasped United States politics on the same level as Letelier, the Popular Unity leaders assigned him to represent them in Washington and to take charge of exile activities in the United States. To carry out his mandate, Beatriz "Tati" Allende, treasurer of the Chilean Socialist Party, authorized Letelier to receive a $1,000-a-month stipend from Socialist Party funds, to offset his expenses and allow him more room for organizing. One of the issues that Letelier had worked for hardest—lifting the quota restriction against Chilean refugees—was verging on success.

In June 1975 Senators McGovern, Abourezk, Kennedy, Church, and Humphrey had pushed an amendment through the Senate Judiciary Committee that would allow four hundred Chileans to enter the United States. They had succeeded in persuading Senator James Eastland, the reactionary chairman of the Judiciary Committee, to allow the amendment to pass. Letelier felt elated, not only on humanitarian grounds but because the more Chilean activists there were on United States soil, the better he could organize. The Socialist Party leadership took note of Letelier's apparently miraculous successes.

IN EARLY 1975 the Leteliers had moved into a spacious house in suburban Bethesda, a twenty-minute drive from Dupont Circle. Orlando could now invite his former IDB colleagues and fellow diplomats to his home.

Isabel Letelier had a thousand stories to tell about life in Chile under the Pinochet regime. Although she and Orlando had a common cause, Isabel never functioned as a "power behind the throne," or as "Orlando Letelier's wife." She led her own life, painted, sculptured, organized cultural events, and formed one half of the Leteliers' social-political life. She had her own style and modes of persuasion, which politicians such as Senators McGovern and Abourezk and their wives came to know well. Because she had lived within the circle of pain and terror experienced by the wives and children of the men imprisoned after the coup, she often reached rarely touched sensibilities within some of the more jaded Washington personages. She established the Chile Committee for Human Rights, to inform United States citizens about Chile and human rights issues.

Isabel, in her early forties, sparkled. Her black hair now flecked with grey, scented with rose perfume, she became a visual and conversational focus at dinner parties. Beyond her physical attractiveness, she exuded a kind of earthy effervescence, a generosity of spirit that showed in her face along with the lines that had formed with the years and with carrying four sons, lines that bespoke determination and stamina.

She had no interest in competing with the traditional male leadership of Chilean exile politics. She was the ideal wife for a man whom the confluence of personal fate and the forces of history had impelled to become a politician, to adopt politics as a vocation. She had imposed upon her own artistic temperament the vocation of exile politics; and although few of her acquaintances realized her political acumen, which blossomed later, no one doubted that Isabel Letelier was a woman of intellectual power, of sensitivity, and of unequivocal determination. "A remarkable woman," Frank Mankiewicz said after a dinner party with the Leteliers and the McGoverns. "She and Orlando are both rare Chileans because they understand United States as well as Latin American politics."

But while the Leteliers worked well as a political couple, their marriage did not regain its easy, flowing vitality. For one thing, Orlando could not, or would not, end the affair with Caridad. What had been presented to Isabel in late 1974 as a temporary fling became by mid-1975 a sticky and unresolved mess. "I think," he told a Chilean colleague, "that it has gotten to be neurotic."

In early 1976, Letelier added two exiled Chileans to the IPS staff: Waldo Fortín, a Socialist, lawyer, and former governor of Santiago and an official of the Chilean Copper Corporation under Allende, and Juan Gabriel Valdés, the son of United Nations official Gabriel Valdés, a left-wing Christian Democrat.

In the spring of 1976 Letelier confided to a close associate that he had decided to leave Isabel and rent his own apartment. "I've become like a crazy man. I can't help myself; I'm in love. I feel torn apart inside, because I also love Isabel, and God knows we have been through so much together and she is the most marvelous person in the world. But I love Caridad."

He moved into a small efficiency apartment on New Hampshire Avenue, near IPS, which he shared with Waldo Fortín. But he did not know how to cook, keep house, or conduct the most elementary shopping expeditions. "He survived concentration camp, but never learned to scramble an egg," Isabel remembers. But slowly he did learn. "He invited me to his apartment for breakfast," said Isabel. "He made an omelette with avocado and everything was very elegant and perfect, but it took him forever. That's how he was: a perfectionist about little things."

Two days after moving in Letelier had a telephone installed. When it rang the next morning, Letelier expected it to be Isabel. "You're a dead man," a male voice said. *Click.* "It was strange," Waldo Fortín said, "because almost no one knew our address, much less our phone number. That was the only time he ever commented to me about DINA's efficiency."

"Orlando woke up about six in the morning even though he normally went to bed late," Fortín recalled. "We customarily listened to cassette recordings of Mozart or Beethoven when we awakened. Then we indulged our common addiction to tangos, which we would sing in turn. Orlando had a beautiful baritone. Normally we didn't cook in the apartment. Someone came twice a week to clean, and Orlando took his dirty clothes to a laundry. He didn't like to be in the apartment. I think it made him feel more strongly the absence of his family. He usually worked until late at night."

The separation did not last. In July Isabel agreed to allow him back into Ogden Court. He had promised to end the affair with Caridad. "An affair," he explained to a friend, "is not something one can cut with scissors and simply end it. Not if one has feelings and honor."

4

CONDOR'S JACKAL

AS HE WALKED the gauntlet of helmeted soldiers and sandbag-ringed machine-gun nests guarding the runway of Santiago's Puda-huel Airport, Michael Townley felt an excited sense of pride and belonging. The first visible signs of the junta's military rule made him straighten his tall frame. He felt one of them, a soldier in the "Move-ment of the Eleventh of September" that had defeated Marxism and defended the *patria,* the fatherland. For Michael Townley, now alias Kenneth Enyart, returning to Chile in late October 1973 meant com-ing home

Home, that elusive abstraction, had caused him anxieties since his nomadic boyhood. He needed to belong, to be accepted.

His parents, Margaret and Jay Vernon Townley, had grown up in tranquil Waterloo, Iowa, but Michael's birth there was only a happenstance of World War II. His father, an administrative em-ployee of the U.S. War Department, stationed at an ordnance plant in Mississippi, had sent his wife back to Waterloo to be with her parents for the birth of their first son December 9, 1942.

An ambitious businessman determined to climb from small time in Iowa to big time in the corporate world, Jay Vernon Townley moved with the opportunity for advancement. His family went with him from city to city and later from country to country. In 1943, with World War II at its height, he left the War Department for an executive position at American Airlines. When Michael was nine years old, the Ford Motor Company hired his father and, after several years work in Detroit, transferred him to the company's new assembly plant in Santiago, Chile, where he soon rose to general manager.

Michael Townley was an introverted fourteen-year-old when the family arrived in Chile in 1957. A family portrait photograph of about that time shows an all-American, clean-cut, apple-pie wholesomeness: gangling but handsome Mike already as tall as his stern, youthful father, pretty little sister Linda next to her slightly plump mother, baby brother Mark on his father's knee.

The Townleys were absorbed into that subculture in Latin American cities known as the "American business community." Climate and scenic settings may vary in La Paz, Caracas, Rio de Janeiro, Buenos Aires, and Santiago, but not the affluent uniformity of the lifestyle of American diplomats and representatives of United States corporations. At the ubiquitous Rotary, Lions International, and Chamber of Commerce clubs, American executives mix fraternally with their local counterparts. For families like the Townleys who did not originally come from the American Brahmin class, life abroad allowed the illusion of having ascended several rungs in social status. Like their executive and diplomatic neighbors the Townleys blended readily into the milieu created by Latin America's thin upper crust, a world of servants, leisure, and disparagement of the poor. They lived in a spacious house in Santiago's exclusive Providencia section. Young women from the outlying slum areas provided round-the-clock, live-in maid service for the equivalent of thirty dollars a month and one afternoon off a week.

The shy adolescent Michael did not adjust at first to life in Chile or to speaking Spanish, though it later became second nature. Although well-behaved, polite, and intelligent, he did poorly in Saint George's School, the exclusive American-style high school run by an American order of priests. He was intimidated by the criticisms and demands of his father, and the father-son relationship deteriorated. Michael's parents sent him back to the United States to attend a boarding school in Florida. His grades failed to improve, but a shop course there introduced him to the basics of electricity and started him on a new and passionate hobby.

Back with his family in Santiago, he tried to finish high school, this time through correspondence courses. Meanwhile, he filled his room with tools, electronic gadgets, old clocks, and radio components. Membership in the youth group organized by the interdenominational Union Church, a social center of the United States business community, provided Michael with a teen-age social life and, most important, friendly adult leadership that contrasted with the critical attitudes of his authoritarian father. He developed a veneer of confidence, having discovered that his serious manner and blue-eyed good looks made him popular with girls. Displays of affability, combined with generous gestures and the proper amount of self-effacement, won him male friendship. The approval he could not win from his father he was able to elicit from his friends.

Outside the home, Michael began to be noticed. His thin, six-foot-three frame was accentuated by a formal wardrobe of dark suit, white shirt, and thin tie. The lost-boy look he had worn when he arrived in Chile had been replaced by an alert brightness and an erect carriage. "He was a leader, and very intelligent," said an adult friend who knew him well. "You would think of him as the kind of boy who would become a successful engineer or lawyer."

At home the confident, affable veneer vanished, for Michael could not fit his father's formula for successful teen-age behavior. While being lectured or scolded, he would study the tops of his well-shined shoes and mumble apologies. To his father, he represented a failure of will and discipline—a high school dropout.

His strained relationship with his father notwithstanding, Michael accepted many of the values that had guided the now successful corporate executive to near the top of the business ladder: ambition, self-discipline, individualism, and a near worship for professionalism and technology in the postwar white-collar world.

Townley senior's modified puritan ethic came heavily peppered with a ferocious anticommunism that he acquired during his years in the paramilitary atmosphere of the War Department and American Airlines. Chile, unlike the United States, had a well-organized communist party amply represented in the Congress and in virtual control of the country's labor-union movement. Senator Salvador Allende, running as the candidate of a Socialist-Communist coalition, received 38 percent of the vote in the 1958 presidential elections, clear evidence for Townley of the impending menace. In Santiago the Townleys for the first time witnessed bloody street fighting between protesting workers and the national police, and that too they blamed on the Communists.

Nurtured in his political formation by the often shrill rightism of his family and his Chilean social milieu, Michael absorbed the text and texture of anticommunism. But agreeing with his father on the "communist menace" to civilization did little to ease the basic tensions between them. At eighteen, Michael began to spend days at a time away from home. Then he fell in love.

Inés Callejas, at twenty-six, had an engaging smile. Her lively, expressive face and rounded figure made her attractive, though they did not place her in the class of beautiful women for whom Chile is famous. Nor did she belong to the upper class; her father worked as a low-paid but upstanding registrar of births and deaths in the small village of Rapel, Coquimbo Province, in northern Chile where Inés was born.

From her early teens, Inés had treated life as a series of urgent crusades. She attacked ideas with a feverish passion, painted her experiences with huge, spontaneous strokes, and punctuated personal relationships with an untiring social and political activism. At fifteen she became a member of the Young Communists, and, though she was not Jewish, had many friends in the Young Zionist League. Her high school expelled her at sixteen for possessing communist literature. She married. After six months the marriage was annulled, and she hired aboard an Italian tramp steamer en route for the fledgling state of Israel. There she married a New Yorker named Allen Ernest, who shared her pioneering zeal on the Skisifim Kibbutz in the Negev Desert. After a year they moved back to New York City with their newborn son, Ronnie. Having "experienced socialism" on the kibbutz, as she would later say, she abandoned it. Her anticommunism was to have that special cast of hatred and fanaticism characteristic of former devotees. In 1960, her marriage with Ernest exhausted, she returned to Chile with eight-year-old Ronnie, three-year-old Susan, and four-year-old Andy.

Michael Townley came with friends to a party Inés gave at her mother's house in La Reina. They danced together, and from then on Michael never wanted to leave her side. Inés, charmed by his teen-age enthusiasm, encouraged his attentions. "I met him when he was seventeen. He looked older, he spoke as an older man, he took charge of situations," she wrote later. Inés took charge of Michael.

In July 1961, despite the adamant opposition of his father, Michael Townley married Inés Callejas. At eighteen and a half, he became a paterfamilias with a strong-willed but economically inactive wife and three small children. A few months later, the Ford Motor Company transferred Jay Vernon Townley to Caracas, Venezuela. After that, Michael's friends in Chile say, he seldom mentioned his father or his American family.

Townley became a salesman, first for *Collier's Encyclopedia,* then for the more lucrative though racy mutual funds of Investors' Overseas Services (IOS). He found his clientele in the American community, the diplomats, businessmen, and technicians who wanted IOS funds as a tax haven. IOS, under flamboyant financier Bernard Cornfeld, guaranteed that income from the fund would not be reported to the U.S. Internal Revenue Service. Townley did so well that he was able to move his family into a spacious house with swimming pool in La Reina, where he became known as a party giver.

True to the dictates of his professional ambition, Townley dressed in expensive suits. He also became seriously interested in technology, and began to buy and experiment with equipment in his self-designed photographic and electronics workshops. He seemed to his friends always to have more money than he could have earned from his work. Inés received child support from Ernest, and people assumed that Townley's father supplemented the income of his son's family. But no one asked.

Townley's favorite customers for mutual funds were the scientists and technicians working at the new NASA Space Station near Santiago. Sales calls there turned into long and informative technical conversations with the engineers and specialists who operated the elaborate electronic equipment and computers at the station. Townley's teen-age hobby had developed into an avocation.

"Mike had a kind of genius," said his wife Inés. "He just had to look at a clock or radio and he would know how to fix it."

He devoured the essays in *Collier's Encyclopedia* and the *Britannica* on electricity, radio, and other technical subjects. He subscribed to *Popular Mechanics,* then to *Popular Electronics,* and taught himself to read and understand the most complicated electronics handbooks.* His technical reading involved hard work and self-discipline. He also developed a less taxing literary pastime. He read detective and spy novels. Technique fascinated him. Nick Carter, Len Deighton, and later Frederick Forsyth became favorites.

In 1964, amid the torrid pre-election climate of the campaign that pitted Eduardo Frei against Salvador Allende, Townley got his first taste of cloak-and-dagger. Several men approached him and easily impressed upon him the danger of violence—possibly even civil war —if the "communists" were to win the election. Townley had already constructed a high-power short-wave ham radio outfit; this might be needed, the men said, in case of emergency. Would he consent to their installing a gasoline-powered generator on his property so that the set would be available for use even during a blackout? Townley consented. But—Frei having won an uneventful election— the generator remained an unused black hulk in Townley's back yard.

Townley's hobbies, his reading, his contact with the NASA scientists, followed a pattern of relationships of the amateur outsider with an organization of highly specialized professionals. For all his skill or even genius, he could never enjoy publicly the status of a full professional.

In 1967 a new United States regulation threatened his livelihood as a stock salesman. Aimed at the booming Cornfeld mutual-fund empire, this law forbade American citizens abroad to buy the stocks as long as Cornfeld refused to report the earnings to the Internal Revenue Service. The Chilean government of President Eduardo Frei also attempted to crack down on the shady Cornfeld operation. In December 1966 a subpoena for Townley's IOS records and a warrant for his arrest were issued by a Santiago criminal court.

The restless Townley and the adventurous Callejas decided it was time to move. Miami offered a good compromise: an American city, yet with the possibility of keeping contact with the lifestyle and language of Latin America.

In January 1967, Townley brought his family to Miami. Christopher had been born in 1964, Brian in June 1966. Townley traded his business suits for jeans and boots; he got a job as a service manager at an AAMCO automatic transmission shop run by José Luaces, a Cuban exile, in the heart of Miami's Little Havana. Luaces appreciated Townley's fluent Spanish, since a good share of his customers were Cubans. At first, the Townleys rented a small house in Pompano Beach. Then Michael bought a house in Southwest Miami after signing a $17,000 mortgage.

Inés soon became restless. She loved causes, which offered outlets for her nervous energy and passionate intellect. No longer a leftist, not yet a rightist, she could not resist the fervent antiwar activism of the sixties. Son Ronnie, now almost of draft age, brought antiwar themes into the dinner-table conversation. Opposition to the war against Asians in Vietnam fit in with the two political convictions that Inés had retained through the years: devotion to the cause of Israel, and opposition to racism in any form. Robert Kunst, the leader of the New Party movement that presented Eugene McCarthy as a third-party, antiwar candidate in the 1968 election, vaguely remembered Inés Townley as a volunteer. "She stuffed envelopes and went to the marches," he said.

Michael preferred the company of some members of Miami's vast Cuban exile community to that of antiwar activists. He shared the Cubans' disgust with the growing remoteness of United States government policy toward the Cuban exile movement.

By 1967, when Townley arrived in Miami, the militant exiles' hopes of launching a United States–supported invasion of the island had all but died with the resolution of the 1962 missile crisis. The CIA downgraded JM/WAVE, its enormous anti-Castro operation in Miami, and each year cut more Cuban exiles from its payroll. Without CIA support, exile organizations could not organize sustained and successful operations. But the agency retained control of the diminished purse, weapons, and access. As a kind of spinoff of its failures, the CIA had also fostered intense rivalry and corruption inside the exile community. Some former CIA agents stayed on the payroll or were found other lucrative employment by the agency, while others were simply dropped, terminated, canceled. Miami-based commando raids, which consisted of shelling of Cuba's coastal cities and terrorist attacks against factories and other installations near the shore, were banned. The raids, once the mainstay of Cuban exile morale, sputtered and died out as the U.S. Coast Guard signaled an end to its past leniency. The CIA withdrawal and the new official hostility to exile terrorism spawned a thousand bitter splits within the Cuban exile community.

Townley spent hours in enthralled conversation with Miguel, a fellow mechanic, who claimed to have participated in dozens of raids in his spare time. But Inés found the Cubans disagreeable. In a collection of handwritten reflections obtained by the authors, she described her misgivings about the Miami Cubans:

Now, you can't work in Little Cuba nor live in Miami without meeting Cubans. I must confess I was always reticent about making friends with them. First, their boisterous tropical temperament clashed with mine. And their language! They destroy Spanish—they don't enunciate, they shout. Finally, I had reservations because the great majority of them are anti-Semitic. It seems that, having been forced to give up the impossible struggle against Fidel, they have concentrated their aggression on the easiest target of all time. For every five male Cubans, there is a political movement that is totally disconnected from the rest, and for most of them the basic goal is not to return to Cuba, but to eliminate the Jews—genetically.

There is a book that circulates among them called *World Defeat*. It justifies Nazism, glorifies the crematories, and blames all humanity's sufferings on the Jews.

We got together once in the house of Pablo C——, a Cuban, who had invited us to meet some of his friends, a group of Cubans from Los Angeles, led by a fat man with burning eyes and a solemn dark man. They were elegantly dressed and [their women] had on many jewels. They looked down on Mike and me, who as usual were decked out in old blue jeans and T-shirts.

We sat face to face. The fat man, whose name I'll never forget, ——, pitched the first question at us:

"What do you think about the World Jewish Conspiracy?"

"I beg your pardon, the what?"

"The Jewish Conspiracy. It's going to destroy the world if we don't fight it. Before we do anything else, we must destroy the Jews."

"It seems to me," I told him finally, "that you have gotten sidetracked on purpose. Fidel is too difficult a target, so you have chosen the perennial target, the Jews. Naturally, it is easier to fight the Jews than the Cubans. And by the way, my name is Ana Goldman."*

In the four years the Townleys spent in Miami, the family enjoyed a tenuous prosperity. Michael, with a loan from his father, bought a partnership in the Hialeah AAMCO. The family bought a motorboat and an air conditioner. But Inés yearned to get back to Chile, where her children would not be subjected to what she considered the harmful effects of American culture.

From Miami, she followed the 1970 presidential campaign in Chile closely and itched to become part of the gathering storm. If Allende's *comunachos*—commies—should win, she told Mike, she wanted to return to Chile as soon as possible. The final showdown between the left and the right would be a scrap she didn't want to miss. Having felt the appeal of socialist ideals in her teens, she now swung like a pendulum to a position that outdid even her husband's visceral anticommunism.

Allende won; the impetuous Inés packed her bags. Later she romanticized her reasons for returning:

My battlefields have been many, but the ideal has always been the same: to make a better Chile, because Chile has been everything to me. . . . So when I left my extremely comfortable life in the United States in 1970, it was to do battle against the government of Allende, which I suspected was nefarious.

*Unless otherwise indicated, this and forthcoming quotations are taken from the three handwritten manuscripts totaling about sixty pages composed by Inés Townley in mid-1978 about her husband's DINA career.

. . . I wrote many letters [to friends in Chile] saying, "Don't leave the country, you have to stay and fight. If you flee, Chile will be another Cuba." So while many of them were flying away from Chile, I was coming back determined to fight.

Townley and his Cuban exile friends were deploring Latin American developments over beers after work. Bolivia and Peru at that time had left-inclined military governments; Chile was about to inaugurate the continent's first elected Marxist president and become "another Cuba." Argentina's military government was weakening, and rumors spread that the Peronists would be allowed to return to the country. What could be done? Townley's friends, veterans of years of CIA-sponsored guerrilla action against Cuba, had ideas. They had been talking about Chile with their former case officers, who, despite the downgrading of the Miami CIA station, maintained close personal contact.

The CIA had received its marching orders on Chile, the retired case officers confided to their former agents. The CIA had orders to stop Allende and the Chilean leftists in their tracks—no holds barred, and help was welcome. Go talk to the CIA, Townley's Cuban exile friends suggested. There's sure to be a lot of action, and with your connections in Chile and your father's credentials, the CIA is sure to want you to play on their team.

Inés, impatient, flew to Santiago with the children November 22, 1970, leaving Townley behind to sell their possessions, liquidate his business partnership, and make necessary preparations for the up-coming adventure. Three days later, Townley stepped over the line that separates those who read spy thrillers from those who partici-pate in them. He called the Miami station of the Central Intelligence Agency. A case officer took the call. "I'm returning to Chile shortly," Townley said. "Would you be interested in talking to me?" The CIA officer asked for his address. A few days later, from his desk in the front office of the AAMCO shop, Townley saw a white Volkswagen pull into the driveway. He had not expected a CIA officer to arrive in a VW Beetle. The man sat down with Townley in the office and identified himself. Townley later remembered only an initial—Mr. H. Conscious of the mechanics in the adjacent garage, he mentally noted that they were out of earshot. Townley also didn't want to appear too eager. Townley later gave a disingenuous description of the conversation:

> I stated simply I would be there. I had the preoccupation of Chile going under the upcoming Marxist government. The Cubans had spoken on many occasions of how they had attempted to use the CIA against the Marxist government of Cuba, and I thought simply that it might be wise for me to have some door of communication open if it became necessary. . . . The man at that time informed me that if they had need or could make use of me that they would contact me in the future. . . .
>
> I didn't ask for employment. . . . I said, "If you need someplace to leave something, to have somebody pick something up, I'll be there, period."

Mr. H., interested, asked for a contact point with Townley in Santiago and wrote down biographical information on him. The interview lasted less than an hour.

By Christmas, Townley had converted his United States possessions into cash. He and Inés had developed a plan to make big money, bigger than ever before—and without Michael working at a nine-to-five job. Inés, inspired by her new cause, also noted that hundreds of Chilean property owners, fearful of the country's socialist future, were abandoning their property at giveaway prices. Large houses, even mansions, were available for a few thousand dollars. Michael would bring United States dollars into Chile. The black market for dollars at that time was offering three times the official exchange rate. As others divested, they would invest. Townley and Inés saw before them a remarkable opportunity for adventure and profit. On January 8 Michael took an overnight flight to Santiago.

In the effervescent political climate in Chile, the Townleys sought and found the outer fringe of militant opposition to Allende. Most of their old friends considered themselves part of the opposition, but only a few became activists in the early months of 1971. Those who looked for traditional rightist leadership shared the National Party's bewilderment over the unanticipated Allende victory and his subsequent support in Congress from the centrist Christian Democratic Party. The National Party retrenched, as the Chilean business and industrial elite tried in the beginning not to ruffle relationships with the new government.

But one group stood out by virtue of its advocacy of taking the battle against the left into the streets. The "Fatherland and Liberty National Front"—in Spanish, Frente Nacionalista Patria y Libertad (PL)—wore black. Its leaders saw the PL as providing the shock troops of the counterrevolutionary forces, and patterned it after Hitler's Brown Shirts.

"We didn't have a common ideology, other than anticommunism," Arturo (not his real name), a member who knew Townley, commented. "The leader was supposed to be Pablo Rodríguez Grez, and he was obviously a fascist, but most of us were just there to fight." Arturo said all of the opposition parties—including the Christian Democrats, who publicly repudiated PL's hooliganism and neofascist political line—sent cadres and funds to PL because it provided a useful second track of operations to harass Allende. PL complemented the traditional parties' parliamentary opposition, which was still restrained by the limits of political propriety. Townley figured out a way to combine business and politics.

The Townleys renewed their friendship with Esteban Vitale, owner of an advertising agency and former member of a short-lived profascist, anticommunist organization declared illegal in the 1950s. Vitale introduced them to friends who were involved with him in PL and in what they called the Nationalist Movement. Townley approached them first with a money-making scheme to buy up cheaply a luxurious mansion in the resort town of Reñaca which he intended to convert into a nightclub. After gaining their confidence, Arturo said, Townley suddenly dropped the idea of the nightclub. "He wanted to work with us politically, said he had resources. He said he had contacts with the CIA, that he had been told to keep alert to political developments in Chile, because when the time came they'd be using him."

Back in Washington and Miami, the CIA had checked on Townley and decided to use him "in an operational capacity." The CIA admitted in late 1978 that Preliminary Operational Approval, or POA, the green light to making a recruitment "pitch" to a prospective "asset," was obtained for Townley in February 1971. The CIA admitted also that the Santiago CIA station attempted to locate Townley sometime thereafter. But when the CIA field officer tried to contact Townley at the address he had given Mr. H. in Miami, he was told the Townleys were no longer in Santiago.

Townley had arrived in Chile and found that Inés was having an affair. Their relationship had already suffered from several previous affairs, including a serious one between Michael and a young Miami woman. When after two months the tension had not abated, Townley abruptly left Chile to return to the United States. Business friends in Miami lined up a job for him at an AAMCO garage in San Francisco. A woman with whom he had had a relationship lived there, and he moved in with her. The marriage with Inés seemed at an end. But in May, Inés flew to San Francisco to retrieve her husband and persuade him to return with her to Chile.* In August she returned to Chile, and Townley followed in November.

Inés rented a ranch-style house on Oxford Street in the affluent Los Domínicos neighborhood. It became the regular meeting place for the small action group in which Townley participated. Inés' eldest son, Ronnie, a university student who had lived away from home for several years, rejoined the family in the Los Domínicos home. Ronnie, an Allende sympathizer, discussed and argued politics with Townley, only nine years his senior.

Townley had caught the San Francisco trend and brought it back with him to Chile. He built an elaborate light and stereo sound system. He and Inés invited friends and even casual acquaintances to watch assorted pornographic films—a rarity in Chile—or to listen to San Francisco sound in stereo as colored strobe lights danced around the living room. The films and equipment, imported from the United States, were part of Townley's plans to make money. He had also brought into Chile a powerful radio transmitter for a yacht he

*Inés told one source that the CIA also followed Townley to San Francisco and offered him a job if he would return to Chile. Townley, according to the unconfirmed report, replied that he would willingly "hide a CIA agent under his bed" if need arose in Chile, but would not become an agent himself.

intended to build at a small boat factory on Panguipulli, one of the southern lakes. Townley told friends he planned eventually to sail the boat to Miami and sell it at an enormous profit. He never finished the boat.

More people on the right were becoming receptive to the violent tactics advocated by Patria y Libertad. Townley and Inés worked with PL to prepare the first massive demonstration against the Popular Unity government. A march was planned for December 1971. The opposition organized around the theme of food shortages, which it blamed on the price-control policies of the Allende government. Thousands of women, banging ladles against cooking pots, poured out of Santiago's affluent sections and marched down Providencia Avenue into central Santiago. Patria y Libertad squads armed with clubs and hundreds of men from other opposition parties marched alongside the women. Townley parked his Austin Mini-Cooper on a side street and led Inés and several members of his group into the action.

The demonstration, which later became known as the "March of the Empty Pots," degenerated into an orgy of violence. The PL squads clashed with the police. Caught between rock-throwing, club-wielding, cursing men, the women converted their chants into screams. The police used clubs and tear gas to disperse the mob.

Inés, in later writings and interviews, mythologized the event:

The roots don't start when he was seventeen, or twenty-one, or twenty-five. They start, I believe . . . when together and helpless we watched an old man, his arm in a cast, being beaten up on the sidewalk with billy clubs and boots [by] Allende's "Special Services." Later, it was us, wet, choking from tear gas in what could have been a peaceful demonstration. It started when we watched, helpless also, the poor people bundled up in ragged blankets, waiting in the street all night to be able to buy a pound of meat or a pint of oil the next day. And we said to ourselves NO to the Democratic Republic of Chile, NO to the "new Cuba," that wouldn't even have been as good as Cuba because our corrupt president behaved like a Central American chimpanzee and drank

Chivas Regal and ate caviar while only a few blocks from his palace, the *people* froze and waited. . . . That, and in many other ways, we learned what the Marxist government was like, and we were disgusted, sick, thinking of the future of our children, and then we said NO, rather not live at all than live in this rotten banana republic that Allende is building. There and then you will find the roots of the crime.*

It is perhaps a good deal more accurate to date Townley's appetite for activism from his approach to Mr. H. of the CIA almost a year before. But he had less interest in ideological nuances of political discourse. Nevertheless Townley followed Inés to discussion meetings at PL's safehouse on Rafael Canas Street.

Patria y Libertad had adopted as its ideological mentor the Spanish fascist José Antonio Primo de Rivera, who was interpreted at PL gatherings by Esteban Vitale and Pablo Rodríguez. A friend recalled Townley clumsily quoting Primo de Rivera and explaining the need for authoritarian government. "The masses are not ready to govern themselves," he would say. "Democracy leads only to mass government, rule by the herd. Power should be reserved for the qualified few, the intellectuals, the philosopher kings." Townley, the friend said, "sounded like a regurgitation of Inés Callejas repeating Pablo Rodríguez repeating Esteban Vitale repeating Primo de Rivera."

Notwithstanding that unkind assessment, Townley must have found a genuine affinity between the idea of rule by a technocratic elite and his enchantment with an elusive professionalism in his own life. The march, the action, the feeling of belonging, while a less dramatic influence on Townley than as painted by his wife, intoxicated the budding activist.

PL leaders considered the "March of the Empty Pots" an unqualified success. The other opposition parties and groups began at least to encourage or condone violence if not actually to practice it.

*Letter to one of the authors, undated, received January 1979. She adds: "But you would never say this, would you, because you had a pair of spectacles through which you saw only what looked good, as so many others did. . . . It's no use, really, looking for a warped childhood or whatever. He led—we led—a happy, normal life. It was communism that changed our style."

Only the liberal faction of the Christian Democratic Party maintained its principled opposition to PL's violence.

By December 1971 it was already a secret *viva voce* among the opposition parties that the money spigot had been turned on at the U.S. Embassy for worthy opposition projects. Armed with its newly won reputation, Townley's group decided to test Townley's claim to have CIA connections.

The embassy's consular section in Santiago is housed in an elegant three-story mansion on Merced Street facing Forestal Park, the city's downtown greenbelt. As long lines of Chileans waited to apply for tourist and resident visas to the United States, Townley, as an American citizen, went directly to a large foyer on the first floor adjoining the richly paneled, high-ceilinged offices of the consul, Frederick Purdy. Several times before, Townley had registered there as an American citizen in Chile, filling out a card and leaving photographs.

Townley thought Purdy might be CIA, but he wasn't sure. He told Purdy he had established contact with Patria y Libertad and was determined to work with them to overthrow Allende's government. He described to the consular officer the kinds of "dirty tricks" he and his group had in mind and indeed had already carried out. The CIA, Townley said, had not recontacted him as they had promised in Miami, but he had done his part by placing himself inside PL.

Townley reported back to his group in the Nationalist Movement on the inconclusive nature of his meeting with the embassy official, but assured them that the contact would remain open. His skills as a radio technician provided Patria y Libertad another way to approach the embassy. Townley discovered a way to pinpoint and monitor the secret radio frequencies used by the Allende government for internal communications. To prove he knew these frequencies, he recorded a number of the intercepted transmissions on a cassette tape. Then, on instructions from his PL comrades, he made an appointment with embassy political officer David Stebbings. He gave Stebbings the cassette as guarantee of *bona fides* and asked him to pass it on to the CIA station, saying he would provide the secret frequencies in exchange for CIA help. For a starter, on behalf of PL he asked the agency to provide a list of names of all officers of the

Chilean military above the rank of captain and to indicate where they could be located.

Arturo,* one of the PL members who had sent Townley on the mission, described the incident in an interview: "We wanted to check out Townley. We had had contact with the embassy through a Mr. Rojas of the labor department. We gave Townley a cassette on which we had recorded a message and sent him to the [embassy], but the political officer never got back in touch with us. We decided that perhaps Townley wasn't everything he said he was."

Stebbings wrote a memorandum about his meeting with Townley and sent it with a copy of the tape to the CIA. The memo was dated December 21, 1971. The CIA Chile station, which had attempted to locate Townley without success some months before, reacted immediately. The same day the CIA operations division notified the security division that "operational interest" in Townley had been canceled. The notice meant that POA—the clearance to use Townley operationally in Chile—was officially withdrawn.†

Townley's intimacy with U.S. Embassy officials grew. His tall, blue-jean-clad figure, his angular face accented by a Sundance Kid mustache reaching almost to his chin, became familiar to the embassy's marine guards and the Chilean receptionists. He stood out from the usual embassy corridor traffic of pin-striped diplomats and businessmen.

The U.S. Embassy, occupying the top four floors of a large office building on Agustinas Street, a hundred yards from La Moneda Palace, had converted itself into the bustling operations center for the United States' effort to undermine and eventually overthrow the Allende government. On one floor were the offices of the ambassador and the four State Department political officers. Townley was frequently seen sprawled in an overstuffed chair at the desk of David

---

*Not his real name.

†Stebbings described the episode in a letter to another political officer in late 1973. The CIA, Stebbings said, showed high interest in obtaining the frequencies but balked at providing the list of army officers. These negotiations via Townley would seem to contradict the CIA's later claims that its agents were unable to locate Townley in Santiago in 1971. The CIA has never explained its cancellation of security approval for Townley.

Stebbings, the junior political officer. In the presence of others, they talked of boats and fishing. Stebbings and his Hawaiian wife, Miku, also visited Townley at his Los Domínicos home. When Stebbings left Chile in mid-1972, he passed Townley on to his successor, Jeffrey Davidow.* John Tipton, the political officer in charge of contacts with Popular Unity sources, recalls Townley as an "embassy barnacle," one of the group of expatriate Americans, money changers, and antique dealers who hang around every American embassy abroad.

Purdy, not much older than Townley and also married to a Chilean woman, cultivated his friendship. He invited Townley and Inés to his home outside Santiago near the picturesque farm village of Lo Barnechea at the foot of the Andes Mountains. Townley repaired Purdy's cars. He had become a valuable embassy informant. Throughout 1972 he provided reliable, up-to-the-minute information about the terrorist activities of PL and about future lines of action. For PL, Townley was a channel to the United States government, a sounding board by which new tactics against Allende could be discussed and coordinated with embassy's own efforts. He offered the advantage of a high degree of deniability for both parties: for the embassy, he was an anonymous Chilean informant; for PL, he was thought to be a CIA agent they were using for their own purposes.

Within the structure of Patria y Libertad, Townley's group was allowed to work independently, initiating actions, securing its own financial backing, and carrying out missions. Such groups roamed the upper-class neighborhoods of Santiago in 1972 and 1973. Gangs of upper-class youths and occasional hoodlums harassed known leftist sympathizers in their homes, threw rocks at marchers, and at times tipped over a bus.

Townley established rapport with the local teen-agers and found that he could recruit them into exciting action clubs that, in the guise of "neighborhood defense units," mobilized anti-Allende sentiment. "Mike was something special," one related later. "He knew a lot about electronics and he would teach us. He also had guns, and he let us take them on loan when we went on missions."

---

*In 1974 Davidow left Chile and introduced Townley to his successor, Michael Lyons. By then, Townley was a DINA agent.

Townley's house on Oxford Street became a nightly gathering place, a hangout for young people seeking excitement, good times, and—increasingly in late 1972—violence. The guests sat on the floor, drank wine, and sang songs as Pedro, a regular, strummed on the guitar. Some smoked the abundant but weak Chilean marijuana. Inés adapted the lyrics of traditional folksongs into fierce vituperations against Allende and taught them to the group. At precisely 10:00 P.M. all would go outside to participate in the ritual of pot banging, a haunting cacophony of protest against Allende that echoed nightly through Santiago's affluent districts of Las Condes, Vitacura, and Providencia.

At the core of Townley's action "brigade" were Milo Baigornee, a tough northerner employed for a time by Patria y Libertad as a guard at headquarters, and Miguel Stol Larrain, whose reputation as a car thief was to frighten away some of Townley's more moderate friends. Townley used the teen-age groupies as "gofers." On one occasion he dispatched Inés' daughter Susan and another teen-ager to pick up seventeen sticks of dynamite from a friend's farm in Linares Province some five hours' drive south of Santiago.

Explosives became Townley's new fascination. Baigornee had some experience in handling small bombs, and another member of the group knew chemistry. Townley educated himself, as he had in learning electronics. *Collier's Encyclopedia,* a U.S. Army Ranger's manual, and a handbook of mining engineering were his textbooks. He handled detonating cord, blasting caps, and nitroglycerine and mastered the technique of kneading dynamite as if it were bread dough. His hands often became chapped and rough from handling the chemicals.

At the same time Townley kept up an active social life. He made the rounds of the city's fashionable discotheques, at times with Inés, often with other women. Edward Cannell, a marine guard from the embassy, became a drinking and nightclub companion. Townley irritated the younger man by flirting with Cannell's date, the daughter of Ambassador Edward Korry. Townley and Cannell met often at the Friday afternoon "Happy Hour" at the luxurious Marine House residence for the embassy guards, a good place to meet other Americans in Chile and to keep in touch with embassy personnel. To

Cannell and others in the embassy who remember him, Townley projected the image of an affable and affluent drifter, who looked a little like a hippie and described himself as an auto mechanic.

In October 1972, a national strike of professionals and truck owners threatened to paralyze the country and unleashed a full-scale offensive against Allende. For three weeks the Chilean Army, called out by Allende, patrolled the streets and imposed an 11:00 P.M. to 5:00 A.M. curfew. All radio stations were ordered to broadcast over a single, government-controlled network. Michael Townley saw an opportunity to use his technical skills. Through Manuel Fuentes, a journalist and PL leader, Townley worked out a plan with PL chief Rodríguez to put a clandestine radio station on the air.

He enlisted the help of PL member Gustavo Etchepare and adapted the two-way radio set he had brought from the United States to use on his planned yacht. Townley modified the radio to transmit to households on an AM frequency. He mounted the apparatus under the back seat of his unobtrusive but speedy Austin Mini-Cooper car. Rodríguez, enthusiastic at the prospect of having an exclusive propaganda outlet and defying the government network, wrote the political texts and recorded them on cassettes.

At night the Townleys and their retinue spent hours practicing and recording Inés' vitriolic songs against the government. Calling itself "Radio Liberation," Townley's station began broadcasting in mid-October. Opposition circles considered Townley's radio, though short-ranged, a strike against the government that drew attention to its deteriorating control. Radio Liberation enhanced Townley's reputation among the opposition as a highly skilled electronics technician and a gutsy operator. The mobile radio station also provided him with incentive to use his newly acquired knowledge of explosives.

In late-night planning sessions with his group, Townley explained techniques for surveillance of the target sites and for preparing and placing the explosives. One of his listeners remembered that he emphasized the need to tie and gag any night watchman or guard who might discover the operation. Like a high school coach, Townley demonstrated a method for tying up a person and had them practice it. "Typical Townley overkill," one of his disciples later called the method, which consisted in gagging the victim with medical adhesive tape, then tying hands and feet together behind the victim's back. The final touch was a loop drawn tightly from the feet to the victim's throat.

Several members of the brigade dropped out in fear. Those remaining began using underground names, battle aliases. Townley called himself Juan Manuel Torres, or "Juan Manolo." The Townley brigade had accumulated an arsenal of dynamite and small arms and made their own Molotov cocktails—gasoline-filled bottles with cloth wicks. In a predawn raid on a municipal bus lot, Townley and his young companions hurled the flaming bottles at the idle buses, whose drivers were defying the opposition strikes. Several of the buses exploded in flames.

Townley had crossed the borderline into violence. For him the increased risks and heightened violence made his life just that much more exciting and fulfilling. By the end of 1972 Michael Townley had become a professional at last—a professional terrorist.

Shortly after the heated March 4, 1973 parliamentary elections, in which the media played a larger role than ever before, Townley asked his journalist friend, Manuel Fuentes, to propose a plan to PL chief Pablo Rodríguez.

The Popular Unity and the opposition forces had fought bitterly in 1973 for control of the mass media. Most of Chile's radio stations remained in private hands and were politically antigovernment. The Catholic Church owned some frequencies and was politically neutral, while the leftist parties bought a few stations to promote the Popular Unity.

But television laws, patterned on United States codes, placed control of the airways with the government. Other legislation allocated exclusive ownership and operation of the country's three television networks respectively to the government, the Catholic University,* and the University of Chile, an autonomous tax-funded institution. Only the Catholic University's Channel 13 was in the hands of the opposition. Its manager was Raúl Hasbun, a firebrand

*The Catholic University television station should not be confused with that of the Catholic Church itself, which maintained official neutrality.

priest who on a television political forum had compared the government parties to "shithouses." Hasbun saw himself as a modern Joshua marching around the walled city of Allende's Jericho, hoping to bring it tumbling down by the force of his righteousness and his verbal horn.

With abundant financing from the opposition parties and businessmen, Hasbun had set up two pirate television stations, one in Santiago and one in the port city of Concepción to the south, using equipment brought in from the United States. The Concepción station, calling itself Channel 5, began transmitting in March without authorization by the government. Its programming interspersed opposition political messages and speeches with old Hollywood movies. Instead of sending the police to stop the illegal transmissions, the government installed a jamming device at an electric power station to distort the picture. Townley and his friend Etchepare had a plan to eliminate the government interference.

Rodríguez took Townley—introduced as Juan Manuel Torres, his *nom de guerre*—to Hasbun to explain the idea. Hasbun called Carlos de la Sotta, the manager of the Concepción station, and told him to cooperate with the plan. On March 15, Townley, Etchepare, and a third man, Rafael Undurraga, drove to Concepción. With de la Sotta's help, they tested the current coming into the station and pinpointed the location of the device causing the interference.

Three days later a Patria y Libertad commando team, made up of a group of teen-agers led by Juan Miguel Sessa, set out for Concepción to break into the electric power station. To facilitate the operation, de la Sotta had obtained keys to a small apartment on Freire Street whose back door led directly to the grounds of the power station.

In the early morning hours of March 20, Sessa opened the door to 382 Freire Street. As his flashlight played around the small room, he saw a man sleeping on the floor in a corner. Jorge Tomás Henríquez, a homeless housepainter who used the vacant apartment as a place to sleep at night, awakened in fright and struggled with the commando members, who pinned him to the floor. Sessa, on Townley's recommendation, had brought rope, chloroform, and a roll of wide adhesive tape. The rest of the operation went smoothly. Townley's description of the location and connections of the interference device, a large oscillator, was accurate. They disconnected the bulky device and loaded it in the car to carry back to Santiago as a trophy to show to Rodríguez and Hasbun.

The next day a Santiago newspaper filled page 1 with a picture of Henríquez, dead of asphyxiation, his corpse grotesquely contorted by the bonds of his overzealous novice attackers. The tie-up method was Townley's. Some of his pupils recognized it.

The murder investigation focused on the three technicians known to have visited Channel 5 a few days before the break-in. Hotel records established that the three men made long-distance calls to PL headquarters and to the home of a militant, Manuel Katz Fried. De la Sotta, the station manager, was arrested. The police arrested and jailed Etchepare and Undurraga in Concepción. Townley, Sessa, and another member of Sessa's operations commando were ordered by PL chief Rodríguez to flee the country.

A PL operative driving a yellow Ford Falcon picked up the three fugitives at their hideout late one night. They drove south all night on the Pan-American Highway, arriving in Temuco before noon the next day. The fugitives knew they had reached safe territory; Patria y Libertad maintained guerrilla training camps in the surrounding countryside and had the support of the conservative landowners. At a small farm outside Temuco the car was met by Eduardo Díaz, the PL commander for the province. Díaz was in charge of the final leg of the escape, the trek on foot to Argentina through the Julia Pass, one of the low mountain passes controlled by PL.

Díaz recognized Sessa, Townley, and Carlos Vial, the commando member, though they were introduced by other names. Townley, he had been told, was a "great technician linked to the U.S. Embassy." To Díaz, that meant Townley was CIA, and he balked at the idea of using PL's most secret escape route for a foreign agent who wasn't even a full member. He would take Sessa and Vial, he said, but not Townley.

Townley argued with Díaz, then pleaded. He wasn't an agent but did have connections with the CIA, he said, and that meant that he would be able to send money and help back to PL from the United States once he was out of Chile.

Diaz was adamant. Later he said he refused to help Townley out of disdain for those proclaiming a "nationalist" ideology yet relying on international power brokers such as the CIA to carry out their aims. A team set out for Junín de los Andes, Argentina, with Sessa and Vial, leaving Townley behind to return to Santiago with the PL driver.

Townley would later claim that he walked with the PL team over the mountain pass into Argentina, and would point to his battered boots proudly and affectionately as the ones that served him so well in his escape from the Allende police. Several other persons in PL, including Rodríguez, back up Townley's story. But other sources, who claim to have been directly involved, say that Townley, after his rejection by Díaz, arranged to fly over the Andes to Argentina in a single-engine private plane.* From Argentina he flew to Miami, arriving in time for the celebration of his parents' wedding anniversary April 2.

The story hit the Chilean press two months later. The tabloid *Puro Chile,* a sensationalist pro-UP daily, published Townley's picture on the front page June 9 with the headline THE MURDERER OF CONCEPCIÓN. The picture caption said Townley was "a man of the CIA" and had been in Chile since 1968 "masquerading as a builder of yachts."

For seven months after his flight, though in his native land, Michael Townley lived the life of an exile. No Cuban exile showed more patriotic zeal for Cuba than Townley exhibited for Chile, which he now spoke of as his country.

Convinced of the imminent fall of the Allende government, Townley made no permanent arrangements in Miami. When Inés and his children flew to join him in June, she bought a round-trip ticket. Michael rented an apartment in North Miami Beach and for $275 a week went back to his former job at José Luaces' AAMCO

---

*These sources also allege that the pilot was Julio Bouchon, the playboy son of a wealthy landowner, who in 1970 flew the escape plane for the kidnappers who killed General René Schneider. Bouchon is said to have landed at a private asphalt airstrip near Mendoza, Argentina, where an "executive-type jet" was waiting to fly Townley to Miami. U. S. Embassy Political Officer David Stebbings, in a letter to another political officer in late 1973, also refers to Townley's escape from Chile by plane.

transmission repair shop. But repairing transmissions was a sideline, a way to keep money coming in. Exile sharpened his devotion to his full-time career as Juan Manolo, counterrevolutionary.

It became a common sight at Luaces AAMCO to see Townley and a uniformed LAN pilot huddled in the small glass-walled office in the far corner of the garage beyond the hydraulic lifts. Anti-Allende pilots and stewardesses flying back and forth on LAN-Chile's daily flights carried messages and small packages, often going personally to deliver the material to Townley at the Eighth Street AAMCO shop. Townley would send back small, flat packages that the pilots would smuggle into Chile as personal gear and deliver to Patria y Libertad, which had been outlawed by Allende in July and had gone underground.

Inside Chile, terrorism became rampant, with an average of one bombing attack an hour in the final weeks before the coup. Townley later revealed his familiarity with the purchase of explosives in Miami at this time. In his testimony to the grand jury he said, "The one thing I found in Miami . . . in the early seventies, late sixties . . . [was that] due to all the stuff that they had obtained from the CIA . . . you could buy plastic explosives on any street just like you'd buy candy—weapons, explosives, detonators, anything that you wanted—and it was exceedingly cheap."

As promised, Townley attempted also to enlist the help of the Miami CIA station. Before he fled Chile, Pablo Rodríguez and Manuel Fuentes had suggested that he approach the CIA. "I think I had mentioned to them the fact that I had called the CIA in 1970," he testified later, "and they suggested that, seeing that you are going to the United States anyway, why don't you attempt to see if you can obtain funds or help, training, whatever, for the resistance movement against Allende."

He dialed the same number he had called three years before in 1970 and reached Mr. H., the official who had interviewed him. Townley said he had returned from Chile and thought it would be to the advantage of both of them to talk. Mr. H. told him he would check whether that would be advisable and call him back. Townley waited four days, then called again. The information about Townley's involvement in the Concepción commando raid had reached the

CIA, and CIA headquarters ordered Mr. H. not to enter into any substantive conversations with Townley. Mr. H. was cool on the phone. He would be glad to hear whatever Townley had to say, he said,·but nothing operational could be discussed.

Townley later said: "But what he stated, it was that the people in the agency who had that particular area were not really interested in talking to me at that time. . . . He said if you want to open up and talk about everything, we will be glad to listen to you only. What he was doing was closing a door. He was saying we are willing to a one-way street, but no two-way street."

What Townley euphemistically described as "that particular area" of CIA operations had proceeded without either Townley or Patria y Libertad. In Chile, the coup countdown had begun among a coterie of Chilean generals.

Tumultuous celebrations greeted the news of the September 11 coup in the Miami Cuban community. General Pinochet and the Chilean junta members became instant heroes among the exiles. Ecstatic, Inés Townley booked passage on the first available flight back to Santiago, arriving September 21. Michael stayed behind for a month to manufacture a new identity for himself. Despite the military takeover, a pending warrant on murder charges still awaited him in Chile.

Townley obtained the Florida birth certificate of one of his customers. With the certificate he obtained a Florida driver's license on October 3, 1973. The next day he went to the Hialeah courthouse and applied for a passport. Kenneth William Enyart described himself on the application as a construction worker living with his wife, Brenda, in Northwest Miami. He listed his destination as "South America, Peru, Venezuela, Ecuador, Colombia, Panama." The clerk waived the normal ten-day to two-week waiting period, and within twenty-four hours Townley had his new, false passport.

Townley's vast library of spy and detective thrillers had served him well. He read them for technique. He learned from them, step by step, the procedures for obtaining false documentation, covering a trail, crossing borders undetected, arranging clandestine meetings, passing information, setting up codes. Tradecraft, the core of a master spy's professionalism, was already replacing electronics and explosives as his obsession. The rudiments of tradecraft gleaned from novels and from association with fellow novices at Patria y Libertad would soon be augmented by training by real professionals.

One of the books on his shelf was Frederick Forsyth's *The Day of the Jackal.* Townley admired Jackal, the anonymous master of weapons and disguise, the manipulator of identities, the face without personality. Though not yet an assassin like his fictional hero, he easily fantasized his future role in Chile in the figure of Jackal, the foreigner called to the service of another country, moving from country to country without identity, without trace. Another Forsyth character described Jackal, whom he was about to hire to assassinate Charles de Gaulle:

> It would be necessary for this man, whoever he is, to be a foreigner. He would not be a member of the OAS [Secret Army Organization]. . . . He would not be known to any policeman in France, nor would he exist on any file. . . . The assassin would be an unknown and therefore nonexistent quantity. He would travel under a foreign passport, do the job, and disappear back to his own country while the people of France rose to sweep away the remnants of de Gaulle's trea-sonable rabble. . . . The important thing is that he be able to get in, unspotted and unsuspected. That is something which at the moment not one of us can do.

Later, Townley would tell one of his interrogators that Forsyth's book was uncannily accurate in its descriptions of the underground arms-supply network in Europe and that only the use of false names separated fiction from reality.

Townley would become a caricature of Jackal, a real-life assassin imitating fiction, a dabbler in tradecraft notwithstanding his training, an undercover man who wore several of his many identities on his sleeve. "He loved all that cloak-and-dagger stuff," a man who knew Townley for many years recalled, "but he never did anything without getting caught."

5

EXTRATERRITORIAL CAPABILITY

TWENTY YEARS BEFORE, the building at Tejas Verdes had been an elegant resort hotel where wealthy Santiagans relaxed by the sea. In October 1973, a naked prisoner lay strapped to a bare metal cot in the former music room. The Army School of Engineers had replaced the vacationers years before, but people still called the barracks Tejas Verdes—the Green Roofs. The Maipo River flowed beneath the spacious terraces, carrying the pulverized black stone of the Andes the last mile to the Pacific. Beaches the color of ashes and charcoal stretched from the mouth of the river north to the port of San Antonio.

Antonio Moreno—the name is false to protect him—screamed many times that day but remembered thinking that no one would hear because of the soundproofing. No one, that is, except the half-dozen men watching the interrogation. An army patrol had picked up Antonio in Santiago and brought him here. On the *parilla*—the electric grill—the soldiers had tortured him until he named several rightist intellectuals as Soviet undercover agents, and now they were torturing him because his confession had been a lie.

The stench of feces filled the room. His soiled pants and body had remained unwashed since his arrest three weeks before. A soldier retched as he moved the electrode from an eyelid to Antonio's penis.

Between jolts of electricity, Antonio fixed his eyes on the face of a bulky man in the uniform of a lieutenant colonel who leaned against a wall watching intently, clinically. The horror of the experience etched this face in Antonio's memory, and later, having survived, he would recognize the heavy jowls, impenetrable black eyes beneath drooping lids, and look of tired contempt. He would learn the man's name: Lieutenant Colonel Juan Manuel Contreras Sepúlveda, regimental commander of the Tejas Verdes army base.

Contreras, at forty-four one of the youngest colonels in the Chilean Army, would later become its youngest general. But he did not seek power through rank alone. Port San Antonio and Tejas Verdes regiment provided a base to build upon until he would stand next to power itself.

The son of a middle-class, social-climbing military family, Contreras was in his final year at the Chilean military academy when Orlando Letelier entered as a lowly plebe. Early in his career, Contreras attracted the attention of one of his former academy professors, Captain Augusto Pinochet. The two, young officer and his mentor, became close friends, and Pinochet crowned their friendship by standing as godfather at the baptism of one of Contreras' children.

As a major, Contreras spent two years—1967 through 1969—at Army Career Officers School in Fort Belvoir, Virginia. While in the United States he joined the Lions Club at Fort Hunt, Virginia, a membership he would proudly continue in Chile's chapter of Lions International. And he opened an account at Riggs Bank in Washington, D.C., which proved convenient later on.

Since there had been no war in their lifetime, the Chilean officer corps were classroom soldiers. Their performance as students in special courses abroad, and as professors in Chile's Military Academy and War College, became avenues to promotion. Contreras always finished first in his class, and later took pains to combine key professorships with the command of troops. Though attached to the Engineering Corps, he developed specialties in military history, strategy, and intelligence, in addition to teaching more typical army engineering courses in explosives and demolition.

Just as Pinochet had nurtured him, Contreras supported a number of young officers, captivating them with his superior intellect and engendering a total personal loyalty by his absolutism and authoritarianism. Manuel Contreras strove always to control: people, situations, the future. He had succeeded in dominating his family, his friends, his junior officers, and had carefully orchestrated his steady, rapid rise inside the military. Two things eluded his control. On social occasions, Contreras could not govern his response to people of different classes and views. He alternated between retiring shyness and argumentative bombast. He would get carried away, excoriating communism, women's liberation, and Christian Democracy. He had also failed to master his appetite. His obesity made him angry, and he channeled his anger into the pursuit of power.

Several months before the coup Contreras received the command of Tejas Verdes, the top military post in the San Antonio area. He had served in that port city for five years in the 1950s, and returned in June 1973 a well-known (if less than endearing) figure to the social circles there. He established iron control over his new regiment, and when the province itself was declared under a state of emergency a few weeks before the coup, Contreras became the effective ruler of the port.

San Antonio was Santiago's closest link to the Pacific. For weeks before the coup the sixty-five miles of highway between the city and its port were almost void of truck traffic, the road being under siege by striking truckers. Ships loaded with hundreds of tons of wheat languished at anchor in the harbor, while in Santiago President Allende announced that the city of four million would run out of flour for bread in three days. An army convoy could have run the gauntlet of truckers and their bands of opposition-party toughs armed only with small-caliber rifles and pistols. But San Antonio had become enemy territory under Contreras. No ships were unloaded, no convoys organized to bring food to Santiago. Days before the coup Contreras ordered army squads to round up young leftists suspected of preparing armed resistance to the impending coup.

On September 11, few shots were fired; the rule of the Popular Unity government had already ended in San Antonio. Trucks lined up once again at the docks to transport grain to Santiago, but on September 13 the radical dockworkers' union staged a sitdown strike to protest the abolition of job-protection rules by the new military

authorities. Contreras invited four union leaders to his office to negotiate on the afternoon of the thirteenth. The next morning, four
bullet-riddled bodies were delivered to the union leaders' families in
sealed coffins. There were no more strikes in San Antonio.

Other bodies began to be washed up regularly on city beaches.
Nurses at the city hospital recognized some of the bodies as persons
who had been brought injured to the hospital after the coup, then
dragged out at night by military patrols. During the first weeks after
the coup, squads of soldiers and civilian collaborators rounded up
dozens, then hundreds of UP militants and sympathizers. By the end
of September the word had spread that Contreras had established a
prison camp at a military storage dump by the Maipo River bridge
near the Tejas Verdes regimental headquarters.

People trying to locate missing relatives gathered daily on the
steep hill overlooking the camp of two dozen ramshackle wooden
barracks. Prisoners being marched to meals or to the latrine could
see the people on the hill waving. They could also see the two white
cement statues that gave the place its name: "The Hill of the Christ
of Maipo." Prisoners arrived daily, many of them brought from
Santiago. Smaller trucks transported groups of prisoners to the former resort of Tejas Verdes, a mile away, for interrogation. Officially
the prison camp did not exist. There were no prisoner lists, and army
officials refused to answer inquiries from relatives. Only the prisoners
and their guards set foot inside the camp. Large shipping crates and
small shacks housed the inmates. An open trench dug in the sandy
ground and lined with planks served as the latrine. There were no
washbasins or showers.

San Antonio constituted a problem area for Pinochet because of
the strategic importance of the port and the strong UP leanings of
its population. Contreras was a godsend who brought a difficult
situation under control with speed and efficiency. As pressures built
up in Santiago to allow international Red Cross inspection of prisons
and the listing of prisoners' names, Tejas Verdes became the destination for prisoners arrested in Santiago and suspected of taking part
in organized resistance. Contreras directed particularly methodical
and productive interrogations. His information on the resistance,
fruit of torture sessions in the Tejas Verdes music room, became the

most complete in Chile, surpassing that of the army, navy, and air force intelligence services.

In San Antonio, Contreras made the rules that governed life. He dismissed a left-leaning judge and imprisoned her at Tejas Verdes. Since Pinochet and the junta had announced that no changes would be made in the judicial system, two national court officials traveled to San Antonio to demand that Contreras respect the court's own procedures for the removal of judges. One of the officials reported that Contreras received them in his office and dismissed their complaints. Standing over the two officials, as was his custom during interviews, Contreras said, "Gentlemen, I am the law, and"—putting his hand on his pistol—"this is the judicial system."

SANTIAGO IN OCTOBER 1973 resembled an occupied city. Army patrols in jeeps and trucks raced through the streets, guns at the ready. Felled trees and sandbags protected guard posts around government buildings, public buildings, and police outposts. At night after the hour of curfew, sporadic machine-gun fire crackled. Morning newspapers—those left after the confiscation of all publications not in line with the new regime—provided daily reports of the number of leftist prisoners killed the night before "while trying to escape."

Michael Townley, his first week back in Santiago, drove through the streets in a state of euphoria, drinking in the sights of total military victory. He waved occasionally to passing patrols when he recognized a former companion from Patria y Libertad riding with the soldiers, proudly brandishing an army-issue automatic rifle. Patria y Libertad, its purpose accomplished, had voluntarily disbanded so that its members could collaborate on an individual basis with the new government. Townley renewed old acquaintances and soon learned which of his PL friends had found work with military mop-up brigades and which had moved into positions of power.

Townley yearned to ride in one of those jeeps, not as a common soldier, but as an officer in the service of the Eleventh of September. He believed that in the officer corps of the anticommunist army of his adopted country, he would find a place to use his talents and skills. Some of his former associates encouraged him, at the same time warning him that even though control of the Chilean state had changed hands, the lower-level bureaucracies would not alter their formal procedures, and that his involvement in the Concepción affair had brought him a certain notoriety. Townley heeded the warning; he didn't want to spoil his chances by moving precipitately.

He reported to the U.S. Consulate on Merced Street. His friend Fred Purdy, the consul, shook his hand warmly and talked enthusiastically about the new regime and the victory over the Allende government. Townley said he needed a new passport.* Purdy said he would be glad to oblige. Purdy knew that Townley was officially a wanted criminal, that he had escaped from Chile a fugitive from charges of murdering a man during the Concepción incident, but the knowledge did not prevent him from helping Townley.

Townley brought several passport-size photos to the consulate and received a new passport. Purdy then brought Townley's American citizen's card on file at the consulate up to date. He recorded Townley's return to Chile and his new address, and glued one of the photos to the card. After Townley left, Purdy wrote a memorandum describing their latest conversation.

Townley felt reassured. He had always made it a rule to maintain honesty with the U.S. Embassy, and felt confident that no one there would be seized by the bureaucratic need to make trouble about his illegal presence. He then turned to the larger problem of quashing the Concepción arrest warrant and the other legal papers that lay in court dockets and prosecutors' files.

The new government had solved similar problems for PL activists and others wanted for terrorist crimes committed during Allende's tenure. The junta had freed Roberto Thieme, former director of PL's clandestine operations, and several men wanted for the assassination of General Schneider had returned from exile in Paraguay. Rafael Undurraga, Townley's companion at Concepción, had been quietly released after spending six months in jail. Townley explained his

---

*Townley told a friend that he had shown the old passport to Purdy and they had discussed Townley's fear that the stamps in the passport would establish that he had exited from Chile and re-entered illegally. Townley told the friend that it was Purdy's idea to resolve the potential problem by issuing a new passport, which would have no stamps.

problem to a PL comrade, Navy Captain Carlos Ashton, who had been given a post in the Foreign Ministry. Ashton assured Townley that discreet communication with the Concepción authorities would end his uncertainty.

Townley settled in once again in Chile. Inés had rented a house in Providencia. To pass the time and bring in a little money while he waited for the hoped-for offer of a job in the military, Townley fixed transmissions and fine-tuned engines at a small auto-repair garage.

COLONEL MANUEL CONTRERAS divided his time between Santiago and Tejas Verdes. He accumulated titles and expanded his power base, muscling in on the territory of several generals but preserving absolute subordination to one man—General Augusto Pinochet. In San Antonio, besides acting as military governor and chief of the emergency zone, he took over the management of the gigantic fisheries complex, EPECH, one of Allende's "social sector" industries conceived as a bridge to a socialist, worker-managed economy. In Santiago, Contreras directed the officers' school and the War Academy and served on the military planning commissions that formulated policy for the government.

The sheer number and prestige of Contreras' many posts, unheard of for a colonel, provided him the power base from which to run the military government's greatest enterprise. In size and resources, only the country's basic industry, copper mining, remained larger. Pinochet had given Contreras the mandate to bring order and efficiency to the gigantic task of eliminating Marxism from the country. He ordered him not to alleviate the violence of the early weeks after the coup, but to intensify, co-ordinate, and rationalize the repression.

The formal organization of state terror in Chile began in November 1973 with a decree that created the National Prisoners Service (Servicio Nacional de Detenidos—SENDET). The new institution was ostensibly a bureaucracy to handle the administration of the dozens of prison camps. SENDET set up its offices in the basement of the deserted National Congress building, and the government announced that anyone seeking news of arrested persons should go there.

Buried in the decree was a clause establishing a Department of National Intelligence (Departamento de Inteligencia Nacional),* "to determine the degree of dangerousness of the prisoners and to maintain permanent coordination with the Intelligence services of the Armed Forces, Carabineros, and Investigaciones." A lawyer working for the newly formed human rights organization, the Committee for Cooperation for Peace, made an educated guess, which he wrote up in a memorandum, that the department would become a new intelligence apparatus. The acronym of the new agency, he concluded, was DINA.

Colonel Manuel Contreras, the secret director of the SENDET "department," now began to build an organization with the dual purpose of instilling terror and gathering political intelligence. He got help. CIA station chief Ray Warren had worked with Contreras before the coup. When he heard that Pinochet had given the task of centralizing Chile's intelligence agencies to a man of Contreras' proven ability, Warren promised CIA help in supervising the planning and organization of the new intelligence structure and in training its principal officers.

Townley and other PL civilians recruited at this time watched Contreras build DINA into a state within a state. "At the beginning of 1974 he [Contreras] had a full set of plans, and six months later he had built an empire," a former DINA agent said. "I thought he was some kind of genius to have built up such a large, complicated apparatus in such a short time—then I found out how much help he got from the CIA in organizing it."†

*Decree 517, printed in Official Gazette, December 31, 1973.

†The source said he was not aware until 1975 and 1976 of the extent of the connections between DINA and the CIA. He said he saw "manuals of instruction and procedure" provided by the CIA. The relationship reached its zenith around the time of Contreras' visit to Washington in August 1975, when he was received by General Vernon Walters, deputy director of the CIA, at CIA headquarters. The relationship cooled, the source said, in early 1977 as a result of the change in CIA top personnel under the Carter administration. The issue of human rights and the Letelier-Moffitt assassinations, so far as he could observe, had no influence on CIA-DINA ties in late 1976.

Chile's five existing intelligence agencies, organized primarily to gather military intelligence, were ill-equipped for the task of rounding up citizens whose crime was that of having unfashionable political ideals. Other governments, including Allende's, had relied on Investigaciones, the political division of the national detective police, to investigate terrorism and subversion, of which there had been few instances in the country's history until the last two years of Allende's government. In the 1960s, the CIA had encouraged the formation of an intelligence arm of the Carabineros, the national police, but SICAR (Servicio de Inteligencia de Carabineros), as it was called, had remained a truncated and unassertive service.

The army's Military Intelligence Service (Servicio de Inteligencia Militar—SIM) conducted operations aimed at potential military threats from outside the country until the 1960s, then, at the behest of the United States military aid program, expanded into counterinsurgency programs. Navy intelligence operated almost exclusively in the port cities of Valparaíso and Talcahuano. The Air Force Intelligence Service (Servicio de Inteligencia de la Fuerza Aerea—SIFA), smaller than SIM, undertook with relish the job of repression. Under the leadership of junta member General Gustavo Leigh, SIFA operated throughout the country and gained a reputation as the most brutal of all the organizations carrying out arrests and detention. Until DINA.

The intelligence services were responsive to their respective hierarchies and engaged on all levels in interservice rivalry. Pinochet, on the advice of the CIA, asserted the need for a full-scale secret police that was under his personal command, independent of any military structure and charged with the coordination of the other intelligence agencies. Other secret police agencies set up for the same purpose, South Korea's KCIA, Brazil's National Information Service, and Iran's SAVAK—all parented by the CIA—provided models for Contreras' organization. He obtained technical and training manuals from the CIA. He handpicked officers to lead his elite corps from among lieutenants and captains at the War Academy, and recruited soldiers who had gained experience at Tejas Verdes. Some officers were sent to Brazil for training. Some $40 million to finance the organization was obtained through the ingenious device of bleeding funds from the EPECH fishery and then borrowing money from the Central Bank to cover the firm's losses. The losses were officially blamed on mismanagement under the Popular Unity regime.

In January and February 1974, with recruitment still incomplete, Contreras' DINA began to operate on a small scale, even though it had as yet no legal existence. Human rights workers at the Peace Committee began to notice an upswing in the number of arrests to almost 250 people per week and to detect a chilling change in methods. Contrary to earlier practice, men in uniform seldom participated in arrests. Those conducting the arrests arrived after curfew, wore civilian clothes, and refused to identify themselves. They blindfolded their victims and threw them into the canvas-topped beds of pickup trucks without license plates. Often a young woman took part in the arrests with a team of four or five men.

THE CHILEAN SUMMER was over. Except for Inés' son Andy, who had enlisted in the U.S. Navy, Townley's family group had spent the vacation season together. Brian, the youngest, had entered second grade. His already gangling brother Christopher was in the fifth. Susan, a pert teen-ager, took boys more seriously than her high school studies. Ronnie, a dark-haired, meditative twenty-two-year-old who inherited his mother's penchant for intellectual pursuits, had departed for New York to resume college. The Townleys were the picture of a close-knit, loving family group.

Lieutenant Colonel Pedro Espinoza, second in command in the fledgling DINA, sat in the Townleys' living room. Inés supervised the maid as she served tea and drinks to her husband, the officer, and an overdressed woman in her late forties. The woman, the owner of the Townleys' rented house, was introducing Townley to Espinoza —a friend of her family, she said, who had wanted to meet Townley.

Espinoza's visit, Michael and Inés soon realized, was a response to the feelers they had put out among their Patria y Libertad friends now working for the government. The thin social pretext for the visit vanished as Espinoza shifted from the forced small talk to reminiscences of the Allende years. He congratulated Townley on his ingenuity in putting the clandestine Radio Liberation on the air under the nose of the Allende government and confided that, as a military intelligence officer, he had received the assignment of tracking Townley's illegal transmitter. "But I didn't look too hard," he said with a laugh.

The Concepción affair, Espinoza chided good-naturedly, was "a bit sloppy." He then delved into intimate details of Townley's activities under Allende and since his return to Chile. Townley studied Espinoza, admiring the straight, military carriage and athletic physique of a man almost as tall as himself. Even when he smiled, Espinoza's Prussian-like bearing and the intensity of his eyes betrayed a military motive, a deadly earnestness of purpose. What Townley heard meant that Espinoza had already checked him out and that he had passed the preliminary test. Townley had read enough spy novels to recognize a recruitment scenario.

Espinoza ended the meeting by inviting Michael and Inés to dinner at his house. He told them to bring the children along. The Townleys reciprocated the dinner invitation. Townley, enthralled by the aura of Espinoza's professionalism, would later describe his relationship with the intelligence officer as a close friendship.

Espinoza sized up his candidate over the coming weeks. Townley was one of a large number of civilians who had come to Contreras' attention because of their audacity as PL terrorists. Though amateurs, they could be trained, and their proven single-mindedness impelled by an ultra-rightist ideology equipped them for tasks that career military men shunned. Contreras and Espinoza had already recruited some of Townley's acquaintances: Vicente Gutiérrez, who had introduced PL to political assassination; propaganda specialists Anthal Lipthay and Álvaro Puga; bomb specialist Victor Fuenzalida; and radio specialist Gustavo Etchepare. Townley scored high in Espinoza's assessment. He had demonstrated his knowledge of electronics, radio, and explosives. Best of all, he was an American with two United States passports, yet devoted totally to the cause of the Chilean military government and willing to go to any lengths, follow any order, to further his adopted cause. Espinoza was impressed by Townley's subservience to authority, his unquestioning, childlike fascination with playing the role of soldier.

Espinoza's offer of work in DINA came about the same time as

Chile's winter rains.* Espinoza hired both Michael Townley and Inés Callejas for a combined salary of about $600 a month. Townley said that he considered it an honor to become a soldier in the service of the Eleventh of September. He told Espinoza about his prior contacts with the CIA and his relationship with the political officers at the U.S. Embassy and with Consul Purdy. Espinoza assured him that the contacts with United States officials constituted no obstacle to becoming a DINA officer.

Inés' later writings on this episode mask her own role in DINA, but appear straightforward in describing some of the factors involved in Townley's recruitment:

> The colonel made a proposition to Michael to work in DINA. His only job at the time was sporadic transmission repairs in the garage of Juan Smith, and he was delighted to accept. At last he would have the chance to work in electronics, his favorite field, and be paid for it. The work, the colonel told us, would surely allow time for Michael to take on other jobs as well.
>
> I'm not insinuating that my husband was an imitation James Bond, nor that he carried out the most important missions. But I certainly can state that DINA found his knowledge of electronics, English, and purchasing extremely useful. Add to that the fact that as an American he had free access to the United States at any moment without having the need for the hard-to-get visas.
>
> My husband, moreover, had qualities that made him especially effective in the intelligence community: a bright mind, an incredible memory, and a fail-safe determination and loy-

*April or May 1974. Townley's testimony leaves vague the exact date of his enrollment in DINA. The dates he gives for his first assignments—October or November of 1974—are contradicted by other documentary evidence. In his second substantive interrogation with FBI Special Agents Carter Cornick and Robert Scherrer on April 17, 1978, he gave perhaps his most straightforward answers about his recruitment. In their summary of that interview, Agents Scherrer and Cornick wrote: "With regard to his DINA affiliation, he advised that he progressively became involved with intelligence operations in Chile, which culminated in October or November, 1974, when he became an operational agent in the capacity of a civilian contract employee."

alty. And he was absolutely convinced that the military government and Señor Pinochet were the best thing that ever could have happened to Chile.

DINA employment carried other perquisites for Townley. Instead of working out of DINA's vast downtown headquarters, he was given the deed to a large house, almost a mansion, on several acres of land in the fashionable Lo Curro Hill district overlooking Santiago. Contreras had bought the house during the Allende days when property carried a low value. At DINA expense, Townley set up a powerful radio transmitter and equipped a full electronics laboratory. The Townleys moved in shortly after their recruitment. Inés wrote later:

> The house was a white elephant, but it turned out to be perfect for our purposes. Michael would have his electronics workshop and his photography lab—another of his hobbies. And I had a third floor with a pleasant and inviting *terraza.* There was a swimming pool—absurdly located off the kitchen at the back—and that made the children happy. The grounds, with its fruit trees, must have been among the best in Lo Curro. Michael put up those enormous antennas that made the neighbors suspicious, so that they denounced us to the police and had us investigated. I think we passed that inspection.

A period of testing, training, and initiation began for Townley over the following months. His superiors wanted to know the limits of their recruit's abilities. He received assignments to test his electronics skill: bugging, debugging, and wire-tapping. He was also given preliminary tasks to perform with explosives. A DINA recruit had to know the fundamentals of tradecraft, and Townley learned above and beyond spy-novel lore the skills and arts of spookdom as practiced in Chile.

DINA had its own initiation procedures, hierarchies, and pecking orders, the idiosyncrasies of a fledgling organization and its directors. Finally, somewhat like the CIA, DINA had an oath of secrecy and loyalty, to be made to Colonel Contreras personally.

Townley signed the oath with ceremony and conviction. He had now become officially a professional spy; Juan Andrés Wilson Silva* was his official DINA name. But most of his co-workers in DINA continued to call him Mike, or "El Gringo"—the foreigner, the American.

Townley's first assignments involved electronic eavesdropping for DINA's various operations sections. His chief was Major Vianel Valdivieso. Using his Lo Curro home and laboratory as a base of operations, he formed a brigade called by the pretentious but typically DINA-esque title of "Quatropillan Center for Technical Research and Development." His working team consisted of a woman secretary, a driver for his DINA-assigned FIAT 125 car, and an army sergeant who also had a DINA car. Both cars had two-way radios, and Townley kept his brigade moving efficiently from assignment to assignment in the manner of a radio-dispatched appliance-repair firm.

But Contreras had not hired Townley to plant bugging devices in flowerpots.

When Espinoza recruited Townley in mid-1974, DINA had about 600 full-time paid military agents and civilian contract employees. About 20 percent of the staff were civilians, mostly recruited in slum areas from among thugs and petty criminals. Townley joined a more elite group handpicked from Patria y Libertad and other opposition groups, most of whom entered DINA in March and April 1974. DINA promised them prestige and positions, including troop commands and ranks equivalent to army lieutenants and captains. At the zenith of DINA power in 1977, Contreras commanded a small army of 9,300 agents and a network of paid and volunteer informants several times as large, honeycombing all walks of life inside Chile and abroad.†

*Townley was issued a Chilean identity card in the name of Juan Andrés Wilson Silva on September 6, 1974.

†Information about DINA size and structure was obtained from United States investigative sources and from independently developed sources inside DINA. The information compiled by the authors from Chilean sources coincides with that obtained in interviews with investigators, who said some of their information was based on classified reports from the Santiago CIA station.

The military government did not admit DINA existed until the publication in June 1974 of Decree 521, the official junta law creating the Directorate of National Intelligence.* Contreras' appointment as director of national intelligence was not made public. Decree 521 contained three secret articles, numbers 9, 10, and 11, that subordinated all other intelligence services in the country to DINA and gave DINA agents unlimited power to raid and search houses and take prisoners without charges.† Technically, DINA was subordinate to the four-man government junta. In practice, all DINA operatives, even those originally from other branches of the armed forces, took orders only from Contreras, and Contreras took orders only from one man: General Augusto Pinochet.‡

DINA covert operations, under the command of Colonel Espinoza, had five sections: Government Service, Internal, Economics, Psychological Warfare, and External (Foreign Operations). The Government Service and Internal sections, the largest and most secret divisions, concentrated on control of opposition forces in the government bureaucracy and in the population as a whole.

Purges immediately after the coup had eliminated thousands of persons identified as members of leftist parties from the universities and government services. But the regime's rulers considered every government office a spawning ground for sabotage and conspiracy, every government employee a potential security risk. Radical and Christian Democratic party members virtually monopolized middle-level government jobs. Many had welcomed the coup but could be counted on to oppose the military as soon as

*Decree 521 described DINA as a "professional technical organ, directly dependent on the governing Military Junta, whose mission will be the gathering of all information on the national level from various fields of activity for the purpose of producing the intelligence necessary for the formulation of policies, planning, and the adoption of measures needed to preserve National Security and development of the country."

†Secret article 11 said DINA was the "legal continuation of the commission designated DINA, organized in November 1973" by the SENDET decree. The secret clauses were never published in Chile, although texts of the articles were leaked to human rights workers in 1975 and then distributed clandestinely.

‡In an interview, Air Force General Gustavo Leigh, a member of the junta until 1978, said DINA activities were never submitted to consideration in junta meetings and that he had withdrawn all air force officers from DINA in 1976 because of disagreements with Contreras.

the plan to dismantle Chile's democratic system became evident.

Informants, called *soplones*—whisperers—provided the only method of instilling fear of discovery and arrest in potential opponents in lower-level and middle-level government bureaucracies. DINA took over a large complex of offices in downtown Santiago, out of which it began to run the vast network of government spies, many of them volunteers or part-time employees. Each informant had his or her case officer; each case officer filed reports to the section chief. Of DINA's estimated 20,000 to 30,000 informants, over half held strategic positions in government offices throughout Chile. Contreras counted on a multiplier effect to increase the network's effectiveness. The mere suspicion that the person at the next desk might be working for DINA was sufficient to extinguish griping and eliminate political discussion in government offices.

DINA's Internal Section had the dual task of extirpating the remaining pockets of organized leftist resistance and enforcing the government ban on all opposition political activity. A formidable assignment, since Contreras regarded the 40 percent of the voting population who had supported the Popular Unity as enemies of the Pinochet government and the 30 percent who had supported the Christian Democratic candidates as potential enemies. Contreras decided to begin his systematic assault with an attack on the far left, the movement with the weakest roots but the largest reputation for courage, conviction, and determination. MIR (Movimiento Izquierdista Revolucionario), the leftist revolutionary movement, had gone underground before the coup and continued to attempt to rally their followers to armed resistance. Next would be the Socialists and the Communists. Finally—but not until late 1975—Contreras would turn his terror apparatus on the Christian Democrats and the Catholic Church.

To bring some 70 percent of the population to their political knees, Contreras resorted to the old methods of arrest and torture, to which he added a new wrinkle: disappearance. The shock troops of Contreras' army, the Brigades of Arrests and Interrogation, were teams of five or six persons under the command of a captain or major. With names borrowed from Chile's Indian past, like Antumapu, Pehuenche, Peldehue, each brigade operated a security house whose location changed frequently. The arrest squads, in civilian clothes, brought prisoners to the DINA houses for torture and interrogation. Those who fell into the DINA category of "incapable of rehabilitation" (*irrecuperable* in Spanish) were wrung dry of information—sometimes by months of interrogation—then taken away by a special brigade and made to "disappear."* DINA issued no warrants; it processed no official arrest records; no bodies were brought to the morgue; no death certificates were filed. The list of "disappeared" grew by fifty persons a month in 1974.

The campaign succeeded: Chile's population became terrified. In a speech in September 1974, Pinochet declared the country to be "an island of tranquillity" in a world of violence. However, not all high-ranking members of Chile's military establishment were pleased by the tranquilization techniques that Contreras was applying to the civilian population. The DINA network functioned not only to control opposition but to influence policy along lines favored by Contreras. DINA demanded, and received, a quota of top-level policy positions in each government ministry. The ministers themselves—many of them generals—began to feel threatened as DINA assumed the shape of a shadow government run personally by Contreras. His tactics grated on even the most callous of the other generals, though probably more out of feelings of rivalry than for humanitarian reasons.

SIFA, the Air Force Intelligence Service, had also initiated a campaign against MIR in 1974 under the direction of Colonel Edgardo Ceballos Jones, whose men made wide use of torture. As Contreras began to assert his power consonant with DINA's secret

---

*Several mass graves discovered in Chile in 1978 and 1979 contained the remains of persons executed by Carabineros and other services, not DINA. The bodies of the DINA victims have never been discovered. It is likely that they were disposed of at sea, thrown from helicopters after the stomach cavity was slit to prevent flotation—a tactic borrowed from United States forces in Vietnam.

DINA officers with access to the DINA card file on prisoners knew which prisoners had been selected for disappearance. Samuel Fuenzalida, a former DINA official now living in Europe, testified about the system in Bonn, West Germany, in connection with a civil suit. If a prisoner had the term "Puerto Montt"—a south Chilean city—on his card, Fuenzalida said, it indicated that the prisoner was to be killed on land. Another term, "La Moneda," was used to indicate that the prisoner "was to be killed by being dropped from an airplane into the sea."

charter to control the other intelligence services, prisoners released by Ceballos were picked up by Contreras' men and reinterrogated under torture, and then often "disappeared." Ceballos, human rights activists reported later, began to hide his prisoners from DINA and arrange with human rights organizations to place them in asylum in foreign embassies so that DINA could not murder them.

Army General Óscar Bonilla, the interior minister with a reputation for dynamism and populism, became Contreras' first declared enemy. At a meeting of the cabinet in mid-1974, Pinochet brought in Contreras to report on the theft of documents from the desk of one of the ministers. The report blamed the theft on leftist infiltrators in the ministry, and it was used by Pinochet and Contreras to justify stiffening of DINA control inside the ministries. General Bonilla, addressing his subordinate officer Colonel Contreras, asked for a show of evidence that leftists had stolen the missing documents. Contreras, according to one of those present, refused to provide further information and remarked pointedly that "certain things can't be said in front of strangers." Bonilla, enraged, turned to Pinochet, but Pinochet backed Contreras.

General Sergio Arrellano, nicknamed by leftists "the Butcher of the North" because of his tour of prisons in the north of Chile a month after the coup that resulted in summary executions of seventy prisoners, protested directly to General Pinochet. In a letter to Pinochet in November 1974, Arellano complained that Contreras, his subordinate in rank, had refused to answer Arellano's inquiries on behalf of prisoners' families. The letter described Contreras' DINA as a "Gestapo" and asked that the abuses be corrected before the situation became uncontrollable.

Pinochet heard the protests, received the letters of complaint, and placated individual generals, but he did not waver in his support of Contreras. Instead, he passed on to him the names of the dissenting officers. DINA penetration and surveillance inside the military was stepped up.

Contreras also had a special interest in the plans being implemented by the government's team of economists, many of whom had received graduate degrees from the University of Chicago and were devotees of Dr. Milton Friedman. The two government ministries dealing with the economy were the only ones in civilian hands, and were least subject to direct military control.

Contreras set up his own economics section in DINA to monitor and keep under control the unrest and discontent among low-income groups and labor unions. But Contreras disagreed with the economic model being implemented and shared the view of political leaders such as PL chief Pablo Rodríguez, who favored a corporativist model combining authoritarian government and benevolent, populist economic policies toward the poor. Contreras' staff of eighteen economists made DINA's Economics Section into a two-edged sword, threatening both the opposition parties and the unions and the "Chicago Boys' " monopoly in junta economic policy-making.*

The economic team that guided the junta's fiscal policies did not at first perceive DINA's methods as a threat, only as a slightly unsavory necessary evil, which was to control the opposition long enough for the new economic model to take root. They saw the tangible reality of rampant inflation, not the abstraction called Marxism, as Chile's number one problem in 1974. The economic managers were businessmen, acting in a rarefied world where the contingencies of international finance counted more than ideological preferences. Contreras, on the other hand, took ideas much more seriously. He was committed, not to replace one economic system with another, but to replace one set of ideas with another. Physical terror required its psychic complement.

DINA's Psychological Warfare Section operated in close liaison with the government's Directorate of Social Communications (Dirección Nacional de Comunicaciones Sociales—DINACOS), the office in charge of press censorship, supervision of foreign correspondents, and pro-junta propaganda campaigns inside and outside

---

*The DINA economists also supervised a battery of accountants and bookkeepers engaged in devising a secret internal budget and payroll facilities, with elaborate mechanisms for laundering millions of dollars of secret funds.

Several hundred businesses that had come under state control during the Allende government were returned to private ownership in 1974 and 1975. Some of the firms, however, were turned over to Contreras, who used them to generate funds for DINA. EPECH, the San Antonio fisheries complex, and Cemento Melon, Chile's largest cement manufacturer, were the largest DINA-controlled firms.

Chile. A second-level post in DINACOS was reserved for a Contreras appointee.

Looming behind DINA's vast apparatus and various departments was an inner circle. Called the General Command, it contained between thirty and forty men that Contreras trusted not only for their total personal loyalty to him but as dedicated professionals in a common cause. Military officers whose primary loyalty was to their own service did not enter the General Command, no matter what their rank. The General Command knew the whole of Contreras' plan and the details of daily activity in the five sections. Everything else remained compartmentalized. The thousands of men and women who drew DINA paychecks, who arrested, tortured, interrogated, and killed, knew only what Contreras decided they needed to know for their assignments.

Contreras designed this structure to impose absolute personal control on every aspect of DINA's work and to undercut the natural tendency of bureaucracies to create vested interests and private power enclaves. Only total devotion to Contreras and to DINA's crusade as he defined it opened the way to advancement and responsibility.

Other DINA operations, so secret that no one outside the General Command knew their full scope, had as their target the Chilean military itself and enemies in foreign lands. The exiles and what Pinochet had branded the "international Marxist campaign" against his government required countermeasures. In response to this new and growing problem, Contreras, in mid-1974, organized his fifth and last division, the "External Section." He had a special role in mind for Michael Townley in the External Section.

Underlying the DINA structural division of labor between Internal and External sections was the concept that the war against communism was a holy crusade without battle lines, boundaries, or physically distinguishable enemies. There were no aggressor's divisions poised on Chile's frontiers, no tangible threat that Pinochet could counter with regular military procedures. Only DINA had the men and methods to counterattack; only DINA could develop the capability of striking the enemy in the protection of his foreign dens. Contreras called this "extraterritorial capability."

The president of Mexico had welcomed the top leaders of the Popular Unity and offered them his capital city as a virtual seat for exile operations. Allende's widow, Hortensia Bussi, accepted the Mexican government's invitation and settled there with her youngest daughter, Isabel, surrounding herself with many of the most able UP leaders. Another pocket of prominent exiles, Christian Democrats as well as leftists, began to organize an anti-junta movement in Rome, Italy. Venezuela's Social Democratic President Carlos Andrés Pérez, an Allende friend and ally in Third World causes, opened his country to a flood of exiles. Caracas became a central meeting place for UP and Christian Democratic leaders, some of whom moved clandestinely back and forth from Chile.

Argentina represented a special threat in Contreras' eyes. It shared over 2,000 miles of mountainous border with Chile and had a burgeoning guerrilla movement. It also sheltered by far the largest group of Chilean exiles in 1974. One man was of particular concern to General Pinochet. General Carlos Prats, his predecessor as commander in chief of the army, was living and writing his memoirs in Buenos Aires. Prats represented the constitutionalist line in the Chilean military, presumably still attractive to some generals after the coup. He had been the greatest obstacle to the coup before September 11, and remained in Pinochet's eyes the most important threat to the unity of the Chilean military. In Buenos Aires, Prats was a mere two-and-a-half-hour jet ride from Santiago.

MICHAEL TOWNLEY ARRIVED at Ezeiza Airport outside Buenos Aires the same day that soldiers in Santiago delivered Orlando Letelier to the Venezuelan Embassy. Townley regretted that his mission would prevent his attending the first-anniversary celebration of the coup the next day, September 11. But this mission would make him or break him in DINA. His orders: Arrange the elimination of Prats —in September. Townley knew that he had barely enough time to make final and detailed plans with the Argentine agents, conduct careful surveillance, prepare the "device," and carry out the operation.

He carried the Kenneth Enyart passport. The octagonal Argentine immigration stamp was imprinted for the second time in the eleven-month-old document. Several weeks before, he had used this passport for the first time since arriving in Chile, also for a trip to Buenos Aires.

An atmosphere of violence hung over Buenos Aires like thick smog. President Juan Perón had died in July and a state of virtual civil war had followed. Combined left-wing Peronist and ERP (Ejército Revolucionario del Pueblo, the Trotskyist People's Revolutionary Army) forces, estimated at 10,000, controlled most of two provinces. Perón's widow and vice-president, María Estela Martínez de Perón, had taken over the presidency with a coterie of right-wing advisers and turned the running of the country over to a Rasputin-like figure, José López Rega. As Townley arrived, a terrorist organization calling itself the Argentine Anticommunist Alliance (AAA) claimed credit for a wave of assassinations of prominent left politicians and intellectuals. Later investigations established that AAA was a blanket name for a variety of rightist terror squads organized by Federal Police Chief Alberto Villar at the direction of López Rega.

Townley made contact with members of Milicia, an AAA affiliate, which specialized in reprinting Nazi tracts in Spanish and promoting anti-Semitism. The group coordinated its underground terrorist operations through a branch of SIDE (Servicio de Inteligencia del Estado), the Argentine military intelligence service.* Townley explained his mission: to kill Carlos Prats. The Argentines agreed to help, but told him he would have to wait a few days. While he waited, five Peronist leftists were kidnapped and killed between September 21 and September 30.

General Prats nevertheless felt safe in Argentina. He had served there as military attaché in 1964 and 1965 and had devel-

---

*The description of Townley's activities and contacts in Argentina is based on interviews with investigative sources in the United States and with former Patria y Libertad members and DINA agents in Chile. The Enyart passport provided documentary evidence of his presence in Argentina and was corroborated by statements from Inés Townley. None of the sources was able or willing to identify by name those who worked with Townley in the Prats operation. A strong physical resemblance to Townley caused an apparently uninvolved Chilean rightist, Juan Ossa Bulnes, to be frequently mentioned in journalistic accounts as DINA's hit man.

oped close friendships with Argentine colleagues over the years. He and his wife, Sofia, lived in the affluent Palermo district in a comfortable apartment with a twenty-four-hour guard. He kept in contact with his friends in the Chilean military through letters carried back and forth by trusted friends. Some of the letters saddened him. They described Pinochet's campaign to discredit him in the military, the orders to remove his picture from the walls of regiments where he had served as commander. His correspondence increased, Prats told friends, as more of his former colleagues began to look to him to express their disillusionment with Pinochet's megalomania.

Prats had begun to write a book about his experiences as army chief under the Popular Unity government. In the manuscript he argued that military intervention in politics would cause the destruction of Chile's military institutions and explained his adherence to the "Schneider Doctrine" of defense of the Constitution. In his book, he answered the charges that by serving in Allende's cabinet he had taken sides in the political battlefield. He revealed for the first time that he had entered the cabinet only after seeking and receiving authorization by secret ballot of the corps of generals. DINA agents reported to Contreras about Prats's writing. Some of Prats's letters fell into DINA hands, and rumors abounded about the spectacular revelations contained in the manuscript.

Townley's operation involved many people. In view of the general level of violence in the country and the cooperation of Argentine intelligence in the project, Townley operated without taking extreme security measures. He saw no need for them. His orders did not include them. Townley's mission to kill Prats came up in Santiago cocktail-party conversation. In Buenos Aires, a police official passed a message back to DINA not to delay the mission any longer because so many people in police circles knew about it that they might have to take action to prevent it.

A few days before Townley's arrival in Buenos Aires, a man imitating an Argentine accent had telephoned Prats: "General, I'm calling to tell you that a Chilean army officer has traveled from Santiago to Montevideo. He intends to hire a group of persons to kill you. The only way to stop the operation is for you to make a public statement saying that you are not plotting against the military junta."

Prats, recognizing the false accent, said to the caller, "Go ahead and talk like a Chilean." The caller refused to identify himself, but talked at length, begging Prats to break off all contacts with Chilean military personnel and to leave Argentina. "It was a warning, not a threat," Prats said when he related the incident to friends.

Uneasy about the growing chaos in Argentina, Prats had applied at the Chilean Consulate for a new passport so that he could travel to Europe to look into job offers there. On September 29, the application was still snarled in red tape. Prats and his wife spent that day relaxing with friends. They drove to a farm a few miles outside Buenos Aires for a country lunch, then returned in the early evening to attend a movie with Chilean friends Ramón Huidobro and his wife. After the film, the two couples went to Huidobro's home for coffee and two hours of conversation.

Shortly after midnight, Prats and his wife drove back to their apartment building. Prats turned into the driveway and got out to open the garage door, then got back in the car to pull into the garage. At that instant Townley's bomb, attached under the floor, exploded. Prats was blown out through the open door, his right arm and leg torn off. Sofia Prats was burned to death in the car. The bomb blast blew parts of the car onto the balcony of a ninth-floor apartment.

Townley's Enyart passport showed five stamps the day of the murders.* He left Buenos Aires on a short flight to Montevideo, Uruguay, just across the broad mouth of the La Plata River. He then took a flight to Santiago, arriving about midnight.

Michael Townley had earned his stripes. Contreras bestowed on him the rank of lieutenant. Townley continued to work at Juan Smith's garage as a cover for his DINA activities. Customers liked him, though they wondered about his long absences, for he was one

---

*Exit Argentina; entry Montevideo; exit Montevideo; entry Santiago Pudahuel Sept. 30, voided; entry Oct. 1 Pudahuel. Enrique Arancibia, who fled Chile because of involvement in the Schneider assassination, returned to Santiago the same day as Townley. Arancibia later worked as a DINA agent, using a job in the Chilean State Bank's Buenos Aires office as cover. His DINA case officer at that time (1977–1978) was Michael Townley.

of the rare mechanics in Chile who could repair automatic transmissions.

Townley's DINA assignments multiplied in variety and grew in importance; he took pride in the more intellectual propaganda and counterpropaganda tasks. He worked in intelligence analysis in the External Section, evaluating agents' reports on exile activity abroad, and preparing memos about the impact of international human rights criticism on the government.

His duties in the field of electronics, besides supervising his bugging team, included the search for sophisticated electronic surveillance equipment. Others at DINA may have known more about electronics, radio, and surveillance, but only Townley could go on buying trips to the United States, the principal source for bugging gear, without attracting attention.

In early December, Townley left with a DINA shopping list for a kind of Cook's tour of the United States' private intelligence suppliers, small and large businessmen whose wares could penetrate the most private meetings or detect electronic surveillance.* In Miami he renewed old acquaintances with Cuban exile activists and established his credentials as a DINA agent in order to buy espionage equipment at Audio Intelligence Devices, a Fort Lauderdale firm.

Townley's father, Jay Vernon, had left the Ford Motor Company and settled in Boca Raton, a suburb of Miami. He had become a vice-president in Miami's South East First National Bank. Townley stayed overnight at his parents' house, and father and son talked business.

On that and future trips to Miami, Michael Townley created the dummy apparatus he needed to buy equipment for DINA and export it to Chile. He set up companies called PROCIN, Inc., and Consul-

*Receipts obtained by United States investigators indicate that Townley, using one or another of his aliases, purchased equipment from Audio Intelligence Devices of Fort Lauderdale; Dektor Counterintelligence and Security, Inc., in Springfield, Virginia; and Criminal Research Products, Inc., of Conshohocken, Pennsylvania. According to the receipts, "Kenneth Enyart" ordered telephone-bugging equipment sent by the United Parcel Service to his father's home in Florida and gave his father's name and address for billing. One of the transactions took place in February 1977—the year Michael Townley told interrogators he never enterd the United States.

tec, Ltd, using the false names Kenneth Enyart and Juan Andrés Wilson. His father helped set up account number 11-192-4 for PRO-CIN at the South East First National Bank. The account was in the name of Juan Andrés Wilson—Townley's DINA alias—and of Jay Vernon Townley, his father.

On December 12 Michael Townley returned to Chile via Mexico, bringing with him the sophisticated equipment he had bought. Contreras personally congratulated Townley on his work, and decided to send him on his third mission abroad.

6

OPEN SEASON

FELIPE RIVERO disliked doing political business at work. His glassed-in office cubicle at Sheehan Buick on Miami's South West Eighth Street lacked privacy, and—worse—cast him in the image of car salesman rather than his preferred role of ideological eminence of the Cuban Nationalist Movement. But as Rivero talked to his two Chilean visitors in February 1975, he was confident that his articulate speech and aristocratic demeanor would transform the mundane auto salesman's surroundings into just the right touch of cover for the discussion of important clandestine matters.

Michael Townley and Inés sat before him in the color-coordinated chairs designed to accommodate nervous couples in their last moments of indecision before they sank their savings and credit rating into a new, $7,000 car. They had been introduced as Andrés Wilson and Ana Pizarro, agents and emissaries of the Chilean military government.

Townley, arriving February 6, 1975, in Miami with $25,000 in his pocket and a mission to perform, had used a circuitous chain of contacts to reach Rivero and establish his credentials as a DINA officer. A name given him by his DINA superior, Colonel Espinoza, led him to the inner circle of the Cuban exile community and, after several false starts with other groups, to the CNM and Rivero.

Townley had been recommended to Rivero by CNM member Pablo Castellón, who vouched for Andrés Wilson's DINA credentials on the word of Vladimir Secen,* a former member of pro-Nazi Croatian groups that fought against Marshal Tito in World War II.

Rivero affected the manner of a baron, and no conversation got very far before he informed a new acquaintance of his family's noble heritage in nineteenth-century Cuba, the last of Spain's New World colonies. Even before he became a dispossessed exile after the Cuban Revolution, Rivero had cultivated an aura of arrogance, charisma, and racial superiority. His intellect, style, and coherent ideology distinguished him from the ranting orators, charlatans, and *machista* braggarts who populated the conspiracy-ridden Cuban community in Miami. His father's newspaper, *Diario de la Marina,* had called itself the *New York Times* of Cuba before the revolution. The extensive Rivero holdings, now in Castro's hands, including a substantial share of the Matahambre copper mines, had also helped him establish his credentials in exile.

Rivero had founded the Cuban Nationalist Movement on an ideology—like that of Patria y Libertad in Chile—that incorporated elements of the thinking of Primo de Rivera and the fascist experiences of Mussolini's Italy and Hitler's Germany. The movement's political philosophy stood out in the exile community by its attempt to tie together theories of nature, history, and the state with the role of the individual in history. Nationalism, a key word, evoked a meaning that went beyond the simple desire to return to the homeland. Rivero believed he had created something new between Marxism and capitalism that guaranteed social justice by mediating the interests of private property and unions—or "syndicates"—under the aegis of an authoritarian state.

He saw himself as a purifying element within the squalid core of exile politics, partly because of his unpleasant experience with the CIA in training for the Bay of Pigs invasion. After landing with the

*Secen, a shadowy figure in the Cuban exile community, was called "the colonel" and had a reputation for being connected with Latin American intelligence circles. A Miami FBI informant reported that Secen, a taxi driver, was an acquaintance of Jay Vernon Townley, Michael's father, through "banking business" and that the elder Townley introduced the two. Townley, in his testimony, said that DINA operations chief Pedro Espinoza gave him Secen's name. In addition to Castellón, Rivero, and Secen, Townley had conversations with CNM activists Ignacio Novo and Sergio Gómez and with Armando López Estrada, the "military chief" of Brigade 2506.

invasion force, he remained aloof from the taint of the CIA. At the
televised 1961 interrogations of the invaders by Cuban journalists,
Rivero had won the admiration of friend and foe in an ideological
debate conducted in the presence of Fidel Castro. Other prisoners,
humbled and demoralized by their defeat, had wept. Some had asked
forgiveness. Not Rivero.

Released by Castro in December 1962 with his fellow invaders,
Rivero stood in military formation with the brigade members at
Miami's Orange Bowl as John F. Kennedy held high the flag of the
invasion force and promised, "I can assure you that this flag will be
returned to this brigade in a free Havana."

Buoyed by the pledge of continued United States support in
overthrowing Castro, some exile groups continued to coordinate
strategy with the CIA's Miami station, JM/WAVE, and to draw on
CIA financial and psychological support. Rivero's Cuban Nationalist Movement, more skeptical, went its own way. Rivero disdained
the futile efforts of other groups to foment guerrilla pockets inside
Cuba and mount new commando raids. In 1964 he publicized the
slogan "War Throughout the Roads of the World" and directed his
followers to perform isolated but dramatic acts of terrorism against
Cuban diplomats and diplomatic buildings and against the ships of
countries trading with Cuba. CNM member Guillermo Novo fired
a bazooka at the United Nations Building during a December 1964
speech by Che Guevara. Rivero was convicted of participating in an
attempted bazooka attack against the Cuban exhibit at Expo 67 in
Montreal, Canada. The bazooka became the CNM trademark.

By 1975 most exile leaders and Bay of Pigs veterans, who had
organized an American Legion–type association called Brigade
2506, shared Rivero's skepticism about the CIA. A decade of exile
frustration and Castro consolidation had convinced them of the
hollowness of Kennedy's 1962 promise. The brigade hired a lawyer
and demanded that Kennedy's heirs return the Bay of Pigs flag. That
same year the brigade announced public allegiance to a new hero of
anticommunism who had promised to support their cause: General
Augusto Pinochet received the brigade's "Freedom Medal," the first
and only such award by the brigade to a foreign leader.

Rivero was a mediocre organizer who left the day-to-day tasks of the CNM to less elevated intellects. He owed his stature in the exile community no longer to the audacity he had shown before Castro in 1961, but to his ability to bring off the bold stroke, the grandiose gesture. He saw the events in Chile as an opportunity to propel the CNM to the vanguard and himself to the top of the pecking order in the militant exile community—a chance to become *número uno.* He began maneuvers soon after the Eleventh of September coup to convince Pinochet to tap him, Rivero, and the CNM as the closest ideological counterpart of the Chilean military government and, most important, to recognize a coalition of CNM and allied militant groups as the Cuban government in exile.

In December 1974 Rivero had sent a delegation of CNM members —Guillermo Novo and José Dionisio Suárez—to Chile to pay homage to Pinochet.

They entered Chile with another exile leader, Orlando Bosch. Novo and Suárez were not received warmly but they got some encouragement. Soon after their return, Novo, Suárez, and three other CNM representatives attended a formal meeting at the Chilean Embassy in Washington with First Secretary Tomás Amenabar to discuss relations and joint projects.*

Now, in February 1975, the DINA agent sitting across from Rivero represented the first response by the Chilean government to the CNM signals. Rivero recalled the meeting in a later interview:

> Lots of people come to see me, some are crackpots. [Townley] didn't have a beard then. He came in with a woman. He said he was an agent of the Chilean government and that his service wanted a link with a militant movement in the Cuban community. I knew he was DINA—CIA or DINA or both—but I didn't think he was an American.† He spoke Spanish like a Chilean. I thought it was a serious offer, but we didn't go into detail. He was a soldier, I was a general—the head of my

---

*Present also were José Ponjoan and Ricardo Pastrana of New Jersey and Humberto Medrano of Miami. The discussion centered on a joint project to pressure Fidel Castro to exchange Cuban prisoners for Chilean prisoners.

†Rivero said he later was aware, however, that one of Townley's parents was American.

movement. I wasn't going to talk to him when I had the prerogative of sending him to my lower officer. Guillermo Novo was under me.

I told him my end of the organization was dormant, but that he should go up to the North Zone, which is the only part of the organization still active, and talk to Guillermo Novo.

Rivero ended the meeting and walked out to the sidewalk with Townley and Inés. Bemused, he watched as they got into a pickup with a camper attached and drove west on "Calle Ocho." He was anxious to call Guillermo and share the news that the Chileans had picked up the bait. "I thought of what kind of help the Chileans could give us—maybe a statement calling the CNM the hope of Cuba. Chile was our pretty baby, our darling in the Cuban community. If we could get them to say we were the best, we'd be the new leaders of the Cuban exile movement. That's what I told Guillermo to demand." He said that he also told Guillermo Novo to negotiate for financial support and "a base in the Antarctic."*

On the plane from Miami to Newark, New Jersey, Michael and Inés Townley discussed their first joint DINA mission and their success with Rivero. Later Townley recounted the orders he had received from Colonel Contreras:

General Contreras told me that some meetings were going to be held in Mexico City on human rights, in which members of the Chilean Socialist and Communist Parties would be meeting to organize world public opinion against Chile. General Contreras wanted to eliminate some of the people that were going to attend this meeting. These persons were to include Carlos Altamirano and Volodia Teitelboim. General Contreras told me to contact anti-Castro Cuban exiles for assistance. . . .

*Rivero made similar statements when called before the Washington, D.C. grand jury in mid-1978. He said he called Guillermo Novo and told him, "There are some Chileans that want to see you. See if you can get the president or the government to say that we're the best movement, and do something to give a slap in the face to our other rivals in the Cuban community."

The Townleys had made contact with various other groups before getting in touch with Rivero. Townley found no one he considered trustworthy. He steered away from those groups that he knew had been penetrated by the FBI and CIA. Felipe Rivero, though cagy and noncommittal, nevertheless showed enthusiasm about establishing a "mutual aid" relationship with Chile. The CNM was a small group, and thus more secure. And it had shown its daring in a long list of terrorist acts over the years.

The meeting had gone well. Now to contact the chief of the "North Zone—" Michael and Inés chuckled at the pretentious titles for an organization with a maximum of twenty-five active members.

On arrival at Newark Airport, Townley called Novo and introduced himself as Andrés Wilson. Gruff and suspicious at first, Novo agreed to a dinner meeting that night. Townley rented a car and drove the few miles north along the corridor of drab industrial towns built on former swamplands between the Hudson and Hackensack rivers. At the agreed meeting place, the Cuatro Estrellas restaurant in Union City, they sat down at a conspicuous table. Inés wrote ANDRÉS WILSON in block letters on a paper napkin and put it in the center of the table. Then they waited. Three men entered the restaurant and approached their table.

"So you're the Chileans who met Felipe in Miami," said one, studying Townley's American clothes and his height and fair hair.

The Cubans introduced themselves: Guillermo Novo, José Dionisio Suárez, and Armando Santana. Skipping the amenities, they grilled Townley about his acquaintances in Miami and made it clear that they suspected him of CIA or FBI connections, that they saw him as an agent attempting to penetrate their organization.

To convince them of his DINA identity, Townley described the detention and interrogation of Novo and Suárez in Santiago a few months before on the occasion of their trip to Chile with Orlando Bosch. The information impressed the CNM militants, but also increased their hostility to Townley and his wife as they recalled their unpleasant treatment at DINA hands. The dinner meeting did not alleviate their suspicions.

Early the next morning, when Townley opened his motel-room door, Novo, Suárez, and Santana pushed their way into the room.

They drew guns and ordered the couple to sit down. Townley rose and closed the curtains. Novo accused him of sending a signal to agents outside. Suárez and Santana searched the luggage and triumphantly produced a United States passport in the name of Kenneth Enyart and a Chilean identity card in the name of Andrés Wilson. A suspicious insignia on a key chain found among their belongings was interpreted as proof of Townley's CIA affiliation. The Cubans kept their guns visible, but not pointed directly at the couple, letting Townley continue his argument, allowing themselves to be convinced.

Townley explained his double identity, keeping his tone friendly. He said he understood and respected their caution, and suggested they call the Chilean Embassy in Washington to check on him. The men placed the call. A voice on the other end of the line vouched for Andrés Wilson. But Novo knew that the CIA or FBI could easily arrange such telephone checks. Moreover, Townley's Spanish had an unmistakable American twang. Townley, using his charm on the suspicious Cubans, explained that he had an American parent. Finally, Novo put away his pistol and extended his hand to Townley.

"Sometimes you have to lose—and trust," he said in Spanish. They sealed their newly won understanding with handshakes all around, and ordered a pot of coffee from room service. A flash of acknowledgment, something in all of their faces, a kindred spark that each person in the room understood, had transcended differences in looks and culture. Had a bottle of brandy and glasses been sitting on the motel-room table, they could have filled and raised their glasses and shouted together a lusty toast: "¡Viva la muerte!" Long live death.

Townley outlined DINA's plan, pointing out that it coincided with the CNM strategy of "war throughout the roads of the world." Contreras wanted the upcoming meeting of UP leaders in Mexico City, the first gathering of exiles and recently released prisoners, to explode in chaos and death. A fast, brutal strike against the Chilean exiles' first organized effort would have immense deterrent effect, as the exiles would believe DINA capable of smashing them even in the most protected of foreign lands. Townley planned to build and plant powerful bombs at the meeting to achieve the double effect of "physically eliminating" the most important UP leaders and terrorizing the rest.

DINA intelligence had provided the agenda, list of participants, and location of the Mexico City meeting. Townley's assassination list started with Carlos Altamirano and Volodia Teitelboim, the exiled heads respectively of the Socialist and Communist parties, and continued with lesser figures. He had a license to kill as many as possible, Townley said, conscious that he sounded like a Chilean 007. Novo agreed to provide the necessary explosives and assigned a CNM member to help on the mission. They would meet in Miami.

Later that same day, Townley answered a knock at his door. A man handed him a bulging brown supermarket bag and closed the door. The bag contained the TNT, detonating cord, and other items he had ordered.

That evening the Townleys met Inés' son Ronnie at a Chinese restaurant in Upper Manhattan. Townley attempted to keep the reunion pleasant. He saw the twenty-three-year-old Ronnie, only nine years younger than himself, more as a brother than as a stepson. Inés kept up a superficial banter, avoiding the topic that had caused so much bitterness between her and her son in Chile—his attachment to the defeated Allende government. It was the last meeting between mother and son. After dinner, Inés and Michael flew to Miami.

A few days later Townley got a call from Novo, who told him to meet an incoming flight from Newark. Using prearranged signals, he greeted a dark-haired, neat-bearded man in his twenties. With the arrival of Virgilio Paz, an unemployed sometime used-car salesman, Townley had completed his team for what he called "Operation Open Season." Michael Townley, Inés Callejas, and Virgilio Paz set off on a nine-month, eight-country DINA mission to terrorize targeted Chilean exiles and the enemies of the Cuban Nationalist Movement. Inés participated as an equal member of the DINA team.

For the operation Townley had invented a special device to set off small, powerful bombs by radio control. With the New Jersey shopping bag full of plastique explosive, TNT, and detonating cord, Townley was ready to build them.

The distinguishing element of Townley's bomb was a paging or "beeper" system commonly used by physicians, policemen, and delivery men. Townley went to one of the Miami stores he had patronized before for electronic equipment, Silmar Electric Company, run by Cuban exile Jorge Smith, who also had provided Townley with intelligence on exile activities. Smith sold him a Fanon-Courier brand paging system consisting of a radio transmitter, a ten-tone encoding device, and six receivers or "beepers." The transmitter and receivers had a single, fixed frequency, and the encoder had ten keys, each producing a separate tone. Only the correct combination of two tones transmitted over the correct frequency would cause the small receiver to beep. In normal usage this would convey some kind of message to the person carrying the device, usually to call an answering service or central office.

Townley had modified the small device so that the signal it received would trigger an electric charge capable of detonating a bomb. This was done by removing the speaker and adding booster batteries, switches, additional wiring, and an electrically activated blasting cap. He adapted the transmitter to run off an automobile cigarette lighter.

As Townley, Callejas, and Paz put the finishing touches on the six detonators and prepared the camper for the drive to Mexico, Chilean exile leaders began to gather in Mexico City for the February 17 opening of the meeting of the International Commission of Inquiry into the Crimes of the Military Junta in Chile. Orlando Letelier flew there from Washington. Clodomiro Almeyda, recently released from prison, came from Caracas, Altamirano and Teitelboim from Eastern Europe.

Townley wasted days in Miami trying to arrange for false papers to avoid entering Mexico under his own name or with the Enyart passport. Finally Novo provided false New Jersey drivers' licenses in the names of Andrew and Ana Brooks. Paz obtained papers identifying him as Javier Romero. The Townleys and Paz packed the camper hurriedly. They planned to drive through the night and finish making the bomb on the way to Mexico City. Paz brought along a high-powered rifle with a telescopic sight, but had second thoughts and disposed of it before crossing the border at Laredo, Texas. The DINA team rumbled incongruously across the arid hills of Mexico in an American Traveler camper mounted on a Dodge pickup, arriving in Mexico City weeks after the Popular Unity leaders had left.*

In Mexico, the trio conducted surveillance on resident Chilean exiles who had set up an exile center, Casa de Chile. Townley contacted pro-junta Chileans and held meetings to recruit a team to continue surveillance of opposition Chileans and report to DINA.† In mid-April, the camper and its healthily tanned occupants rolled back into Miami.

Townley contacted DINA and received orders to follow the exiles he had missed in Mexico City to Europe. Inés Callejas returned to Santiago, and Townley and Paz flew to Spain, which, under the dictatorship of aging Francisco Franco, was hospitable to rightist intelligence operatives. The Chilean Embassy in Madrid harbored DINA's central headquarters for intelligence on exiles in Europe. Townley's operation, involving possible assassinations or "sanctions," to preserve even deeper cover was managed directly by the General Command in Santiago.

With Paz, Townley began to make the rounds of the European fascist circuit. He contacted Corsican gangsters and gunrunners, remnants of the French Secret Army Organization, and a Lisbon-based fascist organization operating as a pseudo–news agency. In Madrid, which was more or less home base, Townley became acquainted with operatives in the Spanish intelligence service and the newly founded Fascist International, inspired by Argentina's AAA.

In early May, Townley waited at Madrid International Airport for the arrival of a flight from Havana carrying Carlos Altamirano. Altamirano later remembered a tall man bumping into him and knocking him down as he rushed to catch a connecting flight to East Germany.

In late May and June Townley returned to Miami and then to

*Townley claims he disposed of all explosives and detonating devices in Mexico City to avoid problems crossing back into the United States. That is probably only partly true; he would have had no reason to throw away a harmless-looking paging device, the most expensive parts of which cost between $250 and $350.

†In court, Townley gave the impression that he arrived only a day or two after the end of the conference, but border crossing records examined by the FBI indicate the trio entered Mexico March 15. The conference ended February 20.

Chile.* In Miami he placed an order with his friend Jorge Smith for another Fanon-Courier transmitter and encoder. He sent the new equipment, adapted for assassination, on a LAN-Chile Airlines flight to Chile and later to Frankfurt, Germany.

In July Townley and Callejas flew to Madrid and rejoined Paz. The team then moved north, traveling in rented cars from country to country. They reported on exile and exile-solidarity organizations and established working relationships with extreme rightist groups willing to carry out DINA operations. Occasionally Paz went on solo missions. He flew to Northern Ireland to photograph British prison camps holding members of the Irish Republican Army. President Pinochet later displayed Paz's photos to foreign correspondents in Chile to prove the hypocrisy of the British human rights criticisms of Chile.

By mid-September, Townley's unit had made contacts, collected intelligence, and carried out operations in France, Brussels, Belgium, Luxembourg, and Amsterdam and other cities of Holland, and had arrived in Frankfurt. There, he arranged for a LAN-Chile Airlines official to act as liaison between himself and DINA's West German collaborators.

IN LATE SUMMER 1975, Contreras himself had embarked on a multicountry junket to organize Latin America's secret police and intelligence services into a cooperative anti-exile strike force. Traveling under a false name, the DINA chief flew first to Washington, D.C., in early August 1975.

General Vernon Walters, deputy director of the CIA, met with Contreras at CIA headquarters in Langley, Virginia. Walters, who speaks fluent Spanish, greeted Contreras warmly. A Nixon political appointee, Walters was responsible for the CIA's liaison operations with friendly foreign intelligence agencies and had overseen CIA organizational and training assistance to DINA during its formative

---

*Townley's itinerary, according to the Enyart passport, was: Miami–Santiago, May 17; Santiago–Buenos Aires, June 1; Buenos Aires–Miami, no date; Miami–Santiago, June 14; Santiago–Rio de Janeiro, July 19. The passport does not record stamps for Europe in 1975, probably because of lax border controls for persons bearing United States passports.

stages in early 1974.* As DINA's superiority over other Chilean intelligence services became evident in the service's first year, he had ordered liaison with DINA upgraded.

What Contreras and Walters talked about remains a secret, but the purpose of Contreras' travels was revealed at his next stop in Venezuela. Rafael Rivas Vásquez, deputy director of DISIP, the Venezuelan intelligence service, met Contreras at Caracas' Maiqueita Airport on the evening of August 27 and took him to dinner at a luxurious restaurant on a hill overlooking the city. The next day DISIP officials held a series of meetings with Contreras and the team of DINA officers who accompanied him. Rivas Vásquez later described the meeting with Contreras:

> During these talks, which of course are subject to each govern-
> ment's approval, he [Contreras] made a formal request—just
> verbally, the way such requests are made—that they wished
> to obtain information about the activities of all the Chilean
> exiles living at that time in Venezuela. We refused to give him
> that information; then he said, well, if at least we could submit
> to him all the travel information on Chilean exiles who would
> be leaving Venezuela for other countries—flight number, date,
> destination—and, of course, on the ones who would be coming
> to Venezuela, just to have them more or less pinpointed and
> have up-to-date information on their activities.
>
> He also explained that DINA was being expanded as an
> intelligence service, that they would have foreign agents in the
> embassies abroad, that they were already training all the third
> secretaries in the Chilean embassies . . . so they could serve
> as case officers abroad.
>
> He said he had been making some good-will trips to get the
> support of different Latin American intelligence services. As
> this works on the basis of . . . verbal agreements, he had been
> traveling quite a lot. [He said] he was building up this grandi-

*Walters, interviewed by the FBI in 1979, told them in his statement that "part of his function as deputy director of the CIA was to coordinate and conduct foreign liaison for the CIA and within that framework he had received General Contreras in 1975 when the latter visited the United States."

ose scheme of a very big and powerful service that could have information—worldwide *information.

According to Rivas, the Venezuelan government of President Carlos Andrés Pérez ordered DISIP to spurn Contreras' overtures. But Contreras, in a move probably designed to facilitate informal cooperation by individual DISIP agents, provided DISIP with a set of codes and ciphers with which they could communicate via telex with DINA in Santiago. He also invited Rivas and DISIP Director Orlando García (a Cuban exile) to fly at DINA expense to a meeting of Latin American intelligence services in Santiago the coming October. The Venezuelans declined the invitation. As Contreras continued on his tour, he repeated the offer to the secret police of Brazil, Argentina, Uruguay, Paraguay, and Bolivia. They all accepted.

IN LATE SEPTEMBER, Townley, Callejas, and Paz loaded their rented car to head south. They had received new orders from Contreras. They stopped in Munich, where DINA had cultivated contacts with former Nazi sympathizers associated with Christian Social Union leader Franz Josef Strauss.† They next made a contact and information-gathering stop in Vienna, then drove west to Innsbruck and south to Italy across the Brenner Pass. They reached Rome exhausted from almost a week of steady driving. Townley nevertheless picked up the phone to call his list of contacts as soon as they found a hotel. He had fallen behind the timetable set for his mission. DINA's orders had been specific: September, the month of Chile, the month of the coup.

Rome had become the central headquarters of the exile Popular

*Excerpts from Rivas Vásquez's testimony of June 29, 1978, before the Washington, D.C. federal grand jury. Contreras told another source that he provided the Venezuelan service with the intelligence that the Revolutionary Coordinating Board (a coalition formed in 1975 of Latin America's most revolutionary underground groups) planned to move its headquarters from Argentina to Caracas. Predictably, he denied to the source having sought information on exiles.

†Strauss visited Chile in 1976 at Pinochet's invitation and emitted predictably effusive praise for the regime. His trip was arranged by DINA propaganda agent Anthal Lipthay.

Unity soon after the coup. Each party assigned representatives to staff the Rome office, coordinate activities in Western Europe, and publish the official exile magazine, *Chile-América.* The Rome organization reproduced in miniature the interparty squabbles that had hamstrung the Allende government. Decisions out of power still required the approval of each party, and each leader spoke first of all for his own party; in exile no one leader represented Popular Unity as such. The lack of unity on tactics and strategy that plagued the exiled UP leadership, however, had one advantage. It allowed them, as representatives of individual parties, to open up a political dialogue with their former adversaries, the Christian Democrats, especially those in the left and center of the party.

The presence in Rome of Chilean elder statesman Bernardo Leighton, a cofounder of the Christian Democratic Party and interior minister during the Frei government, was responsible for this more ecumenical turn in Chilean opposition policy. Before his self-imposed exile in late 1973 Leighton had led a minority in the Christian Democratic Party in implacable opposition to the military coup. By 1975, the mainstream of the party in Chile, including coup enthusiast Eduardo Frei, had followed suit and moved into irreversible if timid opposition to the Pinochet regime.

Back in the vanguard of his party, the sixty-six-year-old Leighton promoted the idea of a Christian Democratic–Popular Unity alliance to restore democracy in Chile. He became one of the editors of *Chile-América* and appeared frequently with UP leaders at anti-junta rallies all over Europe. One of the most popular political figures in Chile, Leighton, nicknamed "Brother Bernardo," enjoyed prominence as well in the international Christian Democratic Movement. The ruling Italian Christian Democratic Party, which had long had close ties to Chile's Christian Democrats, had invited Leighton to live and work in Italy. He cleared and coordinated his political activities with the Italian party.

For a time DINA had operated a surveillance outpost in an apartment directly across the street from UP headquarters.* Now,

*A newspaper vendor who stocked Chilean periodicals mentioned to the *Chile-América* workers that "people across the street" were also very interested in Chile and had been buying Chilean newspapers. After the UP workers began to investigate, the DINA agents vacated the apartment.

after months of telephone threats and petty harassment of the exiles, Contreras escalated the attack. Townley and his team received orders to kill.

The instructions were that Italians should carry out the mission under Townley's supervision. DINA control transmitted to Townley the cover names and phone numbers of agents. On a warm September evening in 1975, Paz, Callejas, and Townley dined with a man whose *nom de guerre* was Alfredo di Stefano and two other men he brought along. They discussed Italian and Chilean politics. Di Stefano and his companions, seasoned warriors of the Italian right wing, belonged to the Fronte della Gioventù (Youth Front) of the Italian Social Movement, a powerful and violent group that proclaimed open allegiance to the fascism of the Mussolini years. Di Stefano bragged to Townley that on December 7, 1970, he had led a group of fifty neo-fascist commandos in a midnight takeover of the Italian Interior Ministry in the Viminale Palace. That, he explained, should have been the first step in a military coup to install their leader, fascist Prince Junio Valerio Borghese. The commandos had sat behind their guns throughout the night, eating sandwiches and drinking coffee, waiting for the military uprising in other parts of the city that never came. In the morning, they left quietly, taking with them 180 submachine guns from the Interior Ministry armory.

Since then, di Stefano boasted, he had become one of the ten or fifteen most important leaders in the right-wing terrorist offensive against the weakened Italian government. Townley interjected that the current Italian situation bore remarkable similarities to Chile under Allende, and that Patria y Libertad, using tactics similar to di Stefano's Youth Front, had emerged as an important factor in provoking the armed forces to overthrow the democratic government. Chile had a Marxist government and a strong Christian Democratic opposition nipping at its heels, he said. Italy had a weak, vacillating Christian Democratic government with a strong Communist Party singing the siren song of center-left unity. In both situations, Townley added, the anti-Marxist forces needed to block any possible alliance between the Marxists and the Christian Democrats. Then the defenders of Western culture could gain ascendancy with the help of the military.

Townley moved from the abstract to the concrete in his argument. In Rome, right now, said Townley, there lives a Chilean exile who embodies that threat of left-center alliance. This man endangers not only our victories in Chile but the cause in Italy and other countries as well. Behind this incipient Christian Democratic–leftist alliance is Bernardo Leighton. His elimination would prove of immeasureable benefit to anticommunist movements all over the world. Paz nodded his agreement as a representative of the Cuban exile movement. Townley explained Leighton's importance, using DINA's intelligence analysis to show that Leighton would serve as a catalyst, "the right man in the right place at the right time" to forge the Chilean antifascist alliance.

Townley's low-keyed approach influenced the Italian fascists to see Leighton as DINA wanted them to see him—a threat to their movement in Italy as well as to the Chilean junta. Over the next few days planning discussions ensued. Paz offered a unique cover-up plan to throw the subsequent investigation off the trail of both DINA and the Italians. The Italians would kill the Chilean target, and the Cuban exile movement would claim credit. September was over. Townley was again behind schedule.

BERNARDO LEIGHTON AND HIS wife, Ana Fresno, lived a quiet life in a modest apartment in Via Aurelia, a few blocks from Vatican City. The cobblestone street had heavy traffic and only a precarious ribbon of sidewalk along the walls of eighteenth- and nineteenth-century buildings. The Leightons, accustomed to upper-class affluence and comforts, had adapted without complaint to a modest exile existence. The threats, which had become more frequent in recent months, worried Leighton, not because he took them seriously, but because his pacific nature rebelled at the thought that someone could want to hurt him. The couple nevertheless agreed to take one precaution: neither would go out alone.

On Monday, October 6, Leighton and his wife were walking arm-in-arm along the sidewalk toward the entrance to their apartment building, number 145. They had just got off a bus at Via Aurelia after a late-afternoon shopping trip. Ana Fresno remembered thinking, as they walked toward their house, that the street was unusually free of cars. Although it was dusk, she could see a man walking toward them on the other side of the street. As they neared the iron gate of the apartment house, she heard the sound of boots on cobblestones and saw the man crossing the street diagonally to a point just behind them. He was young, tall, robust, informally dressed.

A shot rang out. Ana snapped her head around. She saw the man behind them. She saw the gun. Another shot cracked. The bullet hit her right shoulder. She fell. Beside her she saw her husband, his face covered with blood. She tried to turn her head to look at her attacker, but her body didn't respond. She heard the sound of boots running, then silence. A car passed.

A neighbor, Bruno Franscate, heard the shots. He left his television and rushed out into the street, and found the Leightons lying on the bloody sidewalk beside a car. Ana Fresno, immobile but conscious, asked if her husband was alive. Franscate told her that Leighton was still breathing. Then he ran to call the police.*

Leighton and Ana Fresno survived the attack. The bullet, from a 9mm Beretta pistol, struck the back of Leighton's head and exited above his left ear. Though unconscious and then disoriented for several days, Leighton recovered except for a slight hearing loss. The second shot traversed his wife's body at shoulder level and grazed her spinal column just below the medulla. She never regained full use of her legs. Newspapers reported, wrongly, that Leighton had been hit in the forehead, his wife in the neck. Police spokesmen did not correct the errors in later press briefings.

The assassination attempt had the desired effect. Leighton fell silent. The shooting provoked fear throughout the exile community. Without active promotion by the leader who defined himself as a "man of dialogue," and with no one aspiring to take Leighton's place, the tender growth of leftist–Christian Democratic unity withered. Initiative in the Christian Democratic Party reverted to the anti-Marxists around former President Eduardo Frei in Chile.

Townley and Paz left for Miami; Callejas returned to Chile. In

*The street was deserted except for a man inside a telephone booth nearby, from whom Franscate demanded use of the phone. Police tests established that a person inside the telephone booth could not have heard the shots, thus putting to rest early speculation that the man was part of the murder team.

Miami, Townley and Paz met with CNM national coordinator Ignacio Novo, Guillermo Novo's brother and a cofounder of the CNM.

On October 13, a week after the assassination attempt on Leighton, the Miami newspaper *Diario Las Américas,* a pro-exile Spanish-
language daily, received a communiqué postmarked October 10 from
Zero (Cero in Spanish) one of the CNM's clandestine names, claiming credit for the shooting. Before returning to Chile, Townley took
care of a few obligations and loose ends. A Fanon-Courier transmitter and encoder he had ordered were delivered to Miami's LAN-
Chile office. Townley had them sent to Santiago.

On October 15, he drove to Fort Lauderdale to the heavily
guarded headquarters of Audio Intelligence Devices. He signed the
control card "Kenneth Enyart" and was shown to the office of his
friend Jack Holcolm, the AID director. They talked shop. Townley
placed an order for $800 worth of electronics gear to ship to DINA.
Holcolm was expecting Townley, as Townley's father had called
ahead to make the appointment for his son. Late in the afternoon,
his sophisticated equipment loaded and paid for, Townley left for
Miami International Airport to catch that night's LAN flight to
Santiago.

On October 31, a bomb placed under the car seat of Cuban exile
leader Rolando Masferrer exploded, blowing off his legs and killing
him almost instantly. Masferrer, known as "El Tigre" (The Tiger)
because of his stealth and ferocity as a Batista colonel in Cuba in the
1950s, had built his own organization and a reputation in the Miami
exile community. A Communist Party member until 1944, Masferrer
had converted to right-wing repression with zeal. He simultaneously
accumulated a fortune and a private army of retainers, both of which
he brought to Miami. Many in the violent exile community looked
to Masferrer for leadership. The CNM considered him corrupt and
of dubious commitment.

On November 4, 1975, Zero sent a communiqué to the Miami
office of the Associated Press. The message said Zero had executed
Masferrer because he was a divisive force in the Cuban exile movement and accused him of being an agent for Castro's G2 intelligence.
Zero added: "Mr. Bernardo Leighton was shot through the back of
the head in Rome. A 9mm Beretta pistol was used. We are informing

you of this to contradict reports printed in the media and to identify them fully."

The communiqué set off a flurry of Interpol cables between the Italian police, the FBI, and the Miami police. Only someone directly connected with the attackers could have known the details revealed in the Zero communiqué—the make of the gun, the location of the wound.* Suspicion shifted from the Italian Social Movement in Rome to the Cuban Nationalist Movement in Miami.

In Chile, Townley reported to Contreras and Espinoza on the fruits of his long journey. A network now existed to control and mount sanctions against Chilean exiles in Mexico, the United States, and Europe. The most important components for cooperative action were the Cuban Nationalist Movement of New Jersey and Miami and the Italian Social Movement's Youth Front. Townley gave Contreras the names and code names of his collaborators, and suggested that a *quid pro quo* was in order for missions already accomplished.

Contreras agreed. He wanted to see his agents, to submit them to the only infallible evaluation he knew—his own personal scrutiny. Townley proposed bringing several of the Cubans and Italians with whom he had worked most closely to Chile to receive DINA training. Contreras liked the suggestion: foreign agents united in a worldwide struggle against communism, seeking leadership and professional guidance from Chile, from DINA. Just like the CIA, he thought.

Contreras allowed himself to dream, to envision victory against communism on many fronts, all growing out of Chile's Eleventh of September. The fresh shoots of the underdeveloped world would accomplish what the soft-headed, liberal United States had failed to

*There are two theories on the origin of the information in the November 4 Zero communiqué. The simplest is that Townley and Paz were in Rome at the time of the Leighton assassination and got the information directly from Alfredo di Stefano. But Townley claims he left Rome before the assassination attempt. The Zero information, according to Townley, was channeled by di Stefano to DINA in Santiago and from there communicated to Paz in Miami for use in the November 4 communiqué. According to Townley's version, he and Paz would not have known the details of the attack at the time they arrived in Miami and thus Paz was not able to include any convincing details in the first Zero communiqué.

do as leader of the "free world": exterminate communists wherever they could be found.

As Contreras surveyed the world map at the end of 1975, he saw many threats, many remaining enemies. The United Nations had dealt Chile a powerful blow. Exiles had flocked to give testimony to the UN Human Rights Commission, which resulted in a strong condemnation of systematic torture and abuse of rights. As Contreras pored over the intelligence reports from DINA agents in New York, one name in particular stood out as that of an exile who had single-handedly buttonholed and persuaded representatives of countries formerly friendly to Chile to vote against it in the United Nations resolution. This man had entered United Nations foyers as a quasi-ambassador, and other representatives had treated him as a respected peer.

Contreras studied the name: Orlando Letelier.

7

TARGET: LETELIER

GENERAL AUGUSTO PINOCHET UGARTE rose before dawn. It was his habit and his delight to demonstrate to his underlings, his former peers in the generals' corps, that he, the supreme chief of the nation, President of the Republic, General of the Army and Commander in Chief of the Forces of Air, Sea, and Land, absolute leader and incarnation of the movement of the Eleventh of September, worked longer and harder and showed more discipline than any of them.

In early June 1976, at the height of his power, he was sixty years old. In the past months he had begun to look ahead to a decade or two as ruler of Chile, to see himself in his greying years as the leader who turned back communism in Chile, in all Latin America. Another Generalissimo Franco, his civilian aides whispered, just loud enough for him to hear.

At 4:00 A.M., Pinochet donned his loose white karate robes and trousers and tied a brown belt around his waist. A half-hour of exercise in the gymnasium with an army karate instructor, a shower, and an hour of paperwork before breakfast had become his daily routine. The regimen reinforced for him the military values of austerity and discipline and the relentless inner drive to which he attributed his effectiveness.

Colonel Manuel Contreras often worked through the night, for during the curfew hours from 1:00 A.M. to 5:30 A.M. Chile belonged to him and to his DINA commandos. On nights that DINA had no

special operations planned, he retired early and rose in time to prepare for his most important function, the president's daily intelligence briefing. On most days Contreras arrived at Pinochet's
mansion by 6:30 A.M. They would breakfast together there, or depart
immediately for Diego Portales, the government building, riding
together in the back of Pinochet's armored Mercedes, an escort of
screaming motorcycles in front and behind. Contreras reported to no
one but Pinochet, the exclusive consumer of DINA's intelligence
reports. No one but Pinochet could give an order to Colonel Contreras, who, though he commanded no divisions, possessed more
power than any Chilean general.

By June 1976, the four-man junta had become a hollow fiction:
Pinochet controlled Chile. He did so by mastery of detail and by his
swift implementation of ruthless policies, not by force of intellect or
by political brilliance. He demanded to be informed of the movements of everyone in the recognized opposition: the leftist parties, the
Christian Democratic Party, the Catholic Church, the human rights
movement, local and foreign journalists. Contreras provided him
with the details of those activities, and on this intelligence Pinochet
based his power.*

The surroundings Pinochet chose for these briefings were luxurious and protected—the presidential mansion, the armored Mercedes, the twenty-second floor of the Diego Portales Building. But
Pinochet and Contreras, huddled over secret reports, converted the
atmosphere of their surroundings into that of a battlefield tent, themselves the generals, mapping the day's strategic moves against the
enemy, analyzing the previous day's advances and reverses, making
a head count of the foe's losses. They saw the process of government
as war, necessitating deployment of forces on all fronts to defeat the
enemy.

In June 1976 Contreras had much to report, and much to plan
with His Excellency. On the internal front, he could report major
losses inflicted on the enemy. His men had succeeded in picking off,

---

*Only Pinochet and Contreras know the specific content of the intelligence briefings. Outsiders
are limited to a plausible reconstruction based on events and on DINA operations that were
set in motion.

one by one, the top-level leadership of the Chilean Communist Party. Earlier in the year a middle-level party official had broken under torture and provided DINA with information on the locations of most of the party safehouses where clandestine leaders lived or met. DINA knew that the party planned to hold a series of mass protest demonstrations at the time of the meeting of the Organization of American States in June.

Based on the information given by the "broken" prisoner, in April and May DINA arrested the top party leader inside Chile, Undersecretary-General Víctor Díaz. DINA squads had by now arrested a score of leaders and hundreds of others. It would take the party years to re-form a functioning resistance organization.*

The "internal front" was secure. The mopping-up operation against the Communists had obliterated the last center of organized resistance. The Socialist Party and the extreme left group, MIR, had not yet recovered from DINA's 1974 and 1975 offensives against them, which had filled concentration camps and left hundreds missing or dead.

With Bernardo Leighton out of action, the Christian Democratic Party remained aloof from overtures of the leftist parties to form a united front in opposition to the dictatorship. Instead the Christian Democrats maintained a subdued opposition consisting of criticism of the government's economic plan and human rights violations. The Christian Democratic Party posed no immediate threat to the regime.

On the "external front," the situation was more precarious. The foreign press, even in countries the military regime had counted upon as allies, unrelentingly carried stories detailing atrocities and misery inside Chile. Great Britain, Sweden, Italy, and Mexico had with-

---

*One of the middle-level Communist Party leaders arrested by DINA was a CIA agent who had kept United States intelligence informed of party plans. Afterwards a CIA case officer discreetly approached a DINA official with whom he had worked. As a United States official in Chile at the time later told the story, the CIA suggested to DINA that "X," the Communist Party functionary reported as missing or detained, would serve the common Chilean–United States national security cause more effectively if released. The CIA offered, the source said, to "run him jointly," sharing the infiltrator's "intelligence product" with DINA.

DINA never responded. The CIA agent never reappeared. "We assumed," the United States official said, "that DINA had killed him before the approach was made."

drawn their ambassadors. The government press office had compiled a blacklist banning from Chile twenty-four foreign correspondents representing most of the world's major media, but coverage only grew worse.*

Santiago was the site for the upcoming General Assembly of the Organization of American States, scheduled for June 7–18, 1976. Pinochet saw in the OAS assembly a rare opportunity to boost his international image, to rid himself of the international pariah status he had earned through his human rights record.

The United States government had also decided the time had come to help Pinochet put behind him the bothersome human rights issue and begin with a clean slate. First, the State Department exercised its considerable influence in the OAS to override opposition by the nonmilitary governments to holding the prestigious meeting in Santiago. Secretary of State Henry Kissinger was to lead the United States delegation; his preference for the Santiago site was common knowledge.

A month before the OAS meeting, U.S. Treasury Secretary William Simon included Chile in a tour of Latin America. He spent a whirlwind ten hours on May 7 meeting with Pinochet and top government economic officials. He balanced praise for the country's restoration of free-market economic policies and a gentle admonition on human rights. Simon brought with him a list of political prisoners and made it clear to his hosts that he expected a substantial number to be released in connection with his visit. In a later interview with one of the authors, Simon recalled his Chile visit as "playing hardball": "The State Department and the Chilean government were both telling me they needed a high-level United States government official to go down there, to appear there in public," he said. "I told them I wouldn't go unless they freed some prisoners. I played hardball with them; they understood that. I just didn't see why they had to arrest all those people. Their economic plans were working very well."

*The list included Joanne Omang of the *Washington Post,* Rudolph S. Rauch III of *Time,* Juan de Onís of the *New York Times,* William Montalbano of the *Miami Herald,* and correspondents from German National Television, Sweden, Italy, and Mexico. Soviet and Eastern European journalists were banned automatically.

The Chileans obliged. Simon, at a news conference at Chile's Central Bank, announced he had been assured that forty-nine persons would soon be freed.* He said further:

> The United States is prepared to work closely with Chile in the months ahead. We are prepared to assist Chile in its efforts to establish economic stability and promote economic prosperity, but we can only do so within the framework of a system that ensures personal and political freedoms. The elimination of public concern in the United States and elsewhere that will result from this process will pave the way for a dynamic joint effort to move Chile's economic development program to a new level of achievement.

Kissinger sounded a similar note when he arrived in June to address the OAS meeting. He praised the Pinochet government's "progress" and declared that the United States should continue to help Chile economically in order to further improve the human rights situation. Simon had also offered help, and had promised in private meetings with Chilean officials that the Ford administration would fight increased congressional restrictions on economic and military aid to Chile.

Simon's and Kissinger's visits gave the Pinochet regime a legitimacy it had lacked for the first three years after the coup despite heavy United States support. Chile's human rights reputation improved overnight, simply because Kissinger and Simon said it was better.

Contreras reported to Pinochet on the reality behind the façade: DINA's security houses scattered around Santiago were operating at full capacity during the entire time of the Simon and Kissinger visits. Chilean dissidents were undergoing interrogation and torture within a few miles of the official cocktail parties and meetings attended by

---

*Orlando and Isabel Letelier, unknown to Simon, played a role in compiling the list of prisoners he brought to Chile. Simon received the list from Rose Styron, an official of Amnesty International, who assured him of its accuracy. She had spent hours the night before checking and updating the list with the Leteliers.

the two United States officials. More than a dozen of those arrested during the time span of the two visits disappeared into the DINA nether world, never to be seen again.*

On the "external front" the worldwide anti-junta movement gained momentum rather than dying out as time muted the shock of the 1973 coup, as Pinochet and Contreras had hoped. The continuing abuse of human rights inside Chile fueled the campaign, but more important, with the release of UP leaders from concentration camps, there was a great infusion of energy in the exile movement in 1975 and 1976.

Reports on Orlando Letelier's activities began to deluge Contreras. The most disquieting came from the Chilean Embassy in Washington and from Chile's Mission to the United Nations. One of the reports, from retired Admiral Ismael Huerta, the junta's ambassador to the United Nations, outlined Letelier's activities in promoting the UN Commission on Human Rights' condemnation of Chile. A report from Washington said Letelier was preparing to establish a government in exile, that he was gunrunning, that he was preparing a plot to blow up a LAN-Chile plane.

The author of the reports accusing Letelier of plotting terrorist

*A partial list of persons who disappeared is contained in ¿Donde Están?, vol. 2, 1979, published by the Vicariate of Solidarity, the Chilean human rights organization sponsored by the Catholic Church. The book presents documented case histories of 65 persons who disappeared as part of DINA's roundup of the Communist leadership between March 29, 1976, and September 9, 1976. Those who disappeared during the rough time-span of the Simon-Kissinger visits are:

> Miguel Luis Morales Ramírez, CP union leader (May 3)
> Mario Zamorano Donoso, CP Central Committee (May 4)
> Jorge Onofre Muñoz Poutays, CP Central Committee (May 4)
> Jaime Patricio Donato Avendaño, CP union leader (May 5)
> Uldarico Donaire Córtez, CP Central Committee (May 5)
> Elisa del Carmen Escobar Cepeda, CP leader (May 6)
> Fernando Antonio Lara Rojas, CP regional leader (May 7)
> Lenín Adán Díaz Silva, CP Technical Commission (May 9)
> Marcelo Renán Concha Bascunan, CP member (May 10)
> Victor Manuel Díaz López, CP Undersecretary General (May 12)
> Eliana Marina Espinoza Fernández, CP member (May 12)
> Rodolfo Marcial Nuñez Benavides, CP union leader (May 18)
> César Domingo Cerda Cuevas, former CP Central Committee (May 19)
> Juan René Orellana Catalán, Comm. Youth Central Committee (June 8)
> Luis Emilio Gerardo Maturana Gonzáles, CP regional leader (June 8)

attacks on the junta later admitted in an interview that he distorted the facts because his reports were designed only for propaganda. Other reports about Letelier, however, rang more true. His real activities, much more than the inventions, threatened the Chilean dictatorship's lifeline to the United States government. Senators Frank Church, George McGovern, Edward Kennedy, Hubert Humphrey, and others gave Letelier's argument for a total cutoff of military aid to Chile a sympathetic hearing. The bill with the cutoff provision passed on June 16, 1976.

In mid-march, Letelier met with Democratic representatives George Miller of California, Toby Moffett of Connecticut, and Tom Harkin of Iowa, who were planning a trip to Chile. He did not fill them with horror stories about human rights violations, but rather tried to explain the logic of Pinochet's reign of terror, that DINA provided the "Chicago Boys' " free-market model exactly the base it craved: a prostrate and desperate labor force. Letelier asked them to test his thesis about the link between repression and the Chicago model, and gave them names of people and places to visit in Chile. In Santiago, amidst a barrage of headlines denouncing them, the three congressmen met with Letelier's sister Fabiola, a human rights lawyer, and with opposition and government leaders. Harkin attempted to visit but was refused entry to DINA's most notorious detention and torture center, Villa Grimaldi. On their return home, the congressmen began mobilizing congressional support for the amendment cutting off military aid to Chile.

Policy circles were much less receptive than Congress to appeals for action against the Pinochet dictatorship. Letelier succeeded in making contacts in the few places where strong human rights tendencies prevailed. William D. Rogers, assistant secretary of state for Latin American affairs, a strong civil libertarian, lunched with Letelier shortly after his arrival in Washington. With an eye toward the upcoming 1976 elections, Letelier also had made successful approaches to advisers of the leading Democratic contenders, especially to Jimmy Carter's people. Any possibility of a Democratic victory frightened Pinochet and Contreras. At the least it would mean the end of the cozy relationship with the Ford administration and the replacement of Henry Kissinger. At the most, they feared an open break with Washington over the issue of human rights.*

Letelier also gained stature within the exiled Popular Unity. The UP leadership named him to represent Chile at the preparatory meeting of the Nonaligned Conference in Algeria, held during the second week in June. The organization had condemned the junta and reserved Chile's seat in the conference for the UP coalition. Letelier's designation as representative to the Algeria meeting marked his first public appearance in a role that could presage his leadership of the anti-junta coalition.

There was a political logic to Letelier's rise. The Communist Party remained too controversial, too closely associated with the Soviet Union, to provide a unifying figure for the left, especially in view of the Christian Democrats' unyielding rejection of any alliance with them. In addition, the junta still held Communist Party Secretary-General Luis Corvalán in prison, and Senator Volodia Teitelboim, the party theoretician, resided in Moscow. Socialist Clodomiro Almeyda, de facto spokesman for the Popular Unity because of his close association with Allende and his high post in the UP government, was respected but lacked sufficient inspiration and energy to become the central figure in a struggle that many felt might last ten years. Carlos Altamirano, a senator and the Socialist Party's secretary-general until 1979, had national appeal, even charisma. His refusal to abandon Chile after the coup and his underground leadership of the party until finally forced to flee after three or four months enhanced his reputation for courage. But Altamirano could not shake the image that many had of him as politically erratic. With Allende dead, the top leadership post was still vacant;

Throughout 1975 and 1976 Orlando Letelier, never a key member

*Contreras allegedly wrote a letter to Brazilian intelligence chief João Baptiste Figueiredo about the dangers of a Democratic victory in the United States. In the letter, dated August 28, 1975, and leaked to the press after the murder of Letelier and the mysterious death of former Brazilian President Juscelino Kubitschek, Contreras wrote: "I share your preoccupation with the possible triumph of the Democratic Party in the upcoming presidential elections in the United States. We are also aware of the repeated support the Democrats have lent to Kubitschek and Letelier, which in the future might seriously influence the stability of the Southern Cone of our hemisphere." The authenticity of the letter is doubted by United States federal investigators, who ran checks on it.

of the Socialist Party bureaucracy, had matured into a politician who kept his fences mended and seldom alienated anyone. He had cordial relations with the centrist Christian Democrats and had won a certain respect from the Communists and from MIR as well. Outside Chile he had made allies of numerous European Social Democratic parties.

Also, by the process of elimination, the role of unifier fell to Letelier. General Carlos Prats, the constitutionalist general who it was hoped might lead a progressive-military coalition to overthrow Pinochet, was assassinated in Buenos Aires in September 1974. Bernardo Leighton, the former vice-president and the only Christian Democrat considered able to forge a coalition with the left, had dropped out of active politics after narrowly surviving assassination in Rome in 1975.

Coalition sentiment, however, persisted within the Christian Democratic Party's progressive wing, and the initiative was picked up in the United States by Orlando Letelier, former Christian Democratic Foreign Minister Gabriel Valdés, and 1970 presidential candidate Radomiro Tomic. Valdés, whose son served as Letelier's aide, lived in New York and held the post of director of the United Nations Development Program. Tomic, like Leighton, had chosen exile after the coup. He lived for a time in Texas and later Switzerland. The three men had been friends for years, and in early 1976 began to talk informally on behalf of their parties.

In Santiago, Michael Townley received and analyzed reports from DINA informants who surveilled Letelier on three occasions when he met Gabriel Valdés in New York.

These facts and interpretations of Letelier's emergence as the rallying figure in the exile resistance movement weighed more heavily, however, on Pinochet's mind than they did among exile leaders. Contreras saw Letelier's power in Washington turning into an ominous "ambassadorship in exile," undermining the junta's position in the capital of its most important ally. Once DINA's agents abroad realized that Santiago had a keen interest in Letelier, according to an intelligence source, reports began to multiply and to exaggerate his importance. Reports from Amsterdam in early June 1976 may have been the final straw.

In 1975, the Dutch investment firm Stevin Groep had signed a contract with the Chilean government committing it to a $62.5 million investment in mining over a five-year period. The largest single foreign investment since the coup, the contract was a signal victory for Pinochet's economic team, which had based its plans on a generous influx of foreign capital and credits. Stevin Groep planned to introduce highly technical prospecting and mining techniques in order to extract high-grade gold, silver, and tungsten washed down from the mountains into coastal beaches and riverbeds.

Orlando Letelier arrived in Amsterdam on June 11. The Dutch municipality of Groningen had informed Stevin Groep, with which it had dealings on public-works projects, that Stevin's public-works contracts would be canceled if its overseas division went ahead with the Chile contract. Others followed suit, and on June 10 Stevin capitulated and suspended the investment program. The formal cancellation came a few months later. Pinochet, however, held Letelier directly responsible for the loss of the Stevin contract. Intelligence reports accurately assessed Letelier's intention to work for the isolation of the junta, but as always they overestimated his direct influence.

Letelier made four trips to Holland in 1976. Amsterdam had an active Chilean exile community and a strong Dutch solidarity movement, and was the seat of the European division of the Transnational Institute of IPS. Letelier was convinced that Holland was the best country from which to launch an economic boycott against Chile. The Chilean resistance had a strong ally there: the ruling Dutch Labor Party, a social democratic party that also governed several of the major cities. He could count on the Dutch labor unions as well for active solidarity.

At a press conference at the Dutch capital, The Hague, he appeared with representatives of the Chilean labor federation in exile, Central Única de Trabajadores (CUT), and of the Dutch Transport Federation, the federation of Holland's two largest trade unions. He described the suffering of Chile's people and explained how the Dutch people could help.

"A boycott, even by one country, can be effective," he said. "Even if such a boycott may not have direct consequences upon the

Chilean economy, it produces a political effect." In newspaper interviews he elaborated on his argument: "Economic actions abroad are of utmost importance, because of the vulnerability of the junta in its financial dependence on foreign countries." A Dutch firm was planning extensive investments in Chile, he said. Holland had become the number one country on Chile's small list of European investors. "In my opinion any investment in Chile at this moment is immoral," he said, "because it sustains one of the most fascist regimes in the world." He spoke authoritatively and warned that investors should be aware of the commercial risks of investing in Chile. A post-junta government could declare contracts with the present de facto, illegitimate regime null and void.

Letelier sought to prevail on the Dutch government to use its influence and its voice to discourage World Bank loans to Chile at an upcoming meeting of the World Bank board of directors, and to persuade the Dutch to admit more Chilean refugees. He met with the president of the Dutch Labor Party, Ina van der Heuvel, Development Cooperation Minister Jan Pronk, Member of Parliament Relus ter Bek, who served as chairman of the Committee on Foreign Affairs, mayor of Rotterdam Andre van der Luow, and a group of labor leaders including the general secretary of the Dockworkers Federation. Relus ter Bek said after his several meetings with Letelier that he considered him the most reasonable, articulate, pragmatic, and purposeful of all the Chilean leaders he had met in Europe. Only Letelier, he said, understood the intricacies of European politics.

During the June visit Letelier floated an idea that may have served to fuel DINA's idea that he was about to form a government in exile. He proposed the establishment in Holland of a "Salvador Allende Institute" to prepare "blueprints" for a constitutional government and to train potential government officials from among the exiles. The institute's team would be ready to step in with people and programs, including a draft for a new constitution, when the Pinochet government fell. Eventually the institute was founded in Rotterdam under the auspices of Andre van der Luow, the mayor who had met with Letelier in February.

Pinochet and Contreras condemned Letelier to death and set in motion DINA's assassination operation sometime in June.* For Pinochet, Letelier was a traitor. He saw Letelier's anti-junta activities as anti-Chilean; he took them personally. Pinochet anchored his claim to power on the personal identification of himself with the state of Chile. Rage gradually overcame him, the kind of anger that results from feeling one has made a bad decision and projects itself outward. He, Pinochet, had spared Letelier's life, had released him from concentration camp as he released the other UP prisoners. Now this man who literally owed his life to Pinochet's generosity displayed no gratitude.†

The "time frame" for Letelier's death, one of the assassins would later recall, was September—Chile's springtime, the patriotic month, the month of the birth of the nation in 1810 under the sword of Bernardo O'Higgins, Chile's George Washington; the month of Pinochet's 1973 coup, of the 1974 assassination of General Carlos Prats, of the 1975 shooting of Bernardo Leighton. For the September of 1976, Orlando Letelier became the junta's chosen victim.

FOR MICHAEL TOWNLEY, 1976 had so far been a relatively quiet year. Since his return from Europe and Miami on October 16, 1975, he hadn't had to travel and had enjoyed spending time with his two sons, Brian and Christopher, who had been recently enrolled in his old alma mater, Saint George's. He worked out of his Lo Curro home.

Virgilio Paz, Townley's companion in Mexico and Europe, was his house guest from April to June. Contreras' promise to give a full course of intelligence training in return for his services had not been kept. Instead, DINA headquarters kept Paz at arm's length and the

---

*The exact time of the assassination decision is known, of course, only to those who made it.

†There is evidence of a deep-seated personal animosity, the reason for which is not fully understood. A former high junta official described a meeting with Pinochet early in 1974 to discuss appeals by foreign ministers all over the world for the release of Almeyda, who was a respected member of the exclusive worldwide "club" of present and former foreign ministers. "Eighty percent of the letters and telegrams were for the release of Almeyda," the official said. "I asked Pinochet why not release him, and he answered angrily, 'I won't do it, because if I release Almeyda I'll have to release Letelier too.'"

only training he received came from Townley at his home electronics laboratory. Paz, still fascinated by Townley's remote-control bombing device, tried to master its construction. He knew how to set it off, but lacked Townley's tinker's talent to make the modifications that changed the simple beeper into a deadly detonator. Unhappy and bitter, he quarreled with his wife by telephone and goaded Inés Townley with anti-Semitic remarks. Finally, in mid-June, he returned to the United States.

Other members of Townley's international team were also in Chile working with DINA. The Italian terrorist Alfredo di Stefano, from the Leighton operation, had set up a DINA-financed news agency in Santiago to channel progovernment articles to the European right-wing magazines. DINA provided di Stefano and two other Italian comrades* with a large apartment to use as an office and equipped it with a telex machine for their dispatches. The three men also traveled back and forth frequently to Buenos Aires, where they established a working relationship with Townley's Milicia contacts.

Townley's duties included servicing the intelligence and operations network he had set up the previous year for DINA. He divided his working hours between the External Section, under "Lucho Gutiérrez," and the electronics section under Major Vianel Valdivieso. Valdivieso, one of Contreras' closest confidants, was the coordinator of DINA's network of bugging and electronic surveillance. "Lucho Gutiérrez" was the name assigned to whoever happened to be the current chief of the extremely secret foreign espionage and assassination operations. Townley later claimed he did not know the true identity of "Lucho" in mid-1976. But the earlier chief of external operations was a friend, Eduardo Iturriaga, who in June 1976 was on leave taking special courses at the U.S. Army School of the Americas in Panama.

Townley worked closely with the young lieutenants and captains who formed the core of DINA's General Command. Contreras'

---

*DINA sources who met the three Italians during their stay in Chile, which lasted until early 1977, said they used the names Alfredo or "Topogigio," Luigi or "Gigi," and Mauricio. After the information about di Stefano's links to Townley were published in an article by John Dinges in *The Nation* in June 1979, a Rome newspaper, *La Repubblica,* wrote that he had been identified as a fugitive terrorist named Stefano Delle Chiaie.

muchachos adopted the attitude of the conquerer, despising the enemy all the more for his inability or unwillingness to defend himself. They found their appropriate metaphors in the medical jargon: communism was a "cancer on the body of Chile," elimination of the cancer through "bloody surgery" was the only hope of "saving the organism as a whole." "Elimination" became the accepted euphemism for killing.

All UP sympathizers became automatically communists; all communists were *traidores, maricones, huevones, hijos de puta, conchasumadre* (traitors, fags, pricks, sons of whores, mother's cunts). This was the language of hate, necessary to dehumanize their victims, to anesthetize their own awareness that they, who were sworn to defend Chile, were brutalizing and killing their fellow Chileans.

One of the members of the inner circle was First Lieutenant Armando Fernández, who became Townley's friend and shared his childlike earnestness and his devotion to "Mamo"—Colonel Contreras. From a strait-laced military family, he had entered the Military Academy in emulation of his father, retired General Alfredo Fernández. Young Armando graduated from the academy and received his lieutenant's bars in 1969. Stocky, of medium height, and baby-faced, he projected a look of innocence and gravity. Short black hair crept down low on his broad forehead, heavy eyebrows over dark eyes accentuated his olive skin. A typical Chilean of the middle class, definitely not of the aristocracy, but climbing. Those who knew the Fernández family were apt to describe Armando as "a good boy" —*un buen muchacho.*

Most DINA agents had nicknames. Fernández was called "the eagle." He was one of Contreras' favorite *muchachos.* Like Townley, he was assigned to the External Section.

On a quiet day at the end of June, Armando Fernández phoned Townley from General Headquarters. "Pedrito wants to meet with you," Fernández said." It's urgent and top security." "Pedrito" was Lieutenant Colonel Espinoza, whom Townley considered a "deep personal friend," the man who had recruited him, Contreras' chief deputy as head of operations. Espinoza had charge of liaison with DINA's chief intelligence partner, Brazil, and had not spoken with Townley for almost a year. "Top security" meant that the meeting would take place in a neutral location out of doors.

During the coldest part of the Chilean winter, temperatures often drop to around freezing. On Saturday morning, Townley drove down the hill from his house with a thermos of coffee on the seat beside him. He followed the road to the right at the bottom of the hill to Santa María Street along the Mapocho River, passing the national computer firm ECOM. Except for ECOM's modern buildings and parking lot, the scene was rustic. Urban Santiago stopped on the other side of the river.

He knew Espinoza hadn't summoned him to chat, not with these precautions. Townley drove about a mile, then turned right again into a wide boulevard, the sparsely traveled end section of the unfinished Américo Vespucio Avenue intended to provide a traffic artery circling Santiago. It ended five hundred yards away, leading only to Saint George's School. Even on a weekday, he thought, there wouldn't be enough traffic to justify the building of this road, with only schoolchildren on their way to Saint George's. Then off to the left, near a point called El Pirámide, he saw a brown car. He pulled up behind it and stopped.

Espinoza, in civilian clothes—doubleknit slacks and an ill-fitting sports jacket with too-narrow lapels—got out of his car and walked back to climb in beside Townley. His stiff gait, erect posture, and gleaming black shoes marked him as unmistakably a military man.

They drank coffee and talked, at first about their families, then shoptalk about DINA. At last Espinoza got to the point. Would Townley take on another mission outside Chile?

"Elimination?"

"Yes."

Not that Townley had to ask. Orders at Espinoza's level didn't deal with trivial things such as trips to buy bugging equipment.

"This one is in the United States," Espinoza said. "Do you think you can get those Cubans you worked with before to pull it off for us? I don't have to tell you that this operation is of the highest priority. My orders are from Mamo."

That wasn't necessary either; Townley knew that DINA was basically a one-man operation run by Contreras, who answered only to Pinochet. Another assassination, more travel away from home, and Espinoza was asking for his assent without even offering to tell him the name of the victim. Townley showed no enthusiasm. He stalled.

"Things have been running hot and cold with the Cubans," Townley told Espinoza. "We have good relations with one group. They sent a good man to work with me most of last year while I was traveling in Europe, and he has been staying here in Chile with me. DINA has been picking up the tab."

Townley noticed that Espinoza avoided naming the Cuban Nationalist Movement even though he knew all about them and their work for DINA. Looking out the windshield, Townley had a pleasant view of the break in the hills leading to the Conchali district, one of Santiago's poorest areas. From where they were parked, the poverty didn't show. An irrigation canal snaked alongside the steep hill, a thick brown stream. Even there, two men alone planning an assassination seven thousand miles away talked in abstractions. Compartmentalization.

Townley, buoyed by the enthusiasm he felt for DINA, his service, became expansive. Virgilio Paz and his group will help. They need us and are ready for anything. The problem, he explained to Espinoza, is the rest of the Cuban exile community, especially in Miami. They are extremely upset about Contreras giving up Rolando Otero to the FBI. They see that as betrayal. It doesn't matter that Otero was a crazy hothead; he is a freedom fighter and one of them. We can't announce to the whole Cuban community that he was a spy and was lucky to get out of here alive. But I can explain that to my friends in New Jersey, and I'm sure I can convince them that we did what we had to do.

Townley complained that he had already spent most of 1975 away from Chile and that his wife was about to have a hysterectomy. But he expressed no objections to Espinoza's elimination request.

"When?" he asked.

"The time frame will be September," Espinoza said, "as usual."

"I will carry out the mission if given a specific order," Townley replied.

The meeting ended. It had lasted more than an hour. Espinoza told Townley he would be recontacted.

He would follow orders as usual, he concluded during the short drive home. When he arrived, he told Inés that DINA foreign operations had another mission for him. She knew what it meant. Perhaps it was then that Inés "Mariana" Callejas, the girl from smalltown Chile, realized that Mike, the wholesome American boy she had married, had become nothing more than a hired assassin for DINA. Later Inés wrote what she said were her thoughts at that moment:

> He was already too far gone. He had turned into one of them. He was a DINA agent, powerless but respected and, of course, envied. . . . And he was promised, poor man and it made him so happy, an army rank. He'd be a Major. He felt a Major. Only I knew, I just *knew,* that it would never come true.

ALMOST IMMEDIATELY after talking to Townley on the phone, Armando Fernández took a plane to Buenos Aires. This was to be a Condor operation. While Espinoza was setting things up with El Gringo, Fernández would arrange secure travel to Washington. "Tito," the head of DINA's documentation center, gave him two Argentine passports before he left. In Buenos Aires, Fernández contacted DINA's sister service, SIDE, the state intelligence service. He asked SIDE to vouch for the passports and obtain visas from the U.S. Consulate through their contacts with the CIA, the FBI legal attaché, or friends in the consulate. But SIDE turned Fernández down flat.* On July 1, a Thursday, Espinoza reported to Contreras. Another route would have to be found.

Midweek Contreras summoned Fernández to his office and ordered him to accompany Townley to Asunción, Paraguay, obtain Paraguayan documents, and proceed directly to Washington. Fernández asked Contreras to clarify rank on the mission. Contreras placed Fernández in charge. But he also inserted an element of

---

*Fernández' entrance into and exit from Argentina under the name Alejandro Rivadeneira shows up in records of Argentine immigration police. SIDE officials informed FBI agent Robert Scherrer in 1978 of his request.

ambiguity: Townley would receive his marching orders from Espinoza. Contreras told Fernández to call Townley to set up a planning meeting.

LO CURRO HILL, Santiago's most scenic area, some five hundred feet above the city proper, is practically smog-free. The cool breeze and greenery provide a stark contrast to the dirt, traffic, and pollution of the unseen city below. To the east, beyond a saddle a short distance from Townley's house, a broad, lush pasture—a kind of low-altitude plateau—is a picnickers' and kite flyers' paradise in spring and summer. In the distance loom the snow-covered heights of the Andean Cordilleras.

Townley and Fernández drove together to the agreed meeting spot. A few minutes later, Espinoza drove up in a rust-colored Chevrolet Nova, the kind that the junta imported to serve as police cars but that ended up as officers' private vehicles. Fernández stayed in the car while Espinoza and Townley took a walk. More compartmentalization, Townley thought. Espinoza had precise orders to impart, and cut short Townley's friendly banter. The mission he had spoken to him about two weeks before was about to commence. He stressed its urgency.

The target: "ex-chancellor" (foreign minister) Orlando Letelier. "Since his release from our custody," Espinoza informed Townley, "Letelier has been making trouble for the government outside the country. You should make his death seem accidental if possible— arrange an automobile accident, a suicide, something like that. Your friends the Cubans—use them as a backup only," he said.

Townley thought of his Fanon-Courier devices, one of which he knew was in New Jersey ready for use. Quick, foolproof, absolutely lethal. No need to confront the victim face to face. The Townley car bomb would ensure that the job got done. He asked Espinoza if a bomb would be acceptable if other methods proved not feasible.

"Just make sure Letelier is alone," Espinoza said. "Do what you have to do; your orders are to eliminate him by whatever means. Fernández and you are responsible for the actual assassination; let the Cubans help if you need them. Get them involved, but do the hit yourselves."

He laid out the plans. Contreras, he said, has persuaded the Paraguayans to join Condor. He wants to try them out. You and Fernández will get your travel documents and United States visas from Paraguayan intelligence. Fernández will be in charge of that part of the mission, then you and he will be on equal footing. From Paraguay you will fly to Washington. Neither Fernández nor Espinoza told Townley that Fernández had already tried and failed to obtain travel documents through Argentine intelligence, another Condor member.

A few days later, Espinoza called Townley into headquarters in downtown Santiago. Fernández was there too. They received airline tickets marked OPEN for travel between Santiago–Buenos Aires–Asunción–Santiago. Fernández, in a separate meeting, had been given $5,000 in cash. He showed the money to Townley and gave him an envelope containing about $1,000 in United States currency.

After the meeting, Fernández told Townley he wanted to leave right away. Townley argued it would be a waste of time since it was Friday and they wouldn't be able to do anything in Asunción until Monday. Fernández, for reasons of his own, wanted to spend some time in Buenos Aires, so they agreed to travel separately to Buenos Aires and meet there on Monday.

At home that weekend, Townley talked about the mission with his wife and told her the name of the target. Neither of them knew much about Letelier, only that he had been an Allende minister and —a vague personal impression—that he had more style than most of the Popular Unity leaders, a more sophisticated brand of socialism, a bit like the dapper Allende himself, only much younger. Inés felt uneasy, not about the morality of killing but because it would take place in the United States. She wrote later:

Perhaps, I could have avoided it. I could have been determined and stubborn (I usually am) and threatened him with abandonment or indifference. But I didn't do it, although I knew by the fugitive look of his blue eyes, by his evasive answers, that this one was a mission that he did not quite fully understand, an order that he would have questioned, had he ever questioned orders. I said, "I don't like it," but he already knew I didn't like it. He knew I was distrustful of the soldiers to whom he was another soldier at work, and a civilian when the good times for soldiers came.

I watched him pack a small suitcase. I brought him some socks from the laundry room. "Where to?" I asked, "The States again?"

"No," he said, "just Paraguay . . . Look, Paraguayan intelligence has offered cooperation. The chief wants to know what they are like. So we're going to get Paraguayan passports to go to the States . . . I'm going with Captain Fernández.* Don't worry; it's nothing unusual."

ON MONDAY TOWNLEY took an afternoon LAN-Chile flight to Buenos Aires. He rode part of the way in the cockpit talking to the pilot, an old friend named Martín. From Ezeiza Airport, he took a bus to the terminal on Rivadavia Avenue, the contact point.

Fernández was waiting there with another man. Townley greeted his partner and the Argentine contact, a friend and part of his personal network since 1974. Fernández suggested that Townley check into his hotel, El Embajador, on Pelagrini Street, and that they go out to the nearby strip joints that night. Townley declined; he said he had business with the other man that night and would meet Fernández the next morning for the flight to Asunción.

Townley left the terminal with the other man, a member of Milicia, one of Argentina's burgeoning anticommunist terrorist groups operating under the aegis of SIDE. Milicia had earned particular distinction in the trade because of its predilection for stealing Ford Falcon cars to carry out kidnappings and its ideological nostalgia for Hitler and the Third Reich. It owned a publishing house, also called Milicia, that reprinted Nazi texts.

---

*Fernández had been promoted to captain at the time of her writing in 1978.

Townley checked into the República Hotel, into a room with a view of Buenos Aires' Obelisk. Then he and his friend had dinner.*

Townley and Fernández took a taxi the next morning to Ezeiza Airport to catch a 6:00 A.M. Paraguayan Airlines flight to Asunción. It was Tuesday, July 20. Townley and Fernández carried their normal DINA false identity papers: Andrés Wilson and Alejandro Rivadeneira.

COLONEL BENITO GUANES, head of the Paraguayan Army's J-2 division (military intelligence) controlled Paraguay's limited political life in much the same way that Contreras did Chile's. Dictatorship, repression, and corruption in Paraguay were more straightforward than in Chile. Stroessner's twenty-year rule was a relic of pre–World War II *caudillismo.* Stroessner had little need for the fancy doctrines of "national security" that the Pentagon had peddled on the continent since the 1950s. Ringed by Brazil, Uruguay, Argentina, and Bolivia, all safely rightist and authoritarian, Stroessner felt secure in 1976. But the new military dictators who ruled his neighbor countries began to demand new commitments for what they called the continent-wide struggle against subversion. The Chileans were the most fanatic.

For over a year the Chileans had pressured Paraguay to join in a dubious venture to coordinate their intelligence services. They called it Operation Condor, and of course Contreras named himself "Condor One." Paraguay had become an official member of Condor just a few weeks before the two DINA operatives arrived. Special codes and teletype channels had been established. Contreras, in a formal ceremony in Santiago, had presented Guanes with a bronze plaque reading: "In commemoration of Paraguay's joining Operation Condor, July 1976." Now, before July had ended, Contreras was asking for help on a specific mission.

---

*Townley did not identify this man, although he certainly knows his name. It is strange that the prosecutors have not required him to name the man so that he could be located and asked to provide what would be valuable corroborative evidence of Townley's connection with Fernández.

A gibberish of letters chattered out of the teletype machine at J-2 headquarters. The message came over the Condor channel. After decoding, it read:

TO ADVISE THAT TOMORROW, 18 OR 19 JULY, WILL ARRIVE IN THAT COUNTRY FROM BUENOS AIRES ALEJANDRO RIVA DENEIRA WITH COMPANION. FLIGHT NUMBER WILL BE FOR- WARDED FROM CONDOR ONE. I WOULD APPRECIATE ASSIST- ANCE IN THE PERFORMANCE OF THE MISSION IN ACCORDANCE WITH THE REQUEST THE ABOVE-NAMED PER- SON WILL MAKE.

Use of the first person meant that Colonel Contreras personally had sent the message. When the message arrived on Saturday in Asunción, Guanes was on one of his frequent trips to Brazil. An aide phoned him for instructions. Guanes told him to stall until he re- turned. A DINA official followed up the cable with a phone call from Santiago to inform the Paraguayans that Rivadeneira would arrive on the morning Paraguayan Airlines flight on Tuesday.

Townley and Fernández deplaned at Asunción's shabby Presi- dente General Stroessner Airport and paid a dollar each to be waved through a perfunctory immigration and customs inspection. They hired a taxi to take them the fifteen miles into Asunción. The driver recommended the Señorial, a semielegant hotel near Asunción's high-income district and Paraguayan Army Headquarters. It was not yet noon. Asunción's blue skies and springlike temperatures were a welcome change from Santiago's smog and intermittent cold winter rains.

After lunch they took a cab nine blocks up Mariscal López Avenue to a grey-painted gingerbread mansion where a sign above the third-floor windows proclaimed "Estado Mayor del Ejército"— Army Headquarters—in foot-high red letters. A single guard let them in the high iron gates and led them through the elaborately tended gardens to the rear entrance. Captain Sosa, a naval officer, then escorted them to Colonel Guanes' office. There an army major told them they were expected. Unfortunately, the major said, Colonel Guanes was out of the city and could not help them personally, but their request for the documents presented no problem. They should provide two large passport photos and five smaller pocket ID-size photos.

Townley let Fernández do the talking during the meeting. His cover for this mission was as an officer in the Chilean Army, and he knew that despite his fluent Spanish, his American accent would be noticeable after a few sentences. Also, Fernández had acted touchy about rank on this mission and made it clear that he was in charge as long as they were in Paraguay.

They left army headquarters feeling satisfied with their progress. A couple of photos—an inevitable requirement for any identification document—and they would be ready to leave for Washington within a day or two.

In the office they had just left, the army major picked up the phone and called a military installation somewhere in Brazil. Colonel Guanes came to the phone. They're here, the major told Guanes. They want us to provide official passports under false names and request the U.S. Embassy to give them visas. They say their mission is to contact the CIA in Washington and to pick up some Colt silencers for small arms.

Keep them entertained until I get there, Guanes said. I'll be back in a couple of days.

Townley and Fernández had their photos taken at a small shop in downtown Asunción and delivered them to Guanes' office. Moving back and forth between military offices and often with Paraguayan intelligence agents as nighttime drinking companions, they took a kind of spooks' tour of the city that is the center of Latin America's right-wing underworld. Guaranteed absolute protection and anonymity in Stroessner's free zone (sanctuary), Asunción's subculture includes Nazi fugitives, not only from Germany but from Nazi-sympathizer groups in Eastern Europe, and intelligence agents from all the major Latin American countries plus South Africa and Taiwan. Chile's General Viaux lived in comfortable exile in Asunción after the Pinochet government reduced his conviction for murdering General Schneider in 1970 to lesser charges and his prison sentence to banishment. Townley and Fernández went drinking with Captain Sosa and the unidentified major from army headquarters at the Yguazú nightclub on the outskirts of the city. The Paraguayans became boisterous and insisted that two Argentine SIDE agents at a nearby table join them while they enjoyed tender Paraguayan steaks and the voluptuous strippers in the Brazilian-style floor show.

Several days later Townley and Fernández were summoned to the office of the army chief of staff, General Alejandro Freites. Fernández acted nervous. As a lieutenant, he felt intimidated and disconcerted by a face-to-face meeting with such a high-ranking officer. When a major escorted them into the general's office and asked them to introduce themselves, Fernández' discomfort turned into suppressed anger as he heard Townley present himself as a captain attached to telecommunications in the Chilean Army. Townley outranked him.

General Freites politely demanded to know the purpose of their mission. The solicitous major tried to ease their discomfort by reminding the general good-naturedly that the two Chileans belonged to "intelligence" and that such a question bordered on the inappropriate. But the general wanted an answer.

Fernández rattled off part of a cover story. The mission involved both surveillance of suspicious employees at the Chilean Copper Corporation, a government enterprise, in New York and routine scanning checks for electronic listening devices at the Chilean Embassy in Washington: a little in-house bugging and debugging.

The two Paraguayan officers looked askance at one another and the major, suppressing a smile, pronounced the Paraguayan equivalent of "You ask a silly question, you get a silly answer." But Freites wasn't joking; he wanted to make sure Paraguay was covered. He asked the two men standing nervously before him if they would mind if he informed the U.S. Embassy about this.

"That's hardly necessary," they answered. "The Santiago CIA station chief has been fully briefed on this and has given his okay."

Freites said they would have to wait only a short time longer, because Colonel Guanes had returned from Brazil and would personally take charge of their request.

But Guanes had in fact been in Asunción for several days. The passport and visa holdup was due not to his absence but to caution in lending Paraguay's name to an unknown DINA mission to the United States capital. To help a friendly service obtain false documents to cover the tracks of its antisubversive missions to other countries had become routine even before Condor. The United States authorities themselves winked at such operations in other Latin American countries. But this mission in the United States capital was fraught with danger for Paraguay. The Chileans had said that the CIA had given DINA the go-ahead, but Guanes wanted to check directly with the Americans.

There was one difficulty, however. The CIA station chief had recently been withdrawn from Asunción, and at the time of the Townley-Fernández sojourn there the post was vacant. Guanes had no United States intelligence counterpart to turn to. Besides, even if Guanes had decided to risk granting the favor to Condor One, he lacked the high-level contacts in the U.S. Embassy to obtain the visas for the two Chileans. Guanes decided to take the matter outside intelligence channels; he went to talk to "Teruco."

Teruco was Conrado Pappalardo, President Stroessner's fix-it man, officially the Foreign Ministry's chief of protocol. Self-important, arrogant, and foul-mouthed in his dealings with those who depended on him to reach Stroessner's ear, he became obsequious and servile toward anyone he perceived as more powerful than he. One of the most influential men in the country, he used his nickname even in conducting official government business. "Teruco" to the Latin ear suggests shiftiness, chicanery, the Spanish equivalent of "Fast Eddie" or "Tricky Dick."

Teruco told Guanes he would take care of everything, but he too had a problem. Outside of the CIA station chief, only the ambassador had authority to issue visas to the United States for passports known to be issued in false names. And Ambassador George Landau wouldn't return to his office until Monday, July 26.

Townley and Fernández waited. On Friday Guanes agreed to see them. He promised to arrange all matters as soon as possible, and sent them to another office to fill out applications for Paraguayan passports and United States visa forms. Fernández called himself Alejandro Romeral Jara, student, born in Estero, Paraguay. Townley made up the name Juan Williams Rose, an adaptation of his DINA alias Juan Andrés Wilson plus the last name of an English family he knew in Santiago. He identified himself as a student and a native of Paraguay.

In Paraguay, special passports and government cover letters for visas were only a little more expensive to obtain than ordinary passports. Knowing this, the U.S. Consulate did not automatically grant visas for such passports, but required a personal interview, corroborating documentation, and the submission of photos with the visa application. To get around those regulations, the applicant had to have personal connections at the embassy, not just a form letter. Teruco Pappalardo had the connections, and took great delight in showing them off.

On Monday, the matter now in the hands of Pappalardo, Fernández and Townley were summoned early in the morning to the Government Palace, an unimposing colonial-style building near Constitution Plaza in downtown Asunción. Their modest undercover operation had moved out of the shadowy security of secret police headquarters into the public arena of official government diplomacy. Townley recalled later that he suggested abandoning the whole absurd exercise and returning to Santiago without the documents. But that would have meant facing Contreras empty-handed, and Fernández insisted on going through with what they had begun.

When the two young men arrived at the Government Palace, a long red carpet had been unrolled at the main entrance in anticipation of the arrival of some dignitary. Not wanting to mar it with dusty footprints, they skirted the immaculate carpet. They were shown into an office and introduced to Dr. Conrado Pappalardo, a man in his late fifties, who they were told was a high official in Stroessner's office. Later, Townley could remember only the nickname Teruco. Pappalardo was gracious, if somewhat pompous and authoritarian, impressing on them the breadth of his connections and the importance of his position. They politely indicated to him their impatience with the delays. Their difficulties were at an end, he assured them. Their passports were ready, and he personally would see to getting the proper visas from the Americans. That would be no problem because he was good friends with Ambassador George Landau.

Pappalardo had another "good friend" who would help them in Washington, he said. The name he mentioned was that of General Vernon Walters, and he watched their faces to assure himself they were suitably impressed. Give General Walters a call in Washington, he said. Pappalardo dictated a phone number and Fernández wrote it down.

Fernández and Townley had heard Contreras also speak of Walters as his friend. On his visit to Washington in August 1975, Walters had received him at CIA headquarters at Langley, Virginia, the intelligence officer's Mecca. To Contreras, Walters was in another league from the recent run of political appointees, such as the current director George Bush. Walters was a lifelong soldier who understood the military side of fighting communist subversion. He could sympathize with Contreras' arguments justifying the use of disappearance and torture in dealing with Chile's suspected communists.

Townley and Fernández left Pappalardo's office, and in a nearby office an indifferent official filled out Paraguayan passports in longhand as they watched. The official slid the completed passports across the desk for them to sign, then took them back. The visas would be ready the next day at the latest, he said. They walked out of the Government Palace relieved. Though still uneasy about the delays, they allowed themselves to think that the mission remained viable. They took a cab back to army headquarters, where they had felt most at home talking shop among the intelligence operatives.

After lunch they received word that a high-ranking intelligence officer, a lieutenant colonel, wished to meet them. The meeting seemed overly informal. Then their host rose abruptly and left the room, mumbling something about having to make arrangements for a military orchestra to perform at a gala party at his home that evening. Left alone, Townley and Fernández rifled through the papers on the officer's desk.

The papers included their new passports, the applications they had just filled out for United States visas, and a detailed report describing their movements during the past week in Asunción. "Also included in these papers was the name of a United States Army Colonel whose surname began with a 'W,' " Townley wrote later. "I believe there was some notation next to the U.S. Army Colonel's name indicating that he was chief of the United States Military Mission in Paraguay."

The message was clear: The Paraguayans had gotten suspicious, put them under surveillance, and told the Americans about a DINA mission to Washington. The Paraguayans had proved less gullible than Condor One expected.

Tuesday, July 27, Townley and Fernández had agreed would be their last day in Paraguay. If the visas didn't come through that day, they would return to Santiago. They rose before dawn and walked into the large hotel foyer between the street entrance and the empty registration desk. The night guard, a solemn young Guaraní, stood in front of the door to the registration desk, his arms crossed under the ample folds of a dark blue poncho. He summoned the clerk. Fernández paid the bill and left instructions for their bags to be kept ready for departure.

They went to army headquarters to wait. After a few hours they received word that the visas and passports were ready for them at the Foreign Ministry.

Downtown at the Foreign Ministry, they paged through the passports. The visas, embossed stamps on page II, were type B-2 visas dated that day entitling them to enter the United States as tourists or businessmen until July 27 the following year. At the bottom appeared the neat signature of a U.S. Consular officer, William F. Finnigan. The operation had at last begun to function according to plan, they thought. The Americans hadn't asked any questions, had waived the requirements for interviews and pictures, and had stamped in the visas on Pappalardo's recommendation alone.

They walked from the ministry to Constitution Plaza. Before moving to the Washington phase, Fernández said, they had to report to DINA. On their left, they passed the corroded iron hulk of a bullet-riddled tank of World War I vintage, a monument to the glories of Paraguay's disastrous defeat in the 1929 Chaco War with Bolivia.

Eight blocks almost straight ahead they reached the antiquated railroad terminal on Colonel Bogado Street. From the public telephone booth at the station, Fernández placed a collect call to a DINA security number. Townley waited nearby, examining a nineteenth-century steam locomotive standing ready for its afternoon run. Parts of Paraguay seemed lifted intact out of the pioneer era.

"Lucho Gutiérrez" answered.* Fernandez spoke in a simple code. They had obtained the "merchandise" as ordered, but inordinate delays had occurred and he felt uneasy with what had transpired in the process of "sealing the deal." Then Fernandez stopped talking, except for an occasional grunt of assent. He hung up and turned to Townley.

"New orders," he said. "They don't like the way this smells. We are to return to Santiago immediately."

SEVERAL MILES AWAY, on Mariscal López Avenue past army headquarters, in the heart of Asunción's plushest neighborhood, Ambassador George Landau returned to his desk after an early lunch. He opened a folder marked SECRET in red letters that he had just taken out of the combination-locked filing cabinet. It contained a writing pad, several sheets already filled with the first paragraphs of a draft cable. After he completed it, a person with security clearance would type it up and take it to another room where it would be encoded and sent via the most secure telex channel.

It was addressed to General Vernon Walters, CIA, Langley, Virginia, and recorded the first chapter of the story of Juan Williams and Alejandro Romeral. Also on Landau's desk were photocopies he had ordered made of the two Paraguayan passports.

TOWNLEY AND FERNÁNDEZ booked passage that afternoon back to Santiago with an overnight stay in Buenos Aires. There, Townley dined again with his Milicia friend. Fernández, as usual, prowled the

---

*Whoever answered that phone in DINA headquarters identified himself as "Lucho Gutiérrez." It meant the caller was talking to the External Section.

strip joints on Pelagrini. The next morning they took the first available flight to Santiago.

Fernández, still in charge of the operation, reported to Colonel Pedro Espinoza the next morning, and handed over to him the two Paraguayan special passports. Townley called Espinoza a short time later. "I definitely told Colonel Espinoza that I suspected that Captain Fernández' and my intelligence affiliation had become compromised to the United States Government," he wrote later.

The operation had been blown to the CIA.

The delays, the surveillance, the insistent questioning by the Paraguayans, Pappalardo's insinuation that Walters would be expecting their call in Washington: the entire affair made him nervous, Townley told Espinoza. He was told to await further orders. The Letelier assassination, he thought, would no longer involve him.

WHEN ROBERT DRISCOLL went to his office at the State Department on August 6, he found on his desk a manila envelope from the CIA, wrapped with tape and string and marked SECRET. Driscoll, the Chile desk officer, handled the cable traffic to and from the U.S. Embassy in Chile, screened it, filed it, and routed it to appropriate offices at State and other government agencies. He did the same for communications about Chile addressed to State from other agencies. Driscoll opened the envelope.

Inside he found xerox copies of two passports—Paraguayan passports. The names Juan Williams and Alejandro Romeral meant nothing to him. He looked at the pictures of the two men. He noticed that the CIA had included strips of negatives, indicating that they had taken photographs of the passports. A terse "transmittal slip" contained the only explanation why the CIA had sent the packet. It said: "Memo to Harry Shlaudeman* for DIA [Defense Intelligence Agency]. Subject: Transmittal of photos and negatives of Paraguayan passports. We are forwarding photographs and negatives of

*Deputy assistant secretary of state for inter-American affairs.

two Paraguayan passports which were recently sent to Washington from Asunción."

Driscoll scribbled a routing slip, checked boxes for copies and filing, and flipped the packet into his out box.

ESPINOZA AND CONTRERAS received a coded message dated August 7 over the Condor channel from Guanes. The United States representative had informed Guanes that his government had revoked the visas and issued arrest orders and lookouts for the two men at port of entry if they attempted to travel to the United States. Guanes demanded that Contreras return the Paraguayan passports to him by diplomatic pouch. Two days later, he phoned Contreras. Contreras told him that the two agents had not left Santiago and that the passports would not be used.

Espinoza later reported: "Colonel Contreras summoned me to his office and asked me for the passports, saying that the Paraguayan intelligence service had requested their return. I brought them to him, and there in my presence he took out both photographs and destroyed them."

The passports, the now-useless products of what began to be called inside DINA the "Paraguayan fiasco," were delivered to Guanes a month later in the mutilated state described by Espinoza.

MICHAEL TOWNLEY WAS feeling tired and frustrated as he drove home from headquarters. His life had become a series of mostly unrelated missions. He felt a growing remoteness from Inés and the children. He had sandwiched them in between missions and assignments, and even when he was at home he remained subject to call twenty-four hours a day, at the will and whim of "his service." Often he completed a mission, reported to Espinoza, and then learned nothing of its significance or outcome; DINA offered explanations only on a need-to-know basis. Even an assembly-line factory worker eventually sees the whole product to which he has contributed a part.

Assassinations were different. They had spectacular results. His superiors always showed appreciation for such work. But his long absences meant family friction. Inés paid less and less attention to their marriage and was absorbed in the small literary set to which she had gained acceptance.

But soldiers must follow orders, not question them or demand information that their superiors deem unnecessary. Townley knew that in DINA he had found himself, had begun to live as a soldier, to comport himself as an officer. He hoped Espinoza had accepted his expressed reservations on the Letelier mission as within the realm of professional behavior. He had not let his fear show, because in the braggadocio world of intelligence work, fear was as irrelevant as curiosity. Yet Townley ached to know what Espinoza had learned about the CIA's reaction to the Paraguayan incident, and whether the Asunción affair had caused temporary suspension or cancellation of the mission.

He assumed that he would no longer have to think about the Letelier assignment because he had been "burned." Pappalardo had as much as told them that, and he and Fernández had told Espinoza. He deduced from what he knew that the CIA did not support the mission to Washington.*

Townley's character was cut from the American grain even though he had begun to think of himself as more loyal to Chile than to his native country. The audacity of carrying out an assassination in the heart of the United States capital had appealed to his sense of adventure, almost outweighing the dangers.

Inés was finally to have the hysterectomy that had originally been scheduled when he left for Paraguay. Townley was worried. His emotional dependence on her was total, to the point of ignoring her frequent love affairs in order to maintain the relationship. She spent

*In both the Argentine and Italian missions, Townley worked with civilian terrorists with ties to the intelligence service. Milicia and AAA members who helped carry out the Pruts assassination worked directly under an arm of SIDE, the Argentine military intelligence service. The Italian fascist group who had helped plan the Leighton assassination had informal ties to that country's rightist-dominated intelligence apparatus in 1975.

August 7–14 in the hospital. Townley dropped his normal DINA duties and laboratory work and spent most of his days with her at the hospital. But his DINA superiors reached him there and ordered him to report to headquarters.

"Go to Argentina immediately." Townley again wanted to protest. But the good soldier said nothing. He flew to Buenos Aires Wednesday, August 11, and returned the next evening.

Townley later refused to talk about the nature of a mission so urgent it could tear him from his wife's bedside, but the short trip was probably connected with the kidnapping two days before of two Cuban diplomats in downtown Buenos Aires. The two, a consular official suspected of being an intelligence agent and his driver, were kidnapped from their car by SIDE undercover agents and interrogated on their alleged contacts and financial dealings with Argentine revolutionaries. Townley, DINA's specialist in Cuban matters, would have arrived at the height of the SIDE interrogations and torture of the Cubans, and been able to return the next day, having shared his intelligence with the Argentines for use in the interrogation and having gained new intelligence about Cuban operations for DINA.*

A few days after Townley got back to Santiago, the doctors released Inés from Military Hospital but confined her to bed at their Lo Curro home. Winter began to yield to spring. The rains abated and the cold became less intense.

Manuel Contreras considered the Paraguay episode a disappointing setback, but not an obstacle that could not be overcome with a little ingenuity. Most irritating to him was the failure of Paraguayan intelligence to collaborate efficiently as called for by membership in Operation Condor. Contreras began to work steadily with his own documentation people and with friends in the Foreign Ministry to avoid further problems in obtaining secure false documentation.

The Chilean Navy ran the Foreign Ministry. Contreras could not manipulate them. Any DINA operations channeled through the

---

*The bloated bodies of the two Cubans, Jesús Cejas Arias and Crescencio Galamena, their feet encased in cement, washed up on the muddy banks of the Lujan River near Buenos Aires in late October.

Foreign Ministry required the assent of Navy Commander in Chief José Toribio Merino, a junta member. Such procedure functioned well when, a year earlier, Contreras requested and obtained authorization to place DINA agents in foreign embassies under diplomatic cover.

But he had no intention of channeling the Letelier operation through the junta. To avoid hierarchical entanglements, Contreras consulted a friend, Colonel Enrique Valdés Puga, a hard-liner and the highest-ranking army officer inside the Foreign Ministry. Valdés Puga introduced Contreras to civilian career officer Guillermo Osorio, director of consular affairs. Contreras explained his needs: a series of authentic official passports which DINA could fill out with false names. The DINA passports would be "covered" by authentic passports bearing the same numbers issued through normal channels by the Foreign Ministry. Osorio's office would treat DINA's passports as authentic for all purposes.

Osorio agreed. An ambitious man whose wife, Mary Scroogie Alessandri, was a niece of former president Jorge Alessandri, Osorio would later pay a heavy price for his collaboration with DINA. But at the time, Contreras' offer fit comfortably into his political and ideological proclivities. A Germanophile, he had served several years in the Chilean Consulate in Bonn in the early sixties. There he curried favor with ultra-right Germans by bragging about his former membership in a Chilean Nazi youth group. During the Allende government Osorio was associated with Patria y Libertad. Since the coup, his right-wing views had served his career well in the Foreign Ministry; helping out the secret police on the side did not interfere with his lifestyle. And a favor for Contreras, the second most powerful man in the regime, would lead to reciprocal favors.

Osorio became DINA's contact inside the Foreign Ministry. In mid-August 1976 DINA asked him to process a series of passports. Unknown to Osorio, Contreras had set aside seven passports, numbered 525-76 to 531-76, for the Letelier assassination.

· · ·

ON AUGUST 16, 1976, a Monday, at Belgrado II, DINA's central command post, there was a great flurry of activity: phone calls were made, agents summoned, meetings held, papers signed, documents forged, equipment released, expenses drawn, messages sent.

Lieutenant Armando Fernández received his new orders directly from Contreras. In the chief's office, Contreras introduced Fernández to a tall, elegant blond woman in her mid-twenties. Her thin fashion-model figure, her fine features, and her haughty expression spelled aristocrat.

Fernández and the woman were given Chilean passports to sign, and their pictures were taken. They were told they would be given passage on the flight to Washington in a few days. Fernández' identity for the mission, chosen by himself, was Armando Fáundez Lyon. The woman called herself Liliana Walker.

The passports and pictures were forwarded by messenger to the Foreign Ministry, Guillermo Osorio's office. Official stamps and signatures were affixed to the passports, and Osorio filled out the forms identifying the passport bearers as Chilean government officials and requesting visas to the United States. Osorio initialed the forms GOM (for Guillermo Osorio Mardones). By mid-afternoon, a Foreign Ministry messenger arrived at the U.S. Consulate with the completed passports and visa request forms. The passport numbers were 525-76 and 526-76.

DINA agents René Riveros and Rolando Mosqueira answered a call to report to Espinoza's office. "You will leave for Washington before the end of the week," he told them. Contrary to usual DINA practice, they were not allowed to choose their own code names for the mission. The passports Espinoza gave them to sign bore the names of Alejandro Romeral Jara and Juan Williams Rose. Riveros, a military history enthusiast, recognized his new alias, Juan Williams, as the name of a Chilean naval hero of English descent who a century before had claimed the Strait of Magellan for Chile. The purpose of their mission: to act as decoys and to sidetrack any inquiry that might be launched as a result of the suspicion created in Asunción.

Riveros and Mosqueira, using the revived identities of Williams and Romeral, were ordered by Espinoza to attempt to contact General Vernon Walters of the CIA, and achieve a high profile before returning to Chile. If the United States police should attempt to follow the trail left by Townley and Fernández in Paraguay, the clues would lead them to Riveros and Mosqueira's innocuous mission to Washington, with documented departure well before the assassination.

Espinoza gave them expense money and airline tickets. Their passports, with visa request forms describing them as functionaries of the Ministry of Economics, were filled out and initialed by Osorio at the Foreign Ministry.

THE HIGHEST OFFICER at the U.S. Consulate in 1976 was Consul Josiah Brownell. Two vice-consuls assisted in normal consular business. A third consul, John Hall, saw a steady stream of visitors, but they weren't there on consular business. The third vice-consul slot was cover for a CIA case officer.

Unlike the one in Paraguay, the U.S. Consulate in Chile automatically granted visas whenever the Chilean Foreign Ministry sent the official Chilean government visa request form. On Tuesday, August 17, one of the consular officers processed four such requests and stamped visas in four official Chilean passports: Armando Fáundez Lyon (No. 525-76); Liliana Walker Martínez (No. 526-76); Juan Williams Rose (527-76); and Alejandro Romeral Jara (No. 528-76). All four visas were dated August 17, 1976, valid for multiple entry until that date 1977. The visas were type A-2, certifying that the bearers were on official government business.

Riveros and Mosqueira took off the following Saturday, landing in Miami August 22 to begin stage one of Contreras' three-stage assassination plan. Mosqueira, thin and light-haired, bore a superficial resemblance to Michael Townley, enough to allow the physical description on his "Juan Williams Rose" passport to coincide with the description Townley had written for the Paraguayan documents. Mosqueira had filled out the immigration form I-94 on the plane and slipped it into his passport. When it came his turn, the immigration officer took the form and stamped his passport without hesitation.

Riveros, too, passed through immigration without incident. They were surprised. Espinoza had prepared them to be stopped by United States officials because DINA had been informed through Paraguayan intelligence that the United States had placed a lookout for them.

Mosqueira and Riveros spent the day in Miami and departed for Washington the next day, August 23. They made contact with the Chilean Embassy and called on General Nilo Floody, the military attaché. He later described the visit in an interview with the FBI:

> In August 1976, exact date not recalled, General Floody stated he was visited at the Chilean Military Mission in Washington by Captains Mosqueira and Riveros. General Floody advised that Captains Riveros and Mosqueira told him that they were on an intelligence mission for the National Directorate of Intelligence (DINA), and that the purpose of their mission was to personally contact General Vernon Walters of the Central Intelligence Agency (CIA). General Floody recalled that no specific reason was given by Captains Riveros or Mosqueira for their desire to contact General Walters. General Floody advised that Captains Riveros and Mosqueira told him that they had been unsuccessful in their attempts to contact General Walters at CIA headquarters. In an effort to assist Captains Riveros and Mosqueira, General Floody stated he requested his secretary, who was proficient in the English language, to call CIA headquarters in an effort to locate General Walters and set up an appointment. . . . General Floody recalled that his secretary was informed by CIA headquarters that General Walters had terminated his association with the CIA and that he had either retired or returned to active military duty.

Mission accomplished. The CIA had received ample notice of Romeral's and Williams' presence. Mosqueira and Riveros maintained high visibility, hanging around the embassy and going on sightseeing tours in a chauffer-driven embassy car. Floody's son

Ricardo personally showed them around Washington. One evening they dined with Colonel Walter Doerner, a Chilean army officer whose attendance at the Inter-American Defense College was, according to the FBI, a cover for his real job as chief of DINA in the United States.

In Chile, stage two began. Fernández and Walker, who already had their passports and visas, were informed that they would depart on August 25.

Wednesday night's Braniff International flight from Santiago's Pudahuel airport to Miami is one of the few direct flights to the United States and is usually fully booked. Armando Fernández and Liliana Walker looked like an affluent young businessman and his stylish wife on their way to Walt Disney World. Walker stood out in the jumble of people and ungainly hand luggage as they waited to board. The slightly overweight Fernández dressed in a baggy summer suit did not. Fernández was on a mission to map a man's movements in preparation for his murder. His preoccupation, however, as he sat next to the beautiful Walker during the eight-hour flight was whether she would have sex with him as they played out their man-and-wife cover by sharing hotel rooms in Washington. Ignoring Fernández' attempts at small talk, Walker may have wondered about Orlando Letelier, whose picture and background she had studied carefully. She had been chosen for the mission because she was perceived as being the kind of woman Letelier would not be able to resist. She was young but mature, aristocratic, adept at feigning progressive political opinions; sex was part of her equipment, her tradecraft, its use deserving of no more thought than the decision to wear a blouse or a sweater. Her concern was how to get to know Letelier, to seduce him without entering into his circle of friends. The advantage she counted on was the predictable tendency of a married man to keep his affairs with women and his political affairs discreetly separate.*

---

*Fernández, Contreras, and Espinoza were all to deny later ever knowing Walker's real name. The precise orders Fernández and his new partner received that day have never been revealed, or have been obfuscated in the later cover stories. Part of the mission, but probably not all, was to conduct preoperational surveillance on Letelier in Washington: that was Michael Townley's later understanding. But the intended role of the stunning female agent, whose

They arrived at Miami International Airport around 6:00 A.M. and checked through customs and immigration. They transferred to an Eastern Airlines flight leaving at 8:00 A.M., and after a two-hour flight arrived in Washington. Fernández recalled that it was hot and muggy even at that early hour. They booked a room at the Washington Hotel near the White House on 15th Street and Pennsylvania Avenue. The hotel room, number 645, became their base of operation.

On August 26, stage one and stage two of DINA's Letelier operation overlapped in Washington. Mosqueira and Riveros could have contacted Fernández and Walker that day to exchange information. The next day, Mosqueira and Riveros took a flight to Miami, where they spent the weekend at the home of Riveros' sister and visited Disney World.

Fernández had been born in Washington in 1949 during his father's tenure as air force attaché to the Chilean Embassy. A military officer who had grown up in the starchy Chilean military subculture, he felt an almost mystical affinity for Washington, home of the Pentagon, the CIA—the seat of the greatest military power in the world. Like most Chilean officers, he could look forward to a stint of training in the United States as he moved upward in rank.

Fernández' sister, Rose Marie, lived with her American husband, Lawrence Guest, in Centerville, Virginia, about a fifteen-minute drive from the DINA agents' hotel. Fernández spent much of his time with the Guests during the thirteen days he was in Washington, looking the part of a vacationing South American soldier gawking at the sights of Washington. After spending two nights at the Washington Hotel with Walker, Fernández moved in with his sister's family in Centerville.

Liliana Walker left few traces of her activities during those sultry August days in Washington. A receipt from the Washington Hotel indicates that she and perhaps a companion drank two Scotch-and-sodas in the Hotel's Sky Terrace bar. She kept the room until September 6. No other records.

---

identity has been successfully hidden by Chile, remains a mystery. A likely explanation is that she had orders to seduce Letelier and lure him into a compromising situation where the actual assassination could be carried out securely and quietly.

Fernández' sister and brother-in-law later testified that Fernández visited Larry Guest's old place of employment in the mausoleumlike FBI headquarters and spent a day at the Airlie Foundation in northern Virginia, where he had his picture taken with María Eugenia Oyarzún, Chile's socialite ambassador to the Organization of American States. Rose Marie told the FBI that Armando never left her side during those days and could not have engaged in espionage activities. Her husband, however, indicated in his statements to the FBI that on most days he and Armando left the house together and went their separate ways in Washington.

Whatever pretexts Fernández and Walker found to justify their mission, they were frustrated in shadowing Orlando Letelier. He spent less than forty-eight hours in the Washington area from August 26 to September 6. On the day Fernández and Walker arrived in Washington, Letelier was at his 19th Street office between Dupont Circle and Q Street. He had returned the day before from the Rehoboth Beach vacation house his wife had rented to attend an 8:30 A.M. IPS meeting. He spent the nights of August 25 and 26 in Washington, then returned to Rehoboth Friday afternoon the twenty-seventh. On Saturday morning, he drove back to Bethesda and took calls at his home from lunchtime to about 4:00 P.M. Then he caught a connecting flight to New York, and departed that night for Amsterdam. DINA's agents and their intended victim drifted apart; the plot itself seemed to fragment for almost a week, with Letelier in Amsterdam and Fernández and Walker left behind in Washington.

Colonel Espinoza at DINA headquarters received Fernández' and Walker's progress reports. The week in Washington had been almost fruitless because of Letelier's absence. Fernández asked Espinoza for permission to return to Chile; he had received word that his father was gravely ill. Espinoza told them to compile whatever surveillance information they could and proceed to New York. Stage two, less than satisfactory, was ordered terminated.

Espinoza summoned Michael Townley to his office. Stage three became operative. He told Townley that he was to carry out the Letelier assassination according to his original orders: to use Cuban exile terrorists to carry out the actual killing. Townley should be out of the United States by the time it occurred. Espinoza told Townley that Fernández, his original partner, had already arrived in Washington and would provide "preoperational intelligence" on Letelier's movements. Fernández had been instructed to meet Townley at Kennedy International Airport on his arrival. It was September 7. He ordered Townley to leave for New York the next night. Townley was surprised by the orders. He had known nothing about Fernández' mission to Washington.

In Union City, New Jersey, Townley's friends in the Cuban Nationalist Movement laid plans to bomb the Soviet freighter *Ivan Shepetkov* anchored in the Elizabeth, New Jersey harbor.

ON THE EVENING of September 4, Letelier returned from Amsterdam on a KLM flight to New York. Having just missed the last connecting flight to Washington, he stayed overnight with IPS colleagues, Saul Landau and Richard Barnet, in an airport hotel. On the morning of September 5, all three returned to a humid, hot Washington Sunday. DINA's prey was back.

BACK AT HIS Lo Curro home, Townley called Virgilio Paz in New Jersey, then called his friend Fernando Cruchaga at the LAN-Chile Airlines office at Kennedy International Airport.

The next morning, "Tito," DINA's chief of false documents, gave Townley a passport with a visa to the United States. Townley's picture had already been pasted into the passport, which he noticed had been issued two weeks before, on August 24. The name in the passport was Hans Petersen Silva. Another DINA officer gave Townley $980 in United States bills.

Late that night, September 8, Townley drove to Pudahuel Airport and boarded LAN-Chile flight 142 for New York.

IN WASHINGTON, memos and instructions made their tangled but deliberate way from desk to desk, from agency to agency. At the State Department's Visa and Passport Office, Director Julio Arias signed certificates of revocation for visas in two Paraguayan passports in the names of Juan Williams and Alejandro Romeral. From his office he dispatched the documents by diplomatic pouch to the U.S. Embassy, Asunción, Paraguay, where they were received on September 15. Earlier, Arias' office had sent the U.S. Immigration and Naturalization Service a routine request for a lookout on the two names for distribution to border checkpoints and overseas consulates. State was later notified that the two men had arrived via Miami bearing Chilean passports but had not been stopped.

President Salvador Allende

Orlando Letelier takes the cabinet oath

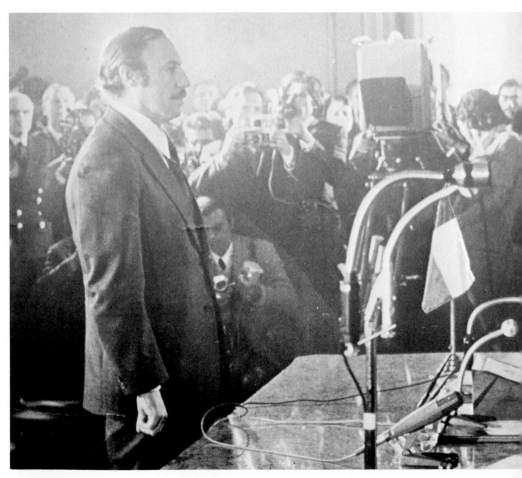

Popular Unity campaign poster

The military coup:
(top) troops in the street; (bottom) arrests

Letelier's arrest

The stadium after the coup

Pinochet and his generals

Sketch of Letelier at Dawson Island

The stone he carved
at Dawson to "Isa"
and the Dawson
drinking cup

Orlando Letelier

Isabel Margarita Morel de Letelier

Isabel Letelier teaching Spanish to FBI agents

Orlando and Isabel Letelier and
young Letelier

Letelier with
Nixon, Castro,
and Kissinger

The Letelier family

Dancing the *cueca*

Ronni Karpen Moffitt

Ronni and
Michael Moffitt

Michael Moffitt

Letelier's car after the explosion

The funeral processions in Washington and Caracas

Michael Moffitt, Fabiola Letelier (Orlando's sister),
and Isabel Letelier

Michael Vernon Townley

Manuel Contreras (second from right, front) with lawyer
Sergio Miranda and bodyguards at the Chilean Supreme Court

The DINA emblem

Inés Callejas de Townley

Michael Townley's house in Lo Curro

Romeral and Williams passport photos

Assistant U.S. Attorneys
Eugene Propper (above) and
E. Lawrence Barcella

Robert Scherrer

Larry Wack

L. Carter Cornick

FBI Special Agents

General Augusto Pinochet

DINA head Manuel Contreras

Colonel Pedro Espinoza

Captain Armando Fernández

Guillermo Novo,
Alvin Ross, and
Chilean United Nations
officials

Ignacio Novo with attorney

Alvin Ross

Virgilio Paz

Rolando Otero

Orlando Bosch

Felipe Rivero

JOSE DIONISIO SUAREZ Y ESQUIVEL

FBI No. 264,663 E
CONSPIRACY TO MURDER A FOREIGN OFFICIAL
F.P.C.: 12 M 1 U 100 13 Ref: 3
         M 3 W MIO   3

DESCRIPTION
AGE: 39, born February 17, 1939, Holguin, Oriente, Cuba (not supported by birth records)
HEIGHT: 5'10"   EYES: brown
WEIGHT: 175 pounds   COMPLEXION: light
BUILD: large   RACE: white
HAIR: black   NATIONALITY: Cuban
OCCUPATION: used car salesman
REMARKS: may be wearing beard and or mustache.
SCARS AND MARKS: scar upper lip under nose
SOCIAL SECURITY NUMBERS USED: 202-70-9712, 262-70-9712

VIRGILIO PABLO PAZ y ROMERO

FBI No. 626,118 L9
CONSPIRACY TO MANUFACTURE UNLAWFUL
EXPLOSIVES; CONSPIRACY TO MURDER A
FOREIGN OFFICIAL
F.P.C.: 4 1 U 11
         1 aUa

DESCRIPTION
AGE: 26, born November 20, 1951, Santa Clara, Las Villas, Cuba (not supported by birth records)
HEIGHT: 5'7" to 5'9"   EYES: brown
WEIGHT: 150 to 185 pounds   COMPLEXION: light
BUILD: medium   RACE: white
HAIR: brown   NATIONALITY: Cuban
OCCUPATIONS: clerk, truck driver, used car salesman
REMARKS: may be wearing beard and/or mustache or clean shaven.
SOCIAL SECURITY NUMBERS USED: 140-44-9630; 071-36-2803

FBI "Wanted" posters

A G R E E M E N T

A. I, Earl J. Silbert, United States Attorney for the District of Columbia, as the representative of the United States in the investigation of the murder of Orlando Letelier, hereby agree to the following:

> 1. That information obtained through the Letelier investigation with respect to actions by Chilean Nationals in the United States may be used to investigate and prosecute violations of law in the United States;
>
> 2. That there will be no other use of this information by the United States and it will be conveyed only to the Government of Chile to be used by its investigators for possible prosecutions; and
>
> 3. That the United States agrees to allow representatives of the Government of Chile to have access to interview Mr. Townley if Mr. Townley and his lawyer agree.

B. I, Enrique Montero, Undersecretary of the Interior, as the representative of the Government of Chile, hereby agree to the following:

> 1. That any information relating to actions by Chileans or persons of any other nationality which relate in any manner to the murder of Orlando Letelier, will be conveyed to the Government of the United States.

It is understood by both Governments that this Agreement relates only to the exchange of information. It does not, in any way, limit the right of either Government to prosecute persons for crimes within its jurisdictions.

_____   _____
EARL J. SILBERT   ENRIQUE MONTERO

_____
DATE   April 7, 1978

THE COURT: Doesn't the document speak for itself?

MR. PROPPER: Yes, Your Honor; possibly I should stick it in evidence and read it to the jury.

MR. GOLDBERGER: I have no objection to him reading it to the jury.

THE COURT: Do other counsel concur with you?

MR. DUBIN: Yes, Judge.

MR. PROPPER: This is United States of America versus Michael Vernon Townley.

"Agreement: Pursuant to Rule 11(e)(1)(C) of the Federal Rules of Criminal Procedure, the United States and Michael Vernon Townley have agreed to the following disposition in the murder case of former Chilean Ambassador to the United States Orlando Letelier and Ronni Moffitt, who were killed in the District of Columbia on September 21, 1976.

"(1) Michael Vernon Townley agreed to plead guilty to one count of conspiracy to murder a foreign official, Orlando Letelier, in violation of 18 U.S. Code 1117. The Government agrees to accept this plea.

"(2) Michael Vernon Townley and the United States agree that the sentence to be imposed will be 10 years imprisonment with the initial parole eligibility to be after three years and four months, in accordance with 18 U.S. Code 4205(b)(a).

Townley's plea-bargain agreement
with the United States government

◀ The Silbert-Montero Agreement

"(3) The United States agrees to provide for the safety and protection of Michael Vernon Townley and as necessary and appropriate for the safety and protection of his wife, children, parents, and brother and sister while they are in the United States.

"(4) Michael Vernon Townley agrees to provide complete, candid and truthful information concerning the murder of Orlando Letelier and Ronni Moffitt, including but not limited to testimony before the grand jury and in any subsequent trials. Mr. Townley's cooperation shall be total and without reservation.

"(5) Michael Vernon Townley further agrees to provide complete candid and truthful information with regard to any investigation into any other criminal activities within the jurisdiction of the United States or affecting United States citizens by individuals of which he is aware. This cooperation likewise will be total and without reservation and will include but not be limited to testimony before a grand jury and at any subsequent trials.

"(6) United States agrees not to prosecute Michael Vernon Townley for any further crimes that might become aware of which occurred prior to the date of this agreement. It is understood that the United States has no knowledge as of the date of this agreement of any crimes of violence involving Michael Vernon Townley in the United States excluding the case involving Orlando Letelier and Ronni Moffitt.

"The United States further agrees not to prosecute Michael Vernon Townley's wife, Mariana Inez Callejas de Townley for any crimes of which it might become aware. This agreement not to prosecute her does not extend to crimes of violence as those terms are defined in Title 23, D.C. Code, Section 13314.

"It is understood that the United States has no knowledge as of the date of this agreement of any crimes by Mariana Inez Callejas de Townley.

"(7) It is clearly understood by Michael Vernon Townley that if it is found that any part or portion of the testimony, statements, or other cooperation is knowingly false, he can be fully prosecuted for perjury and/or false declarations.

"(8) Any breach of this agreement by either party, including that referred to in Paragraph 7, will confer upon the other party the right to request that the plea be set aside.

BY MR. PROPPER:

Q   Mr. Townley, is that your recollection of the agreement?

A   That is.

Pinochet

The Letelier-Moffitt Memorial Medallion

8

AN ACT OF TERROR

RONNI KARPEN MOFFITT's intermittent humming provided a kind of background sound track as she and Michael drove with Orlando Letelier to IPS the morning of September 21, 1976. She improvised with her voice as she did with her flute, maintaining a structural control, then flying into unknown passages. She loved her music and her husband, Michael Moffitt.

At age twenty-five, Ronni had moved from a confined suburban childhood into the world of international politics. She had grown up in Passaic, New Jersey, where her parents, Murray and Hilda Karpen, owned a delicatessen store. The attention that Murray and Hilda Karpen lavished on their lox and pastrami took second place to their children, for whom the deli afforded the means to college.

Ronni, the oldest of the three Karpen children and the only daughter, graduated in 1973 from the University of Maryland and began to experiment with life careers. She worked in an advertising agency, taught third grade, opened a community music center in Washington's poor and racially mixed Adams-Morgan area so that people who could not afford to buy instruments could use them. By 1975, along with her community activities, she had begun to work full-time at the Institute for Policy Studies. A secretary at first, she quickly acquired the knowledge to become IPS's fund-raising coordinator.

For Michael Moffitt, a young economist working with Richard Barnet at the institute, Ronni was joy incarnate. After a fast and romantic courtship, they were married on Memorial Day, 1976. IPS staff and fellows drove to Passaic for the ceremony in the Karpen's back yard. A sumptuous wedding lunch—chopped liver and lox, fresh rolls and pastries, champagne—lay under a canopy where the guests ate, drank, and danced until evening.

Four months later, wedding guests would remember little incidents, such as the wind blowing away the top of the *chupah,* the arch that covers bride and groom in Jewish wedding ceremonies, and Ronni's stumbling as she walked toward the rabbi, and they would discuss these things as omens.

On the morning of September 21, 1976, Michael sat in the back of Orlando's car, reading, looking out the window, listening to and sometimes participating in the conversation Ronni and Orlando were having about a book they had both read as children. Orlando, though not a slow driver, did not have an aggressive style at the wheel. "If I was driving," Moffitt remembered thinking, "I would be driving a lot faster."

The day had that muggy, mildewed feeling characteristic of Washington from June through September. The sky was overcast. Ronni embodied all the brightness the day lacked. When she turned her head to talk to Orlando, Michael would admire her profile. He felt contented as he cracked his window just enough to let Orlando's incessant cigarette smoke curl out and away.

Letelier's car, tailed by the grey sedan, passed the Chilean Embassy on the left and entered Sheridan Circle. The driver of the grey sedan pressed one key on the instrument plugged into the cigarette lighter, then pressed a second key.

Michael Moffitt heard a hissing sound, "like a hot wire being placed in cold water." He saw a flash of light over Ronni's head, then a deafening, crushing sound overwhelmed him.

William Hayden, an attorney driving behind Letelier's car, was snapped out of his early-morning lethargy by the flash and a shock wave. "I saw an automobile actually coming down out of the air," he said later. "There were flames coming out." Letelier's Chevelle crashed down into a parked Volkswagen and rolled to a burning halt in front of the Rumanian Embassy, leaving behind a trail of glass, blood, and bits of metal and flesh.

Black-uniformed Executive Protection Service police, guarding the nine embassies around the circle, materialized from every direction, running across the circle toward the wreck and moving traffic out of the way.

"The car was picked off the ground," Moffitt recalled. "I started to smell the most unbelievable stench that I have ever smelled in my life . . . and there was a lot of heat. . . . We seemed to come to a stop. I was on the floor on my knees, and I couldn't feel anything below my waist, and there was smoke."

Moffitt tumbled out of the car, one shoe off, stunned. He pulled fresh air into his seared lungs. "I saw Ronni from the back, kind of walking or stumbling toward the curb." He did not see Orlando.

Moffitt ran around the wreckage to the driver's side. Then he saw him. "There was a huge hole in the car, and Orlando was turned around, facing the back of the car, and his head was more or less hanging back and he was moving his head back and forth . . ." "Orlando," Michael cried, slapping the face of his mentor, "this is Michael, can you hear me?" He saw Letelier "trying to utter something, but he never said anything I could make sense of." Moffitt reached into the smoking car, around jagged metal edges, and "managed to get my wrists and part of my forearm under his shoulders and tried to lift him, and he just seemed to be very heavy . . . I looked down and I could see the bare flesh, the bottom half of his body blown off."

Michael exhausted a strength that he drew in desperation from the deepest reserves of his body and still could not lift Orlando from the smoking chassis. He withdrew, sweat streaking his blackened face, and in rage and frustration screamed, "Assassins, fascists!"

Then he saw Ronni lying on an embassy lawn "and there was a woman who was kind of bent over her, and I said to her, 'Do you want me to help?' and she said, 'No, let me try to stop the bleeding.' "

The woman tried to reach into Ronni's throat and position her head to cut the blood flow. "Blood was just pouring out of her mouth," Moffitt described.

"She had blood gushing out of her mouth, blood all over," said Officer Walter Johnson of the Metropolitan Police. Johnson had rushed to the scene minutes after receiving a radio call from an Executive Protection police officer. Johnson saw the wrecked car and raced toward the vehicle.

"As I ran closer, I could see a foot in the roadway. . . . I could observe that apparently the vehicle had skidded across some 50 or 75 feet, leaving debris in the roadway, including the foot. I got closer to the vehicle. I looked into the car, and immediately saw a white male sitting there on his buttocks, on the pavement. The whole floor panel of the car was gone. He was missing his legs someplace above the knees. There was blood everyplace. The inside of the vehicle was all blackened, charred. He looked up at me . . . motioning to me."

Johnson spotted a Fire Department car, asked the driver to summon an ambulance if one had not already been called.

"Then I saw a white male . . . running around, very upset. The front of his hair looked to me as though it had been singed. He was yelling words to the effect that the fascists had planted a bomb."

"The fascists killed him," shouted Moffitt. "DINA killed him. Pinochet, the murderer."

Detective Johnson felt nausea welling up. He heard shouts, saw more blood, severed legs. Vehicles arrived, and more police and sirens. A crowd gathered and swelled.

The ambulances arrived, preceded by hoarse siren blasts as they wormed their way through the maze of stalled traffic. Letelier, limp, a widening pool of blood beneath him the measure of his swiftly ebbing life, was lifted free of the wreckage by a police officer and hefty ambulance attendants. The paramedics groped about the stumps of his legs, tying and clamping blood vessels. The ambulance screamed off. Letelier was dead by the time they reached George Washington Hospital, half a mile away.

Four men in civilian clothes emerged from one of the cars that had managed to penetrate Sheridan Circle. They surveyed the scene and began to issue orders. A second ambulance carrying Ronni Moffitt sped off to George Washington Hospital. A policeman refused to allow Michael Moffitt to accompany his wife.

AS THE LAST ambulance drove away, FBI Special Agent L. Carter Cornick forced his mind to absorb details without losing the larger picture. He noticed, he recalled later, that the ambulances had driven off with the victims but had left behind on the pavement a severed foot, still inside its shoe. Cornick ordered a tight police cordon and then "vectored" the entire area—divided it into numbered sections to facilitate precise identification of each location where evidence would be found.

More FBI agents arrived, among them the top officer of the Washington Field Office, Special Agent Nicholas Stames. Informed of Letelier's identity, Stames anticipated lots of publicity, probable political involvement, and pressures from many groups. He walked over to Cornick. "It's your case. Do it," he told Cornick.

"Mike Moffitt was still there," Cornick recalled later. "He was in a daze, shouting DINA, DINA. I didn't know what DINA was. But it wouldn't take me long to find out."

A police car finally took Moffitt to the hospital, where he was told Ronni was receiving emergency treatment. He rang IPS. Receptionist Alyce Wiley, hearing his voice, began her usual teasing. "He said, 'Be quiet, Alyce,' and I knew something bad had happened," she recalled. "I remember he said that there had been an explosion in a car and that Orlando was dead and that DINA had done it or something like that. He wasn't too clear about it. I didn't know who DINA was, it sounded like a girl's name. Michael told me they were working on Ronni and he didn't know about her condition, and he told me to call Isabel. I asked Lilian to call Isabel."

In a small treatment room, a doctor removed a fragment of metal from Moffitt's breast bone; his cuts were cleaned and bandaged. "They told me Ronni was hurt very badly, but that they were working on her, and it seemed like an eternity . . . and they took me in a little room and put me on one of those examining tables and made me lie down and there were several people standing around and one of the doctors came over and said, 'Your wife is dead.' "

Lilian Montecino, Orlando Letelier's secretary, telephoned Isabel and told her there had been an accident involving Orlando's car, and that Isabel should go to George Washington Hospital. Mechanically she added, "Don't worry, everyone's all right." Lilian was nervous as she descended the stairs to the street. Less than three years earlier she had received a similar phone call in Santiago, Chile: her oldest son, Cristián, had met with an accident. Two DINA agents had arrested him, apparently mistaking him for someone else. Lilian's son had died while being tortured.

A few minutes later Alyce reached Saul Landau at his home. "Terrible accident . . . Orlando dead . . . Ronni . . . Ronni . . . Come to IPS. Marc and Dick are at the hospital . . ." She was sobbing. Landau rushed to the institute in a cab, arriving a few minutes before reporters and other outsiders began to drift into the lobby. He asked them all to leave and locked the door.

At the hospital emergency room, Marcus Raskin and Richard Barnet were told that Orlando was dead. The hospital authorities, realizing the unusual nature of the event, succumbed to bureaucratic caution and withheld all information. Not until Barnet's wife Ann arrived about 10:30 A.M. and was able to use her physician's status to get information did the IPS codirectors have absolute confirmation that Ronni was also dead, a victim of drowning in her own blood. Her carotid artery had been severed by shrapnel. The blood had rushed through her punctured windpipe into her lungs.

Ann Barnet saw Ronni. Her face, burned raw, charred black in places, possessed none of its living qualities. It bore signs of excruciating pain.

"Lilian's call made me very nervous because her voice told me that she didn't know what had happened," Isabel Letelier remembered. "I thought to myself, 'If there was an accident I hope it wasn't Orlando's fault because he would never forgive himself if he caused bad injury to Michael or Ronni.' " Isabel shouted to her housekeeper, Illa, that she had to rush to the hospital. She glanced quickly in the mirror as she normally did before leaving the house. "I was dressed in a black leather pants suit, and I somehow knew that I could not wear that outfit. I told Illa, 'I cannot wear this.' I changed and went outside and saw it was raining. I got a kind of premonition that something horrible had happened. What if he had skidded? I couldn't bring myself to drive so I called a taxi. A strange thing to do. I can always drive.

"The taxi driver seemed to take forever. You know how Washington gets when it rains, everyone slows down, and then we approached the Mosque on Massachusetts Avenue and traffic was blocked off in both directions. Panic welled up inside me. I told the driver, 'My husband was driving the car that caused the accident.' I felt terrible. Orlando would rather be dead than have someone hurt because of his driving.

"I saw Michael Moffitt just after I arrived, and people told me it was a bomb and Michael cried, 'They got my baby,' and we embraced. My chest hurt and I felt very weak."

Isabel demanded to see Orlando's body. The hospital authorities and police tried to stop her. "No." "Impossible." "Out of the question." "Regulations don't permit." They cited rules, laws, routine, higher authorities. Isabel persisted. "I knew that I had to see him. It didn't matter how he looked, but seeing him dead was very important." Finally with Ann Barnet's help she entered the room where Orlando's body lay.

"I saw his body without legs. It was important to see what the enemy had done. Orlando was life, life, life. I felt a sense of terrible loss. My marriage could have collapsed, and we could have not only separated but divorced, but he would have remained my friend and taken care of me in some ways, as he did when we were separated. And he was the father of the boys. When I entered the hospital and people told me he was dead, I felt my legs might collapse. I had nothing to hold on to. The lack of Orlando caused a pain in my chest. A darkness filled up inside me where he had been.

"When I saw him with half a body I became very angry. A rush of energy went through my body, which had been feeling so weak. He loved his body, his legs, and the enemy had done this. I was ready to fight them.

"I could see on his face the pain and the surprise. Those must have been his feelings when he died. I could not dwell on the pain in my chest, on my desire to cry. I had been right to demand to see his body. It meant that nothing had changed. I had been fighting against these murderers since the day of the coup."

She recalled the day in Chile when Moy Tohá received news of her husband José's death in prison and she had gone with her friend to the hospital. The authorities had said his death was "suicide." Isabel had whispered in Moy's ear, "Demand to see the body." Moy did and found evidence of murder.

"I remember how Moy turned so serene after that. And how calm Tencha was after Salvador died. I thought to myself that I could never achieve such serenity, that I would be hysterical and cry and not be able to think. I wanted very much to be alone and cry and to allow my sorrow to rush from my mouth. But I could not. A pattern began with the coup. When Pinochet kills, the survivors must do what is necessary to carry on. It had become a way of struggle. I knew I had to do all in my power to make Orlando's death costly to the enemy that killed him."

When IPS fellow Ralph Stavins arrived at Sheridan Circle, a five-minute walk from the institute, huge police vacuum cleaners had begun to suck up the glass and metal fragments from the road and the embassy lawns. The rain had washed away most of the blood, and men were climbing the sides of buildings searching for fragments, while other teams walked the Sheridan Circle rooftops picking up bits of glass, metal, car upholstery, shreds of clothing, and fragments of human bone.

More IPS personnel and friends of the victims arrived. They crayoned their outrage on makeshift posters and began to form a picket line in front of the Chilean Embassy. The Executive Protection Service officers dispersed the angry crowd, citing an ordinance that forbade demonstrations within one hundred feet of an embassy.

Chilean Ambassador Manuel Trucco told a radio journalist that Letelier might have been attempting to throw a bomb at the Chilean Embassy as he drove by and the bomb might have exploded instead in his hand. Advisers conferred with the ambassador, who quickly retracted his remark—too late to keep it from appearing in the evening news.

. . .

JOHN DINGES, a resident correspondent in Chile for *Time* magazine and the *Washington Post*, sat at his desk in the offices of a small magazine in Santiago.

Bernardita, the secretary, took the call and, not understanding English but hearing my name, passed it on to me. It was ten minutes to ten. Washington Post foreign editor Ronald Koven was unusually succinct: an explosion in Washington a few minutes ago, bodies not identified but car definitely belonged to Orlando Letelier, one man—probably Letelier—dead. Write the "Chile angle." More editors came on the phone, outlining how the story was being covered.

I had never met Letelier, but I reacted like a friend of the family. While he was on Dawson Island, I became friends with his sister Fabiola, and we often discussed her struggle as a lawyer to gain his release. Through her I had met Isabel Letelier, and while in Washington that July had visited her at the Leteliers' Bethesda home, and remember being disappointed that Orlando was not there.

I ran the three blocks from my office on Matias Cousino Street to the Plaza de Armas and rushed through a door under a chipped sign that read "Manantial Bookstore." Inside, an unobtrusive side door led upstairs to the Catholic Church's Vicariate of Solidarity, the center of human rights activity in Chile. The security guard at the door recognized me and waved me past. "Mataron a Letelier!" I shouted as I bounded up the steps. "They've killed Letelier!"

I told what I knew to a group of lawyers, clergymen, and others who had gathered in the office of Vicariate Director Christian Precht. A lawyer hurried out to find Fabiola, who, since her brother's release two years before, had worked tirelessly as a member of the human rights legal team to pressure the timid Chilean courts to act on the thousands of illegal arrests and hundreds of cases of missing persons. Someone turned on the radio, but there was no news yet. Fabiola arrived, in shock, her face grey. Then she became enraged as the first news flash confirmed that Orlando Letelier was dead, his legs blown off.

No one spoke, no one bothered to say that DINA had done it. As an institution, the Vicariate had survived three years of arrests, imprisonments, and harassment of individual members working under what they liked to call "the umbrella," the precarious sanctuary afforded by their association with the Catholic Church and various international human rights organizations. Conversations started but stopped suddenly. Fear seized the office. If DINA can kill Orlando Letelier on the streets of Washington, how can we be safe here, church or no church?

I went upstairs to the archives of the Vicariate, the only place in Chile where complete files on DINA activity and human rights violations are stored and analyzed. As on countless other "human rights" stories, the Vicariate workers offered to help me. They pulled down files.

My notes that day contain this outline, "D" meaning dead, "A" meaning assassinated, "M" meaning missing after arrest by DINA:

D-A Schneider	*Oct. 1970*	*Mil[itary: Commander in Chief of Armed Forces]*
D-A Prats	*Sept. 1974*	*Def[ense Minister Military: Commander in Chief of Armed Forces]*
D-? Toha (suicide?)	*1974*	*PS [Socialist Party] Def[ense Minister], died in prison*
D-A Letelier	*Sept. 1976*	*PS Def*
D-? Bonilla	*Mar. 1975*	*Mil Def*
M V. Díaz	*May 1976*	*PC [Communist Party chief]*
M Carlos Lorca	*June 1975*	*PS chief*
A Leighton	*Oct. 1975*	*PDC [Christian Democratic Party leader], survived*

| D-? Alberto | 1974 | FACH [Air Force], |
| Bachelet | | pro-Allende, died in prison |

I phoned my dispatch to the Post *that afternoon from a public booth, using a false name:*

> *The murder of exiled Chilean Orlando Letelier . . . fits into a remarkable pattern of terrorism inside and outside Chile that has eliminated potential threats to the military regime of General Augusto Pinochet.*
>
> *Observers here believe that while the plot against Letelier was carried out in the United States, it was conceived here in the office of the DINA, Pinochet's secret police.*
>
> *The common denominator in all the murders or questionable accidents is that the victim was an immediate military rival to Pinochet's rise to power or continuation in power or that the victim was a civilian opponent with strong ties to the generals surrounding Pinochet.*

U.S. ATTORNEY EARL SILBERT, after consulting Donald Campbell, head of his Major Crimes Divison, assigned Assistant U.S. Attorney Eugene Propper to the case at midday.* The designation of the junior member of the division reflected Silbert's judgment that "the assassination was an obvious terrorist act that would be practically impossible to solve." But Propper, he said, "was industrious and resourceful and had a relatively uncluttered case load." Propper was having midmorning coffee in the cafeteria of the U.S. District Court building when Campbell told him of the assignment.

Stanley Wilson, a veteran member of the Metropolitan Police, maneuvered to get the assignment to cover the Letelier-Moffitt bombing from his department as soon as he learned the identity of Letelier. Born in the Canal Zone, he spoke Spanish.

*Silbert and Campbell served as United States prosecutors in the investigation and trial of the Watergate burglars. The third Watergate prosecutor, Seymour Glanzer, who had gone into private practice, was retained in 1978 to represent Michael Townley.

. . .

ON THE AFTERNOON of September 21 the scene in and around IPS shifted from chaos to order and back to chaos. Shortly after Raskin and Barnet returned from the hospital, reporters came in and television camera operators lit the seminar room on the ground floor.

Waldo Fortín and Juan Gabriel Valdés secured from Lilian Montecino the keys to Orlando's office half a block away. With Saul Landau they quickly went through documents in Letelier's files to ensure that materials that could compromise the Chilean resistance inside Chile or in exile would not fall into the hands of the FBI. Valdés, filled with an understandable blanket mistrust of the government that had helped overthrow his own, was convinced that the FBI would turn over to DINA any names it found. The three men discovered no lists of names in Orlando's office. But they did not know what papers Letelier had been carrying in his briefcase or on his person. Whatever information those documents contained now was in the hands of the police and the FBI.

Raskin and Barnet began the news conference. They described the murders as assassinations, containing their grief with effort, and demanded that President Ford and FBI Director Clarence Kelly investigate the case fully. Barnet then accused DINA: "I believe there is sufficient evidence based on what has happened in Rome, in Buenos Aires, and now here in Washington, D.C., to show a pattern of conduct by Chilean intelligence agencies."

Michael Moffitt, wearing a green hospital shirt, vowed to work to enlist "people on Capitol Hill to cut off aid to the dictators in power." He forced himself to look almost dry-eyed into the national network television cameras: "The United States government helped to overthrow the government of Allende and to put these dictators in power. And they're responsible for killing my wife."

The press conference over, the police arrived and evacuated the institute so that a bomb squad with trained dogs could inspect the building. The dogs had already barked themselves into a frenzy over a car near Sheridan Circle. The car belonged to a well-known CIA critic, and the police immediately took all security precautions. Later inspection revealed the presence of a few marijuana seeds, which provoke in the trained animals the same reaction as do explosives.

The dogs sniffed their way through the institute's halls and offices. Outside Ralph Stavins' office they barked and growled, signaling to their handlers that they had found something interesting. The discovery turned out to be a chemical used on mimeograph paper which strongly resembles the odor of certain explosives.

Outside the street was cordoned off by police. Saul Landau showed a police officer Michael Moffitt's car where he had left it disabled the night before, and made a move to open the door. The policeman jumped and grabbed his hand, shouting, "Don't touch that car, it could be wired."

At about 2:00 P.M. the FBI arrived on the scene, anticipated but heightening the general unease. The bureau had entered the case because Letelier had been a member of Washington's diplomatic corps, a lifetime status according to protocol, within federal rather than local jurisdiction. The directors, fellows, and staff of IPS greeted the agents' arrival as if they were carriers of bubonic plague.

In 1974 IPS had filed a suit for damages against the FBI. Based on the reports of two former FBI informants, the institute charged the bureau with illegally planting informants inside IPS, tapping its phones, opening its mail, and keeping its fellows under surveillance over the years 1968–1972. In addition, the IPS brief accused the FBI of systematically rifling its garbage and on one occasion reconstructing from discarded typewriter ribbons a letter written by one of its fellows. The FBI admitted to a House Investigating Committee in 1975 that it had placed 62 informants in IPS. The suit was still pending in September 1976.

So when the FBI agents asked to interview the various IPS staffers who had been closest to Letelier, the institute leaders demanded that Stavins, a former attorney and professor of political theory, be present. Throughout the afternoon of September 21 the FBI agents, uneasy about this distortion of their normal procedures, asked their questions. Landau was among the first interviewed.

"Who do you think might have killed Letelier and Moffitt?"

"Pinochet."

The agents looked puzzled. "Again, please."

"Augusto Pinochet Ugarte, the president of Chile." Landau spelled the name. The agent taking notes asked him to slow down. Landau described Letelier's activities against the junta.

"Would anyone else that you can think of want to or have reason to kill him?"

"No."

THE EVENING OF September 21 at a friend's house, Michael Moffitt, still wearing his green hospital shirt, a bandage covering a cut on his head, regained his equilibrium. The cordite residue had left stains on his face; his eyes were red.

"There was a hissing sound, a white flash . . . Jesus," he repeated. Grief and anguish exuded from him, from the lines that had formed in his face that day and still have not disappeared. Still in the grip of shock, he shuddered frequently but fought for control and handled the frequent phone calls from reporters with composure. He told them what had happened and always gave the same message: Pinochet and DINA had murdered his wife and Orlando Letelier.

He had not seen Ronni's body. He knew that Ronni was dead, but his last sight of her alive remained to haunt his imagination, to cause him pain and agony. Unafraid to show his grief, he directed his passion toward revenge. As soon as his battered psyche recovered, he would seek the killers. He began his political work, however, before the trauma had healed. For the next six months he heard the hissing sound, saw the white flash, asked himself the inevitable "Why didn't I fix the car? Why didn't I sit in the front seat?"—questions as normal as they were irrational.

MICHAEL TOWNLEY'S HANDS shook as he held a glass of beer, both elbows planted firmly on the varnished table. Ignacio Novo and his wife Silvia sat across from him at a window table of the Viscaya Restaurant in the heart of Miami's Little Havana. Ignacio, a CNM member, had been the first to tell him of the explosion in Washington.

"You're shaking. What's the matter?" Silvia Novo recalled asking Townley.

"I'm nervous by nature," he answered.

Townley was anxious to get out of the country. His plane didn't leave until midnight. He didn't know whether Silvia was in on the operation, so he evaded her probing questions about whether DINA was involved. He figured Ignacio had told her about it, and she was as militant as a woman can be in the *machista* Cuban exile world, but it was best to play it safe.

Events had been nerve-racking for Townley since his arrival in Miami from Newark late Sunday night. All day Monday he kept expecting to hear news of a bombing in Washington. He imagined a dozen things that could have gone wrong. The bomb could have fallen off, been discovered, not worked, or Paz and Suárez could simply have gotten disgusted and gone home, leaving the device under the car.

"All this time all sorts of worries started going through my mind. I was considering having to go back to Washington myself to follow up," Townley said later. He contacted Felipe Rivero, the titular head of the CNM, but the enigmatic Rivero wouldn't let on that he even knew an operation was in progress.

He had used the time in Miami to check on equipment he had ordered for DINA from Audio Intelligence Devices in Fort Lauderdale and to visit his parents. He had gone shopping and bought souvenirs for his sons Brian and Chris. When he finally heard the news on the radio, Townley fretted because a woman had been killed with Letelier, and wondered why they had detonated the bomb almost in front of the Chilean Embassy.

Townley gripped his beer glass tighter to steady his hands as Silvia Novo bantered on. He was not an unemotional man, not the Jackal, someone who could kill as if he were squashing a bug. The woman's death wouldn't bother his superiors in Chile, he knew. But it did him; it touched what remained of the moral sensibility he had acquired as a boy growing up in mainstream America. His trembling was also evidence of the dizzying high that goes with having killed, having possessed the highest power and committed the greatest sin. Townley wished the shaking would stop, cursing it as a show of weakness. But he savored the exhilaration, the tingle of pride mixed with the revulsion and fear.

Silvia and Ignacio Novo drove Townley to Miami International Airport the night of September 21 and watched him step over the baggage scales into the LAN-Chile office. Townley had only a few dollars and a ticket in Hans Petersen's name that did not match his passport alias. He could not persuade the LAN-Chile ticket agent to exchange the Petersen ticket so he could catch the LAN flight that night. The next day a LAN pilot he knew gave him a voucher for a one-way ticket to Santiago in the name of Kenneth Enyart.

IN WASHINGTON, Saul Landau began to act.

The morning after the assassination I awoke and calmly washed, dressed, breakfasted, gathered papers I wanted to take with me to the institute. I walked out to my car and fished the key out of my pocket. When I tried to insert the key into the car door, my hand began to shake, causing me to make tiny scratches in the paint around the key slot. Shock had ended; fear had begun.

I used both hands to get the key into the ignition and closed my eyes and bit my lip as the engine turned over. I imagined sound, flame, smoke, pain, but my Plymouth Fury simply started. The trembling stopped. The involuntary daydreams launched themselves like fast-moving ships inside my head.

By the time I arrived at the IPS building I had conceived a myriad violent deaths for myself, most of them revolving around a car bombing. I also realized that I had to either run away from the whole affair or decide to live with this fear. I could allow my imagination to write horror scripts and invent murderous scenarios, and I could continue to work and function. No conscious decision arose from these thoughts; I simply began to do what had become necessary. Orlando was my friend, my colleague, and my comrade. So was Ronni.

I didn't tell Ralph Stavins my fears; he didn't tell me about his. We just set out with clenched jaws, to push as hard as we could to bring the killers to justice, or at least to expose them.

The majority of people we knew and loved, those who worked with us and lived with us and would have to share whatever consequences our efforts brought, those from afar who cared about justice and who loved Chile, those in power who had liberal views, who knew Orlando, the religious people who wept and said that a great sin had been committed—all these people, as with one voice, told Ralph Stavins and me that we were absolutely crazy to attempt an investigation of these murders. All had different reasons, but all agreed that nothing but more pain and suffering would result from our efforts. Only Isabel Letelier did not object. She wasn't optimistic about our chances for success, but at least she did not disagree with our plans. That was all we needed. We ignored the rest because we did not like their advice. Our reasons were ethical and political. We felt we had to pursue the killers in any and every way that we could.

THE CHILEAN MILITARY GOVERNMENT delivered its reaction through *El Mercurio.* An unsourced story from Washington on September 23 alleged that Letelier and his two friends were on their way to bomb the Chilean Embassy when the explosion occurred.

Officially, the Foreign Ministry condemned the assassination as a "regrettable and despicable act of terrorism." Its statement added: "It is clear to any normal person that what has happened can only harm the Chilean government, because it immediately becomes part of the propaganda campaign of the Soviet Union against us."

El Mercurio headlined the Washington memorial service for Letelier as "North American Extremism at Letelier's Funeral." In an editorial a few days later, the newspaper noted that Letelier had spent many months in a Chilean prison, and that if Chile had wanted him dead, "there was time enough to carry out the deed in our own territory without notoriety and with complete impunity."

Another statement from DINACOS, the presidential press office, noted that the assassination of "Mr. Carlos Prats and his wife" and the shooting of Bernardo Leighton also occurred during the UN General Assembly, and that the Leighton attack happened the day the Chilean foreign minister addressed the assembly. "In view of these facts," the statement continued, "there is no question of coincidence, but rather of a cold and ruthless plan. . . ."

MURDER DOES NOT ALWAYS unify friends and relatives. Letelier's death underlined rather than obscured some of the differences within the Chilean and the American left.

Isabel Letelier, still dry-eyed, emerged beyond her widow's role into that of political leader. While dealing with Gawler's Funeral Home on Wisconsin Avenue where Orlando's body lay in state and handling phone calls and telegrams from around the world, she mediated, arbitrated, and calmed the political disputes that arose around the nature of the memorial service. Firmly, by phone and messenger and in person, she established herself as the final authority.

On Sunday, September 26, several thousand people gathered at a small plaza one block south of Sheridan Circle. Many carried posters with pictures of Ronni and Orlando. Murray Karpen's first public words after learning of Ronni's death were printed beneath his daughter's profile: "Orlando Letelier was fighting the junta in Chile. He accused them of barbaric acts, and to prove they were not barbaric, they murdered him and my daughter." Under Orlando's picture was a quotation from his speech eleven days before his death: "I was born a Chilean, I am a Chilean, and I will die a Chilean. They, the fascists, were born traitors, live as traitors, and will be remembered forever as fascist traitors."

At the head of the march, walking abreast, were Isabel and Fabiola Letelier, Michael Moffitt and the Karpens, and three other women whose loved ones had fallen victims to the junta: Hortensia Bussi, Salvador Allende's widow; Allende's daughter Isabel; and Moy Tohá, widow of José Tohá.

The four Letelier sons and Ronni's two brothers walked alongside Senators George McGovern and James Abourezk, former Senator Eugene McCarthy, and Congressmen George Miller, Tom Harkin, Pete Stark, and John Brademas. Diplomats, exiles, bureaucrats, technocrats, academics, workers, and street people walked together, ten or more abreast. Buses had brought people from other cities.

A man with a deep voice intoned, "Compañero Orlando Letelier . . ."

The crowd responded, "¡Presente!"

The man: "Ahora . . ." (Now . . .)

The crowd: "¡Y siempre!" (And forever!)

The chant was repeated for Ronni and alternated between the two names at a slow, solemn pace.

Only five hundred people were able to squeeze into the cathedral, each one checked at the door. The police and dogs had already inspected the church interior and plainclothesmen were scattered throughout the crowd.

Senator McGovern said from the pulpit, "If Orlando Letelier must die at the age of forty-four and dear Ronni Moffitt must die at the age of twenty-five because of the unbridled power of madmen, then there is no security for any of us."

Controlling his own grief, the IPS board chairman, attorney Peter Weiss, spoke of Ronni Moffitt, who "shared [Orlando's] ideas, his comradeship and his total dedication, but who did not know that this made her a soldier and that Washington, D.C. had become a battlefield." Weiss vowed personally and for IPS "to make the DINA assassins, and their protectors and counterparts around the world wither under the rays of merciless exposure; and to free [Orlando's] beloved Chile from fascist tyranny."

Hortensia Bussi, with a fierceness emanating from her thin voice, declared: "The junta is very much mistaken if it thinks that in assassinating the popular leaders every September, it will break the will to resist and end the battle of the Chilean people."

Inside the church an almost deafening silence reigned as Michael Moffitt rose to speak. "I am finding it difficult to get along without my wife," he began quietly. "Ronni taught us that none of us can shut out the world. . . . If the purpose of the junta is to silence the voice that speaks for a free Chile and for the freedom-loving people everywhere, they have not silenced that voice, but have multiplied it a hundredfold."

Bishop James Rausch concluded the service, speaking of Orlando as one whose voice "sought to proclaim release to the captives and set at liberty the oppressed." He left the altar, and into the profound silence stepped Joan Baez, who began, without accompaniment, to sing "Gracias a la vida" (thanks be to life, which has given me so much). And the tears came at last for Isabel.

AT THE INVITATION of President Carlos Andrés Pérez and Caracas Governor Diego Arias, Isabel and the boys flew to Venezuela to bury Orlando Letelier on Latin American soil. Large crowds of mourners lined the route to the cemetery. Isabel had worked hard to make a political point in two capitals and had succeeded: masses of United States and Latin American citizens had responded to the assassination by public protest and a show of solidarity with the Chilean cause. Events in other cities, organized by Chilean exiles and by indigenous Chilean solidarity groups, also signaled to the junta that the murders of Letelier and Moffitt had aroused worldwide indignation.

For the Chilean exiles who marched, the shouts and slogans also masked the gut-wrenching fear germinating inside them with every new death, every report of torture, every midnight arrest; a sense of defeat and failure tore at them. The conclusion they were forced to draw from Orlando Letelier's assassination pushed even the most modest among the Popular Unity exiles to the terrifying realization: The same could happen to anyone who becomes a public symbol of resistance to Pinochet and his government.

For United States supporters of the Chilean cause, Letelier's assassination meant that their homeland was no longer off limits to the terrorism sponsored by the Pinochet dictatorship. Of Ronni Moffitt's death, each could say, "It could have been me." Every one of the hundreds of Ronni and Orlando's friends and colleagues felt they personally had had a brush with death.

The bombing continued to disrupt the lives of everyone involved and to destroy the veneer of security. "After it happened it seemed as if evil emanated from everywhere," recalled a woman who witnessed what she thought was a terrible wreck on her way to work on September 21. She found out an hour later that it had involved three of her friends and that it was no accident. "I never needed more comfort than in those next days; but I felt too exposed to ask for it up front. . . . We all tried to help each other, but that sense of predictability that you have with friends was obliterated. Looking back, you can see that was the effect of terrorism . . . we knew it firsthand for the first time."

Everyday acts, such as riding in a car, became traumatic. The bombing challenged the very idea of "my car" or "my house"—with the implication not just of possession but of shelter and security. Familiar places became sinister, faces hardly noticed or often seen became objects of suspicion.

The confusion extended to the leaders of IPS. Who exactly was in charge of exactly what areas? Raskin, Barnet, and Landau tried to decide what to do, whom to trust, and how to delegate the added work. No one had known, no one could have known, what a bomb could do before it had really happened. Terrorism had been something read about in the papers, seen in the movies.

Some IPS fellows began to object to the presence of the Chileans in the institute, identifying in them the object that had attracted violence to the institute for the first time in its fourteen years of existence. One fellow spoke in anger about the IPS leadership having "signed us up for a death trip without asking." Some of these same people had risked their lives in the civil rights movement in the South, had faced angry White Citizens Councils, armed Klansmen, and vicious sheriffs. But even the hateful and murderous pique of Southern racists somehow paled before the car bombing on Embassy Row. An act of terrorism directed by an actual government in power signifies a brutal audacity that few felt capable of confronting.

The murders were successful—at first.

9

THE INVESTIGATION

ON THE AFTERNOON of the assassination Eugene Propper returned to his fourth-floor office in the U.S. District Court building and called Captain Joe O'Brien, head of the Homicide Division of the Washington, D.C., Metropolitan Police. He assumed that the Letelier-Moffitt murders, like the dozens of other felonies he had handled, the robberies, rapes, homicides, frauds, and drug cases, came under D.C. Police jurisdiction.

Captain O'Brien gave him a rapid, fact-studded description of the crime, gleaned from radio reports of officers at the scene. No one had been seen leaving the scene; there were no obvious explanations as to who had set off the bomb or how. O'Brien promised to send over written reports.

By mid-afternoon, Propper began to realize that the murders had international overtones, and that the FBI would be involved because Letelier, as a former Chilean ambassador, came under a special federal statute protecting diplomatic personnel. As he called professionals and friends in government agencies around Washington and read reports as they came in, a bewildering cacophony of buzzwords began to engulf him: Communists, Allende, Marxist government, CIA role, military coup, concentration camps, torture, human rights, DINA, friendly intelligence service, IPS, left-wing think-tank, comsymps, political assassination.

Having lost only one felony case at trial, Gene Propper had

earned a reputation for relentless energy fueled by ambition, a swift, impetuous kind of intelligence, and a lawyer's instinct for useful fact. He was brash, irreverent, ambitious. He carried himself with an almost insolent air, redeemed from outright arrogance by spontaneous friendliness. Outside the courtroom, he peppered his conversation with hyperbole and sarcasm.

Propper's small, drab, institutionally painted office had acquired the easygoing, cluttered look of a college dorm. Doonesbury cartoons taped to the wall above his desk and a drooping plastic basketball hoop affixed to a wall above the wastebasket served as contrasting decor to the filing cabinet with a combination safe lock near the door.

Although his beard and his motorcycle gave him a slightly unconventional image, Propper was an apolitical man who occasionally expressed vaguely liberal views about race and civil liberties. The Washington U.S. Attorney's Office, to which he felt unabashed loyalty, also offered unique experiences in that its major cases involved both federal and local law, and Propper, like most young prosecutors, saw his job as a career stepping stone. But this case fascinated him from the outset. He was angry when he saw the official police photographs of the two victims.

On September 22, Propper met for a strategy-planning session with Joe O'Brien from D.C. Police and Carter Cornick from the FBI Washington Field Office. Propper told the investigators that he would take a direct part in coordinating the investigation. He worked out jurisdictional questions with the two law enforcement agencies, which, in Washington's unique federal-local legal amalgam, often find themselves in competing roles.

"Assassination" had not yet become part of the official investigative vocabulary, but O'Brien agreed to defer to the FBI if political motives began to predominate or carried the case abroad where D.C. Police had no operational capacity. In the meantime, he said, the murder of Ronni Moffitt fell exclusively within D.C. Police jurisdiction, and his department would continue a full-scale investigation while maintaining liaison with the FBI.

Cornick noted that either of the victims could theoretically have been the target. Motive? Passion. They had found preliminary indications that Letelier was involved in a love affair and until recently had been separated from his wife. Ronni and Michael Moffitt both had former boyfriends and girlfriends who required routine checking. Letelier and Moffitt had bank records and insurance policies to be checked out.

The three investigators, trained in crime-busting, followed the traditional "rule-out" method. None of them had anything but vague impressions of recent Chilean history, but what they learned during the first twenty-four hours after the murders convinced them that an understanding of those events might hold the key to the case.

Propper ordered books and articles on the Allende government. The CIA kept cropping up. He learned that DINA—that word repeated by Michael Moffitt and the IPS people—was the secret police whose reputation for brutality had earned Chile condemnation by the UN Human Rights Commission the year before. He read about MIR, the Chilean revolutionaries who advocated armed struggle, and, in the Church Committee reports, about United States involvement in undermining the Allende government, about CIA support of the right-wing groups that killed General René Schneider. If DINA or another Chilean intelligence agency were involved in the assassination as charged by Letelier's associates, Propper concluded, the investigation would necessarily run in tandem with—or afoul of —the Central Intelligence Agency.

Propper introduced the case to an already convened federal grand jury. The FBI began a systematic search for suspects. The filing section sifted through past reports and leads on groups and individuals known to use bombs. From the first week, the search focused on Cuban exile groups who had a history of bombing. Thick dossiers and memorandums soon accumulated on Propper's and Cornick's desks.

Early editorial comment offered predictable cries of outrage and regret, but uncharacteristically the conservative *Washington Star* pointed its accusing finger at Chile, then wagged it at the United States government:

This whole chain of events began, of course, with the fall of the Allende regime, in whose undermining the U.S. had played a covert role. There is a lesson there if only this country and its leaders would heed it. To the extent that we interfere illegally in the internal political affairs of other nations, we assume responsibility to the same extent for the lamentable aftermath.

But another note also appeared in news stories and editorials. Respectfully muted at first, the theory was floated that left extremists had killed Letelier to create a martyr. Chile had been trying to improve its human rights image in recent months, the *New York Times* said, and it was "difficult to believe" that Chile's government was involved. The editorial posed as an open question whether Letelier's murder had been committed "by the government of Chile or by leftist extremists who will stop at nothing to heap discredit" on the Chilean junta.

Senior officials at the State Department, in internal memorandums analyzing possible implications of the case for United States policy, emphasized the friendly partnership between the United States and Chile. For most of them, it precluded the possibility that an agency of Chile's military government would perpetrate a crime of violence on United States soil. Instead, State Department Chile experts stressed that the harm done to Chile's government by the assassination and charges of DINA participation exceeded any conceivable benefit that could be gained by the elimination of a critic like Letelier.

A Defense Intelligence Agency cable September 28 said in part:

Santiago had taken away the former ambassador's citizenship on 17 September [*sic*] and was known to be making inquiries into the nature of his activities and those of his interest group. . . . It is difficult to pin the blame on Santiago at this point for several reasons. The reach of DINA—cited as responsible—almost certainly (80 percent) does not extend to the United States. Chilean image-building received a severe setback by the killing, something that planners of the attempt would have foreknown and considered. Moreover, the event occurred, as had two previous attempts, during the convening of the

UNGA [UN General Assembly] in New York—poor timing
for a Chilean attempt. Chile will attempt to ride out the storm
of protest, but its position in the UN has likely been damaged.
The incident may never be fully explained, or the culprits
identified to the satisfaction of Chile's critics.

The Marxists were considered more likely suspects. By killing
Letelier they had created a martyr, a focus of outrage against the
Chilean government. "Letelier has hurt the Chilean junta more dead
than alive," became a stock phrase at State. The proximity of the
explosion to the Chilean Embassy and the fact that the assassination
occurred on the opening day of the UN General Assembly were cited
as proof that the Chilean government was the victim and not the
perpetrator of the crime.

During the week following the crime, as he made the rounds of
other government agencies and talked to representatives of the Chilean Embassy and the pro-junta Chilean community in Washington,
Propper heard the martyr theory over and over. Some of Letelier's
former colleagues at the Inter-American Development Bank even
provided anecdotes of leftist animosity toward Letelier.

Special Agent Carter Cornick of the FBI heard the same drum-
beat. Some senior FBI officials referred to Letelier and the IPS as
"pinkos" and "commie preverts." They dropped suggestions to Cornick to direct the investigation at the American left and Chilean
exiles. Cornick, a staunch anticommunist, resisted.

Saul Landau and Ralph Stavins set out to conduct an independent investigation on behalf of IPS. They felt their efforts were
needed to monitor the official investigation, to keep it on the track
leading to DINA. More than providing clues and leads, they intended to make United States investigators understand the political
context of the assassination, to tread the fine line between cooperation with and criticism of the United States effort.

*We started with far more general knowledge than the FBI. We
knew what DINA had done inside Chile because we had met
torture victims and heard countless tales of arrest, harassment,
imprisonment, and murder from victims and their relatives.*

The pattern of attacks on and threats against Chilean exiles in other countries convinced us that DINA also operated abroad.

Press clippings and information gathered from Chilean exiles told us that both journalists and police in Argentina had suspected DINA in the car bombing of General Carlos Prats and his wife in the fall of 1974, and several European reporters had named DINA as a likely suspect in the nearly fatal shooting in Rome of Bernardo Leighton and his wife in October 1975. Other material alluded to DINA attempts against leading Chilean Popular Unity and Christian Democratic leaders in Costa Rica and in several European countries. From this we felt secure in leveling our charges. We left open the possibility that a paramilitary group like Patria y Libertad or a rival intelligence service from the Chilean Air Force or Navy might also have had motive and capability to kill Letelier on foreign soil. From discussions with former Chilean military officers, however, about the rigid military command structure we had no doubt that Pinochet himself had to have known about and authorized the hit.

I had met Carter Cornick at Isabel Letelier's house on the night of the assassination. When we insisted that one of us or an attorney sit in on each interview the FBI conducted with any of our people, Cornick looked shocked. Absolutely not. Against all procedure. We remained adamant, accusing him personally of having tapped our phones, opened our mail, rifled our garbage. He shook his head, confused. "I don't know anything about that," he said, "but I'll tell you one thing. We're on the same side in this one." We probed him to explain this elliptical reference. He looked me straight in the eye: "Saul"—I had to decide whether or not to take offense at his taking the liberty of using my first name—"I want to get the people who did this. I want all of them. And I can promise you that we'll go wherever we have to go to get them." His tie was loose; a tuft of hair had fallen over his forehead. He pursed his lips to emphasize his determination. He swore that he had no connection with anything in the past between the FBI and IPS, that he was nothing

*more than a criminal investigator assigned to the case. I be-
lieved him.*

*I could not project my stereotype of the FBI agent as both
a symbol and an embodiment of persecution onto the real-life
figure of Carter Cornick. He answered our questions about
what was known on the case, mostly with "I don't know," and
agreed to allow an IPS person to stand outside the door of the
interview room in case the person being interviewed felt the FBI
agents were asking improper questions. As Cornick talked
about the horror of the crime, I no longer saw J. Edgar Hoover
and his apparatus in front of me: I saw and heard a man who
I thought was an honest cop.*

*We developed sources in Miami and New York to look for
two things: Cuban exile groups and individuals with clear and
overt connections to Chile, and Cuban exiles with bombing
histories. It became important to maintain close and friendly
ties with Eugene Propper, so we had long phone conversations
with him, visited his crowded office, and kept track as best we
could of his whereabouts. We fed him the information we received from our own sources and told him our theories. We
learned to persist in the face of his put-downs and overt indifference to our information. Our cooperative strategy faced another
problem. We assumed that all of the Chile-Cuban exile-terror-
ist ring connections were established with CIA knowledge, if not
its active blessing. If the CIA had penetrated DINA, and also
possessed the most elementary knowledge of the right-wing terrorist operations, most likely it would have had warning or
actual knowledge of the Letelier-Moffitt assassinations. If it
had foreknowledge, it had obviously withheld it. Why? It defied
logic that the CIA would allow a bombing assassination in the
heart of Washington, D.C. If they did, it was unlikely that the
FBI would pursue them. So, should we trust the FBI to solve
this case? Our only answer was obvious: The official United
States government cannot afford to allow acts like the Letelier-
Moffitt killings to occur—and especially not in Washington—
even if renegade CIA types are involved. But would the FBI
have the will to take on the national security apparatus that we*

assumed already knew who did the murders? If the FBI had support from Congress, and pressure from the press and the public, they stood an outside chance. We decided to gamble on that long shot and help to provide that support and pressure.

The FBI made the investigation a "special." They gave it the code name CHILBOM. The status gave Cornick and Propper the authority and the budget to command immediate action by hundreds of FBI agents across the United States. Preliminary laboratory reports crossed Propper's desk as experts began the tedious examining and analyzing of the wreckage of Letelier's car and the contents of scores of plastic bags containing debris swept and vacuumed from the ground at Sheridan Circle. The media pressed for indications of progress in identifying the kind of bomb and method of detonation. Propper and Cornick imposed even stricter than usual secrecy on the investigation and refused all on-the-record comment.

In the end the experts concluded that the bomb that killed Letelier and Moffitt was the work of a skilled and experienced technician, not an amateur. The assassin had shaped the charge—either TNT or plastic—so that its force blew upward to ensure that Letelier, the driver, would receive its maximum impact. Ronni Moffitt, they believed, was not the intended target, but rather the victim of stray pieces of shrapnel. The investigators found no remnants of conventional fuse and detonating equipment, but identified pieces of Radio Shack–brand batteries and gnarled brass pins. The FBI lab men concluded that most probably a remote-control signal had detonated the bomb—some kind of radio device. The face and body of a large pocket watch and a minute hand found in the area at first baffled the investigators. But the watch face was almost unscarred by the blast; it could not have been part of the bomb. Someone close to the investigation leaked the finding of the watch parts to the *Washington Post,* along with the interpretation that the bomb used a "relatively unsophisticated timing device."

The *Post*'s story of September 25 reported accurately that the investigation was now focusing on Letelier's last days and hours. The agents hoped that, as in the majority of murder cases in which the victim knows his assailant, Letelier's life and work would provide the hidden answers to solving the crime. Inside a grey-black Samsonite briefcase found in the bombed car, intact except for a single shrapnel hole, investigators found Letelier's working papers, address books, schedules, letters, a tape recording, a black sleeping mask, aspirin. The contents provided a rough personal and political biography of Letelier's last months of life.

Cornick decided to have FBI agents interview each person listed in the address book. Within days, scores of persons received phone calls and visits from FBI agents. Some agents, following methods learned in the J. Edgar Hoover FBI, probed for details of leftist activity and contacts. Some implied that the left had a motive for killing Letelier.

One of Cornick's first steps in the investigation was to contact an official at the U.S. Immigration and Naturalization Service, whose offices on 4th and I Streets were a short drive from FBI headquarters. If Chilean extremists or secret police agents had entered the country to kill Letelier or contract others to do the killing, Cornick reasoned, their names would appear in the computer files of the INS listing all foreigners entering the United States. INS prepared a computer printout listing almost 1,000 names of Chileans entering or leaving the United States from September 2 to September 22 and of non-Chileans who had traveled from Chile to the United States. Cornick assigned agents the task of checking the names.

The IPS investigators thought they had found the killers. A switchboard operator in a New York hotel had contacted Chilean exiles with hot information. A Chilean man and woman had checked into the hotel in mid-August; two other Chileans joined them on September 15. The four made phone calls to Chile and Costa Rica and to a number in Washington, D.C. Five days before the assassination, all four checked out—at 3:27 A.M.

One of the numbers called in Chile was traced by IPS investigators to a right-wing family whose son had been involved in the Schneider assassination. One of the Chileans, naval officer Herman Ferrer, held militant right-wing views. Another naval officer, Ivan Petrovich, was attached to DINA, Chilean exiles claimed. The number of persons—four—coincided with the report of four suspected

DINA agents arriving on Lufthansa, although the dates of arrival differed. The hotel clues also seemed to jibe with the report from Letelier's maid that on the day of the assassination she had seen three men and a woman sitting in a car outside the Letelier house.

The FBI promised to check out the leads. "Nope," Cornick told Landau a few weeks later. "There's funny stuff happening at the hotel and with the military mission, but it's not connected to the bombing."

SPECIAL FBI AGENT ROBERT SCHERRER had covered the Southern Cone of South America since 1972. His title at the U.S. Embassy in Buenos Aires—legal attaché—was leftover but no longer secret "cover" from the old spy days, when the FBI maintained an intelligence network in Latin America and bore the responsibility of monitoring pro-Nazi activity there during World War II. Now, the CIA having taken over the FBI's spying operations abroad, the legal attaché's task involved tracing drug traffic and tracking down fugitives. But Scherrer did more: he was an intelligence specialist. From Buenos Aires, he covered Argentina, Chile, Paraguay, Uruguay, and Bolivia, maintaining liaison with the police and intelligence services in each country. He had made it his business to get to know Chile's Manuel Contreras.

Wiry, five and a half feet tall, red-haired, and soft-spoken, Scherrer in appearance reflected the Irish origins of his mother. His toughness came from his strict German father, and from growing up lower-middle-class and Catholic in Brooklyn. J. Edgar Hoover's FBI recruited him when he was eighteen, gave him a job as a filing clerk, and sent him to Fordham University to get a law degree. FBI work was more than a job for Scherrer; it approached a religious vocation.

He fielded the cables from Washington after the assassination, and went to work. He asked around, informally, at the Argentine military intelligence services. Within a week, he struck pay dirt. A source came to Scherrer and said he was sure killing Letelier was the result of a "wild Condor operation."

"Those lunatics in Santiago are going to ruin everything. This will hurt us all, tremendously. If you're talking about MIR, Tupamaros, stuff like that, it's all right with me. I don't care. But the other stuff is bad business—going way outside into Europe and other countries. Condor was a good operation; this will ruin it."

The source, a veteran intelligence officer, dealt with murder and torture as daily routine. Scherrer knew the man's position and knew that it gave him access to reliable and sensitive information. The officer spoke to Scherrer with anger in his voice. Scherrer's expression remained friendly. He drew out the source, savoring the experience, one of those rare, intimate moments in intelligence work when one agent passes hard, hot information to another.

So they called it Condor. Scherrer told the source that he had heard vague reports about exchange of intelligence data, about a computer setup in Santiago. Only phase one, said the source: interchange and storage of data on Marxist terrorists. The real purpose of Condor was phase two and phase three. Scherrer's source said he had heard that phase three operations were under consideration for Portugal and France, but he didn't know of any actual phase three assassinations. He said he had reason to believe Letelier may have been the first victim.

Scherrer listened, storing the information for recall later. He did further checking. On September 28, one week to the day after the Letelier assassination, he sent his top-secret report to Washington.

SUBJECT: Operation Condor,
        possible relation to Letelier assassination.

Operation Condor is the code name for the collection, exchange and storage of intelligence data concerning leftists, communists and Marxists which was recently established between the cooperating services in South America in order to eliminate Marxist terrorists and their activities in the area. In addition Operation Condor provides for joint operations against terrorist targets in member countries. . . . Chile is the center for Operation Condor, and in addition it includes Argentina, Bolivia, Paraguay and Uruguay. Brazil has also tentatively agreed to supply input for Operation Condor.

A third and more secret phase of Operation Condor in-

volves the formation of special teams from member countries
to travel anywhere in the world to non-member countries to
carry out sanctions, [including] assassinations, against terrorists or supporters of terrorist organizations from Operation
Condor member countries. For example, should a terrorist or
a supporter of a terrorist organization from a member country
be located in a European country, a special team from Operation Condor would be dispatched to locate and surveil the
target. When the location and surveillance operation has terminated, a second team from Operation Condor would be
dispatched to carry out the actual sanction against the target.

Theoretically, one country would provide false documentation
for the assassination team, which would be made up of agents from
a different country. The Letelier assassination, Scherrer concluded,
"may have been carried out as a third phase of Operation Condor."

Scherrer learned that Manuel Contreras—"Condor One"—had
personally provided the inspiration and organizational impetus for
the creation of Condor, which had begun to function in late 1975.
Chile had provided much of the financing for Condor in its formative
stages, and had conducted a series of organizational meetings in
Santiago at DINA expense. Chile also provided the system's elaborate computer capacity and acted as center of operations.

The purpose of Condor was to prevent leftist resistance leaders
from one country from taking refuge in another. Condor's member
intelligence services had permission to execute suspected leftists from
any Condor country. On request, leftists arrested in one country
would be turned over secretly to their native country for interrogation and execution.*

· · ·

---

*Most examples of Condor operations involved phase two, or two-country operations. They
included the arrest of Chilean MIR leader Edgardo Enríquez in Uruguay in April 1976 and
his subsequent secret execution in Chile; the assassination in Argentina in June 1976 of former
President Juan Torres of Bolivia; and the assassination of two Uruguayan congresspersons in
Argentina in late 1976. The CIA later told a Senate investigating committee it had headed off
Condor operations in Portugal and France by informing authorities.

IN THE FIRST WEEK after the assassination, Cornick took the unusual step of cabling all outlying bureaus to ask agents' opinions and analyses of "where he should look." Agents in the New York and New Jersey area and in Miami put their networks of informants to work and cabled Cornick with what "the street" was saying about the assassination. The stool pigeons and informants provided a remarkably coherent picture. They pointed to Cuban exile groups, and to one group in particular, the Cuban Nationalist Movement. Some of the informants said they had heard that Guillermo and Ignacio Novo were involved.

Agents digging through their memories and files discovered a past incident of probable Cuban exile–Chilean collaboration in the 1975 assassination attempt against Bernardo Leighton in Rome. Zero had sent communiqués to Miami news media claiming credit for the wounding of Leighton and his wife and for killing Cuban exile leader Rolando Masferrer. Both attacks had occurred in October 1975. The FBI gave credence to the Zero communiqué about Leighton because it provided details of the attack that only the assassins could know. A powerful bomb placed under his car had blown off Masferrer's legs; the bomb was similar in power and placement to the one that killed Letelier and Moffitt. On the basis of the files, Cornick and his men reasoned that the Leighton attack had been a "contract" from the Chilean military government and that Zero had served as Chile's hired gun. The FBI's best information had it that the Cuban Nationalist Movement used the name Zero for terrorist operations and that its members included CNM chief Guillermo Novo, his brother Ignacio, and a turncoat member of the revolutionary Cuban army, José Dionisio Suárez, who had gained the nicknames "El Cepillo" (The Brush) and "Charco de Sangre" (Pool of Blood) for his work in carrying out executions since the revolutionaries' victory.

TWO WEEKS AFTER the assassination it became evident that the murders would not be solved quickly. Propper, in reports to the office of Attorney General Edward Levi, indicated that the FBI had narrowed its investigation down to political motives, and that it would likely spill over beyond United States borders. He informed his superiors around October 2 that the FBI had uncovered leads pointing to DINA or another Chilean intelligence agency. Allegations that the Pinochet regime had instigated the assassination had no place in the official administration picture of Chile, and official "spokesmen" took care not to link the two publicly. Behind the scenes, however, the problem had to be faced: to press for an investigation that might show a Chilean role in the killings. A second problem: Should the CIA assist in the investigation? And if so, to what extent?

Attorney General Levi argued that an all-out effort to solve this heinous crime would become an important first step in healing the deep wounds left by Watergate and Vietnam. It would help restore public faith in the government bureaucracies, Levi asserted, if all government agencies could work together efficiently to solve this case.

The Justice Department and the CIA struggled to define mutually acceptable ways of working together. What Justice needed and what the CIA feared amounted to the same thing: information that would find its way into court, into public scrutiny.

The CIA's charter allowed it to protect information that might reveal "sources and methods." Moreover, a recent executive order growing out of the Senate investigations of CIA abuses prohibited the CIA from gathering "domestic intelligence." The prohibition extended to collecting foreign intelligence that would be used in a domestic criminal case. The CIA was in liaison with the FBI, the bitter rivalry of the J. Edgar Hoover years having healed, but the CIA took the position that its business was intelligence and not law enforcement. It further maintained that if its Latin American stations provided information in the Letelier case and this became known, it could destroy CIA ties to all Latin American intelligence services.

Finally, the CIA was leery about cooperation because, according to its "worst case" scenario, the investigation might reveal that someone the CIA had worked closely with in Chile in the past was directly involved in the assassination. The prosecution of that person or persons would inevitably result in the disclosure of "national security" information. A Chilean culprit, moreover, would be in a position to blackmail the United States by threatening to tell about CIA activities in Chile.

On October 4, J. Stanley Pottinger, assistant attorney general for civil rights, and Eugene Propper met with CIA Director George Bush and CIA General Counsel Anthony Lapham to hammer out a solution to the problem of CIA cooperation. Bush said the agency was willing to help if Pottinger and Propper could "solve his problem" about the executive order banning domestic intelligence gathering. In the course of their discussion of developments in the case, the subject of Scherrer's discovery of Operation Condor came up. Bush said that if Attorney General Levi would write him a letter requesting that the CIA initiate an investigation of Operation Condor, they would have a solution to the quandary about CIA cooperation. The existence of an international hit squad with the capability of operating on United States turf, he said, was definitely a serious matter of national security within the realm of the CIA's mandate. He foresaw no legal problem in turning over to the FBI the by-products of such a CIA effort.

Over the next few days, Pottinger arranged for the presidential order, and he and Propper ironed out the details of a Justice-CIA agreement for secret, circumscribed cooperation. The CIA would provide "relevant" information from CIA files, but Justice could not use the information in court unless it had independently obtained it from a separate source. In case the outcome of the investigation turned on a particular piece of CIA information or a CIA witness, the decision to use the information would be made by the president.

Propper felt more than satisfied; he was impressed. He had become a member of a very special club. CIA couriers began to deliver to the FBI and then to his office stacks of documents with top-secret classifications. Much of the material dealt with Chilean leftists suspected of being terrorists. But the CIA withheld from Propper the information that Deputy Director Vernon Walters, a few weeks before the assassination, had learned about a covert mission to Washington by two Chilean intelligence officers using the names Juan Williams and Alejandro Romeral. Director Bush had personally handled the cable from Ambassador George Landau reporting on the Chileans' projected trip and had discussed with Walters what action to take. Nor was Propper told that the CIA had received a telephone call in late August 1976 establishing the presence of agents Romeral and Williams in Washington. According to a source with personal knowledge, Bush made no mention of the mysterious Chilean agents or of his discussions with Walters at the meeting with Propper.

Instead of providing the information it possessed that pointed to Chile, the CIA became a public advocate of the martyr theory and for the view that DINA was innocent of the Letelier-Moffitt murders. In the coming weeks, the CIA slant on the case received prominent coverage in the major news media. *Newsweek*'s "Periscope" column for October 11 said:

> After studying FBI and other field investigations, the CIA has concluded that the Chilean secret police were not involved in the death of Orlando Letelier . . . . The agency reached its decision because the bomb was too crude to be the work of experts and because the murder, coming while Chile's rulers were wooing U.S. support, could only damage the Santiago regime.

In a story headlined "LEFT IS ALSO SUSPECT IN SLAYING OF LETELIER," *Washington Star* reporter Jeremiah O'Leary wrote:

> Probers are not ruling out the theory that Letelier might just as well have been killed by leftist extremists to create a martyr as by rightist conspirators. It was pointed out by several officials, however, that Chile's rightist junta had nothing to gain and everything to lose by the murder of a popular and peaceable Socialist leader at a time when Chile's financial problems were coming up for review in Washington.

The *New York Times* reported on October 12:

> [Ford Administration] intelligence officials said it appeared that the FBI and the Central Intelligence Agency had virtually ruled out the idea that Mr. Letelier was killed by agents

of the Chilean military junta. . . . [They] said they understood DINA was firmly under the control of the government of Gen. Augusto Pinochet and that killing Mr. Letelier could not have served the junta's purposes. . . . The intelligence officials said a parallel investigation was pursuing the possibility that Mr. Letelier had been assassinated by Chilean left-wing extremists as a means of disrupting United States relations with the military junta. . . .

On November 1, the *Washington Post* reported:

CIA officials say . . . they believe that operatives of the present Chilean military junta did not take part in Letelier's killing, according to informed sources, CIA Director Bush expressed this view in a conversation late last week with Secretary of State Kissinger, the sources said. What evidence the CIA has obtained to support this initial conclusion was not disclosed.

10

TWO NAMES
IN THE FILES

JUST AFTER 1:00 P.M. on October 6, a Cubana Airlines DC-8 took off from Barbados' Seawell Airport en route to Kingston and Havana. Once a week Cubana flight 455 journeyed between Havana and Georgetown, Guyana, stopping at Trinidad-Tobago, Barbados, and Kingston. The flights, begun in 1972, symbolized a break in Cuba's isolation from its Caribbean neighbors. Among the plane's seventy-three passengers and crew, twenty-four young members of Cuba's fencing team were celebrating their gold medals won in competition in Venezuela a few days earlier.

Two men who deplaned in Barbados had left small packages hidden on the plane. One of them placed a phone call from a hotel lobby to Caracas, Venezuela. A hotel clerk listening in remembered a cryptic phrase: "The bus is full of dogs."

On board flight 455 the pilot turned off the No Smoking sign as the plane ascended over a calm, hot Caribbean. At Seawell's control tower, nine minutes after takeoff, the Cubana pilot's voice broke into the routine exchange of messages:

"Seawell. Seawell. CU-455. We have an explosion on board. We're descending fast . . . We have fire on board . . . Request immediate landing permission." From the ground horrified spectators watched smoke pouring out of the plane. Then a second bomb blew up on board. "Shut the door!" the pilot shouted to one of the crew members. "Total emergency," he told the tower. Toxic fumes poured into the cabin, the plane's nose dipped, and the DC-8 with seventy-three people crashed into the Caribbean some eight miles from the shore.

No one survived.

Hernán Ricardo and Freddy Lugo, the two men who had left the plane in Barbados, made their way back to Trinidad on another flight. That evening the *Miami Herald* received a message from a man with a Spanish accent who said he represented "El Condor." He claimed credit for the bombing in the name of the anti-Castro movement. Another call came in to a Miami radio station from a woman who claimed that the bombing had been carried out by "CORU."

In Trinidad, Ricardo telephoned again to Caracas. He wanted instructions. The man who answered the phone told him in a pseudo–code language that he thought the line was tapped. It was. Ricardo and Lugo were arrested by Trinidadian police the day after the bombing. A cab driver had reported their "odd" conversation, as had the hotel operator in Barbados who listened in on their call to Caracas. Ricardo and Lugo later told reporters that the Trinidadian police threatened to kill them if they did not confess immediately. Ricardo and Lugo confessed, and named Orlando Bosch and Luis Posada Carrilles as part of the conspiracy.

News of the bombing unleashed a flood of informers' reports into police agencies throughout the Caribbean and the United States. The dominoes began to fall. In Caracas, DISIP officers arrested Posada, a forty-seven-year-old Bay of Pigs veteran who had parlayed his CIA security training into a job with Venezuela's secret police and later set up his own private detective agency. DISIP then arrested Orlando Bosch, the current *número uno* of the violent Cuban exiles, a kind of Godfather of the exile terrorists.

FBI investigators in Washington working on the Letelier case gave *Washington Star* reporter Jeremiah O'Leary exclusive information—which he published on October 8—that they also wanted Orlando Bosch for questioning in connection with the Letelier assassination. Bosch had founded and organized CORU, a new "umbrella group," in summer 1976 to coordinate Cuban terrorist activities against Castro. He knew who had killed Letelier and Moffitt, the investigators said, and might have played a role in the hit himself.

Ralph Stavins read the news of the bombing and came into Landau's office enraged. "I bet you it's the same gang of Cuban exiles," he said. In the days that followed they called Isabel Letelier's contacts in Venezuela, most of whom were old friends of Orlando. Bosch and CORU, the Venezuelans confirmed, meant the same thing. They referred to a mysterious meeting held in Bonao, a mountain resort in the Dominican Republic.

Stavins and Landau believed that Bosch held the solution to the case. A Venezuelan newsman from *El Nacional* informed them that his paper would report that Bosch had named Guillermo Novo and Ignacio Novo as the authors of the Letelier-Moffitt bombing.* Landau and Stavins phoned Propper to tell him about their findings, and advised him to leave immediately for Venezuela to question Bosch.

On October 11, the U.S. Department of Justice officially requested that Venezuela make Bosch available for questioning in the Letelier case. Reporters began to converge on Caracas, confident that a major story on international terrorism was about to break. The IPS investigators, feeling they were in tandem with the official investigation, perhaps even in the forefront, assembled a thick dossier on Orlando Bosch, and a picture emerged of the compleat terrorist and prime suspect for the Letelier assassination.

Behind thick glasses that slid down the bridge of Bosch's nose blazed a pair of dark, intense eyes. A pediatrician who had taken his residency in Toledo, Ohio, and fought briefly in the Escambray Mountains of Cuba against Batista, Bosch had renounced his medical career and from 1960 on had built a consistent image of himself as the most militant, the hardest, the most zealous and committed of Castro's exiled enemies. The vulnerable look on his round, babyish face, softened further by thick, protruding lips and a puckish mustache, did not fit the stereotype of the modern terrorist. But Bosch had won his terrorist stripes and stars by his deeds. In 1960 the CIA had placed him and his followers in the Everglades for training—for

El Nacional published the Novos' names on October 18.

the Bay of Pigs invasion, they told him. But the agency found him too wild, too uncontrollable and unpredictable, to include in their effort. They left him stranded in Florida while the other exiles disembarked from Puerto Cabezas, Nicaragua, for Playa Girón in Cuba.

When the April 1961 invasion failed, Bosch attacked the CIA and served notice on the United States and Cuban governments that as far as he was concerned, terrorism launched against Cuban targets from United States soil had both a moral and a legal mandate, and that he would use any pretext as cover for his mission.

"We have a right to work for Cuba here or anywhere in the world. If the CIA breaks the laws, and [John F.] Kennedy broke the laws [by ordering the Bay of Pigs invasion], why can't we do the same?" he asked an interviewer in 1966. For a short period of time Bosch worked in a Coral Gables hospital, but it soon became apparent to the hospital director that the hospital was serving as a front for other activities. "He had filled the hospital with explosives," a friend of Bosch told the *Miami Herald* after Bosch had been fired.

By the mid-1960s, Orlando Bosch had launched a series of bombing and commando raids against the Cuban mainland. Police and Coast Guard patrols arrested him several times on a variety of charges. Once police discovered six live aerial bombs in the trunk of his car. Working with less than a dozen dedicated disciples, Bosch conceived grandiose projects that required elaborate financing. He seldom failed to raise the money. Rich exiles found it hard to say no to Orlando Bosch.

By mid-1967, the United States government had become selective about the Cuban exiles they allowed to launch attacks against Cuba from United States bases. Bosch and his group did not fall into the CIA's favored category. In the summer of 1967, federal police caught Bosch and his followers in the act of firing a bazooka at a Polish freighter anchored in Miami harbor. No legal technicalities or "CIA" arguments could get around the testimony of Ricardo Morales, an FBI informer who had penetrated Bosch's group. The exiled pediatrician served four years in prison. He still had six years of his ten-year sentence left when he was paroled in 1972.

Bosch emerged from prison angrier and more militant than ever. The United States, at the instance of Henry Kissinger, had signed an anti-hijacking treaty with Cuba in 1973. To Bosch, this was further evidence of United States betrayal of the holy war against Castro. Bosch began to look for sponsors among more resolute anti-Marxist governments. He set off on a two-year peregrination of Latin America, and in so doing violated his parole.

He called his new organization Cuban Action, and launched a fund-raising drive to raise $10 million—$3 million to contract for the assassination of Castro, and the rest to launch bomb attacks against Cuban consulates and embassies. As special targets of his fury, Bosch singled out institutions that symbolized a thaw in the cold war against Castro. In November 1974 he was arrested in Caracas and linked to two bombings. The United States government, informed of Bosch's arrest, declined Venezuela's offer to expel him to serve the rest of his sentence in the United States.

Bosch felt at home in Venezuela and hated to move on. Caracas had a large and influential Cuban exile community, and several Bay of Pigs veterans had found jobs in Venezuela's secret police in the 1960s. Bosch's friend Orlando García had been appointed head of DISIP. Another Cuban, Rafael Rivas Vásquez, held the number two post. Luis Posada was still DISIP's chief of operations. Bosch's past and future betrayer, Ricardo "Monkey" Morales, had become a DISIP special agent. All had received CIA training.

Bosch's cronies apologized for arresting him, but warned him that the current political climate in Caracas would not allow him to continue his anti-Castro activities there. After his release he flew to the Caribbean island of Curaçao, and a short time later, on December 3, to Santiago, Chile.

IPS sources had many suspicions but few facts about what Bosch did for the next year and a half in Chile. Landau and Stavins read that he had met personally with Pinochet, and noted that during his stay in Chile, attacks on Cuban diplomatic installations occurred in neighboring Peru and Argentina. According to the *Miami Herald,* Bosch had traveled to other South American countries with Chilean bodyguards.

In February 1976 Bosch made headlines again. Costa Rican police arrested him for plotting to kill Henry Kissinger, who visited
that country on February 24. Costa Rican Foreign Minister Gonzalo
Facio disclosed that Bosch had entered the country on a false Chilean official passport in the name of Héctor Davanzo Cintolesi and
that he had a second mission: the assassination of Chilean MIR
leader Andrés Pascal Allende and his companion, Mary Anne Beausire, who had recently fled a DINA manhunt in Chile.* Again the
United States declined to take Bosch into custody and return him to
prison. He left Costa Rica after a few days of detention and interrogation, and flew to the Dominican Republic in late March. There,
over the next several months, he began to organize a new coalition
to overcome the exiles' long and bitter internecine strife and channel
their collective violence toward a new anti-Castro offensive.

In early June, Miami buzzed with rumors about a large group of
exile heavies converging on Bonao, a mountain resort town in the
Dominican Republic. The alleged organizers of the meeting were
Bosch and Frank Castro, a Cuban exile who had married into an
influential Dominican-based family.† The meeting ended in mid-
June with a consensus for action and the formation of a new group,
CORU, the Commando of United Revolutionary Organizations.‡

Word reached Miami that CORU—which sounds in Spanish like
a rooster's crow—had an impressive membership. Although Bosch's
minuscule Cuban Action group was listed first, CORU included the

---

*The information that led to Bosch's arrest was given to the Costa Rican government by the
U.S. Secret Service, who received it from the FBI. The FBI source was Bosch's old friend
Ricardo "Monkey" Morales.

†Frank Castro's wife was the daughter of retired Admiral César de Windt, an intimate of then
President Balaguer

‡In a prison interview with journalist Blake Fleetwood (*New Times*, May 13, 1977), Bosch said
of CORU: "The Dominican government let me stay in the country and organize actions. I
wasn't going to church every day. We were conspiring there. Planning bombings and killings.
. . . People were coming in and going out. I was plotting with them. . . . the story of CORU
is true. There was a meeting in the Bonao mountains of 20 men representing all different
activist organizations. It was a meeting of all militaty and political directors with revolutionary
implications. It was a great meeting. Everything was planned there. . . . At least we had all
the Cuban revolutionary fighters and leaders together, after 17 years. We decided to upscale
the action after that. We wanted to beat [Castro] or at least make his life impossible."

leaders of the Bay of Pigs veterans' Brigade 2506, the largest and most respected of the exile groups, with almost a thousand active members; Frank Castro's Cuban National Liberation Front (FNLC) and Felipe Rivero's CNM—groups that claimed adherents with long action records.

CORU patterned itself on the Palestine Liberation Organization: ideologically undefined, but united in support of the tactics of world-wide terrorism to focus attention on their struggle to recover their homeland. CORU members accepted the CNM stragegy of "war throughout the roads of the world." Reports filtered through to Miami that CORU had reached a tacit "understanding" with United States authorities. Some informants claimed that CORU had agreed not to carry out any acts of terrorism in the United States; others said the agreement simply restricted CORU from claiming credit for acts of terrorism in the United States. There was no dispute about one fact: the FBI had "covered" the meeting, meaning its informers had penetrated the meeting and the organization. Some sources in Miami said the Bonao gathering and the creation of CORU had the active support of the CIA and at least the acquiescence of the FBI, and that CORU was allowed to operate to punish Castro for his Angola policy without directly implicating the United States government.*

A wave of bombings, killings, and kidnappings swept North and South America, most of which were claimed by CORU or eventually traced to its operations. Up to October 6, the attacks had cost the lives of three Cuban diplomats. On that day, CORU's toll rose to seventy-six dead.† With Orlando Letelier and Ronni Moffitt, seventy-eight had died in less than four months.

---

*The scenario was never confirmed, although several sources in Miami investigative circles told the authors the same basic story in 1979 about the creation of CORU. One source, a veteran of the Miami police's fight against terrorism, said, "The Cubans held the CORU meeting at the request of the CIA. The Cuban groups—the FNLC, Alpha 66, Cuban Power —were running amok in the mid-1970s, and the United States had lost control of,them. So the United States backed the meeting to get them all going in the same direction again, under United States control. The basic signal was 'Go ahead and do what you want, *outside* the United States.' "

†CORU members carried out the following acts of terrorism from July to October 1976:
  July 14: Bombings of the British West Indian Airline Office in Bridgetown, Bar., and of a car owned by the manager of Cubana Airlines in Bridgetown. July 17: Cuban Embassy,

. . .

ATTORNEY MICHAEL TIGAR asked, on behalf of Isabel Letelier, Michael Moffitt, and IPS, for an appointment with Attorney General Edward Levi to discuss the progress of the investigation. The request was granted on October 21. Levi, flanked by Propper and Stanley Pottinger, assistant attorney general for civil rights, for the government, expressed optimism that the case could be solved and gave assurances that recent press leaks exonerating DINA were inaccurate and had not originated in the Justice Department. Facing them were Tigar, Isabel Letelier, Saul Landau, and IPS Codirector Marcus Raskin.

As in Watergate, Tigar said, the investigation should be under the control of a special prosecutor. In addition, he said, the special prosecutor should have the power to subpoena CIA files on Letelier, DINA, and any other relevant persons or matters.

Tigar and Raskin explained their fears that, because of past political persecution of IPS by the Justice Department, the FBI might turn the investigation against the left. The FBI's illegal surveillance and

---

Bogotá, raked with machine-gun fire; bombings of the Air Panama office in Bogotá (Air Panama handled Cubana Airlines business in Colombia) and of a car owned by a Colombian government official in charge of dealings with Cuba. July 22: Unsuccessful kidnapping attempt against Cuban Consul Daniel Ferrer Fernández in Mérida, Mexico, in which kidnappers killed Fernández' companion, Cuban Fisheries official Artaignan Díaz. Two Cuban exiles—Gustavo Castillo and Gaspar Jiménez—who attended the Bonao meeting were arrested in Miami pending extradition. July 9: Bomb exploded in luggage about to be loaded aboard Cubana Airlines flight in Kingston, Jamaica. If the plane had taken off on schedule, the luggage would have been aboard and in the air when the bomb exploded. July 24: Three CNM members (Santana, Gómez, and Chumaceiro) arrested in an attempt to plant a bomb at New York's Academy of Music, where an event celebrating the Cuban Revolution was being held. August 9: CORU claimed credit for kidnapping-murder in Buenos Aires of Cuban Embassy officials Jesús Cejas Arias and Crescencio Galamena Hernández, which the authors learned in 1979 was carried out in conjunction with the Argentine secret police (see Chap. 7, "Target Letelier," p. 197). August 18: Two bombings in Panama, at Tocumán International Airport and in Panama City at offices of Cubana Airlines. September 7: Bombing of Guyanese Embassy in Port of Spain, Trinidad-Tobago. Guyana welcomed Cuban use of its airports to refuel troop planes en route to Angola. September 16: Bombing of anchored Soviet ship *Ivan Shepetkov* in Elizabeth, N.J., claimed by Omega 7. September 21: Bombing killing Orlando Letelier and Ronni Moffitt in Washington, D.C. September 23: Bombing of Palladium Theatre in New York, claimed by Omega 7. October 6: Bombing of Cubana Airlines flight killing 73 persons. CORU claimed credit in communiqués called "war dispatches" for actions July 14, July 17, August 9, September 7, and October 6.

harassment of the institute and the CIA's actions against the Allende government, they said, vitiated those agencies' ability to investigate.

Levi, former president of the law school Raskin had attended, spoke slowly, showing that his words must have been chosen with great care: "My belief is that the most important healing process for this country would be for the regular agencies to solve cases like this. I would be horrified if the investigation became diverted. But there are restrictions on information."

"Given those agencies whose past would give them a motive—" Tigar began, and Levi snapped abruptly, "In those cases we would be particularly vigilant to get the information."

"On the procedural question—" Tigar began again, pushing for a decision on subpoenaing CIA files.

"I can't use subpoena based on the information available right now," Levi replied.

The meeting seemed over when Isabel Letelier spoke: "According to Mr. Propper the idea of a passion crime has been dismissed. Yet he still persists in questioning me about it."

"There was a woman in California. She wasn't interviewed, however, because of bad health," said Propper. "And the questioning on the bank records?" Tigar inquired. "You have them in the briefcase," Isabel interrupted. "Why are you interviewing Maruja del Solar [Letelier's aunt]?"

"I can't be responsible for every FBI agent," said Propper. "You can have the briefcase in two weeks."

In the hall waiting for the elevator, Tigar almost whispered to Propper, "Why not subpoena the CIA?" The elevator bell rang.

Propper looked at Tigar like a teacher repeating a lesson that he assumed the pupil should have learned long ago. "If I issued a subpoena for CIA records and they didn't want to produce them, they'd just say they didn't have them, and then they'd destroy them." The IPS people filed into the elevator and nodded goodbye to Propper.

THE NEXT DAY—though unrelated to the meeting at the Justice Department—a State Department official called in the FBI's liaison officer to offer "something that might be useful in the Letelier investigation." The liaison took with him a memo outlining the information: There was a strange incident in Paraguay a few months ago involving Chilean Army officers named Juan Williams and Alejandro Romeral. They tried to obtain visas to the United States by using Paraguayan passports. The United States ambassador got suspicious and took pictures of the passports, including the page with the men's passport photos. The visas were canceled, but the two men subsequently arrived in Miami August 22 with A-2 diplomatic visas in official Chilean passports.*

Carter Cornick received the memo, and a few days later copies of the passports of Romeral and Williams arrived in his office via State Department courier. Cornick noted the physical descriptions of the two men: Alejandro Romeral, dark hair and eyes, 1.74 meters (5 feet, 10 inches), 26 years old; Juan Williams light hair, blue eyes, 1.89 meters (6 feet, 2 inches), 34 years old. Immediately he checked the names Romeral and Williams against the INS computer list he had received several weeks before. Not finding the names, he ordered an agent to doublecheck with INS whether there was any record in their files to confirm the State Department information. INS answered that its computer listing of the I-94 forms all foreigners must fill out and present to immigration officers on entering and leaving the United States showed no record of Romeral and Williams. Cornick then asked agents of the Miami Field Office to check for reports of the two suspected Chilean agents there. Again he drew a blank. He put the photographs aside. He continued to assign other leads already uncovered in the case higher priority than suspicions about Chilean intelligence officers.

LARRY WACK'S FAVORITE toy as a child was a fingerprinting set. Growing up in Willingboro, New Jersey, Wack was also a cops-and-robbers fanatic, and he always wanted to play the cop. At age twelve, he wrote to J. Edgar Hoover asking how to become an FBI agent. Hoover wrote back and told him what to do, and he did it. After his

---

*Cornick, asked in 1979 about the handling of the Romeral and Williams lead, said he considered the incident "something a little bit unusual, that's all."

high school graduation in 1967, Wack went to Washington and got a clerical job at FBI headquarters. He fit criminology courses at American University around his working hours.

When he graduated from the FBI's academy in September 1975, he walked with a slight swagger, head held high. He talked out of the side of his mouth, and occasionally let his jacket fall open; a holstered service pistol protruded from his belt. Wack had blond, blue-eyed, all-American looks and a smooth, boyish face. He grew a rugged-style blond mustache to toughen the image. But on the job, on the street, Wack *was* tough. He had been working in the New York Field Office's Bomb and Terrorism Squad for only six months when he was assigned to handle the Letelier-Moffitt murders—his first big case.

On October 11, a tall, thin-faced man in blue jeans walked up to Elizabeth Ryden at New York's East Side Air Terminal and said "Hi." Ryden, an airline stewardess, was waiting for the Carey bus to Kennedy Airport to make her flight assignment. An hour later, at a gathering point for stewardesses at Kennedy, Ryden saw the same man walking toward her. He stopped close to her.

"Your little friend had better keep his fucking nose out of Chile's business. Or you won't be so pretty any more. Boom, Boom. You know what I mean?" He looked straight at her a moment longer, then turned and disappeared into the crowd. Ryden noticed that he was balding at the crown of his head. She rushed to a telephone and called her "little friend," who was also her fiancé, Larry Wack.

An exciting assignment became for Larry Wack a personal quest. He commandeered an FBI car and raced to Kennedy Airport. In an American Airlines office, Wack coaxed out of his fiancée a full description of the man. An FBI artist worked with her, and together they arrived at a composite drawing. Wack arranged protection for his fiancée.

He thought back over his dozens of calls and interviews over the twenty days since the assassination. None of them fit Elizabeth Ryden's description of the man who had threatened her. Most of the people he had interrogated belonged to the left, associates of Letelier's. But he had also spoken to the head of the Chilean UN Mission,

Admiral Ismael Huerta, and had asked direct questions about Chile's contacts with Cuban exiles.

Wack shared the general view inside the bureau that if Chileans were involved, it was probably the leftists. Eight formative years with the bureau had taught him to view leftists as enemies. For a time, this attitude showed in his interviews of Chilean exiles. Jaime Barrios and Monica Villaseca of the New York Chile Democrático office told Landau in Washington that Wack's probing amounted to harassment. In early November, Wack dropped into the office of Chile Democrático, near the United Nations, without phoning first. He asked Jaime Barrios, who ran the exile effort in New York, if he could spare a few minutes—"nothing really special." "Do you think," Wack asked, "that the assassination could have been a mistake, meant for someone else?"

"It's possible," replied Barrios.

"Did Letelier have money problems?"

Barrios shook his head.

"How did he live? You know his salary didn't amount to much. Is it possible—this is a wild guess—that he stole money from IPS, and that that somehow resulted in someone killing him?"

"I doubt it," said Barrios, "but I can check on it."

Wack then asked questions about Letelier's personal life. Barrios and Villaseca maintained that they knew nothing about Letelier's private life. Wack also asked questions about Letelier's United Nations contacts.

After Barrios told Saul Landau and Isabel Letelier about the incident, they complained to Cornick and Propper and later to the attorney general. But Cornick assured Landau: "Don't you worry about Larry Wack. That's a helluva good man, and he's doing a helluva job investigating this case. Barrios must be wrong."

Cornick was right. Wack resisted his personal biases and heeded other, more solid leads. He learned that the Bomb and Terrorism Squad had developed information on three other recent bombings and bombing attempts in the New York–New Jersey area. In July, New York police had arrested three young members of the Union City branch of the Cuban Nationalist Movement in the act of planting a bomb outside the New York Academy of Music, where a pro-Castro celebration was being held. On September 16, a bomb planted by a frogman dented the side of a Soviet ship, *Ivan Shepetkov,* in the Elizabeth, New Jersey harbor. Two days after the Letelier assassination, a bomb exploded outside the Palladium Theatre in New York, where a Cuban film was showing. Omega 7 claimed credit for both bombings. The FBI knew that Omega 7 was the clandestine-operations arm of the Union City branch of the CNM.

Wack had picked up and reported to Washington the early "street" information that named the CNM and the Novo brothers as being involved. He had read Cornick's dispatches reporting that terrorist Orlando Bosch had also named the Novos after his arrest in Venezuela.

He sifted through the FBI files on the Novos and the CNM. In one of the folders he found photographs clipped from Cuban exile publications which showed Chilean diplomat Mario Arnello sharing a podium with Guillermo Novo and other top CNM leaders at a benefit rally billed as "Cuba and Chile Against Communism." Beside the podium stood another CNM activist, Jorge Gómez, one of those arrested in the abortive bombing attempt July 24 at the Academy of Music. The rally had taken place just a year before in the hall of Union City's San Rocco's Church, decorated for the occasion with banners and pictures showing twin lightning bolts destroying a hammer and sickle. The photos proved no criminal activity, but cemented a high-level political connection between the Chilean government and the CNM. And Wack already had evidence that CNM members liked to play with bombs.

He shifted his investigative energies from the left to the right. He began to work the streets of Union City. He stopped in the small shops and hung out drinking beer at the Bottom of the Barrel bar. The Cubans almost got used to him. FBI agents had become a part of their lives in the past few years, and Wack was more *simpático* than most. They began to call him the "hound dog," because of his persistence.

During the first week of November, first one, then several exiles agreed to meet Wack secretly in secure locations in New York City. They told similar stories. About a week before the Letelier murder, they said, they saw CNM members hanging around town with a tall, fair-haired man from Chile. One of the informants had seen the man with Alvin Ross and Virgilio Paz at the Bottom of the Barrel late at night. Another said the Chilean had been in Union City before, and that the association with Guillermo Novo and Suárez went back at least a year. One said that he knew at first hand that the blond Chilean was a member of DINA. The man spoke perfect English, with no trace of a Spanish accent, said another.

Wack noted down each description. They agreed in the general outline: blond or light brown hair, over six feet, slim, athletic build, blue eyes, early thirties. Wack persuaded the informants to meet with an FBI artist. The artist drew a composite sketch that they accepted as a fair likeness.

ROBERT DRISCOLL, AS THE State Department's Chile desk man, maintained contact with most of Washington's official Chilean community—the ambassador and his staff, the military attachés, the businessmen, the OAS mission, and the international bureaucrats alternating between government service and jobs at such organizations as the World Bank, the Inter-American Development Bank, and the International Monetary Fund. Driscoll had a problem. One of his Chilean contacts—whom he liked to refer to as sources—had told him an unsettling story with possible ramifications for the recent Letelier-Moffitt killings. The source said that two DINA officers were in Washington about the time of the Letelier assassination, "hanging around the Chilean military mission."

In October 1976 the State Department had issued no directives indicating special interest in the Letelier-Moffitt deaths. No one had asked State Department experts to think of possible leads to turn over to the FBI. And Driscoll, who fielded, sorted, and analyzed cable traffic about Chile at the Andean Area offices on the fifth floor of the main State Department building, had learned in his twelve-year career that unwarranted head-scratching was a decidedly perilous endeavor.

Relations with Chile were good. They had been excellent immediately after the coup, then had undergone a dicey period in 1975 when

Pinochet reneged on a promise to the State Department to let the UN Human Rights Commission visit Chile. In 1976, relations had taken a definite upswing. The morning of the assassination, in fact, a Chilean delegation headed by Finance Minister Jorge Cauas had arrived in Washington for a round of cordial interviews with high State Department officials and top United States bankers. Cauas had made friends with U.S. Treasury Secretary William Simon and arranged Simon's visit to Chile in April, and had impressed Secretary Kissinger when Kissinger visited Chile a month later. Cauas, in the State Department's opinion, was a man of the old school, a man who could be trusted to keep his word. And Cauas assured them that the ascent of "moderate" civilians like himself to posts previously monopolized by erratic military men and fanatic rightists meant an improvement in the human rights situation in Chile.

Driscoll looked to the policies formulated by those above him for clues on how to handle the sensitive information he had received. Secretary Kissinger had announced to the press on October 15, "We have seen no evidence yet as to who was behind this assassination." Driscoll had also received clippings from *Newsweek,* the *New York Times,* and the *Washington Star* quoting "intelligence sources," saying that Chile's DINA had been virtually eliminated as a suspect in the Letelier-Moffitt slayings.

Driscoll's information seemed to contradict these reports. At the very least, he now knew that Chilean intelligence had been conducting a secret mission in Washington at the time of the assassinations. His source had also given him the names of the purported Chilean agents—Juan Williams Rose and Alejandro Romeral Jara—and a tip that the same two men had earlier attempted to enter the United States surreptitiously from Paraguay.

He checked his files and fed the names into the computer. The computer responded: positive. A flurry of cables referring to Chilean officers Romeral and Williams had passed into the Chile desk file in July and August. References existed to cables sent as late as September 15—and, incredibly, September 22, the day after the murders. Working back chronologically, he read them.

The September 22 cable, sent by overnight traffic to Santiago, had actually been composed the day of the assassination. It advised the Santiago consulate not to issue visas to anyone using the names. The September 15 cable, addressed to the U.S. Mission in Paraguay, was a formal certification of revocation for visas granted Romeral and Williams on July 27, 1976, at the U.S. Mission in Asunción. Another cable about the same date informed Washington that U.S. Ambassador to Paraguay George Landau had received from Paraguayan authorities as requested two passports in the names Romeral and Williams, in order to physically revoke the visas stamped in them.

In late August, a brief memo noted that further information had been received by the State Department Visa and Passport Offices. Driscoll didn't bother to check there, but went on. The next item jogged his memory. A hefty manila envelope marked August 6 contained an attached memo on CIA letterhead addressed "To Harry W. Shlaudeman, Assistant Secretary of State for Inter-American Affairs, for DIA." Driscoll remembered receiving the packet and looking at the photos inside. He looked again. The same two faces on the same photos—a dark-haired man with a broad, unlined face and a light-haired, angular-faced man with a short-cropped mustache and goatee. The accompanying memo stated only that the photographs were of "two Paraguayan passports which were recently sent to Washington from Asunción."

Driscoll found Ambassador Landau's original order that a lookout be posted at all ports of entry to the United States for the two men. The messages explained that two Chileans using false identities had tried to obtain visas to the United States from the consulate in Paraguay. One of the cables contained the annotation "reftel" followed by a code number, indicating reference to a telegram sent on July 28 via the top-secret "Roger Channel" directly to the office of Secretary of State Kissinger and bypassing the central State Department communications network. To look at that telegram Driscoll knew he would need special clearance.

Driscoll knew that it was standard for friendly foreign intelligence agents to be allowed to enter the United States using false names and documents. He himself and his predecessors had received visits from Chilean intelligence agents seeking information from the Chile desk.* The unusual factor was that Chilean agents had used passports from a "third country"—Paraguay—rather than Chilean passports for an intelligence mission. Driscoll's new information that the same two agents—or at least two agents using the same two names—had managed to enter the United States and come to Washington despite the lookouts gave him additional grounds for suspicion. In the context of the assassination of Letelier and Moffitt and the ensuing accusations against the Chilean government, the new information was sizzling.

Driscoll knew that in the State Department, the favored interpretation of the assassination was the "martyr theory." He thought twice and even three times before advancing a maverick theory that would fly in the face of official policy. He decided not to make waves. He wrote a memo.

The purpose of the memo was to inform Driscoll's superior, Harry Shlaudeman, about the presence of the two Chilean agents in Washington without placing the incident in the context of the Letelier assassination. Shlaudeman, equally capable of putting two and two together, would decide whether to blow the whistle. If he did not place the "Paraguay incident" into the Letelier-Moffitt murders context, there would be nothing on paper to suggest the possible linkage.

Driscoll sent the memo to Shlaudeman November 11. He explained that the two Chileans, probably army officers, had entered the United States after obtaining visas from the U.S. Embassy in Paraguay, under false pretenses, and after Ambassador Landau had ordered the visas revoked and lookouts placed. He said he heard that "these guys were over at the Chilean Embassy, " ten days earlier and that "they had been there thirty days or so." What he wanted, Driscoll said, was to ask Shlaudeman's opinion on possible courses of action. For example, should the two men be expelled from the country to teach Chile that the United States government would not tolerate such behavior?

*Manuel Contreras and his entourage paid a call to the Chile desk during their visit to Washington in August 1975.

Driscoll's memo was a model of bureaucratic evasion. Nowhere did it mention DINA, or indicate an intention to link Chilean officials to the Letelier assassination. Yet Driscoll had done the correct thing. He had reported a suspicious incident to his superior and recommended action. Let Shlaudeman put on paper that there was circumstantial evidence suggesting Chilean official involvement in the Letelier-Moffitt murders.

Shlaudeman, however, was equally determined to avoid belling the cat. He penned a simple reply: "Bob, don't cancel the visas, but inform the FBI."

Driscoll checked the file again and discovered that a memo on the Paraguay incident had already been turned over to the FBI liaison October 22. He decided that was sufficient notice to the FBI. He ignored Shlaudeman's instructions and simply added his memo to the file.*

CORNICK HAD BEGUN TO put in long working days on the case. His agents in the field chased down hundreds of leads, most of them specious. Cornick sifted through the cabled reports and gleaned those significant enough to call to Propper's attention. Even after Cornick's preliminary selection, he dispatched daily more than one hundred pieces of FBI paperwork to Propper's already cluttered office. Cornick and Propper met frequently, occasionally joined by Donald Campbell, chief of the Major Crimes Division, and E. Lawrence Barcella, deputy chief and also Propper's superior.

The FBI provided Propper with a list of Cuban exiles who had

---

*More than a year later, FBI agents interviewed Driscoll at his new post as consul in Maracaibo, Venezuela. He said he remembered little about the whole affair and could not recall who had given him the information that Romeral and Williams were in Washington. He said he had had "over two hundred contacts" with Chilean sources that month and couldn't remember which one told him about the two army officers.

On another occasion, however, a fellow State Department officer asked Driscoll the same question out of curiosity, intending to congratulate him on his fine work in coming up with what became the major lead in the Letelier-Moffitt case. Driscoll stiffened, and got "officious," the other officer said, and replied that his sources were confidential and that he would reveal that information only through "proper channels if necessary."

traveled to Chile since the military coup, and Propper began calling them before the grand jury. The disgruntled exiles, responding to subpoenas against their will, yielded little new information.

On October 27 Ignacio Novo, then two days later his brother Guillermo, were led before the grand jury. Their answers were consistent: neither had known anyone from DINA; the CNM had dropped out of CORU; the United States was using the Letelier-Moffitt case to persecute the Cuban freedom fighters. Guillermo, asked if he had ever traveled to Chile, took the Fifth Amendment.

BOB SCHERRER KNEW SOME of the Cuban exiles from the mid-1960s when, as a member of the FBI's "Tamale Squad" in New York, he monitored both pro- and anti-Castro activities.* In the weeks following the assassination, Scherrer fed Cornick names of Cubans whose entry into Chile he was able to verify through confidential contact with the Chilean police.†

Scherrer knew the intelligence turf in Latin America—the spies, the agents and double agents, and the complex secret deals between them. He understood the mentality of the Latin American intelligence agents and secret police. They saw themselves fighting a secret war against communism for two decades beneath the façade of changing governments. Often they found they had much more in common and greater reason for loyalty to each other than to their frequently changing political bosses. Scherrer had observed squads of men drifting into outlaw status without its altering their relationships with the rest of the intelligence brotherhood.

Patria y Libertad in Chile—outlaws under Allende—were treated as equals by Brazilian intelligence, and many members became intelligence agents under Pinochet. Argentina's AAA had flourished in an alliance with Argentine intelligence under the weak

*In 1967, the Novo brothers and their CNM cohorts in the New York area had publicly announced plans for massive terrorism against EXPO 67 in Montreal—especially its Cuban exhibition. A special target of Tamale Squad surveillance was Ignacio Novo, then the most active Novo brother.

Peronist government, then found itself out of favor when the military took over in early 1976. Venezuela, with its democratic, vaguely liberal government, could turn its intelligence apparatus over to fanatic right-wing Cuban exiles like Orlando García and Rivas Vásquez, then in turn grant safe haven and false papers to active terrorists like Orlando Bosch. The Cuban exile terrorists—"out" because of the Castro revolution—belonged to the secret Latin American anticommunism club.* Scherrer had followed the vicissitudes of the CIA as it alternately encouraged and discouraged the men on the fringes of intelligence work—torturers, kidnappers, the men who did the dirty work.

Scherrer felt ambivalent about his immersion in the sordid Latin American intelligence atmosphere. He talked and traded jokes with torturers and executioners, appreciating their anticommunism but hating their methods. He had to work with them, to gain their confidence, while clinging to the principle that the ends do not justify the means. He struggled to fight evil, and to touch it without letting it contaminate his soul.

On November 26, Scherrer sent a long analytical report to Washington via diplomatic pouch. He provided evidence from his files and personal experience to support his conclusion: Chile's military government maintained a "special relationship" with the anti-Castro militants, and that relationship included joint murder missions. The cable answered Cornick's early request for agents around the world to share their thoughts and speculations on the Letelier-Moffitt killings. It supplemented Scherrer's report of September 28 on Operation Condor.

Chile had offered the Cuban exile movement the kind of support and encouragement once given by the CIA. Scherrer's sources had described a full program of Chilean-Cuban exile relations that could provide an inviolable base of Cuban exile operations. Pinochet, said

---

*The gangsters and drug dealers also had a place in this sophisticated, changing game. Pinochet turned over to the United States drug enforcement administration a planeload of cocaine dealers rounded up after the coup. Their drug dealing could be blamed on Allende's ousted government. Then Pinochet's right-hand man, Contreras, could set up his own men with DINA protection in the same cocaine factories and shipping points. The anti-Castro Cubans had a piece of the action. The enormous profits went to supplement DINA's clandestine budget. The Cubans' share went into individual pockets and to the anti-Castro cause.

these sources, had committed his government to recognize a Cuban government-in-exile based in Chile. Such diplomatic recognition, even by one country, brought with it the right to wage war against Cuba and to seek arms and allies from other anticommunist nations. Orlando Bosch was the man who had elicited this commitment from Pinochet. He had lived more than a year in Chile. According to Scherrer's exile sources, Pinochet had promised to accept Bosch as president of the Cuban exile government. Some activities had already begun: Chile was providing arms, explosives, and false documents to the Cuban exiles. Safe haven for fugitives under prosecution for terrorist activities had been given Bosch and several others.

Chile promised to establish a training camp and provide military and intelligence instruction. Some of the exiles were taken to a large, secure farm south of Santiago to a site that had been especially reserved for their camp.

Scherrer noted that the buildup of the Cuban presence in Chile coincided with DINA's organizational impetus to Operation Condor, but said he had no evidence of an official Cuban exile role in that organization. He reasoned, however, that the Chilean government's red-carpet treatment of the Cubans had to involve a substantial *quid pro quo.* The Cubans who had become involved with Chile were logical suspects in the Letelier-Moffitt assassinations. Terrorism was their currency, and they owed Chile a great debt.

Bosch remained the primary suspect since he was known to have tried to organize an assassination for Chile in Costa Rica. But informant information from the New York area linked the CNM to the murders, and Scherrer knew that Guillermo Novo and Suárez had been among the visitors to Chile. And there were two dozen others who had laid burnt offerings at the shrine of Pinochet. The contract could have been given to any one of them.

One of the Cubans who had come to Chile in 1976 was a special case. Rolando Otero, of Frank Castro's FNLC, had gone directly from Chile to an American jail a few months before the assassinations, and had recently faced trial in Miami on multiple bombing charges. Scherrer had personally carried out Otero's capture by prevailing upon the Chilean government to hand him over in handcuffs on an airliner bound for the United States.

Otero, like Bosch a close friend of the ubiquitous "Monkey" Morales, had informed Morales in February 1976 that he had accepted an assassination contract from DINA as a way of showing *bona fides.* The intended victims were Andrés Pascal Allende and Mary Anne Beausire, the same targets another Chilean intelligence service had given to Bosch. Morales, who also had learned of the Bosch assignment, passed the information to the FBI, which told Costa Rica of the double plot. After Bosch was arrested in Costa Rica, Otero returned to Chile. He was kidnapped by DINA a few months later and kept in a torture center.*

Otero's expulsion from Chile in May 1976 had disrupted the whole pattern of Chilean-Cuban exile relations. Otero hated Scherrer for setting up his capture, but hated the Chilean government even more. He and many other Cuban exiles considered the arrest a violation of the trust established between the Chilean government and the exile movement. Scherrer referred Cornick to the Otero file and suggested that a carefully orchestrated approach to Otero, as he sat in prison in Miami, might be fruitful. The fiery Otero's hatred might open a window onto DINA's handling of the exile terrorists. He added that Cuban exile resentment over Otero's betrayal was so great that the FBI should seriously consider the possibility that the bombing in front of the Chilean Embassy was done by Cubans acting alone to cause trouble for the Pinochet regime.

DETECTIVE STANLEY WILSON OF D.C. Homicide called Chilean press attaché Rafael Otero (no relation to Rolando Otero), whom he had been cultivating since the assassination, and arranged to meet him in a restaurant a few blocks from the Chilean mission. "I've got something to show you," said Wilson. "And by the way, who is 'Tati'?"

*The Chilean government first denied having Otero, then offered to turn him over in a coffin. The U.S. Embassy insisted on expulsion and told the Chilean government that if Otero were not turned over to the FBI, Secretary of State Henry Kissinger would cancel his scheduled June 1976 visit to Chile to attend the General Assembly of the Organization of American States. On May 19, Chilean police dragged a dirty and half-starved Otero aboard a plane with Scherrer bound for Miami.

"She's Allende's daughter—her real name's Beatriz Allende. Lives in Cuba now. There's more about her, but tell me why you want to know."

"I've got a letter here, to Orlando, signed 'Tati.' Sent from Cuba."

The two men spoke in Spanish. Each considered the other a "source." They had been meeting regularly. For Wilson, Otero was a conduit of information from inside the Chilean government. For Otero, Wilson provided a way to keep tabs on the Letelier-Moffitt investigation and learn how close it was getting to Chile.

Otero, who sometimes referred to himself by his less than flattering nickname "the Dwarf," had a reputation in Chile for venomous journalism. Once an admirer of Fidel Castro and an employee in the Cuban news agency Prensa Latina's Chile office, by the late 1960s Otero had become a fierce anticommunist. He filled a small political weekly that he published during the Allende years with insulting cartoons and scatological references. He bragged of being arrested twenty-eight times, implying he had been a victim of Allende's political persecution, but in reality most of his arrests were in the pre-Allende years and involved petty theft and fraud. Orlando Letelier had considered him a DINA informer in Washington.

Wilson's telephone call in late November signaled to Otero that Wilson was ready to "trade" classified investigative material for Otero's cooperation in providing access to Chile's files on Latin American terrorists. Otero chuckled to himself as he put on his overcoat and left the embassy.

Wilson couldn't be sure that Otero worked for DINA, but he knew Otero had access. The FBI had bungled the case so far, Wilson thought. The agents had barged into the Chilean Embassy and interviewed embassy personnel, but they had not managed to get any real information. The Chileans had shut up tighter than clams. Wilson used a different tactic, and it had produced results. He had convinced Otero that by working together they could keep the investigation's focus where it belonged: on the Marxists, on the Cuban exiles acting alone, and on Orlando Letelier as a supposed communist agent. Wilson doubted that Chile was involved in the murders. He had won Otero's trust, and access to DINA documents.

Wilson found the files Otero showed him "incredible." Virtually every active terrorist in the Western Hemisphere, including pro- and anti-Castro Cubans, had a dossier. Wilson was convinced now he could beat the FBI in solving the case. Only the CIA had files like these, and the CIA wasn't sharing.

Otero was already sitting at a table when Wilson arrived at the restaurant. Wilson laid a thick sheaf of papers on the table before shaking Otero's hand and sitting down. Wilson, a soft-spoken man with a gentle demeanor, took out several xeroxed sheets clipped together and began to read key paragraphs in Spanish.

"Political office expense sheet—until October 1975. Received: Two payments, one for $3,000 at the beginning of the year, and the other for $5,000 in May 1975. Total received: $8,000."

Wilson shoved the papers he was reading across the table to Otero; they contained a month-by-month expense ledger. From the items listed it was obvious to an informed Chilean like Otero that the ledger had belonged to Orlando Letelier.

"This is incredible. Where did you get all these things?" Otero asked excitedly.

"Wait. This is only the beginning. Now I'll read to you a letter telling you where he got the money."

He read, looking up occasionally for effect:

Havana, May 8, 1975

Dear Orlando:
I know that Altamirano wants to communicate with you to offer a solution to the problems that have arisen there, and he has asked me to inform you that, from *here* [Wilson stressed the word] from here, we will send you, in the name of the party, a thousand dollars ($1,000) per month to support your work. I am sending you five thousand now in order not to have to send it monthly.
A big hug for you and Isabel Margarita from
[signed] Tati.

Wilson shoved the letter across for Otero to see that it was signed. "That's money from *Cuba,* my friend, to operate a resistance movement in the United States. And there is another letter referring to another five-thousand-dollar payment just a month before the assassination. All this stuff comes from Letelier's briefcase. We impounded it from the car as evidence the day of the assassination and copied everything," Wilson said.

Wilson and Otero huddled in the mid-morning quiet of the restaurant for more than an hour, handing papers back and forth and talking animatedly. Otero told Wilson all he could think of about "Tati": she was Allende's favorite daughter, in her thirties, and a high official in the Chilean Socialist Party. During the salad days of the Popular Unity, she had met and married a Cuban diplomat. After the coup she and her husband, Oña Fernández, and children had gone to live in Cuba.

"Fernández' connection with the Cuban government is perfect," Otero said. "He worked abroad; who can say he isn't an intelligence agent? Letelier receives money from the Cuban agent's wife—he thus becomes a paid Cuban agent himself. It couldn't be better if we had written these letters ourselves."

Otero said he didn't want to take any of the papers himself. It would be damaging to Chile, he reasoned, if it became known that the embassy had access to the papers before they became public, and there would soon be charges that the embassy had leaked them. He told Wilson to give the papers first to friends of Chile on Capitol Hill.

Three weeks later, on December 20, the Jack Anderson–Les Whitten column was headlined: LETELIER'S HAVANA CONNECTION. It read in part:

Secret papers found in Chilean exile Orlando Letelier's attaché case after assassination show he had been collecting a mysterious $1,000 a month through a "Havana Connection."

We have seen some of these hush-hush papers.

Intelligence sources contend that the money couldn't have been transmitted to Letelier without the Cuban government's approval.

His contact was Beatrice "Tati" Allende, daughter of Salvador Allende. . . . The woman now lives in Havana with her husband, a Cuban official. . . .

We reached Tati Allende in Havana by telephone, but she declined to reveal the source of the payments. Her letter to Letelier, she said, was personal and she couldn't understand why it would be made public "unless it was to hurt" Letelier's cause.

ISABEL LETELIER HAD begun to pick up the pieces of Chilean exile work that Orlando had left behind. Dressed always in black, she presented a dignified and sober image to television cameras and the press. She spoke at churches and at unions, at universities and at public meetings. Her message was simple: "Pinochet killed my husband and Ronni Moffitt, an American citizen. They are but two of many he has murdered, tortured, imprisoned, exiled. Justice in the case of my husband and Ronni Moffitt will also mean justice for the majority of the Chilean people. I do not seek revenge. I seek only justice."

In addition, she was deeply involved in the institute's independent investigation. She struggled over the meaning of each new lead or fact, over the interpretation of data, over the extent to which the institute could and should work with the FBI and the U.S. attorney's office. But in contacts with Cornick and Propper she always managed to coax out bits of information about the investigation. In her speeches she refrained from making broadside attacks on the United States government. But perhaps more than anyone else at IPS, she harbored a visceral mistrust of that government and its officials, not only for what she knew they had done to Chile, but because they operated an imperial system, cloaked in democratic and anticolonial rhetoric. As she listened, often silently, during meetings with Propper, Cornick, and other government officials, she occasionally smiled. "I keep thinking," she later explained, "of the days when I taught FBI agents Spanish, and I would wonder if when someone can learn a language, it means he is open to learning other things. And these very polite men with short haircuts and clean-shaven looks, who dressed alike and had similar expressions on their faces, would repeat after me the words, phrases, and sentences in Spanish.

And sometimes I would wonder if I said, 'Socialism is the only solution for Latin America and the Third World,' would they repeat it?"

By December, three months since the assassinations, the investigation, as if caught in a whirlpool, ceased its forward motion and began circling around the leads developed in the first weeks after the assassination: the Novo brothers, Orlando Bosch and CORU, the ephemeral Venezuelan connection, and the even more elusive Cuban-Chilean connection. Agent Larry Wack's composite sketches circulated among FBI field offices, Drug Enforcement Administration agents, and even CIA staffers stationed abroad.

By Christmastime, hundreds of false leads that FBI agents all over the country had pursued were finally eliminated. Cornick kept the FBI's interest in the case alive by providing thick "progress reports" (one of them one thousand pages long) to all FBI offices. But the flow of paper across Propper's desk and reports of new information had slowed down. Propper began to grow impatient with the nebulous "informants' reports" repeating the same few, unsubstantiated facts. He needed proof—something he could use in court. So he continued to march a procession of Cuban exiles into the grand jury room on the third floor of the district court building.

As the weeks went by without any progress in the investigation, the honeymoon with IPS and Isabel Letelier grew strained. Isabel wanted some indication that the investigation was centering on DINA, some official word that DINA and the Pinochet government were at least on the list of active suspects. On December 8 Isabel Letelier and IPS fellows met with Attorney General Levi a second time. Propper announced: "We've eliminated all leads except the political motive, the South American connection, the Chile–anti-Castro Cuban connection, and that's where the great bulk of the investigation is going." Before the arrival of the IPS contingent, Levi asked Propper, "Why don't you just tell them you are investigating DINA?" Propper said no. IPS would immediately give it to the press and "any sources we had down in Chile would dry up immediately."

Cornick and FBI bomb experts were puzzled that Michael

Moffitt had been able to survive the blast with only minimal cuts and scratches. Cornick felt that Moffitt's extraordinary memory of the sounds and sights just before the explosion might hold further clues. He thought that Moffitt might have subconsciously hidden away some additional details that could yield further clues. He came to IPS and told Moffitt that the FBI would pay to fly him to Rochester to see a doctor who specialized in a kind of hypnotism that had occasionally helped people recall memories they had buried. Moffitt agreed—although the suggestion was never followed up—but then exploded at Cornick over the sluggish pace of the investigation and the FBI's reticent attitude toward the Chilean Embassy and Chile itself.

Cornick listened to Moffitt, shouted back in his own defense, and finally admitted his sympathy with Moffitt's feelings of rage. Cornick left IPS. Moffitt calmed down as he began to realize that Cornick's visit meant that the government's investigation was grasping at straws.

More than anyone else, Moffitt had suffered the trauma of the assassination. He had seen and heard the explosion; the experience was etched into his mind forever. Yet he went on television within three days of the assassination, wrote an angry but reasoned editorial in the *New Republic,* and gave a moving oration at Saint Matthew's Church. Only then had he taken several weeks off to rest and recoup his equilibrium. He returned to institute work two months after his wife's death and finished writing the pamphlet he and Letelier had worked on together the night before the murders.*

In tandem with the IPS investigation,† he contacted reporters, trying to persuade them to follow up IPS leads and to pressure the government into releasing details of their investigation, and briefed congressional staffers on the the case's progress, or lack of it. By the dull grey winter of early 1977, as Propper's and Cornick's optimism faded and the press could not find sufficient "hard" news to keep the

---

*In 1977 the Transnational Institute published the pamphlet entitled *The International Economic Order* over Moffitt's and Letelier's by-lines.

†After the murders IPS had created the Letelier-Moffitt Fund for Human Rights, which among other projects helped pay for the independent investigation.

issue in the public eye, Isabel Letelier and Michael Moffitt carried the ball. They took speaking assignments throughout the United States to drive home the facts about the Pinochet regime's systematic violation of human rights. They made headlines in college and local newspapers where the murders themselves had received scant space. They appeared on radio and television spots, met with college presidents and church leaders, and spoke to numerous groups, trying to keep public concern alive over the dormant investigation and indefatigably building up pressure to place Chile on the new president's human rights agenda.

IN EARLY MARCH, half a year after the murders and months since the last new lead, Propper and Larry Barcella flew to Caracas, Venezuela, to interrogate Orlando Bosch in his cell at La Pastora Military Prison. During much of the seven-hour flight, Propper briefed Barcella on the prior course of the investigation.

In Caracas, a Ministry of Justice official introduced them to Cuban exile Rafael Rivas Vásquez, the second in command of DISIP. A member with Orlando Bosch in a Miami exile organization in the early 1960s, Rivas had dropped the militant MIRR group for closer connections with the CIA, which in turn led him into intelligence work. Bosch opted for terrorism, but the two former companions did not lose touch. Rivas told Propper and Barcella he had talked to Bosch for what seemed like hours after Bosch was arrested in early October. Bosch had ranted about the betrayal of the Cuban movement by the CIA and about his arrest and the betrayal of the Cuban movement by the Venezuelan government. In the course of his tirade, Rivas said, Bosch talked about the Letelier case, and made the almost offhand assertion that the Novo brothers had done it for Chile.

Propper and Barcella elicited from Rivas a promise to come to Washington to repeat this story before the grand jury. They asked about connections between Bosch and Guillermo Novo and between Cuban exiles and the Chilean government. Rivas became vague, talking generally about the efforts of Manuel Contreras to get foreign intelligence services like DISIP to monitor Chilean exiles and activities. He said he knew that Bosch and Novo had traveled to Chile together in December 1974, because he had met them in a hotel in Caracas just before they left. They were, he said, with another exile figure, José Dionisio Suárez, and he said DISIP would be glad to provide immigration records establishing Novo's presence in Venezuela. Rivas was unhelpful, however, when Propper and Barcella asked to interview Bosch, and Venezuelan government officials made no move to expedite the matter. U.S. Ambassador to Venezuela Viron Vaky was cool toward the investigators' suggestions that he "lean on" the Venezuelans a bit. The lack of U.S. Embassy and Venezuelan interest gave Bosch little incentive to cooperate. Neither carrot nor stick could be brought to bear, and finally Bosch, through his lawyer, turned Propper down flat.

But the trip was not a total loss. Rivas had unexpectedly provided evidence that Propper and Barcella could use in court to prove that Guillermo Novo, by traveling to Venezuela, had violated parole and could be returned to prison. The Venezuelan trip also convinced Propper and Cornick to follow up a lead that Scherrer had offered shortly after the assassination. Rolando Otero, the FNLC terrorist whom Scherrer had brought out of Chile in handcuffs the previous May, had been acting on DISIP instructions when he made contact with DINA, the DISIP agents told Propper and Barcella, and had provided them with abundant and useful information about DINA foreign operations.

Back in Washington, Propper, now working closely with Barcella, decided to call the principal Cuban exile suspects for a second round before the grand jury. The Venezuelan trip provided additional reasons to renew the focus on the CNM. Propper subpoenaed Guillermo and Ignacio Novo, Alvin Ross, José Dionisio Suárez, and an assortment of suspected CORU meeting participants.

Cornick advised Scherrer in Buenos Aires of the renewed interest in Guillermo Novo and CNM. One of Scherrer's informants had told him that the CNM's contact with Chile was a blond DINA agent who had at least one American parent. Scherrer combined that information with FBI Agent Wack's reports from New Jersey that Guillermo Novo had been seen with a blond Chilean shortly before the assassination. Armed with the FBI composite drawing based on the description of the blond Chilean provided by Wack's informants, he flew to Santiago. He wanted to see whether the mysterious blond Chilean-American might by some stroke of policeman's fortune have his photograph on file at the U.S. Consulate.

Scherrer spent April 5 and 6, 1977, inspecting one by one some 1,500 cards of United States citizens registered in Chile, most of which contained photographs. Each photograph he compared with the composite sketch. Seven men vaguely fit the description given by the informants, albeit far from the composite: fair-haired, early to mid-thirties, blue-eyed. They all had Spanish surnames. He began the familiar policeman's routine of checking them out. None had any conceivable connection with either the Chilean government or intelligence work.

In New Jersey, Larry Wack showed the photos of the seven to his informants. They shook their heads: No. Neither Scherrer nor Wack, in their search for men who might fit the descriptions of the light-haired suspect, had seen the FBI file containing the photographs and passports of Juan Williams and Alejandro Romeral.

COMING HOME
TO ROOST

A FEW DAYS after searching the consular records, Robert Scherrer went to see DINA director Manuel Contreras, as had become his custom on each trip to Chile. The inner offices at DINA headquarters near downtown Santiago displayed a flashy aura of elegance derived from seemingly unlimited resources. The reception area was presided over by a bevy of young secretaries whose dress, make-up, and cultivated good looks could have qualified them as models. Glass and chrome tables, designer lamps, and low-slung suede chairs completed the Southern Cone* imitation of Madison Avenue atmosphere.

Contreras' private office was dominated by an enormous world map behind a large wooden desk and a console of elaborate telephone, television, and radio communications equipment. Scherrer had been meeting with Contreras since early 1976 when, as a result of the negotiations over the expulsion of Cuban terrorist Rolando Otero, the FBI and DINA had established formal liaison. After the Letelier assassination, the relationship became more adversarial, but remained within the polite bounds of *caballeros.*

*"Southern Cone" refers to the cone-shaped southern portion of South America, comprising Argentina, Brazil, Chile, Paraguay, and Uruguay.

Scherrer found himself in the awkward position of dealing with a fellow officer as a primary suspect in a murder case. At their first meeting after the murders, in late November, Contreras had offered Scherrer "confidential information" that Ronni Moffitt was actually one of Orlando Letelier's lovers and that the FBI should consider Michael Moffitt the most likely suspect, since he obviously had contrived to sit in the back seat instead of next to Letelier on the morning of the bombing. When two Latin men ride in a car with a woman, the DINA chief told Scherrer authoritatively, they always sit together in the front. Contreras had also repeated the official Chilean government position that the assassination was designed to damage Chile's image and was part of a Marxist plot. He therefore had promised to help Scherrer in any way he could in his investigation.

In subsequent meetings, Scherrer had begun to bore in on DINA's relationship with the Cuban exile militants who had visited Chile. Contreras fielded the questions confidently, self-assuredly, revealing nothing. Now, in April, Scherrer detected a difference in Contreras' answers. He sensed that he sat before a man no longer at the peak of power. A strange insecurity had replaced the DINA chief's inscrutable, Buddha-like demeanor.

They reviewed Scherrer's facts and Contreras' denials, DINA's relationship with Rolando Otero, Orlando Bosch, Guillermo Novo, and José Dionisio Suárez. While they talked, Contreras strode about the grey-carpeted expanses of his office, then stood at his desk fondling the bronze paperweight that bore the DINA emblem, a mailed fist delivering a downward blow. The two men accepted the necessary assumptions of their charade: that the discussion implied no accusations, no interrogation; only Chile's willing cooperation in clearing up a crime committed by others.

Suddenly a change in the picture on one of the television screens interrupted them. On the screen the unmoving black gate outside DINA headquarters switched to the image of President Augusto Pinochet sitting at his desk three-quarters of a mile away in the Diego Portales Building. Contreras returned to his desk, pressed a button, and greeted Pinochet. Scherrer saw the stationary television camera high on the wall to his left, trained on them both. Pinochet asked whether Contreras had completed the report on "the Admiral." Addressing him with the familiar *tú,* Contreras indicated discreetly that he would report back to Pinochet with the information.

Scherrer used the interruption to break off the uncomfortable conversation. In a cable to Washington, he said that Contreras, in that interview and subsequent ones, seemed to be "waiting for the other shoe to drop" in the Letelier case.

Scherrer knew only part of Contreras' troubles. In the murky waters of the power politics inside the military government, the tide had turned against Contreras and DINA. Pinochet, for the first time in almost three years, had imposed trammels on Contreras' power. Faced with budget cuts and orders to halt the extermination of leftists through disappearances,* Contreras had entrenched himself along with his most trusted followers to defend his DINA empire.

For three years Contreras had thrived on repeated challenges to his power. Progressive General Óscar Bonilla, one of the original coup plotters and Pinochet's principal rival in the army, had attacked Contreras. But that challenge ended with Bonilla's death in a mysterious helicopter accident in March 1975. General Sergio Arellano, another giant in the generals' corps, had complained to Pinochet about Contreras' "Gestapo" and had expressed his disagreement with other Pinochet policies. Arellano received his retirement orders. Also in late 1975, General Odlanier Mena, the chief of the Army Intelligence Service (SIM) faced down Contreras over the issue of DINA spying on army officers. Pinochet named Mena ambassador to Panama and later Uruguay—in effect, diplomatic exile. Contreras, by controlling most of the flow of information to Pinochet, had skillfully cast all opposition to DINA in the light of opposition to Pinochet. Their alliance seemed eternal, their fates indissolubly joined.

Now pressure came from quarters he could not control. The United States had a new president who had made Chile an issue in the election.† The nonclandestine opposition leaders had gathered

---

*Human rights officials of the Catholic Church reported that for the first time since the coup, no one had disappeared in the three-month period starting in January.

†Candidate Jimmy Carter, in one of the pre-election debates with President Ford, had said, "I notice that Mr. Ford didn't comment on the prisons in Chile. This is a typical example,

in the ballroom of the Santiago Sheraton San Cristóbal Hotel on election night and cheered Jimmy Carter's victory as if he belonged to their party. The pro-Pinochet businessmen, technocrats, and economists also observed the reaction at the hotel. Pinochet's non-military supporters understood the vicissitudes of United States power. It was part of their education, of a lifetime of business and professional contacts with what they called their "neighbor to the north."

Now that Carter was president, human rights in countries such as Chile had become a major foreign policy thrust. Some of the men of power and property inside Chile began, slowly at first, to react. They wanted to restore the government they had helped create into the good graces of the United States. Their loyalty to Pinochet would remain firm, as long as His Excellency showed some flexibility. Pinochet, the realist, allowed them to choose a hitherto sacred target: the burgeoning empire of Manuel Contreras.

These men had worked together since before the coup, sometimes formally, but sharing a consensus, a community of political and economic interests. Never a numerical majority among Chilean businessmen, they nonetheless possessed the economic and political power to shape the country's economic future in postcoup Chile. No more than twenty or thirty at most, they clustered at the poles of power. In banking and industry, Javier Vial and Manuel Cruzat, first together, then separately, had built the largest financial empire the country had ever seen in the short years since the coup. Cruzat and his new partner, broker Fernando Larrain, could count among their executives—their subordinates—five cabinet ministers or former cabinet ministers in Pinochet's government.* Close behind the Vial

---

maybe of many others, that this administration overthrew an elected government and helped establish a military dictatorship."
*The five ministers with past or present executive positions in Cruzat-Larrain holdings are Jorge Cauas, minister of finance and economics; Fernando Leniz, minister of economics; Pablo Baraona, economics minister and Central Bank president; José Pinera, minister of labor; and Alfonso Marquez de la Plata, minister of agriculture. According to research by Chilean economist Fernando Dahse, the conglomerates created by Cruzat-Larrain, Vial, and Edwards together with four other conglomerates controlled 101 of Chile's largest 250 companies, including most of the private banks. The Cruzat-Larrain group, the largest conglomerate, controlled 37 of the 250 firms. See Fernando Dahse, *Mapa de la Extrema Riqueza: Los Grupos Económicos y el Proceso de Concentración de Capitales* (Santiago, 1979).

and Cruzat-Larrain groups in political clout came the Agustín Edwards empire, owner of El Mercurio Publications. They had built their economic base through control of junta economic policy and access to the large United States corporations and banks. The Cruzat enterprises had earned the cozy nickname of "The Piranhas."

In publishing, members of the group competed among themselves, but held undisputed and growing control over the print media. El Mercurio Publications owned the major newspaper by the same name, plus two of the three remaining Santiago daily newspapers. El Mercurio owner Agustín Edwards had been a factor in persuading President Nixon in 1970 to order covert action by the CIA against Allende. Edwards' top lieutenant, Hernán Cubillos, was, until the coup, the CIA's principal agent and conduit of covert funds to opposition groups through El Mercurio, of which he was president in Edwards' absence.*

Pinochet, soon after assuming power, had conferred on a group of economists associated with these empire builders the task of restoring pure capitalism to Chile after the years of Christian Democratic and Popular Unity reforms. These were proper, well-dressed men, mostly in their late thirties or early forties, from well-to-do landowning or industrialist families. They had studied at the Catholic University and received Ford Foundation or similar scholarships in the early 1960s to take advanced degrees in economics or business administration at the University of Chicago. Pinochet did not get involved in their plans; he knew nothing about economics. He merely asked what they needed to carry out their aims—and demanded that

---

*Lord Cochrane Publications was partially owned by the Edwards family that owned *El Mercurio,* but the publishing house was under the control, by 1977, of Hernán Cubillos, who had left El Mercurio in 1973 after a money dispute with Edwards. Lord Cochrane and a third publishing house, Andean Publications, filled Chilean newsstands with slick, made-in-Miami, Spanish-language, American-format magazines such as *Vanidades, Cosmopólitan,* and *Mecánica Popular.* Only one mass-circulation magazine in the entire country, the Christian Democratic *Ercilla,* had been independent of the major publishing houses. It too fell into the fold in late 1976 when bought by a Cruzat subsidiary. *Ercilla*'s editor then raised money in the United States and Europe and started his own magazine, *Hoy.*

Cubillos' CIA status was revealed during an October 23, 1978 court hearing in the case of ITT official Robert Bergellez, charged with lying to a Senate subcommittee in 1973 about ITT-CIA anti-Allende activity (*Washington Post,* November 14, 1978).

they not interfere in the military task of extirpating the Marxist cancer.

Jorge Cauas, a pleasant-looking, rotund little man with the air of an academician rather than a banker, led the government economic team as minister of finance and held the officially conferred title of "superminister." Sergio de Castro, minister of economics, and Pablo Baraona, president of the Central Bank, surrounded themselves with men who looked, dressed, and thought like themselves—bright young men convinced that the technocratic enlightenment which they embodied had finally been given a free hand to pull a backward country into the modern world. When Cauas was appointed ambassador to Washington in March, everyone moved up a step—de Castro to finance, Baraona to economics, and Baraona's vice-president Álvaro Bardon to president of the Central Bank. They were steely-eyed, ambitious men—though charming in a particularly Chilean way—to whom human rights in the early years of the junta were worth, in the Chilean idiom, "not a cumin seed." When Jimmy Carter became president, however, they suddenly saw the light.

The editorial page of *El Mercurio* and a drab newsweekly *Que Pasa*** acted as their unofficial voice. Their line on economic development called for the opening of Chilean markets to foreign competition to spur healthy—that is, unprotected—domestic industries, which could then compete abroad. They believed in controlling inflation through the sole mechanisms of manipulating the money supply and creating a free labor market (Pinochet guaranteed this by dismantling Chile's once enormous union movement). Their intellectual mentor, economist Milton Friedman, taught them that political democracy was the natural—if not necessarily immediate—outgrowth of an untrammeled free-market economy.

---

*Que Pasa was founded by Hernán Cubillos, Pablo Baraona, and right-wing ideologue Jaime Guzmán in the first year of the Allende government. During the Allende years, *Que Pasa* was heavily subsidized by the opposition. It was printed in the same residential building that housed the Institute of General Studies, a think-tank, and many other groups. IGS, whose president in 1973 was Baraona, was later described in the Church Committee report on covert action in Chile: "The CIA also funded progressively a greater portion—over 70 percent in 1973 —of an opposition research organization. . . . Many of the bills prepared by opposition parliamentarians were actually drafted by personnel of the research organization." *Covert Action in Chile, 1963–1973* (Washington, D.C., 1975), p. 30.

In early 1977 the group decided that Contreras' DINA had out-
lived its usefulness.* *El Mercurio* editorials began to suggest that the
time had come for the military regime to shed the battle dress of the
first three years and put on more institutionalized mufti. The present
"political immobility" could jeopardize the solid economic gains, the
paper said, and it warned against "fanaticism," "fascism," and the
temptation to use "outmoded Francoist models" in the government.

WHEN EUGENE PROPPER and Carter Cornick decided to recall certain CNM members before the grand jury, they fixed on a new tactic
—a combination of divide-and-conquer and carrot-and-stick. They
granted José Dionisio Suárez and Alvin Ross Díaz immunity in
exchange for their testimony. This had the effect of preventing the
two from pleading their Fifth Amendment right to remain silent,
since the immunity guaranteed that they could not be prosecuted for
any crimes they revealed in their testimony.

Both men refused to talk. On April 20 a U.S. District Court judge
held Suárez in contempt of the grand jury and jailed him either until
he changed his mind or until the end of the grand jury term in March
1978. Ross, however, was released. Propper and Cornick's informants had advised them that it was Suárez who played the role of
enforcer. He had earned a reputation for maintaining discipline
within organizational ranks. Suárez intimidated people. Cornick and
Propper hoped that if he stayed in jail, Ross, the "blabbermouth,"
would feel less inhibited about exercising his tongue. In addition,
Propper's informants told him that Ignacio Novo had developed a
serious drinking problem and often boasted of his crimes when

*A factor in the decision to go on the offensive against DINA in early 1977 may have been
DINA's role in exposing a large-scale money-market scandal. The folding of several small
financieras, quick-turnover money operations that had sprouted in 1976 to take advantage of
20 to 30 percent *per month* interest rates, threatened to undermine the whole overindebted
economy until a Central Bank guarantee stemmed the tide of financial failures. During the
height of the crisis, DINA agents fed Santiago journalists inside information that fueled the
crisis, and claimed the crisis itself was proof that the "Chicago Boys' " economic team was
a failure. One of the firms that folded was La Familia, linked to Pinochet adviser Jaime
Guzmán. It had made loans to students at 24 percent per month, using short-term deposits
from Catholic University, a Guzmán fiefdom since the coup.

drunk. With Suárez in jail, Novo too could indulge his vice more freely.

Propper and Cornick had a third reason for keeping Suárez and freeing Ross: to sow suspicion.

While Propper waited, hoping for results from this plan or for anything else that would revive the stagnant case, a New York City policeman in early May made a routine arrest of Ricardo Canete de Céspedes on a charge of passing a bad check.

At the police station a veteran desk sergeant recognized Canete from previous arrests and ordered the patrolman who brought him in to search him thoroughly. In Canete's pocket were several marijuana joints; he had a roll of counterfeit twenty-dollar bills in his wallet and a small handgun hidden in his crotch. He also had a false New Jersey driver's license under one of his aliases. The desk sergeant watched Canete's face as the charges multiplied. Worry turned to fear. The sergeant made his move. He invited Canete to step into a private office, ordered a six-pack of beer, and put up his feet on the desk.

"We can do this the easy way, or we can do it the hard way, Ricky," the sergeant said, "and I think you're the kind of person who will want things easy."

Canete read the policeman's badge and gun the same way a vice cop reads needle tracks on a junkie's arm. What Canete did not understand, he thought he understood. The bottom line was clear: He could become an informer, or he could go to prison. Canete traded his information for his freedom. Each charge against him bid up the amount of information he had to offer. Over the next several weeks he helped a Secret Service agent infiltrate the counterfeiting ring that had sold him the fake twenties.

The New York Police Department's Arson and Explosives Squad was interested in information about the CNM. Canete told Sergeants Robert Brandt and George Howard that he had dropped out of the CNM in the mid 1960s, but that he would try to renew the acquaintance. Canete's friendship with Ignacio Novo dated back to 1960 when, along with Felipe Rivero and the Novos, he helped found the organization that later became the Cuban Nationalist Movement. Whatever ethical battle he fought with himself over the betrayal of an old friend, he resolved it quickly. He dialed the number for Center Ford in Union City where Ignacio worked as a salesman.

Ignacio Novo recognized the voice. They went through the necessary amenities before Canete suggested to Ignacio that they renew their friendship on the basis of mutual assistance. Ignacio knew that Canete sold forged papers. Canete knew that the CNM members perpetually needed such documents. But Ignacio went further on the phone: "If Guillermo goes to jail, there will be war. We'll get Propper. We'll get Bell. We'll get Fiske [assistant U.S. attorney in New York]."

Canete reported the conversation to the police. On May 2, 1977, officials from the U.S. Secret Service, whose mandate includes protecting cabinet officials, debriefed Canete. He now informed for two police agencies. On May 12 the NYPD told Canete that they had found another charge to bring against him. Canete began to fret and fume. A classic police double cross. They had used him to crack the counterfeiting ring that passed the bogus twenties and other criminal operations that he had been connected with. He had ratted on Ignacio Novo, an old friend, and possibly placed him in deep trouble. And after all that he would still go to prison.

The Secret Service officer shook his head. "Sorry," he said. Tears welled up in Canete's eyes. "There might be a way out," the officer said. He led Canete into an adjoining room. In it Special Agent Larry Wack sat waiting, a smile on his face.

Wack saw before him a cocky street hoodlum who talked the authentic slang of the gangster-hipster underworld. Underneath the façade he knew there was the cynicism of a man who thinks he has found the secret of life and has decided it is too boring for his taste. Wack recognized a rare and brief flickering in the eyes, a distress signal, a sign of *Weltschmertz,* that the lost creature occasionally flashed as if he were calling for help or intimating his ultimate vulnerability.

Wack held Canete's freedom in his power. To Canete, freedom meant visiting topless bars and "bullshitting," buying "smokes" and snorting cocaine. It meant hustling with his street cronies, forging certified checks and leaving the bank exhilarated. It meant he could play and hang out on the street with the "nudniks" and talk in criminal lingo in Spanish, English, or Spanglish. For Canete, freedom meant the doglike sniffing out that hoodlums practice on each other, looking for signs of character weakness—that someday could be used to advantage. The street gangs who never grow up, but do grow bald and develop liver and kidney ailments, still punch each other playfully and jokingly threaten each other with death in various forms. Their flashy clothes in the topless discotheques show them as pathetic creatures, but they are nevertheless men capable of killing, stealing, and hurting. This was Canete's street life, his freedom, his sense of continuity from one day to the next, from a decade of fascism in the 1960s to a decade of crime in the 1970s.

When Larry Wack began his verbal sparring with Canete, he saw a pale and sensitive face, partly hidden by a well-trimmed black beard. The stains on the teeth came from chain-smoking imported English cigarettes made from Turkish tobacco. To Wack, Canete looked like an informer.

Beneath Canete's façade of a petty hoodlum, Wack detected a resourcefulness and quick intelligence. The FBI wanted Canete to become their man inside the Cuban Nationalist Movement. He accepted it as just another part of the same inevitable game, a normal twist in his life, to be passed from one police agency to another.

Recounting his life story to people he hardly knew, Canete mixed fact and fiction in stylized anecdotes that were an attempt to give the impression of a man who was born ten thousand years ago and had translated the wisdom of the ages into street savvy. For Canete, his political career began during the Castro-led insurrection against Batista in the late 1950s. He claimed to have smuggled guns for Castro's Twenty-sixth of July Movement. Castro, he proudly related, begged him to return to Cuba when the bearded guerrilla leader left New York after a triumphal visit in 1959. In 1960 Castro allegedly offered Canete an opportunity to come to Cuba for KGB training— preparatory to joining Cuban intelligence. He refused both offers, and instead accepted the CIA's recruiting pitch in 1960 and joined Brigade 2506 to invade Cuba. Because of his special skills and intelligence, the agency made him the interpreter for exiled political leader

Tony Varona. On one occasion this assignment led him to Hyannis-port, where he posed for a photograph with the Kennedy family.

So great was Canete's value to the agency that they pulled him out of the invasion force two weeks before its fateful disembarkation for the Bay of Pigs and recruited him for service in a secret squadron called Operation 40. Designed under Attorney General Robert Kennedy, this Cuban exile Waffen-SS was to mop up pockets of resistance after the successful invasion and neutralize dissident elements inside the invading force. In this venture Canete associated with legendary CIA figures like Colonel Rip Robertson and Grayston Lynch. The CIA also enlisted him along with Mafia hit man John Rosselli and Mafia mistress Marita Lorenz in ZR/RIFLE, the CIA acronym for the plot to assassinate Castro.

In 1964 Canete participated in the CNM's bazooka attack on the United Nations building, which "Guillermo [Novo] fucked up by letting the bazooka slide into the mud." He also "knocked off some ass" and "blew away some niggers" with the Novos at a 116th Street whorehouse in Harlem. By 1966, however, his fascist imagination surpassed the narrow limits of the Castro-obsessed CNM, and Canete drifted away from the Cuban exiles and joined—or infiltrated —the American Nazi Party of George Lincoln Rockwell. "Those were one bunch of crazy fuckers."

Sometime in the 1960s he found his way to Vietnam, where the CIA placed him in the Phoenix program. He specialized in throwing Viet Cong out of helicopters—attached to a rope so they would not hit ground—to make them talk. In the United States in the late 1960s he alternated his time between selling shoes and petty racketeering. Throughout his dangerous career Canete always consulted the spiritual leaders of his *santería* cult, the Yoruba protectors who shielded him from peril. He practiced the appropriate rituals with his beads, which he wore under his shirt. Canete also allied himself with Chinese Tongs and branches of the Brooklyn Mafia, and learned Tai Quan Do.

He also learned forgery in the 1970s, as well as other crafts designed to make him quick money for little work. He did specialized jobs for the South African secret police, BOSS, and for the Israeli MOSSAD. He "took a hit contract out on PLO leader Yasser Arafat and personally kept the son of a bitch from coming to the United States for more than three weeks."

Now, as Wack's agent, Canete kept on meeting with Ignacio Novo, who introduced him to Alvin Ross. Novo gave him specifications—age, height, coloring—for the false papers. Canete turned over copies of the papers to Wack, who cemented the relationship by giving him $300, for which Canete signed a receipt.*

The Novos knew from the questions asked before the grand jury and from the attention the FBI continued to pay CNM members that it would not be long before they discovered that Guillermo had traveled to Chile without permission, thereby violating his probation. Suárez was in jail. Guillermo made plans to flee. Canete forged the first sets of documents using the name Frederick Pagan, with a New Jersey driver's license, Panamanian passport, and baptism certificate to match the age and description of Guillermo Novo. On June 20, Novo failed to appear at a court hearing to consider revocation of his parole, and a warrant was issued for his arrest. Novo disappeared into the protective underworld of Miami's Little Havana.

IN SANTIAGO A BUNGLED DINA operation involving the kidnapping of a sixteen-year-old boy gave the magazines *Ercilla* and *Que Pasa* the pretext for their first exposé stories of DINA abuses since the coup. *Ercilla* led with a four-page story in early June, giving full details of the kidnapping, identifying DINA agents as the probable perpetrators, and illustrating the story with vivid drawings of fierce agents applying lighted cigarettes to the bare skin of the bound and gagged boy. *Que Pasa* followed with excerpts from secret court testimony contradicting DINA denials that their agents were involved. In issues throughout June the two progovernment magazines took their readers step by step through the nightmare lived by the boy, Carlos Veloso, a labor organizer's son, at the hands of DINA.

*Wack arranged for the remaining charge against Canete for possession of counterfeit money to be dismissed with a proviso that he waive his right to a speedy trial, and that if he stopped cooperating the indictment could be reinstated.

The story provided most Chileans their first view of the DINA nether world of torture and lies that constituted the military government's reign of terror.*

Carlos Veloso had gone after school on May 2 to his father's office at the church-sponsored Cardijn Foundation. It was dark when he left the office alone around 6:30. As he walked toward a bus stop three men jumped out of a car, grabbed him, and threw him on the floor of the back seat. They took him to a house and tortured him with cigarettes, electric shock, and drugs for six hours while questioning him about his father's labor activities. Then they dumped him out of a car on a residential street just before curfew. A passer-by helped the dazed boy reach his home.

Two days later other DINA agents came to Veloso's house and told his parents they were investigating the kidnapping and wanted to take the boy and his father, Carlos Héctor, for questioning. At the interrogation center DINA agents separated the boy from his father and told him that his family would be killed if he did not memorize a detailed false story of what had happened and identify four of his neighbors—all opposition labor leaders—as the kidnappers. The agents at one point showed him his father through a one-way window. Young Carlos saw a man with a shotgun trained on his father. He recognized the armed agent as one of his original abductors.

Three DINA agents took up residence at the Veloso home. They again drugged and hypnotized the boy. His father was told that Marxists had raped his son during the kidnapping. On May 25 the DINA agents called a press conference at which, under the agents' close supervision, young Veloso identified pictures of neighbors he said had kidnapped him. The four men whose names were given to the press had been reported as "disappeared" since May 4. DINA officials then announced that the four men were Marxists and subver-

---

*The first time any reference at all to DINA appeared in the Chilean press was in November 1975, when most newspapers printed a DINA press release describing in a favorable light the events surrounding the arrest of British physician Sheila Cassidy during a raid in which another woman was killed. A *Que Pasa* cover story in August 1976 described some DINA procedures, such as the use of hoods, and hinted at disappearances, but congratulated DINA for cleaning up the Marxists.

sives and had been turned over to a military court to face kidnapping charges.

The true story of the boy's ordeal came to light when a Catholic bishop investigated and took the boy and his family under church protection. In early June, the family made sworn statements to a military judge denouncing the DINA kidnapping, then flew into exile in Canada.

On June 28, a Tuesday, *Que Pasa* editor Jaime Martínez left his office at dusk and got into his car, which was parked across the street. As he reached for the ignition a man rose up from the back seat and put a gun to his head while another armed man opened the door on the passenger side and got in. Martínez, a slight, intellectually inclined man in his late forties, bolted from the car shouting for help. A group of *Que Pasa* employees saw what was happening. One of them noted the license number of a late-model Peugeot that raced up to Martínez' car and picked up the two would-be abductors.*

THE SAME DAY, in Washington, Carter Cornick and Eugene Propper paid a formal call on the new Chilean ambassador, Jorge Cauas. Cauas received the young prosecutor and FBI agent graciously in his office. It was not normal protocol for an ambassador to receive callers of Propper's and Cornick's rank on official United States government business. But Cauas' tenure as ambassador to the Jimmy Carter White House had been fraught with difficulty.

Cauas saw himself as an economist, a technocrat who eschewed politics. Once a Christian Democrat with a position on the Frei government's economic team, he had embraced the Pinochet dictatorship with enthusiasm and energy as a unique opportunity to apply his economic theories in a test-tube environment free of political pressures. His former friends were dismayed, but continued to think of Cauas as a breed different from the Pinochet stable. During his

*When checks were made, the license number was found to have been "withdrawn from circulation." But Martínez harbored no doubts that his attackers were sent by Contreras and that open battle had begun.

almost three years at the helm of the Chilean economy, he kept his public statements analytical and apolitical. He never expressed concern over insistent reports of political repression, torture, and murder practiced by his government. That was not his department.

No other Chilean could bring to Washington the kind of prestige and personal capital that Cauas possessed. He bore a certain similarity to Orlando Letelier in that and in the fact that he had lived in Washington before, as director of development research for the World Bank. Cauas considered himself "ambassador" to New York and the private banking community as much as ambassador to the White House. In that he was unsurpassed. Starting in 1976, while he was putting the finishing touches on the country's most severe austerity program in its history, the spigots of private international credit opened and allowed Cauas to avert an $800 million balance-of-payments deficit.

In diplomacy he had considerably less success. Named ambassador by Pinochet six weeks after Carter's election, Cauas arrived in Washington in February only to cool his heels for more than a month before Carter granted him the formal interview to accept his credentials. Relations were icy and getting worse as the Carter administration unfolded its human rights campaign and made repeated references to Chile. In early June Rosalynn Carter pointedly omitted Chile from her tour of Latin America, and a week later Vice-President Walter Mondale and National Security Adviser Zbigniew Brzezinski were receiving former President Frei in the White House.*

The Letelier case caused Cauas discomfort. A contemporary of Letelier's though not a friend, Cauas respected Letelier and was familiar with his Inter-American Development Bank work. But when President Pinochet in mid-1976 placed the decree removing Letelier's citizenship on the table at a cabinet meeting, Cauas had signed it. Now he sincerely wanted to believe that Chile had nothing

---

*Socialist Clodomiro Almeyda, the top UP exile leader, got similar treatment befitting his rank as former foreign minister. He was received at the State Department by Deputy Secretary Warren Christopher. Such protocolar visits by opposition leaders are unusual, though not unprecedented, and were a clear signal that Washington did not consider the Pinochet government the sole spokesman for the people of Chile.

to do with the assassination, nor with the attack on Leighton or the bombing of Prats.

Now Propper and Cornick had come to his office to lay the Letelier matter on his desk. Propper, with great deference, talked about the Justice Department's efforts and determination to solve the crime. The investigation, he said, had uncovered the names of several Cuban exile militants known to have visited Chile, and he would like to request Chile's help in obtaining information about the activities of three men—Guillermo Novo, Orlando Bosch, and Rolando Otero.

Cornick handed Cauas a brief data sheet on the Cubans' date of entry to Chile and possible aliases. They wanted, he said, to find out what contacts and meetings the three men had had with members of Chile's intelligence services. Cauas assured them he would convey the request to the highest Chilean authorities and that he was anxious to help personally in the investigation in any way he could. The United States and Chile had a common interest, he said, in identifying the criminals responsible for Letelier's and Moffitt's horrible deaths. Chile, in particular, had been gravely damaged by the constant accusations of its involvement in the assassination. Only by solving the crime could Chile's name be cleared.

The two investigators left. A few days later Propper received a telephone call from an official at the embassy informing him that the president of Chile had personally ordered Investigaciones, the civilian detective force, to begin an investigation so that the questions about the three Cubans could be answered.*

The reply to the questions that was transmitted by Cauas to Propper over a month later, a three-page memorandum marked "Highly Confidential," contained no information that had not already appeared in the press about Bosch and Otero, adding only their addresses while in Chile. Guillermo Novo, who entered Chile under his own name December 3, 1974, and departed December 19, was a "tourist" about whom no "negative actions" were known. The report

*Pinochet had not, however, ordered the investigation at that time, according to Investigaciones chief, retired General Ernesto Baeza, who told Scherrer in Santiago on July 15 that he was unaware of any queries about the three Cubans.

ignored Propper's question about the Cubans' suspected contacts with DINA. The important thing for Propper, however, was that one part of the Chilean government had committed itself in action to cooperation with the United States investigation.*

ON JULY 8, Agent Larry Wack's bedside phone rang at 2:00 A.M. Rick Canete's voice was shaking. Wack knew Canete had planned to meet Alvin Ross that evening to turn over false documents, but hadn't expected to hear from him for a debriefing until the next day. Canete began to pour out a story while Wack forced his mind to full alertness. When Canete said something about the "Letelier bomb," Wack interrupted him and told him to start over, that he was going to hook up a tape recorder.

"Now go back over the conversation sentence by sentence, as you remember it. Calm down," Wack said as he pushed the record buttons.

"I go over to meet Al at work, at Ascione Ford, where he's a salesman. He closes the place up when I get there—it's late, he's got keys to the place. We get in his car and go get a drink at a restaurant. I notice an open briefcase on the front seat, it has two manila folders, one says Orlando Letelier and the other says Chile. At the restaurant he's real polite, asks me if I want a drink or whatever while he goes to make some calls. I have a lemon coke.

"Then we go back to the garage. I need a typewriter to fill out the documents I brought for him. I'm typing away and he wants to bullshit—you know? I began to make up a set of IDs for one Frederick Pagan. I'm bragging about my work—you know, to fill out those DD214s† you have to have all those United States Army codings in your head, one mistake and you're dead, it's no good.

"And Al, he says, 'I'm pretty good at my work too,' he says, and he starts to brag about making bombs, he says he once made a bomb out of a flowerpot. I didn't believe him. I didn't really want to be

*Soon after the June 28 meeting, Cauas arranged for an embassy official to submit to a lie-detector test about meetings with the Cuban exiles at the embassy.

†Army discharge identification cards.

bothered with his bullshit. So I'm typing away and I says, 'Yeah Al, sure.'

"And he says, 'I'm not kidding, I'm serious, my bomb was a beautiful thing, even the professionals admired it.'

" 'Yeah, yeah,' I goes, typing away, I'm almost finished with the DD214. He's getting a little annoyed.

"He says to me then, 'Look, I made the Letelier bomb, made it right here. Used plastic explosives because they are the easiest to mold and they can be used for penetration and they produce the necessary amount of heat I needed. I used a clock with backup acid device.' "

Wack broke in: "Rick, will you take a lie-detector test that all this really happened?"

"Sure," he said, as Wack cut off the tape.

The next afternoon, Wack met his informant at a bench in Central Park.

"This is crazy," Canete said. "I'm in too deep. I didn't know you were putting me in the middle of a bunch of killers. I don't want any more of this stuff. I want out."

Wack had had little experience in handling informers, but he knew Canete was terrified and he appreciated the real danger to his inside man. He tried unsuccessfully to persuade him not to drop out, to keep up the contact. Canete refused. He said he would keep his next meeting with Ross to deliver more documents, and that was all. The two men walked off in separate directions.

SITTING IN A CELL at Florida's Raiford Federal Penitentiary, Rolando Otero fanned his rage against Augusto Pinochet, the man who personified the latest betrayal in his life, who had promised him asylum in Chile, whose thugs had humiliated him like a rat in a trap and turned him over to the hated FBI.

Otero, unlike the pedestrian, paunchy Orlando Bosch, fit everybody's—and his own—image of the idealistic terrorist. At thirty-five, with dark, roughly sculptured features and slight, muscular build, he looked younger and less jaded than most Miami Cuban militants. While others sold shoes and cars, Otero devoted full time to his

paramilitary activities and maintained a flamboyant lifestyle—
clothes, girls, nightclubs, lots of travel, and skydiving as a hobby.

Rage dominated Rolando Otero's life. Fidel Castro and the revolution had enthralled him when he was a young boy, until—his
aristocratic family having taken him into exile—he wallowed in
feelings of betrayal and vowed to kill the object of his former adula-
tion. When he was sixteen, the CIA recruited him and he became the
youngest member of the Bay of Pigs invasion force. He hated Castro
all the more for having defeated him and subjected him to long
months of imprisonment. Betrayed, in his mind, once again by the
CIA, he became a maverick terrorist, available to any group that
offered adventure and financing.

Many of the Cuban militants were disillusioned with the United
States government for putting the cause of overthrowing Castro on
the back burner in the 1970s. But Rolando Otero struck out. In his
rampage of anger in October and December 1975, practically every
symbol of the United States establishment in Miami was hit by a
bomb: Miami International Airport, two post offices, FBI headquarters, the Social Security Office, the Federal Building, and a large
private bank. The FBI was convinced Otero did the bombings. Otero
went on a trip to the Dominican Republic and then to Caracas,
Venezuela, leaving each country just a jump ahead of United States
extradition papers.

He found a haven in Santiago, Chile, in early 1976. He expected
a chance to admire at close range the true "nationalism" of the
Pinochet government and to participate in Chile's victorious ongoing
war against communism. But there too he met betrayal.

Gene Propper read the reports on Otero. Despite Chile's disclaimers, there was solid evidence that Otero had been in contact
with DINA up to the time of his expulsion to the United States in
May 1976. He had been on the inside, had gone on missions for
DINA, and at his trial in January he had signaled his resentment of
Chile and his willingness to talk. In July, Propper made arrangements with Otero's lawyer and laid out the ground rules for an
interview. Otero would provide information openly, said his attorney
William Clay, and cooperate fully on information about Chile and
the Chilean secret police, but any questions about Cuban exiles

would be out of bounds. Propper agreed. He obtained a writ and arranged to have Otero flown to Washington.

The interview took place in the U.S. Attorney's Office in Washington in July. Otero was nervous, crossing and uncrossing his legs, pursing his lips, and clenching his large jaw so that the muscles showed on the side of his face. He spoke rapidly, shotgun fashion. At first he vented his anger, talking incoherently about the injustice of his expulsion from Chile, his betrayal, his hatred for Special Agent Scherrer, his hatred for Manuel Contreras. Propper let him go on, then bored in point by point. He wanted information, detail by detail, of every personal contact Otero had had with DINA officers. Over the next three days the story unfolded.

In Caracas in late January 1976, Otero said, he was staying in the apartment of his old friend Ricardo Morales. Venezuela, aware of the FBI's efforts to extradite Otero, had allowed him to enter the country on the understanding that he would move on immediately to Chile. Otero knew that "Monkey" Morales was then employed by DISIP, the Venezuelan secret police. Propper also knew that Morales freelanced as an informant for the FBI. Morales persuaded Otero to "double" while in Chile: to work with DINA as he had planned but also to inform DISIP about DINA operations abroad.

Otero flew to Santiago on February 3 and checked into the elegant, colonial-style El Emperador Hotel. From there he went to the Chilean Foreign Ministry in the wing of La Moneda Palace that had remained intact. He identified himself as a captain in the Cuban exile army and, after a cordial welcome, was told by a Foreign Ministry intelligence officer that DINA would make contact with him at his hotel within several days.

A few days later three DINA officials, two men and a woman, came to his hotel room. They wore civilian clothes and behaved in a gruff, authoritarian manner. Otero told the officers, according to Propper's report, "that he expected to fight Cuban communism wherever it existed, and that his purpose was to contact DINA on behalf of the Cuban anti-Castro exiles. Otero said that he was contacting DINA in order to buy explosives and other equipment from them, in return for which he could give information on communists of interest to them in Latin America."

He described the three officers. The woman seemed to be present only to take notes and said nothing. She was thirtyish, heavy-set, and dark-complexioned. The officer who appeared to be in charge identified himself as Major Torres and was in his forties, olive-skinned, tall, and muscular.

The third member of the interviewing team said little, but asked incisive questions exhibiting detailed knowledge of Cuban exile affairs. He was "five feet ten inches tall, skinny build, blond hair and blue eyes." Otero estimated his age at approximately thirty-two to thirty-five, and said he seemed taller than he actually was because of his skinny build. He said this officer "appeared to have a very fair complexion but spoke Spanish with a North American accent."

Propper's expression did not change. He gave no signal to Otero that the description of the tall blond DINA officer was any more interesting than anything else Otero had told him, but his mind raced. Wack's informants had reported a tall blond Chilean in the company of Guillermo Novo around the time of the assassination. Another informant had added the detail that Novo's "DINA contact" was a Chilean-American. Now Otero seemed to have closed the circle: he had personally met in Chile a tall blond DINA officer, an expert in Cuban exile affairs, and this man had spoken Spanish with an American accent.

Otero continued the story of his odyssey with DINA. He told of another DINA agent becoming his case officer and assigning him to carry out the assassination of Andrés Pascal Allende and Mary Anne Beausire by traveling to Costa Rica at his own expense. He had got as far as Caracas, fully intending to carry out the assassination, and reported to Morales, then got cold feet and returned to Santiago. He said he had met the tall blond DINA agent on several other occasions.

After Otero was taken away, Propper and Cornick analyzed the information. They surmised that the man who enlisted Novo's help in the assassination might be the DINA agent who interrogated Otero in Santiago. They debated whether to take the interrogation one step further and show Otero the pictures given to the FBI as part of the Paraguay incident. The pictures had circulated to some FBI field offices, but agents were strictly prohibited from showing the pictures to anyone who was not a law enforcement officer.

The pictures and the Paraguay incident had not been an important part of the investigation, and Propper had to refresh his memory. They included the facing passport page containing Romeral's and Williams' personal data and physical descriptions. Although the black-and-white photographs were overcontrasted, which made it difficult to distinguish the color of hair, the description of Juan Williams on the documents fit.

When the agents debated whether to show the Williams and Romeral pictures to Otero, some argued that Otero might be working both sides of the fence still, despite his overt hatred of DINA, and might get word back to DINA through Cuban friends that the pictures were being used in the Letelier investigation. Propper was undecided. For months he had placed great hopes in the possibility of developing a source inside the Chilean government or DINA. Any sign that the investigation was zeroing in on individual agents, as Romeral and Williams were suspected to be, would "dry up the source immediately." Finally, they agreed that the risk had to be taken.

On July 12, the photos, mixed with other pictures, were shown to Otero. He didn't hesitate: the blond DINA officer he had met in Santiago was the man in the picture. The picture he identified was that of Juan Williams Rose. Over eight months had passed since the State Department had handed over the passports to Propper. Almost a year had passed since the pictures came into the possession of U.S. Ambassador George Landau in Paraguay.

The mysterious Juan Williams became the center of the investigation. Teletypes alerted field offices as to the renewed importance of the two pictures.

Robert Scherrer received the news in Buenos Aires. Since he had handled Otero's expulsion the year before, he had a special interest in the long cables that summarized the results of the three days of interviews. He cabled Washington, adding his analysis to the voluminous information. Otero's identification of Williams as a DINA agent in contact with Cubans in Santiago was, he concluded, "a momentous development" in the case. He scheduled another trip across the Andes to Santiago.

· · ·

RUMORS THAT PINOCHET had plans to curtail DINA began to circulate in Santiago political circles in July. They came from two sources: the Catholic Church hierarchy and the U.S. Embassy. And the rumors fit into the general thrust of political events that month.

On July 11, Pinochet gave a speech at a candle-lit hillside ceremony organized by the government-sponsored National Youth Front. He outlined for the first time the kind of government Chile would have after the military government, and promised that the transition to that new "institutionality" would soon begin. Chile would have a "new democracy," he said, but one that would protect the country from ever again falling into the clutches of Marxism. It would be "authoritarian," "integrating," "protected," and based on the "principle of subsidiarity" and "free economy." Pinochet's plan called for parliamentary elections sometime in the early 1980s and contained a provision that virtually ensured that the first elected president in the new system would be himself.*

But he did commit himself for the first time to the prospect of elections. *El Mercurio* and *Que Pasa* heaped praise on the speech, which they immediately dubbed the "Chacarillas Plan" after the hill where it was given. It was their plan, conceived in the technocratic businessmen's minds and written by one of them, Jaime Guzmán.

The U.S. Embassy saw it also as a response to their painstaking efforts to persuade Pinochet to move away from absolutism and toward elected government, no matter how far distant. Copies of the speech had been given to the embassy days in advance so that an immediate congratulatory statement could be issued in Washington. In Santiago, Chargé Thomas Boyatt, the top man in the embassy since the resignation of Ambassador David Popper, called personally on Foreign Minister Patricio Carvajal the next day and talked to Chilean journalists afterwards. Boyatt said he "came to officially visit

---

*According to the system, Pinochet would personally appoint one-third of the members of Congress, and the other two-thirds would be chosen by popular election. The congressmen would then hold an election to choose a president. Thus, if Pinochet were a candidate, and everybody assumed he would be, he would need only 26 percent of the vote in addition to his hand-picked congressmen.

Chancellor Carvajal to express to him in the most cordial and formal way the positive reaction there has been within the government of my country about the advances toward a new institutionality made by His Excellency the president. My government is very pleased to see Chile on the way to a governmental regime generated by election."

The opposition leaders screamed in anguish that Boyatt should congratulate Pinochet on a plan they considered a "farce" and a "mockery of democracy."* But Boyatt knew something the opposition didn't: that the civilians in the government and the moderate military had persuaded Pinochet to make substantive moves toward improving relations with the United States. Boyatt, a longtime friend of Pinochet's, also knew that changes in DINA were next on the agenda.

Manuel Contreras understood the implications for him of the presidential announcements. They meant that Pinochet had opted against the governmental model favored by him and his supporters, a rigid authoritarian state without elections or political parties in which the government, as ultimate arbiter, controls both business and labor. Worse, Contreras' informers brought him the news that some time ago Pinochet had requested that Contreras' rival, retired General Odlanier Mena, draw up a plan for the restructuring of Chile's intelligence service. In addition, Pinochet had appointed Colonel Jerónimo Pantoja, from outside the Contreras circle of intimates, as DINA's new number two man.

On August 13, during an official visit of U.S. Assistant Secretary of State Terence Todman, a government spokesman announced that DINA had been dissolved and that a new intelligence organization, the National Information Center, would be formed. DINA, the announcement continued, "had completed the delicate national security functions with which it was entrusted." Contreras remained as director of the new organization.

Robert Scherrer arrived in Santiago one week later. He needed

---

*A State Department spokesman put their fears somewhat to rest a few days later in a clarifying statement, saying that the administration remained "very concerned" about human rights violations in Chile and that Carter would "prefer" an "earlier return" to democracy than that promised by Pinochet.

to find out who Juan Williams and Alejandro Romeral were without Contreras getting wind of his interest. It was not hard to conclude that if Juan Williams was actually involved with the Cubans in the Letelier assassination, and Contreras knew Scherrer was on the trail, Juan Williams, whoever he was, would become just another statistic in DINA's missing-persons list.

Scherrer made the rounds. A surreptitious check at the Chilean National Identity Cabinet, the agency responsible for issuing ID cards to all adult Chileans, came up negative. There were no records of anyone named Juan Williams or Alejandro Romeral. Next he went to the Defense Ministry and was allowed to examine the current army roster. No Captains or Lieutenants Williams or Romeral.

He then went to see U.S. Consul Josiah Brownell. They had met several times before, and relations had been strained. Brownell countered his request to examine consulate documents by insisting on express authorization from Washington. Fortunately, Brownell had received the "operational memos" allowing the search, and he showed Scherrer to the grey cabinet where official "form 257-A" visa applications were kept. Scherrer quickly found the cards for Juan Williams and Alejandro Romeral and asked to photocopy them.

Since they were official visas, he knew there was likely to be a so-called "note verbal" from the Chilean Foreign Ministry requesting the visas for official government business. Brownell showed him where the notes were stored. He had to go through hundreds of pages of probatory documents that visa applicants had furnished with their applications. All the papers were punched and filed daily in loose-leaf binders in chronological order. The note was there—one for both men. It was a form letter saying that Romeral and Williams were going to the United States on official business for the Ministry of Economics.

Scherrer emphasized to Brownell that the consulate records were of utmost importance in the Letelier investigation and cautioned him not to allow any records to be removed or destroyed. After a check with the Economics Ministry confirmed that nobody by those names worked there, he cabled his report. Romeral and Williams were fictitious names. They had sought and obtained official visas with the help of the Chilean Foreign Ministry for a covert mission to the United States about a month before the Letelier-Moffitt assassinations. Otero's identification of Williams as a DINA captain dealing with Cuban terrorists was ample reason to consider him a suspect in the case—if it could be established that he actually was in Washington.

Scherrer asked Cornick for copies of the Romeral and Williams pictures and the Paraguayan passports, and a rundown on all FBI information that might answer the basic question: Was Williams in the United States around the time of the assassinations?

SEATED BACK AT HIS DESK in the U.S. Embassy in Buenos Aires two weeks later, Scherrer studied the photographs of the two men and the data on the Paraguayan passports. The telephone rang. To his surprise, Colonel Manuel Contreras was on the line. "I want you to come here right away. It's something really important to me," Contreras told him. Scherrer stalled. Such short notice. "I don't even have a Chilean visa to enter your country."

"Don't worry about the visa," Contreras practically shouted. Scherrer speculated on possible reasons for the urgency in the DINA chief's voice. "I've made a reservation for you already," he told Scherrer. "I'll have someone from my personal staff meet you at Pudahuel." DINA Captain René Riveros met Scherrer at Santiago's airport and whisked him through immigration and customs without so much as a flash of papers or passport.

Without looking around, walking in his casual stride, Scherrer perused every DINA official's face as he entered Belgrado II. None resembled the two photographs. "I want visas for His Excellency's trip to Washington," Contreras told Scherrer, "and I need them immediately if the president and his wife are to have adequate security." President Carter had invited all Latin American heads of state, including Pinochet, to attend the signing ceremonies of the Panama Canal Treaty. "I am asking you as a personal favor to intervene in this affair, and cut through the red tape that has developed in your embassy these days. "Fifty-five people is what we need. After all, there is a great deal of hostility against us in certain quarters these days," Contreras explained. He also wanted gun permits for all his agents.

Scherrer promised to do his best. He returned to the embassy and assembled a photographic team to accomplish several hours of work. The next day he phoned Contreras on the direct line to his office. "I was able to pull a few strings," he told him. "The bottom line is that I have some good news for you. Just send me the actual passports so I can personally stamp the visas into them and get them right back to you."

A DINA messenger brought the passports to the U.S. Embassy. Scherrer chuckled as he examined each one before handing it to the photographer to be copied. Some faces he recognized, such as Colonel Victor Barría Barría, DINA's man in Buenos Aires, and DINA electronics chief José Fernández Schilling. He wrote down all names and numbers of the passports. Then he saw another familiar face. The civilian government employee's name was given as Morales Alarcón. The face belonged to Manuel Contreras. The passport's issue date was September 22, 1976, the day after the assassination.

He was disappointed not to find the names Romeral and Williams nor their photos among the passports. He noticed, however, that the Fernández Schilling, Barría Barría, and Morales Alarcón passports bore serial numbers that belonged to the Romeral and Williams sequence.*

On September 5 Pinochet and his entourage landed in Washington and checked into two floors at the Embassy Row Hotel, two blocks from the Chilean Embassy on Massachusetts Avenue. Pinochet considered the invitation to visit the United States capital an important step in restoring his tarnished image. President Carter had scheduled personal meetings with each of the Latin American heads of state, and Pinochet was looking forward to being treated as an equal by the president of the United States.

Senator James Eastland of Mississippi hosted a luncheon in Pinochet's honor. Between toasts, Eastland recounted to another senator,

---

*Scherrer used his favor to reduce the gun permits from 55 to 13. He also sent the photos of each of the 55 agents accompanying Pinochet to FBI headquarters, in effect "burning" each one. Contreras did not make the trip, but DINA's man in the Foreign Ministry, Guillermo Osorio, did accompany Pinochet.

"I told Pinochet that I was in favor of hanging all communists and putting all rabble-rousers in jail. And Pinochet said to me, 'That's exactly what I'm doing.' "

Later, waiting with Pinochet for his appointment with the president, his translator noticed that his knuckles showed almost white as he clutched the arms of his chair outside the White House Oval Office. Carter welcomed Pinochet; they shook hands. Then Pinochet gave the president of the United States a lecture on the progress he had made in eradicating communism and restoring law and order. Carter politely waited his turn to discuss items on his agenda. Neither raising his voice nor ceasing to smile, he told Pinochet that human rights remained high on the United States priority list and that he expected full cooperation on the Letelier case. Pinochet voiced ignorance about Carter's concern, but assured him that he would personally guarantee full cooperation.

Shortly afterwards Pinochet gave a press conference. A reporter asked him to comment on the accusations that Chile had ordered the assassination of Orlando Letelier. Pinochet placed his thumb and forefinger to his lips, the symbol of the sacred cross, and swore innocence. The Latin gesture escaped the Washington press corps, but the oath did not: "I am a Christian, not an assassin. I swear that nobody in the Chilean government ever planned such a thing."

Les Whitten from Jack Anderson's office had confirmed almost the exact opposite from FBI sources. On the day of Pinochet's departure, Thursday, September 8, the Anderson column appeared in hundreds of newspapers throughout the world: "Chile's shadowy secret police chief was the man behind the murder. . . . Some Justice Department sources speculate that Chilean President Augusto Pinochet personally suggested the assassination."

While Pinochet was in Washington, Special FBI Agent Larry Wack discreetly made the rounds of his Union City contacts, including those he knew would refuse to cooperate as well as those who had given him information in the past. Since Ricardo Canete's conversation with Alvin Ross, Wack had become doubly careful. A slip on his part, any signal that would lead one of the CNM inner circle to suspect who his informants were, could result in someone's death.

He had read the reports on the Washington interviews with Otero and on Scherrer's Santiago investigation into the Romeral and Williams names and pictures. He had received the pictures a few months before, but could not use them "on the street." Now, however, he had authorization to show the pictures to his informants who had told him the previous November about a blond Chilean hanging around with Guillermo Novo and other CNM members.

He arranged a separate, secure meeting with each of them. Urgent, he told them. Yet the meetings took time to arrange—Wack had to establish tight security, using backup agents to ensure that the informants were not followed. He needed other FBI agents to keep watch. Hand gestures, the position of a magazine in a coat pocket or under an arm, were the "all clear" or "danger" signals for the clandestine meetings.

One by one, Wack showed his informants the Paraguayan passport pictures. Some of them had originally recalled the man as clean-shaven, so Wack had the FBI laboratory remove Williams' beard in one of the photos.

On September 16, Wack teletyped Cornick his results: all his informants agreed that the Williams photo matched the man they had seen with the CNM members. None of them recognized Romeral.

IN WASHINGTON, CARTER CORNICK reorganized his priorities in the case. For the first time he placed the Romeral and Williams pictures and the Paraguay incident at the top of his list.

Cornick reviewed the thin file and found it contradictory. A State Department memo gave seemingly precise details about the entry of Romeral and Williams in Miami on August 22, a month before the assassination. The data on the memorandum showed A-2 diplomatic visas and Chilean, not Paraguayan, official passports. This checked with the visa applications discovered by Scherrer in Santiago. The memo led Cornick to a logical hypothesis: Romeral and Williams had returned to Santiago after getting the Paraguayan passports, had obtained new passports and visas, and had traveled to the United States on the same covert mission.

But according to the Immigration and Naturalization Service, no one using those names had entered the United States. How, then, did the State Department know that Romeral and Williams had entered the United States, and how had it learned the details about their passports?

Cornick compared the Paraguayan passport information with the visa applications. The personal descriptions varied slightly. The two Paraguayan passports were in the names of Juan Williams and Alejandro Romeral. They omitted the second last names, or matronymics, ordinarily used by all Spanish-speaking persons. The men who were reported entering at Miami were listed as Juan Williams Rose and Alejandro Romeral Jara. The difference could conceivably have caused a filing error.

Cornick decided to cover the ground once more with both the State Department and the INS. He called the State Department's Chile desk and spoke to the new desk man, Robert Steven, who had recently replaced Robert Driscoll.

Steven knew Chile well, and felt a strong affection for and a sense of identification with the country—a phenomenon not uncommon among Foreign Service officers who had served there. He understood the intricacies of Chilean politics and took charge of the desk with an authority and enthusiasm that were immediately evident to Propper and Cornick, who had often complained about Driscoll's lackadaisical response to their requests in the Letelier-Moffitt case.

Cornick gave Steven no indication why he wanted a file search on the Romeral and Williams matter. He presented the request as routine. The two men chatted about the case. Cornick showed optimism, but volunteered few facts about the recent progress.

Steven took on the task with relish. An Ivy Leaguer of Massachusetts Brahmin stock, he viewed Foreign Service work as a pleasant duty and a privilege. The Letelier-Moffitt case interested him. Steven had spent considerable time during his first weeks on the Chile desk putting the haphazardly stacked files on the case in order.

ON SEPTEMBER 21, the Chilean springtime begins: the season of elections in the past, of political assassinations and punitive police campaigns against the left in 1974, 1975, and 1976. In the bright, warm days of spring 1977, the most bitterly fought power struggle since the coup took shape.

Contreras remained at the helm of Belgrado II. Opposition leaders cited this as proof that the police state, with its arbitrary disregard of basic citizens' rights, would continue. They pointed to the similarity of wording between the old DINA charter and the presidential decree creating the new National Information Center (Centro Nacional de Información—CNI). Contreras, however, clung to power with a sense of desperation. He could no longer count on the president of Chile and the commander in chief of its armed forces as an absolute ally.

In September and October, Contreras drew closer around him the DINA civilians who had always given him unconditional loyalty. Career army officers, like Operations Director Colonel Pedro Espinoza and Captain Armando Fernández, were unlikely to stake their future on a crumbling empire. They began to drift away from DINA, obtaining transfers to military posts.

The cadre of loyalists around Contreras carefully avoided using the word CNI (pronounced say-nee). They referred to "The Service," which for them would always be DINA. They prided themselves on their toughness, their unflinching hard line. In September a score of small bombs exploded, targeted at El Mercurio, Citibank, and a former Pinochet residence. The press dutifully printed the perfunctory government accusations that pointed the finger at "left extremists." But among journalists and among U.S. Embassy staff it became an open secret that Contreras' men had planted most if not all of the bombs as a warning to those pushing a softer line.*

Contreras had been outmaneuvered. As if the very Marxist laws that he had vowed to disprove and to eradicate had crept up like a sneaky ivy on the DINA walls, economic interests had dictated the turn of events.

---

*The new CNI agents also played rough. Shortly after the bombings, Victor Fuenzalida, a former Patria y Libertad activist, was found drugged and dazed in his car after a three-day disappearance. CNI agents had tortured and interrogated him, his wife told the press. She also confided that Fuenzalida had worked for DINA as an explosives expert since shortly after the coup.

The economic gang of technocrats had used DINA, had relied upon Contreras' ruthless will to destroy the labor unions of Chile, to silence all political voices, to rid the nation of all institutional obstacles that lay in the path of their economic model. But this accomplished, the "Chicago Boys" found DINA and its methods an obstacle and, without a drop of sentiment or loyalty, now actively plotted for its removal and for the removal of its chief, its designer, its mainstay.

As a colonel, he had wielded the might of ten generals at the apex of his power. But with DINA formally abolished and Pinochet no longer solidly behind him, he discovered what he had suspected: he had no independent constituency within the military. He had friends and admirers, but nowhere near as many as he had enemies. And even his staunchest supporters did not possess the will or organized strength to confront the generals' corps to defend his position without the clear backing of Pinochet.

Contreras, forced to retreat, gathered his loyalists and prepared to do battle to recapture Pinochet's support, to convince His Excellency that the economic group who had persuaded him to dissolve DINA and kowtow to the United States had in fact deceived him and betrayed the *patria*.

Before he could take the offensive, Contreras had to take precautions. Pinochet was replacing him with General Odlanier Mena, his rival, a man jealous of his predecessor's power. Contreras did not want any damaging evidence to fall into his hands. Before he turned his offices over to Mena, Contreras supervised his men in a weeks-long task of expurgating DINA files of material relating to clandestine arrests, brigades, interrogation and execution centers.

On October 22, Contreras attended a noon reception at the Peruvian Embassy. Among the Foreign Ministry officials he saw his friend Colonel Enrique Valdés Puga, who had serviced his false passport needs. Guillermo Osorio, Puga's man who took care of the day-to-day details, was standing across the reception room. Contreras and Puga smiled at him. Osorio had begun drinking even before he saw Puga and Contreras at the reception. When they approached him he swallowed the rest of his red wine and ordered more. Observers watched the trio leave together at one o'clock. They took Contreras' car to Osorio's home.

A white-faced Osorio entered his house alone. As his maid served him lunch he continued drinking. He ate little and refused to answer his wife Mary's questions about his obvious distress. She did not press him. She had learned not to probe.

The frail, middle-aged career diplomat rose unsteadily from the lunch table and said he would "lie down for a while." He asked his wife to bring him an Alka-Seltzer. In the bedroom he removed his trousers, drank the Alka-Seltzer, and lay down. His wife left him alone. A few minutes later she and the maid heard a shot. They rushed to the bedroom. Osorio's hand held a gun, dangling from his thumb, the very gun he kept in the nightstand. From a tiny hole in the middle of his forehead trickled a thin stream of blood.*

THE FIRST WEEK OF NOVEMBER the government officially announced that Manuel Contreras had resigned as director of CNI. Simultaneously it was announced that Contreras was among eight army colonels promoted to brigadier general. Contreras, the announcement said, had been designated special adviser to the president on national security.

Since 1973, Contreras had been a shadowy figure whose name was seldom mentioned, a symbol, almost in the abstract, of the terror that gripped Chile. Few outside the army knew what he looked like. On November 3 the cloak of mystery was officially lifted. Contreras' picture was distributed along with pictures of the other seven colonels elevated to brigadier general. That afternoon Contreras' face appeared on the front page of the tabloid *La Segunda*.

The new CNI director, Odlanier Mena, was called out of retirement to resume active duty. Mena had returned from his ambassador's post in Uruguay only days before. When he went to take charge of DINA headquarters in mid-November he took with him a dozen personally selected military aides. They entered the Belgrado II

*Puga returned with General Forestier to Osorio's house when his wife telephoned them. They arranged for the coroner to waive the autopsy.

building guardedly, like an occupying army. The file rooms still bore the signs of hasty ransacking by Contreras' men. His office had been stripped of much of its electronic equipment.

The next three weeks, as Mena and his men went over personnel lists, over one thousand agents, most of them civilians, resigned or were fired.

In Washington Robert Steven combed the Chile desk files for material on Romeral and Williams and the Paraguay incident. Knowing the usual working procedures of State Department officials, he reasoned that the most sensitive material about what had happened in Paraguay might be stored in the personal file safe of Harry Shlaudeman, who had recently left the job of assistant secretary for Latin America. After obtaining authorization, he went to Shlaudeman's vacant office and opened the files for classified materials.

He had reasoned correctly: there were several folders relating to the Paraguay incident and to the Romeral and Williams passports. Because of their classification, copies had never circulated through normal State Department channels. As he uncovered relevant documents, he forwarded them to Propper by courier. In some cases, he asked Propper to come personally to the State Department to read documents whose high-secrecy classification prohibited physical transfer or the making of copies.*

The key document was a cable from Ambassador George Landau to Vernon Walters, deputy director of the CIA in 1976, sent to the CIA via the State Department back channel known as the "Roger Channel." For the first time Propper directed his full attention to what had happened in Paraguay in July and August 1976, to the events that led to the United States government having possession of the pictures that had now become the center of his investigation.

General Vernon Walters, Propper learned, had traveled to Paraguay in June 1976 to remove the CIA station chief from his post because of a dispute with Ambassador Landau. The CIA chief had

---

*Propper, Barcella, and their two superiors, Donald Campbell and Earl Silbert, received maximum interdepartmental security clearance allowing them access to classified material from any department of the government.

deceived Landau, putting him in the embarrassing position of having denied to the Paraguayan government that a certain Paraguayan was a CIA agent, then being proved wrong. Walters' trip to Paraguay had the double purpose of summarily removing the CIA station chief and trying to convince the Paraguayans not to kill the unfortunate CIA agent who had been arrested and was being accused of involvement in a plot to overthrow President Stroessner.

The assignment was routine to Walters, a longtime Latin American hand and close friend of many of the most important figures in the military governments controlling the region. He considered the trip somewhat of a junket prior to his scheduled retirement from the agency. Paraguayan official Conrado Pappalardo had received Walters on his arrival and arranged interviews for him with other Paraguayan officials, including President Stroessner. The visit had been cordial. The CIA station chief was packed off to Buenos Aires and back to the United States, but the fate of the CIA agent, who had been tortured and remained in prison, had not been resolved when Walters departed the last week in June.

Landau had then gone on vacation for two weeks and on his return, Pappalardo had presented him with a request Landau described in the cable as "bizzare." Pappalardo said that President Pinochet of Chile had asked President Stroessner to provide passports to two Chilean DINA agents, Captain Juan Williams and First Lieutenant Alejandro Romeral, to conduct a mission in the United States. Pappalardo indicated that he understood that the Chilean mission had been arranged in Santiago with the CIA and that the two men were to contact General Walters on arrival in Washington. Pappalardo was at once informing Landau of the Chilean mission and requesting that Landau facilitate the issuance of visas to the United States.

Landau said he was suspicious of the matter because he considered it unusual for the CIA in Chile to arrange for a DINA mission to the United States using passports from a third country. But it appeared, he told Walters, that the request to go along with the Chilean DINA mission to the United States was the *quid pro quo* that Paraguay was demanding in exchange for sparing the CIA agent's life. Landau said he had issued the visas after having tried unsuccessfully to call Walters to check out the matter. But, he said, he had taken the precaution of having the entire passports photocopied and was forwarding the copies to the CIA so that it could control the visit by the DINA agents.

Then Propper read Walters' August 4 answer. Walters said he had not made any arrangements with Pappalardo about collaboration on such a Chilean DINA mission. He said he had discussed the matter with CIA Director George Bush and they had agreed that the agency wanted nothing to do with the DINA matter and desired no contact with agents Romeral and Williams. The Paraguayan request, he said, was "highly irregular" and "a strange way of doing business."

Ambassador Landau, Propper learned, took immediate action to repair his misstep in issuing the visas. He cabled the State Department that the visas for Romeral and Williams should be canceled and that lookouts should be posted by INS to prevent the two men from entering the United States. Landau reported to the State Department that he had called Pappalardo and demanded that the passports be retrieved from the Chileans and turned over to the U.S. Embassy so that the visas could be physically canceled.* Over the next few weeks, Landau called Pappalardo ten times, until finally in mid-September the unused passports were delivered.

It was clear to Propper that the Paraguay incident had caused considerable stir in the upper echelons of the CIA and the State Department, certainly more than was usual for a visa cancellation —a matter usually handled by consular officers and the State Department's Passport and Visa offices. He conceded that perhaps it could be attributed to the "extreme sensitivity" of the other matter, the removal of the CIA station chief and the discovery of the Paraguayan CIA agent.

Propper followed the paper trail left by the Paraguayan passports. The State Department Chile desk received the Romeral and Williams passport pictures on August 6.

---

*Paraguayan intelligence chief Colonel Benito Guanes, in a signed memorandum obtained by the authors, said Ambassador Landau asked him on August 6 to "contact his [Guanes'] friend Manuel Contreras" to demand that the passports be returned.

Propper was already familiar with the next set of papers: the memos from the State Department that had accompanied the pictures of Romeral and Williams and other documents when they were forwarded to the FBI a month after the assassination. And there was also the October 22 State Department communication notifying the FBI that Romeral and Williams had entered Miami August 22 with Chilean passports.

Propper had discounted that information after Cornick informed him that checks with INS were negative—no record of Romeral and Williams ever entering the United States. Cornick had repeated the INS check after Otero identified the Williams photo as a DINA agent, and had received the same negative answer.

But the new documents provided by Steven included a startling discovery. Propper read a memo dated November 11, 1976, from Chile desk officer Robert Driscoll to Harry Shlaudeman, his boss. It said that the two Chilean officers, Romeral and Williams, had been seen in Washington during a time period overlapping the assassination. Shlaudeman had ordered Driscoll to turn the information over to the FBI. Driscoll had not done so.

The questions were obvious. If INS had no record of Romeral and Williams entering the country, who then had informed the State Department that two men using the same names had entered with Chilean diplomatic passports on a precise date, August 22? Who was the source of Driscoll's information that someone had actually seen the two men in Washington? Why had Driscoll disobeyed his superior's order to inform the FBI?

The biggest questions remained: Who was Juan Williams, and who was Juan Williams Rose? Were they two persons or one? Whatever his real identity, the Juan Williams whose picture appeared in the Paraguayan passport was a Chilean army officer, a DINA agent who handled Cuban exile terrorist matters, and he had been identified in the company of Guillermo Novo, the presumed assassin, around the time of the assassination. Juan Williams had to be located and questioned.

Propper met with Cornick to discuss strategy. Cornick pouched the newfound State Department information to Scherrer in Buenos

Aires. Scherrer, at about the same time, had learned a bit of historical information that further stimulated interest in the figure of Juan Williams. At an early November cocktail party in Buenos Aires he had casually brought up the name Williams in a conversation with a Chilean army officer. The officer told Scherrer that the name was originally English and that a nineteenth-century navy captain named Juan Williams had played an important role in Chile's military history. Williams, he said, had beat the French in a maritime race in 1843 to claim the Strait of Magellan for Chile. Scherrer hid his amazement when the army officer told him the date in 1843 of Williams' famous landing on the Strait—it was September 21, the same date as the Letelier assassination.

The investigation could move no further without, in one way or another, demanding information directly from the Chilean government about Juan Williams. The question was how. A false step might cause the mysterious Juan Williams to disappear for good.

The removal of Contreras from CNI/DINA had radically changed the balance of power within the Chilean military and police forces. It was conceivable for the first time that a discreet approach through police or diplomatic channels could be handled confidentially without immediate leakage of the information to Contreras. It was also conceivable that even if Contreras learned of the United States interest in Williams, he would no longer be in a position to eliminate Williams.*

Propper favored broaching the Juan Williams matter to Chile in Washington through Chilean Ambassador Jorge Cauas. But the first attempt the previous June to enlist Cauas' cooperation in the investi-

---

*The extent of Contreras' real power during the months following his removal from CNI/-DINA was a subject of great speculation, even inside the civilian part of the Chilean government. Contreras officially had returned to his post as head of the San Antonio Army Engineering School, but there were credible reports that he retained a substantial secret budget with which to maintain a secret police squad parallel to General Mena's CNI. U.S. Embassy observers gave serious consideration to reports that President Pinochet, forced to remove Contreras by international and internal pressure, continued to cooperate with Contreras in the establishment of an autonomous "Death Squad" led by Contreras and DINA loyalists. The idea that Pinochet continued to rely heavily on Contreras was bolstered in December when it was learned that Contreras had traveled to Argentina to conduct crucial negotiations with that government on the Beagle Channel border conflict.

gation had turned into an embarrassing failure, First, Cauas had given Propper assurances that President Pinochet himself had ordered a special investigation of the activities of Cuban exiles in Chile. That claim turned out to be a lie, though United States officials were convinced that Cauas himself, in communicating the Chilean assurances, thought he was telling the truth. Then, when the Chilean answers to Propper's questions about the Cubans arrived, they contained further lies and served only to convince Propper that the Chilean government was actively involved in a cover-up in the Letelier case.

Scherrer, in a cable from Buenos Aires December 7, laid out a proposed course of action. Given what was known about the Paraguay incident, especially the fact that President Pinochet allegedly made the request for passports to President Stroessner, Scherrer said, it was likely that the Chilean government would deny all knowledge of the names when asked officially. To undercut that possibility and in effect to put the Chilean officials between a rock and a hard place, Scherrer recommended revealing specific details of damaging evidence held by the FBI which, unless satisfactorily explained, could be extremely embarrassing to the Chilean government. In addition to the names Williams and Romeral, the Chileans should be told that the FBI had established that the two men had obtained official visas at the U.S. Consulate on August 17, 1976, and that they had traveled to the United States during that same month.

Then he proposed a ruse to conceal the true extent of United States knowledge of the Paraguay incident. The Chileans should be told that FBI computers had discovered records of the attempt by Romeral and Williams to use Paraguayan passports to obtain visas at Asunción in July 1976. The Chileans, he reasoned, would be impressed by the knowledgeability of United States computers and worry that the FBI had even more information than was being disclosed.

Instead of going through Ambassador Cauas, Scherrer proposed approaching General Ernesto Baeza, the head of Investigaciones, the Chilean civilian police, in order to place the request for information on a strictly police-to-police basis. Baeza had cooperated with the

FBI and other United States criminal investigative agencies frequently in the past, and Scherrer knew him well. Baeza was also one of the Chilean generals who had expressed opposition to Contreras and the operations of DINA, and he had provided Scherrer with information on the activities of Cuban exiles in Chile and with immigration records on Cubans' travels to and from Chile.

Scherrer's plan to use police channels had the added advantage of heading off inevitable Chilean protests that the United States was using the Letelier case for political ends and was seeking to overthrow the Pinochet government. A week after Scherrer's December 7 cable, the plan was approved by Propper. After Christmas, Scherrer flew to Santiago.

GEORGE WALTER LANDAU, a tall, gaunt man in his late fifties, now ambassador to Chile, strode from his office to greet Scherrer and lead him into his private office. Scherrer took from his locked briefcase the two pictures of Juan Williams and Alejandro Romeral, and the draft of a letter to Investigaciones chief Baeza outlining the United States' request for information. Landau recognized the pictures. They existed because, seventeen months earlier when he was ambassador to Paraguay, some instinct had led him to order the two passports photographed and sent to the CIA.

Landau promised full embassy support, and a glint of enthusiasm showed through his usually staid demeanor. The matter would be treated as purely police-to-police, but Landau insisted that he be informed and consulted at every step.

The letter and pictures were delivered Thursday, December 29. Baeza was on vacation in the south of Chile in Punta Arenas, Scherrer learned, but his second in command, J. F. Salinas, said the letter would be sent to him for immediate attention.

A week passed with no word from Baeza. Then Scherrer, who had returned to Buenos Aires, got an urgent call from Landau politely but firmly ordering him back to Santiago to push Baeza on the Romeral and Williams matter. In Santiago, Scherrer and Landau met daily. Baeza was still in Punta Arenas; they suspected he was simply avoiding the issue. Scherrer called on Investigaciones acting chief Salinas every morning, then reported to Landau. After a week, Salinas set up a radio-telephone contact between Scherrer and Baeza.

He had received the letter and pictures, said Baeza. But he had "gone through channels" and delivered the United States request to Minister of the Interior General Raúl Benavides, the official superior of CNI/DINA under the new CNI charter. Scherrer, crestfallen, broke off the conversation and went to report to Landau. Scherrer felt that Baeza had caved in, had washed his hands of the whole matter and kicked it upstairs, where it had evidently been blocked.

Landau and Scherrer huddled in Landau's office and then cabled their separate reports to Washington. With Baeza's refusal to handle the case as a police matter, the investigation had become the concern of the State Department as well as the Justice Department. From this point on, diplomacy and the selective use of United States international power would have to take precedence over the investigators' sleuthing in determining the outcome of the case.

Ambassador Landau, unwittingly involved in the case since before the murders because of his former position in Paraguay, joined Propper, Cornick, Wack, and Scherrer in viewing the case as a personal challenge. Like most of the Latin American hands in the Foreign Service, Landau had favored the "martyr theory." He had resisted the idea that the unusual passport incident in Paraguay was connected to the Letelier-Moffitt case. After the murders he had made no attempt to bring the incident to the attention of the FBI.* In his mind, he had done the appropriate thing by reporting the

*Landau said the following when questioned during the trial:

Q. What did you do with the passports?

LANDAU: First I looked at them and found out that there was no picture in it, and that they were unused, and then I put them in my files. Nobody ever asked for them.

Q. Did they stay in your files?

A: They stayed in my files for—came with my files actually from Paraguay to Chile and as far as I was concerned, they were unused passports. They were of no use. I just didn't know what to do with them and it was not until '78 when this whole thing became active and the names of Williams and Romeral came up that I told the FBI man, when he came through, and I said, "Are you aware that I have those passports," and he said, "No," and I said, "Look. They are just a piece of paper, no picture on it. They are unused, but if you want them, if you will give me a receipt, I will give them to you," which I did.

incident to his superiors at the State Department and to the director and deputy director of the CIA. He had nothing to add to his August 1976 cables and reports.

Landau girded for a tough game of what others at the State Department would call "hard ball," an Americanism Landau eschewed. Born in Vienna, he had become an American citizen as a soldier during World War II. He still had an aristocratic European air that set him apart from most of his fellow United States ambassadors. But his deeply lined face, tanned the year round, bore the veteran diplomat's mixed expression of affability and toughness. A trace of an Austrian accent added an authoritative touch to his English.

Landau had excellent credentials for the task he was about to pursue with the military government. He had risen to the rank of colonel in U.S. Army Intelligence, then left uniformed service in 1947. Entering private business, he had spent several years in Colombia as general manager of an auto-manufacturing plant. In 1957 he became a Foreign Service reserve officer and was assigned to Montevideo with the title of commercial attaché.*

Much of his diplomatic career had brought him into intimate contact with right-wing dictatorships. He served in Spain as chief political officer under the Franco regime, and specialized in Spanish and Portuguese affairs for a time before being named ambassador to Paraguay in 1972. While in Spain he had gained a reputation as an ardent defender of the Franco government, but by 1977—at Senate confirmation hearings on his appointment as ambassador to Chile—he declared himself "personally highly committed to the cause of human rights." Once convinced by Scherrer's evidence that DINA agents, not leftists, were the most likely suspects in the murders, Landau turned single-mindedly to the task of forcing the Chileans to produce the key witness in the case: Juan Williams.

In Washington, Propper felt vindicated on learning that Scher-

---

*Landau was thirty-seven years old and lacked a college degree when he joined the State Department. Yet he began with the rank R-4, the rough equivalent of his former army rank of colonel. The designation "R" remained attached to his name for three years. He received a two-year "Associate of Arts" degree from George Washington University in 1969. By then, he had reached the top rank of the State Department, O-1.

rer's attempt to use Baeza had failed. Although they had never met, Propper and Scherrer had frequently disagreed on what tactics to use in approaching potential Chilean sources. He felt strengthened by the presence of a tough, decisive ambassador like Landau. And he had reached the conclusion that regular investigative tactics had been exhausted. The only card he had left to play, he felt, was Juan Williams' picture.

Propper was painfully aware how weak his case against Williams was and how little he really knew about the mysterious agent. His informant's evidence linking the DINA agent to the Cubans was solid and convincing, but virtually useless in court. At this point it was doubtful that it could even win convictions of Guillermo Novo and Alvin Ross.

Propper could count on other strengths, however. With the support of the State Department, he could bid up his hand so high that perhaps the Chilean government, aware of its own guilt and uncertain of the extent of United States knowledge, might be compelled to cut its losses by dropping out of the betting. The image of a gigantic poker game stayed uppermost in Propper's mind. He was not a heavy gambler, but he loved the challenge of poker and its central gambit: the bluff.

The legal mechanism Propper chose for his move was letters rogatory, which were a request for international judicial assistance. This device allowed the court of one country to ask the court of another to carry out certain judicial procedures. Such requests were routinely reciprocated in international business matters in the courts of most nonsocialist countries. The procedures included putting witnesses under oath and asking them questions provided by the party asking assistance. Propper began to prepare a list of questions for Juan Williams and Alejandro Romeral.

AT HIS HOME electronics laboratory on Lo Curro hill, Michael Townley spent much of his time in January 1978 teaching himself computer technology. His work at DINA had changed radically over the last year, and after Contreras' resignation, Townley had considered himself lucky not to have been purged by General Mena along with many of the other civilian agents. He poured over technical handbooks and journals with the same zeal as he had once studied the technology of terrorism—electronics and explosives. Already he had established business contacts with two computer supply firms in the United States, making purchases for DINA and a growing private clientele.

He gave little thought to the Letelier mission. A lot of water had gone under the bridge since then, and missions to Argentina had more recently occupied his attention. DINA co-workers had allayed Townley's nervousness* about the Paraguay fiasco by assuring him that two other men using the names Romeral and Williams had traveled to the United States to clean up the operation by giving it an innocent face. As far as he could tell, the United States' investigation of the murders had concentrated almost exclusively on the "Cuban connection" and had been unable to tie the killings to Chile or DINA.†

In late January, as he and his family were packing for a vacation in the south of Chile, Townley received a call from Miami. The caller identified himself as "Fernando," and Townley recognized the code name and the voice immediately as Guillermo Novo's. They talked in euphemisms. Novo wanted money. He was apologetic but firm in his demand for what he called a "loan" of $25,000. The case had gotten too hot, he said, and the "organization" needed the money to "relocate some of the members."

Townley was sympathetic. He knew Novo had been in hiding since the previous June, wearing a wig and moving from safehouse to safehouse in Little Havana. He said he would pass on the request to Contreras, who was at his vacation home in Santo Domingo on the coast. The next several days, Townley received more calls and

---

*An April 12, 1977 article in the *Washington Post* by Watergate reporter Bob Woodward gave Townley a few panicky days by mentioning an Edmund Wilson as a former CIA operative and suspect in the Letelier-Moffitt case—a name too close for comfort to Townley's DINA alias of Juan Andrés Wilson.

†Townley's perception, expressed in his courtroom statements, was that Investigaciones chief Baeza did not give the Romeral and Williams pictures to DINA.

requests for money—first from Novo again and then from Virgilio Paz and Alvin Ross. Each used a different approach. Novo continued to call the money a loan. Paz said he considered it a matter of honor and friendship between himself and Townley and between the CNM and DINA. Ross growled and cursed and threatened dire consequences if DINA did not pay up on the "debt."

Townley drove to Santo Domingo in his battered grey Austin Mini to speak to Contreras. Santo Domingo was barely an hour's drive from Santiago. He had to pass through the city of San Antonio, the port, then down a long hill to the cement bridge that crossed the dark Maipo River. As he gunned the car over the bridge he could see to his right the outline of Tejas Verdes and the army engineering headquarters where he had spent many days training early in his DINA career. Overlooking the bridge on a hill to his left was the white cement statue of the Christ of Maipo, and below were the ramshackle remains of the abandoned concentration camp. Five minutes later, Townley reached the black cliffs known as the "Rocks of Santo Domingo" and drove through the placid bougainvillea-lined streets to identify himself to the guard patrol at Contreras' street.

Contreras, still in rough clothes from a day of fishing, greeted Townley warmly. Townley told him of the new developments. Contreras asked for his analysis of the Cuban request. It was unlikely, Townley answered, that the FBI had developed a strong case against the Cubans. One CNM member, José Dionisio Suárez, had been in jail almost a year for refusing to testify to the grand jury, Townley added, and the United States authorities had been unable to charge him with the crime.

Contreras rose to signal that the meeting was at an end. No money, he said. Tell them they can send their families to Chile to live if they want, and they will be taken care of. But the members of the assassination team would have to fend for themselves. Contreras added that he no longer had that kind of budget to spend.

Townley moved toward the door, and then, in a burst of uncharacteristic audacity, made a last appeal. If you can't command that kind of money yourself, he said, couldn't you . . . you know . . . go up higher?

"I can't," Townley quoted Contreras as saying. "No one above me knows about the operation. I can't ask for the money."

ON FEBRUARY 17, Assistant Secretary of State Warren Christopher summoned Chilean Ambassador Jorge Cauas to the State Department. Christopher handed Cauas a ten-page sheaf of papers tied with official red ribbon and bearing the dual seals of the Department of State and the Department of Justice. The documents bore the signatures of Secretary of State Cyrus Vance, Attorney General Griffin Bell, and William B. Bryant, chief judge of the U.S. District Court for the District of Columbia.

Christopher told Cauas that an identical document would be officially presented to the Chilean Foreign Ministry in Santiago by U.S. Ambassador George Landau. Cauas read through the documents quickly. They consisted of a letter from Judge Bryant to the Supreme Court of Chile and a list of fifty-five "questions for Juan Williams Rose and Alejandro Romeral Jara."

Point three of Bryant's letter said:

It has become known to the Attorney General of the United States . . . that two members of the Chilean military entered the United States one month before the Letelier and Moffitt murders. At least one of these men met with one of the persons believed to be responsible for these murders. Both of these men had previously obtained visas to enter the United States using fraudulent documentation from a country other than Chile. These visas were revoked by the United States on August 9, 1976, after the fraudulent nature of the documents was discovered. They subsequently obtained official A-2 visas from the United States Embassy in Santiago, Chile, on August 17, 1976, by presenting official Chilean passports.

The letter described Williams and Romeral and added: "It is believed that these men have knowledge and information concerning these murders. It is therefore requested that you cause each of these men to appear in Court to answer under oath the written questions which are attached to this request." Cauas finished reading the letter and glanced at the four pages of single-spaced typed questions. Attached to the questions were photographs of Williams and Romeral and the Paraguayan passports.

Cauas repeated the Chilean government's pledge to cooperate fully with the United States' request, but the words rang hollow. The evidence presented in the documents clearly laid the Letelier-Moffitt case on the doorstep of the Chilean government for the first time. Cauas asked Christopher about publicity. He said he assumed the letters rogatory would be handled as in the past—that the State Department would keep all contacts on the case secret. Christopher replied that that was no longer possible. The Bryant letter would be filed publicly in U.S. District Court.

The meeting ended. It had lasted less than half an hour.

THE NEWS OF THE letters rogatory reached Santiago front pages the following Thursday, after having appeared first in the *Washington Post.* Propper's elaborately orchestrated poker game now began to unfold publicly one card at a time.

A cascade of official denials and disclaimers issued forth from the Chilean government and military. There was no Juan Williams or Alejandro Romeral in their official records, said spokesmen for the army, navy, air force, and Foreign Ministry. No civilians by those names either, said the Cabinet of Identification after a check of registration records. "The Last Name Romeral Doesn't Exist in Chile," headlined the official government newspaper *El Cronista.* "It's up to the United States to explain how the U.S. Embassy in Chile granted visas to Williams and Romeral," said one official.

The next day U.S. Embassy officials, in briefings for several American correspondents, played another of Propper's cards. "We know the names are fictitious," a spokesman said. "We have a signed letter of request for visas in those names from the Chilean Foreign Ministry, saying that Romeral and Williams were going to the United States on official business for the Ministry of Economy. Let them explain that."

Michael Townley spent most of February vacationing with Inés and two of the children at a cabin on a lake in southern Chile. He filled the dull hours and earned some extra money by installing radio equipment for wealthy farmers in the area. The time spent relaxing and talking with Inés had strengthened their faltering relationship. Inés' three children had already left home. Ronnie and Andy had left two years before, and now Susie was planning to get married.

Michael and Inés talked about the future and about money. The private school, Saint George's, was more expensive every year because of the economic changes being implemented by the "Chicago Boys." Townley's DINA salary had less buying power each year and was now approaching insignificance. Already the major share of his income came from his moonlighting jobs in private industry and from the lucrative import of tariff-free electronic equipment—the latter a perquisite of his DINA status.

Inés urged him to get out of DINA for good, to work full time at the computer-import business he had begun. Townley was tempted. Since Contreras had been removed, DINA had changed. But his loyalty to Contreras had not diminished, and he nursed the hope—discussed in hushed tones at gatherings of DINA stalwarts—that Contreras would regain power.

The Townleys drove back to Santiago and found the name of Juan Williams headlined in every newspaper. Townley cursed, called his CNI/DINA secretary, and found the expected message waiting. He was to call Colonel Vianel Valdivieso, a Contreras loyalist and his chief in the electronics section. Valdivieso told him to come that night to "Nico's Pizza," a sleazy drive-in on the outskirts of the city.

Valdivieso picked up Townley at his home and drove him to the drive-in. They found Fernández already at the restaurant, sat down with him, and ordered a pizza. Townley was glad to see Fernández. A few minutes later a grey Peugeot pulled into the parking area. Valdivieso watched, then made a sign with his hand. Townley and Fernandéz walked out and got in the back seat of the Peugeot. Townley saw that the driver was Eduardo Iturriaga, his former chief in the External Section. Beside him sat Manuel Contreras. Iturriaga backed out and drove into the street. Another car that Townley presumed to be Contreras' guard patrol followed.

"I have arranged for you both to go down south, to the farm, where you will be safe from all this in case something should go wrong," Contreras told Townley and Fernández. He had, he said, anticipated problems in light of what had happened in Paraguay. "But the cover operation should take care of it nicely. Riveros and Mosqueira will answer the questions for the *gringos.*"

Townley stiffened. "Down south," he thought, they would disappear like hundreds of prisoners before them. The betrayal he feared had come from the man he admired almost as much as His Excellency the president. Obviously he and Fernández had become men who knew too much, and Contreras was planning to get them out of the way.

"I suggest that Fernández and I keep up the cover story as long as possible," Townley said. "I won't leave Santiago." It was the first time he had ever refused a direct order.

Fernández let Townley do the talking as Contreras grew angry. But Townley had come prepared—at his wife's insistence—with an intelligence operative's life insurance policy. He had, he told Contreras, arranged for certain files on his DINA activities to be kept by trusted friends outside the country.

A FEW DAYS LATER, the United States investigatory team played another card. The pictures of Romeral and Williams were given to veteran *Washington Star* reporter Jeremiah O'Leary, along with a full background on the government's determination to force Chile to produce the two agents for questioning. Two persons with inside knowledge of the case, who themselves had access to the photos, admitted that the leak to O'Leary was officially authorized and arranged. The *Star* printed the pictures on March 3 under a banner headline: U.S. THREATENING TO SEVER CHILE RELATIONS. The story said: "Officials of at least two federal agencies told *The Washington Star* that an uncooperative attitude by Chile toward the U.S. request could result in the recall of Ambassador George Landau at the least, and a rupture of diplomatic relations at worst."

The next morning in Santiago, wirephotos of Romeral and Williams appeared in *El Mercurio*. Ignacio Peñaflor* picked up the paper from his doorstep and gasped. "¡Chicha! El gringo," he cried. He had seen the "Juan Williams" in the picture only a few weeks before. He had known Michael Townley since 1974, when Townley had worked on his car at Juan Smith's garage.

They had become friendly at the garage, and Peñaflor had invited Townley home for drinks one evening. Townley had brought his wife, who he remembered wrote short stories using the pen name "Mariana" and had once won a writing award from *El Mercurio*. Townley had come across as affable but mysterious. He was obviously many cuts above the average Chilean auto mechanic, both in social graces and in his standard of living. Townley had also bragged about his days as a militant with Patria y Libertad.

Peñaflor, an ardent supporter of the Pinochet government, called an *El Mercurio* editor who was a trusted friend. Later in the day, the *El Mercurio* editor gave a reporter the go-ahead to write the story. A search of old precoup newspapers turned up a clip of Townley's picture from a leftist tabloid headlined THE MURDERER OF CONCEPCIÓN. A reporter was assigned to interview Inés Callejas Townley. As the day progressed, several other persons called with similar information.

The stories and pictures covered most of page 1 the next morning. The Williams picture was run side by side with the 1973 story showing a younger, disheveled-looking Townley. The man in the two pictures was clearly the same. An unsigned story implied that Townley was a CIA operative, and told the story of his Patria y Libertad past. In a separate story, Inés Callejas was identified as a "close friend" of Michael Townley. She was quoted as saying she hadn't seen Townley for four years. None of the coverage linked Townley to the Chilean government or to DINA. An *El Mercurio* editorial the same day urged the Chilean government to cooperate fully with the United States' request, which had been dubbed the *exhorto*—the exhortation.

The *El Mercurio* story, appearing in the country's most progovernment and authoritative newspaper, unleashed a flood of journalis-

---

*Not his real name.

tic energy in Chile. Reporters interpreted the lack of government reaction to *El Mercurio's* revelations as a green light to investigate. They published dozens of reports of persons who had known Townley. Townley's father, Jay Vernon Townley, was reached in Florida by the *Washington Post* and confirmed that his son lived in Chile, but said he had not seen him for three years. In Santiago, Patria y Libertad chief Pablo Rodríguez told the press Townley was a "collaborator" with his organization in the fight against Allende.

Townley was depicted as the American connection, as the hand of the CIA in the Letelier-Moffitt assassinations, but reporters didn't dare print all they learned. One Chilean journalist who had once lived near the Townley house in Lo Curro found out that two Chilean men entering and leaving the house regularly had admitted to being DINA employees. The journalist, convinced by a private conversation with a right-wing leader that Townley was a CIA agent, did not publish the story. Other journalists, deeply opposed to the Pinochet government but determined to preserve what little opposition journalism remained, were simply afraid to break new ground in the case.

Several days after Townley was identified, an opposition journalist received a telephone call from an old friend asking for a personal meeting. At the meeting, the friend told the journalist he knew the identity of the man in the second picture. Alejandro Romeral was Army Captain Armando Fernández, he said, and he showed the journalist a xeroxed page of the 1969 *Cienáguilas,* the yearbook of the military academy. The Fernández in the graduation-day picture was unmistakably the same person as Romeral. The friend said he had been alerted to the true identity of Romeral by two army classmates of Fernández who were troubled about possible Chilean military involvement in the Letelier assassination.

Fernández had been attached to DINA since its creation, the sources had said. The journalist knew his identification would effectively remove much of the red-herring aspect of Townley being American. If he wrote the story, there would no longer be any doubt about the connection of the Chilean military and DINA to the Letelier case. That, he feared, would not be tolerated by the government censorship overseers. When he got back to the office he called John Dinges, the *Washington Post*'s resident correspondent.

The story identifying Romeral as DINA officer Fernández appeared in the *Post* the next day, March 8. A number of Chilean journalists had been tipped off in the meantime that Dinges was doing the story, and began submitting queries about it to the local Associated Press office. By mid-afternoon, the wire service had transmitted the story. Now that the story was based on a foreign publication, the local Santiago media no longer feared that printing it would bring reprisals. *El Mercurio,* in its coverage, put the Romeral picture and the *Cienáguilas* picture of Fernández side by side.

In the same issue, *El Mercurio* reported President Pinochet's first public reaction to the letters rogatory. "This government," he said, "had nothing to do with the crime against Mr. Letelier." He added that he had the impression that the whole matter was "a very well elaborated campaign—like all communist campaigns—to discredit the government."

THE IDENTIFICATION OF Juan Williams as Michael Townley, an American, set off a round of feverish activity in the office of Assistant U.S. Attorney Eugene Propper. Propper had been prepared for the possibility that "Williams" had an American parent and spoke English, but not that he might be a full-fledged American with possible connections to the CIA. Propper knew there was no question that Townley had contacts with U.S. Embassy officials. By coincidence the former consul Frederick Purdy was in Washington to be interviewed on another matter by another assistant U.S. attorney. Purdy mentioned that he knew Townley, and Propper was called to interview him. He requested full record checks on Townley by the CIA. The CIA answered that Townley had "been in touch" with the agency on several occasions during the Allende period, but had never been a paid agent. Propper believed the CIA report.

The FBI had no record of Townley, but Cornick ordered agents all over the country to find out about him, and the Townley file grew quickly. Agent Larry Wack located Townley's younger sister Linda in North Tarrytown, New York, where she lived with her husband, Fred Fukuchi. She was wary and vague but said she remembered that her brother had visited her during a trip from Chile. By calling a friend who had seen her brother during the visit, she narrowed the date of the visit to around September 1976. She also remembered that Townley had made several phone calls during the visit.

Wack asked if she kept the monthly telephone bills. Fred Fukuchi pulled out the household records and found the bills, including the listing of toll calls, going back several years. Wack took the records for September 1976 back to his New York office and traced the numbers. He discovered that two collect calls had been placed to the Fukuchi household on September 9 from the Union City, New Jersey, Bottom of the Barrel bar, a Cuban Nationalist Movement hangout Wack knew well. On September 19, two days before the assassination, there was a call from the Fukuchi phone to 201-945-7198—the number registered to Guillermo Novo.

Additional new evidence came from an informant in Miami who tipped off the FBI that Townley had frequented an espionage equipment company, Audio Intelligence Devices, in Fort Lauderdale. AID president Jack Holcolm confirmed that he knew Townley and provided sign-in records establishing that Townley, using the name Kenneth Enyart, had visited the AID plant and talked to Holcolm September 21 and 22, 1976. In New Jersey, an FBI visit to an apartment formerly used by Alvin Ross yielded a variety of bomb-making equipment and a receipt for purchase of paging devices that bomb experts said could have been used as remote-control detonators of the type used in the assassination.

Propper kept in touch with events in Santiago by immediate courier delivery from State Department cable traffic. The embassy reported that the Chilean government had pledged its full cooperation and had opened an internal investigation to determine the origin of the passports used on Romeral and Williams' trip to the United States. But the Chileans had taken no substantive steps to produce the two men, and the embassy cautioned that the offer of cooperation might be a maneuver to gain more time.

Propper was prepared to leave for Chile on short notice. He wanted to be there to monitor the interrogation proceedings. On

March 18 word came from the embassy that the Chileans were ready to produce Romeral and Williams. Propper and Cornick boarded a plane that night and arrived in Santiago the next morning, a Sunday.

THE FIRST SIGN that President Augusto Pinochet was in trouble had come when Jorge Cauas flew back to Chile a few days after receiving the letters rogatory. He announced that he was resigning as ambassador to the United States. Before leaving Washington he had told friends at the State Department that he was disillusioned. He had finally come to accept as true many of the accusations of DINA brutality that he had, as ambassador, denounced as lies. The revelations linking his government to the Letelier assassination, he told a friend, was one of the reasons for cutting short his tour as ambassador.

In Santiago, Cauas found consternation among his civilian friends in the government. No other event in the four-odd years of military government had so threatened the future of the regime. Without the good will of the United States, their plans for Chile were totally illusory. He talked with businessmen and bankers and with those who determined the editorial line of the major media. The language was guarded, but they were of one mind: Contreras could not be allowed to prevent the government from coming to terms with the United States.

Over the next two weeks, as the Chilean front pages were filled with revelations about Townley and Fernández and the bogus passports, the men who considered themselves members of the "enlightened" right formulated a strategy.

At dinner meetings attended by no more than half a dozen men and at hours of informal gatherings in their high-rise offices, a common approach emerged. The civilians found that they were not alone in their point of view. They had the support of five top generals: Sergio Covarrubias, the army chief of staff; Héctor Orozco, chief of military intelligence; Odlanier Mena, director of CNI/DINA; René Vidal, a cabinet minister and secretary-general of the government; and Enrique Morel, head of the military region of Santiago. All of them—civilians and military alike—were staunch Pinochet loyalists. Some believed firmly that if DINA had carried out the Letelier operation,

Pinochet had not been informed; others were concerned only that any participation outside of DINA should never be proved. All had reasons of their own for considering Contreras a potential enemy.

They agreed that the Letelier case need not become Chile's Watergate. It need not cause a radical change in course for the regime other than to reinforce the already increasing grip of the civilian economic group and their military supporters on the government. They had effective control of the press and would know how to mute the damaging effect of new revelations. The damage, they believed, could be focused on sectors of the regime they wanted to weaken, namely Contreras and their adversaries on the ultra-right who wanted to curtail their economic model. The option of abandoning their support of Pinochet and rallying around an alternative figure was discussed actively in these circles in early March. The option was soon dropped, principally because no one else was available and because an open break with Pinochet would have necessitated a coup, thus ending the façade of unity of the Eleventh of September Movement.

Their task, then, was to convince Pinochet to adopt their strategy —in effect, to accept their leadership in managing the crisis. In exchange they offered the united support of the most powerful sectors of the civilian and military establishment. Hernán Cubillos, a former naval officer with unrivaled access to the U.S. Embassy, emerged as point man for the businessmen and civilian officials in the process of bringing Pinochet to their point of view.

Opposing them were the followers of Contreras, and Contreras himself. The Contreras camp proposed isolation and a declaration of independence from the United States. Its representatives urged Pinochet to proclaim that the United States' letters rogatory violated Chilean sovereignty and to refuse to cooperate with the American investigation in any way. Inside the military there was strong sentiment that cooperation in finding "Romeral and Williams" constituted a betrayal of the military code of honor according to which a commanding officer alone takes responsibility for actions resulting from his orders.

Contreras, in a series of meetings at his Santiago home, gave Bonaparte-like speeches to assembled military and civilian supporters. DINA, he said, had served as the most efficacious instrument in eradicating Marxism and creating the new Chile that served them all.

"We have served in the darkness and bloodied our hands so that Chileans might live in sunshine and tranquillity," one of those present recalled Contreras saying. "Now there are those who propose that we turn over to a foreign power the boys who, loyally following orders, were the soldiers in the front lines of the battle against communism."

Contreras argued that DINA's work and that of the whole Eleventh of September Movement would be in vain if Chile were handed over to the bankers and big businessmen whose only principle was profit and whose first loyalty was to Uncle Sam. Contreras knew his own followers were extremely loyal but few in number. His only hope was to convince President Pinochet personally to adopt his course. He asked for a face-to-face meeting.

General Augusto Pinochet expected to be president of Chile until 1990 and had never wavered in that resolve. That and anticommunism were his only guiding principles. Since 1973 he had successfully juggled competing forces within his regime and had given each faction a piece of the action. He had left the economy to the pro–United States businessmen and economists, against the wishes of the extreme rightists, who urged upon him a state-managed economy along fascist lines. Pinochet had turned over the task of eliminating Marxism to the fascists, and had given them a free hand to organize an authoritarian police state.

Pinochet, in handling the Letelier matter, was determined to continue to straddle the fence, to avoid being forced to choose one faction in such a way so as to lose the loyalty of the other. He was in a unique position. The Letelier assassination mission had been carried out by Contreras, but only Contreras and Pinochet knew the answer to the question in everybody's mind: Had Pinochet given the order or approved the Letelier assassination and other DINA assassination missions? Whatever Pinochet did, he must dissociate himself from Contreras without so alienating him that he would declare publicly that Pinochet had given the order. He had confidence in Contreras as a tough-minded man who would understand what Pinochet had to do. There was a phrase Contreras had often used in their daily intelligence sessions, in the old days when he was still head of DINA. The first job of the chief of intelligence, Contreras had said, was to "administer the silence." Pinochet devised his strategy to ensure that Contreras would continue to follow that maxim.

Contreras came to the Diego Portales Building and took the top-security elevator to the twenty-second floor, Pinochet's suite of offices. Instead of being shown into Pinochet's private office, however, he was taken to the conference room, where he found Pinochet presiding over a meeting of the eighteen members of the cabinet.

After Contreras was seated, Pinochet turned to him and asked for a report on the Letelier case for the benefit of the members of the government. Pinochet said there were three questions in particular that required specific answers: Was Michael Townley a DINA agent? Did DINA have anything to do with the Letelier assassination? Was there any reason the government or the military should refuse the United States' request to interrogate "Romeral and Williams"?

Contreras answered as Pinochet knew he would. He said the answer to the first two questions was no: Michael Townley had done "telecommunications" work for DINA on a contract basis but was not a full-time DINA agent. DINA had had nothing to do with the Letelier assassination. There was no reason that "Romeral and Williams" could not be interrogated; they had nothing to do with the Letelier matter and, moreover, they were not Townley and Captain Fernández. The two men who traveled to the United States in August 1976 as Romeral and Williams, Contreras explained, are René Riveros and Rolando Mosqueira, both captains of the army formerly attached to DINA. Their mission was conducted with the knowledge of the Central Intelligence Agency and involved routine intelligence tasks. While in Washington they made contact with CIA headquarters.

Contreras ended his report, rose, and walked out. Pinochet had maneuvered him into lying before the whole cabinet and making it appear that Pinochet himself was totally innocent.

EUGENE PROPPER ARRIVED IN Santiago on the bright Sunday afternoon of March 19, thinking the Chilean government had decided to cooperate. Cornick and Scherrer came with him on the plane. Propper was picked up by an embassy limousine and taken to the U.S. ambassador's luxurious hillside estate bordering on Santiago's lush mid-city golf club, Los Leones. Cornick and Scherrer were dropped off at the Carrera Hotel near the embassy. On Monday the three met at the embassy. They were led through the ambassador's office on the ninth floor, through a maze of code-locked doors and guards, to the top-security section marked POL/R—the quarters of the CIA station in Chile. They needed top-security facilities for their work.

During the day, the Chilean government informed the ambassador that the two men who had traveled to the United States with the Williams and Romeral passports would appear on Wednesday before the Chilean judge handling the letters rogatory. The judge, a woman named Juana González, would conduct the interrogation according to the United States' questions. The U.S. Embassy had hired a Chilean lawyer, Alfredo Etcheberry, who would represent the United States prosecutors at the hearing and would be allowed to ask follow-up questions

Ambassador Landau and Propper conferred on strategy. Townley's American citizenship changed the situation radically. The Chilean government would be hard put to it to refuse a United States demand to turn over an American citizen wanted for a crime, Landau suggested. After Townley's interrogation—and predictable refusal to answer the questions—Propper should demand his immediate deportation to the United States. Landau said, "We'll tell them: 'Give him to us. He's ours.'" Propper agreed.

Agent Scherrer was intrigued by the fact that Juan Williams had turned out to be an American citizen. He went to the U.S. Consulate to recheck registration files for United States citizens. He had gone there almost a year before looking for the "blond Chilean-American" and had found nothing. At that time he had checked every one of the consulate's 1,500 cards on file. He wondered why he hadn't noticed Michael Townley's name and picture in the files.

He found several 5 × 8 cards filled with writing and stapled together. Michael Townley had registered at the consulate in 1957 when he arrived as a boy with his parents, in 1964 and 1966 when his children were born, and in January 1971 and October 1973. But there was no picture. In the space for a passport-size photo on the upper card Scherrer found only dried glue and shreds of paper. Townley's picture had at one time been attached to the card. Someone had removed it before Scherrer's first search in April the year before.

On Tuesday, the Chilean Army announced that General Manuel Contreras had resigned "voluntarily." Pinochet told a group of newsmen at a lunch a few days later that Contreras had lied to him, and had left active service in order to avoid associating the armed forces in the Chilean investigation of the false-passport affair.

Late Wednesday evening Army Captains René Riveros and Rolando Mosqueira appeared before Judge Juana González and the lawyer for the United States, Alfredo Etcheberry. The two men identified themselves and said that they had traveled on an official mission for DINA to the United States in August 1976 using passports in the names of Juan Williams and Alejandro Romeral. They said they were ready to answer the United States' questions.

Etcheberry barely looked at the two men; he had expected to see Townley and Fernández. "These are not the men we are looking for," he told Judge González. "They don't in any way match the pictures of the two men that we have enclosed in the letters rogatory packet. The identifications of the two men that are the basis of the United States' request were made from the pictures, not from the names, which we have long assumed to be false. I request on behalf of my client, the government of the United States, that the court suspend these proceedings and refrain from revealing the contents of the questionnaire to these two men."

Propper was furious when he heard that the Chileans had attempted to palm off two strange men as Romeral and Williams. Scherrer was bemused. He had long wondered about the minor discrepancies in the descriptions of Williams on the Paraguayan passport and Williams on the Chilean passport that had actually been used to enter Miami. The Paraguayan passport listed birth date October 18, 1942, height 1.89 meters; the Chilean document listed March 12, 1949, and 1.75 meters. He and Cornick had discussed with Propper the possibility that two pairs of men had used the Romeral and Williams identities. Scherrer and Cornick had always been bothered by DINA's apparent irrationality in sending the same two men with the same false names to kill Letelier, knowing that the United States authorities were already suspicious of Romeral and Williams. Now that made more sense. Townley and Fernández had indeed traveled to Paraguay and obtained passports and visas under the false names Williams and Romeral. They could not have known that Ambassador Landau had made copies of their false passports, but they did know that the Americans had become suspicious and had ordered the visas canceled. Two men uninvolved in the Letelier assassination mission—now identified as Captains Mosqueira and Riveros—had used the names Romeral and Williams to provide an innocent explanation for what had happened in Paraguay. Cornick later learned that Mosqueira and Riveros, as "Williams and Romeral," had informed the CIA of their presence in Washington. The second Romeral and Williams journey, they deduced, was a cover operation intended to sidetrack the FBI should the Paraguay incident be brought to their attention after the assassination.

It had almost worked. But Landau had ordered the Paraguayan passports copied, and there could be no question that "Williams" was Michael Townley and that he was the man the FBI wanted.

Ambassador Landau was also outraged by what he regarded as a ploy by the Chileans to avoid turning over Michael Townley. Early Thursday morning he called the Chilean foreign minister and demanded a meeting. By noon all of the officials concerned with the case had gathered in the office of Foreign Minister Patricio Carvajal. The Chilean officials included Deputy Foreign Minister Enrique Valdés Puga, CNI chief Mena, deputy CNI chief Jerónimo Pantoja, Deputy Interior Minister Enrique Montero, and Miguel Schweitzer,* a lawyer. Sitting with Landau around the crowded conference table were Propper, lawyer Etcheberry, and Thomas Boyatt, Landau's deputy chief of mission.

When Landau rose to speak, one of those present was reminded of a Prussian general lecturing to his corporals. In measured, perfectly articulated Spanish, Landau explained the consequences of

---

*Schweitzer, the son of Pinochet's former justice minister of the same name, was one of five candidates suggested by the U.S. Embassy to represent the United States government in the letters rogatory matter.

Chile's failure to turn over Michael Townley. All niceties of international protocol were dropped as Landau hammered home his argument to the Chileans.

The United States government considered that the entirety of its relations with the government of Chile depended on one thing, that Michael Townley be presented to answer the United States' questions about the Letelier murder, Landau said. The argument that Townley is not under government control and cannot be found is not a credible position. Our investigators have firm evidence that Townley is linked in some way to the Letelier assassination, and we hold the Chilean government responsible for his apprehension. Failure to cooperate on this matter could oblige our investigators to make public the information in their possession that tends to cast the Chilean government in the role of accomplice in the Letelier assassination.

Attorney Miguel Schweitzer, speaking for the Chilean side, clung to the official position that Michael Townley had nothing to do with the Chilean government and that Chile had fully cooperated with the United States investigation. The United States, he said, by refusing to disclose all the evidence it possessed on the case, had not reciprocated that cooperation.

Before the meeting ended, the Chileans pledged to turn over Townley for questioning on the condition that the embassy continue to tell the press that Chile was cooperating in the case.

A week later, Michael Townley made his first public appearance. He was photographed running from a CNI/DINA car into the Ministry of Defense to testify before General Héctor Orozco, who as head of army intelligence was conducting an internal army investigation into the use of the false passports. Townley's statement to Orozco followed the lines of the cover story worked out with Fernández. Manuel Acuña, an attorney representing Townley, said his client "had seldom left his home" since his picture appeared in the press. The following day Townley and Fernández went to CNI headquarters at Belgrado II where, by special arrangement, Judge González and attorney for the United States Etcheberry were waiting to hear their answers to Propper's fifty-five questions. Townley answered six questions about his personal appearance and education and refused to answer the rest on the grounds of self-incrimination. The testimony was taken on April 1—April Fools' Day.

Townley was released without charges, but he guessed correctly that the United States would next demand his expulsion from Chile into the hands of the FBI. With Acuña, his lawyer, he devised a strategy to stay safely in Chile, although it would involve spending time in jail. The plan seemed perfect. Acuña arranged for the Concepción murder case to be resurrected. The long-dormant murder warrant for Townley's arrest was reactivated and would be served. The 1973 charges pre-empted the United States' demand for Townley's expulsion, Acuña contended, and thus would make it impossible for the Chilean government to turn him over. Despite willingness to cooperate, the government's hands would be tied. Officials close to President Pinochet had assured Townley that the government would not stand in his way.

While Townley schemed to save himself, Deputy Interior Minister Enrique Montero and attorney Miguel Schweitzer flew to Washington armed with authorization to negotiate Townley's expulsion. During long hours of discussion at the State Department with prosecutors Propper and Larry Barcella, the terms of the agreement were ironed out. Schweitzer and Montero demanded that the United States agree to keep the Letelier investigation from going beyond the identification of Townley's role. The Chilean government, Schweitzer argued, feared that the Letelier case would be used by Chile's enemies in the American government to seek the overthrow of the Pinochet government. The case could be used as a fishing expedition to delve into the whole range of DINA activities at home and abroad, they said.

The United States prosecutors assured them that was not the intention of the United States. They said they could not promise to limit the scope of the Letelier investigation but—in order to obtain Townley's expulsion—would agree to keep all other information about DINA activities from the press and from other governments where DINA crimes might have occurred. They agreed that extradition proceedings, not expulsion, would be used for future defendants.

Propper also agreed to keep the agreement itself a secret. The Chilean negotiators said they had to clear the final text with Santiago. The night of April 7, negotiator Miguel Schweitzer called prosecutor Eugene Propper at home. He said approval had been obtained and that the agreement was ready for signing. Propper called Larry Barcella. It was after 10:00 P.M., and Propper was entertaining guests at home in celebration of his twenty-ninth birthday.

The agreement had to be signed immediately. The prosecutors feared that the Chilean government would change its mind. Barcella, who had the draft agreement in his briefcase, drove immediately to the Chilean Embassy, where Schweitzer and Enrique Montero were waiting. At the embassy Montero signed for Chile and Barcella signed for the United States in the name of his boss, U.S. Attorney Earl Silbert. Below the name he placed his own initials ELB in nearly indecipherable script.

To the Chilean government, the agreement meant that the United States would not use information obtained in the Letelier investigation to expose DINA crimes to the world. To Propper and Barcella, the agreement was a fair price to pay to obtain the expulsion of the man they believed had arranged the Letelier-Moffitt murders.

Unstated in the agreement was the Chilean commitment to put Townley on a plane to the United States.

Barcella stayed a short while to chat with Schweitzer and Montero. Barcella asked about the situation in Santiago. Could anything go wrong?

"Things are very confuse in Santiago," Montero said in hesitant English.

Schweitzer, more fluent, corrected him: "Confusing. I can't predict what is going to happen. You can't tell who's in charge down there any more. Things change by the hour."

IN SANTIAGO, Michael Townley was confident that the reports of his impending expulsion were a ruse. He believed that Pinochet, while appearing to give in to the United States, would go along with Townley's "Concepción gambit"—to pre-empt the United States' expulsion demand by facing murder charges for the 1973 homicide in Concepción.

President Pinochet had informed the other three members of the junta three days before of his decision to turn Townley over to United States authorities. Air Force General Gustavo Leigh protested that such an important decision should not be made by the president alone but by the junta as a whole. Pinochet overruled him, and as had become usual in the meetings of the four men, Leigh remained unseconded in his dissent. Pinochet did not mention that Schweitzer and Montero had gone to Washington to negotiate a secret agreement on the terms of Townley's expulsion.

At mid-afternoon on Friday, April 7, CNI/DINA official Jerónimo Pantoja called Agents Cornick and Scherrer to his office at Belgrade II. He showed them an official paper signed by Interior Minister Raúl Benavides decreeing the expulsion of Michael Townley, but refused Cornick's request for a copy. He said the expulsion decree would be issued as soon as word was received from Chile's negotiators in Washington that the agreement had been signed with the United States prosecutors.

Townley must not know about the decree before he turns himself in to Investigaciones, Pantoja told them. "Townley has got a smart lawyer and they are maneuvering. We may not be able to get him out of the country until Sunday—Saturday night at the earliest."

At 6:30 P.M. Townley drove with his attorney, Manuel Acuña, to the headquarters of Investigaciones to turn himself over to authorities on the homicide warrant. He was nervous, but in high spirits. Acuña, the owner of a private plane, had arranged with Investigaciones officials to fly Townley to Concepción in custody of a detective the next day. Many of the detectives at Investigaciones knew Townley from his DINA work, and they invited him to their recreation room to play pool. Acuña departed, saying he would talk to Townley the next day. There is nothing to worry about, he said. Even if an expulsion decree is issued before we get to Concepción, the law provides twenty-four hours to file an appeal before the Supreme Court.

At 8:30 P.M. Chilean radio stations interrupted their programming to broadcast a special government announcement. By virtue of government decree 290, the spokesman said, Michael Townley's residence permit had been revoked and he would be expelled from the country. The government had determined that Townley had committed numerous violations of Chilean law by illegally entering and leaving the country.

Around the pool table at Investigaciones, the detectives' banter took on an edge of meanness. The detectives knew of Townley's plans to become a prisoner in Concepción to avoid expulsion from the country. The Concepción jail is full of political prisoners, they reminded him. Many of the Concepción prisoners are "extremists" they said, one a convicted murder. They laughed, but Townley blanched. "I'll bet you don't last a day down there," one of the detectives put in. Townley racked his pool cue and walked out of the room. Guards followed him. He went to a telephone and began making calls.

Robert Scherrer and Carter Cornick awoke the next morning at the Carrera Hotel and met in the Copper Room for a leisurely breakfast shortly after 8:00 A.M. They joked about the tense waiting the night before for the issuance of the expulsion decree. Their job in Santiago was almost over, and it had been successful. Townley was securely in custody at Investigaciones headquarters and would be put aboard that night's Braniff International flight to Miami. They would be on board to receive him.

Scherrer, dressed in blue jeans, returned to his room about 9:00 to brush his teeth. The phone rang. The man on the other end refused to identify himself.

"Get out to Pudahuel Airport right away. Townley will be on the Ecuatoriana Airlines flight 052 scheduled to leave at nine forty-five. Don't worry about tickets and reservations. We'll take care of that. Please hurry, Townley's lawyer is maneuvering."

Scherrer called Ambassador Landau at home. He said there was a risk in taking Townley out of Chile on a non-American airline, especially an Ecuatoriana Airlines flight with intermediate stops in Ecuador before flying on to the United States. Landau listened closely to Scherrer's analysis, then decided. "It may be our only chance to get him," he said. "We have to take the risk."

Scherrer changed into a suit and called Cornick away from his third cup of coffee in the Copper Room. Minutes later, leaving their bags behind and the hotel bill unpaid, Scherrer and Cornick raced out of the hotel and into a waiting embassy car.

A half-hour later, the van with the two FBI agents arrived at Pudahuel Airport and drove directly out onto the runway next to the multicolored Ecuatoriana Airlines plane. The scheduled departure time had passed, but airport authorities denied permission for take-off.

Scherrer and Cornick waited at the bottom of the narrow aluminum stairway. They watched as a caravan of police cars rounded the curve leading to the airport. A few minutes later a group of men with machine guns emerged from the airport building, and a car headed toward the plane. The tall, jeans-clad figure of Michael Townley got out slowly. Handcuffed with his hands at his waist, Townley walked up the ramp and into the plane with one of the guards. He looked at Scherrer and recognized him from having seen him months before at DINA headquarters during one of Scherrer's visits with Contreras. He had seen Cornick's picture in the Santiago newspapers. They led him to a window seat at the rear of the plane, and took the other two seats. The plane lifted off the runway over an hour late, on its twelve-hour flight to the United States. Michael Townley raised his manacled hands to his face and cried.

"Mike," Cornick said, "you understand, don't you, that you are in deep trouble and you will be arrested as soon as we reach United States soil?"

Townley, ashen-faced, answered in a cold, angry voice, "I didn't think you were taking me on a picnic with these handcuffs."

Cornick, seated next to Townley, adopted the role of the hard-nosed, crime-hating cop, telling Townley gruffly about the charges that he faced. Scherrer, in the aisle seat, was friendly, even cajoling in tone. He spoke as one intelligence officer to another. The conversation wove by indirection in and through the investigation that had brought them together. The hours passed according to the flight rhythm of drinks, meals, and idle time.

"I wonder what's going to happen to Fernández?" Townley said. His voice trailed off. He spoke of his wife and children, and the tears came again. Then he stiffened. "This will be the end of Chile,"

Scherrer recalled him saying. "The Christian Democrats will take over, and they'll leave the door open to the communists again. Just like the last time. All our work will have been in vain."

It was then that Scherrer sensed that Townley had crossed the line from intelligence operative to defector. He knew that Townley would eventually tell all. They would arrange the appropriate protections and provisos, but those were mere details. Townley showed a compulsion to tell his story, to unfold his store of information to men like Scherrer and Cornick whom he respected as officers and whose respect he so earnestly desired. They would understand his hatred of communists, his childlike devotion to Contreras and soldierly obedience to his commands.

THE ECUATORIANA AIRLINES flight with Townley aboard was diverted from New York for security reasons and landed at Baltimore-Washington International Airport. Townley was confined at Fort Meade Army Base and saw Cornick and Scherrer daily in the top-security facilities once used for Watergate defendants. A week after his arrival he signed an agreement with the U.S. attorney to plead guilty to one count of conspiracy to murder a foreign official. The agreement stipulated that he could not be required to provide information about any DINA activities except those involving the Letelier case. He was guaranteed a sentence of no more than ten years in prison with the possibility of parole after three years and four months. Over the following weeks and months Michael Townley told the story of the DINA operation to assassinate Orlando Letelier.

The week after Townley was expelled the members of the Chilean cabinet resigned at Pinochet's request. The new cabinet had, for the first time since the coup, a majority of civilians, the most prominent of whom was the new foreign minister, Hernán Cubillos.

On April 14, Miami police and FBI agents located and arrested Guillermo Novo and Alvin Ross, who had been hiding in Miami's Little Havana. Ignacio Novo was picked up a few days later in Union City, New Jersey. Two Cubans remained fugitives: Virgilio Paz and José Dionisio Suárez. Suárez had been released from jail only four days before Townley arrived in the United States.* On August 1, a United States grand jury returned indictments charging seven men with the murders of Orlando Letelier and Ronni Moffitt. The accused were Manuel Contreras, Pedro Espinoza, Armando Fernández, Guillermo Novo, Alvin Ross, José Dionisio Suárez, and Virgilio Paz. Ignacio Novo was charged with lying to a grand jury and covering up the crimes.

---

*Suárez was a suspect in the Letelier case and had been jailed for contempt of court for refusing to testify before a grand jury after having been granted immunity. He was released because the term of the grand jury was about to end.

A MEASURE
OF JUSTICE

THE TENSION could already be felt at the entrance to the U.S. District Courthouse a few blocks from the Capitol, a half-mile from the White House. The armed guard operating the metal detector scrutinized each entrant with the zeal of an El Al Airlines security officer. In the elevators a nervous mood prevailed. Then the crowd poured out on the sixth floor to be searched a second time. Spectators and press, Ronni Moffitt's parents and brothers, Isabel Letelier and her sons, and the defendants' families all lined up single file, emptied their pockets into trays, placed briefcases and purses on a belt where they could pass through an X-ray box. Then the people themselves passed once more through a metal detector.

Over 200 people waited in the hall outside the courtroom, hoping to fit into the 150 seats, 50 of which were reserved for the press.

Along the corridor stood United States marshals in plain clothes, identifiable by their unsmiling faces, their almost military carriage, and the bulges under their suit coats. Outside the courtroom a small sign announced the day's proceedings: "January 9, 1979; 9:30 A.M. The United States of America vs. Guillermo Novo Sampol, Alvin Ross Díaz and Ignacio Novo Sampol."

A group of Cuban exiles from Union City, New Jersey, held a brief demonstration outside the courthouse to proclaim that the

Novos and Ross had fallen victim to a United States government plot designed to suppress the Cuban Nationalist Movement. They claimed that shops and other businesses in Union City had closed that day as a gesture of support for the three defendants on the opening day of the trial. Later in the day one of the CNM militants pasted an Omega 7 decal on the wall of the sixth-floor men's room. The marshals summoned the police bomb squad, which brought its dogs to scour the area. The dogs found no explosives, but the incident heightened the tension.

The marshals escorted two of the three defendants from the security room to the courtroom itself. Then Ignacio Novo, free on bail, walked in with the spectators. The three defendants embraced. The television artists began their sketching. The defendants could have passed for members of the same family; Ignacio Novo resembled Alvin Ross as much as he did his brother Guillermo.

Guillermo Novo and Ross faced charges of conspiracy to murder a foreign official, murder of a foreign official, first-degree murder of Orlando Letelier and Ronni Moffitt, and murder by use of explosives. All five counts were punishable by life imprisonment. Guillermo Novo was also charged with lying to a grand jury. The government charged Ignacio Novo with two lesser counts: perjury before the grand jury and "misprision of a felony," meaning that he knew about the crime and failed to report it.

According to the indictment, Novo and Ross had helped Michael Townley organize the assassination and obtain the lethal explosives, but it did not allege that either of the two was present in Washington at the scene of the assassination. The most prominent persons accused in the indictment, the three Chilean DINA members, were conspicuously absent from the courtroom. The United States government had formally requested that Chile extradite retired General Manuel Contreras, Colonel Pedro Espinoza, and Captain Armando Fernández, and the Chilean court had ordered the three men confined to Santiago's Military Hospital, in comfort but nevertheless under arrest. José Dionisio Suárez and Virgilio Paz, accused of helping Townley plant the bomb and detonate it, remained fugitives.

The trial that was about to start would be the first public airing of the two-and-a-half-year investigation by Assistant U.S. Attorney

Eugene Propper and the FBI. The importance of the trial rested on the strength of the United States' evidence linking the Chilean military regime of President Augusto Pinochet to the plot to kill Letelier, not a simple homicide but a grotesque act of international terrorism. The Chilean Supreme Court had found pretexts to delay a decision on the extradition of the three DINA officers, awaiting the outcome of the trial and the public reaction to Chile's role in the murders.

Adding to the charged pretrial atmosphere was the projected role of the only DINA agent in United States custody. Michael Townley had not been indicted with the rest, but had been permitted to plead guilty to a single count of conspiracy to murder a foreign official. Even though his involvement in the murders was more serious than either Novo's or Ross's, the government had cast him in the role, not of a defendant, but of star witness, the man upon whose performance the outcome of the trial depended.

Guillermo Novo looked the part of the leader among the three defendants. He sat with his back to the press and spectators, but when he looked around, his face expressed defiance, confidence, authority. Inside his close-fitting three-piece suit was a lithe and nervous body whose movements appeared to spring from some inner coil, even if just to propel him from a sitting to a standing position. His legs twitched and fidgeted despite his efforts to control them. He showed no signs of emotion apart from an acknowledging nod to his friends, family, and supporters in the spectators' section.

Novo was born in Cuba in 1939 and came to the United States with his family in 1954. He became an American citizen and studied chemistry. After the Cuban Revolution, which had originally attracted him, he became a believer in the fascist ideology of Felipe Rivero and, with Rivero and his brother Ignacio, founded the Cuban Nationalist Movement in late 1959. His ideology, which he believed would liberate Cuba from Castro, from communism, and from the corruption that had plagued it, had led him into contact with Chile, with DINA, with Michael Townley, and now into a courtroom facing trial for a double murder.

Alvin Ross Díaz was born in Havana, seven years before Guillermo Novo. From a lower-middle-class family, Ross drifted into a job as a blackjack dealer at the Tropicana nightclub's gambling casino. For him, the revolution meant the closing of the casinos. After fleeing his homeland, he returned as part of the CIA-trained invasion force at the Bay of Pigs in 1961. Like the Novo brothers he occasionally sold used cars for a living in Union City. He had developed a facial tic, a slight flutter of his right cheek, made more conspicuous by the unpredictable but frequent movements of his head and eyes. His round face, which he had deliberately molded to look mean and dangerous to match his tough-guy reputation, had lost the clear outlines of youth, and the skin had begun to sag.

Ignacio Novo, two years older than Guillermo, lacked the physical energy and mental edge his brother projected. The only one of the three defendants free on $25,000 bail, he had tried to raise funds for the defense and organize community support.

Shortly after 9:30 A.M. the marshal inside the courtroom shouted, "All rise." All rose. A short middle-aged black man with grey-white hair entered. Judge Barrington Parker, Jr., walked laboriously on crutches, having lost a leg in an automobile accident some years before. With dignity he slowly climbed the three steps to the judge's dais, adjusted his rimless glasses, and nodded left to the prosecutors, right to the defense table. He took his seat. Everyone sat down.

A former Republican Party national committeeman, Parker was appointed to the federal court bench in 1969 by President Nixon and had presided over some of the most controversial cases on the national docket. He had gained a reputation for a crusty and strict courtroom manner, and for skepticism toward the claims of United States government agencies that "national security interests" entitled them to special protection in the courtroom, claims that promised to play a part in the Letelier trial.*

Below Judge Parker to his right sat the three Cuban defendants

---

*Parker handled the case of former CIA Director Richard Helms, indicted in 1977 of lying to a U.S. Senate committee about CIA involvement in covert action in Chile. Parker reluctantly agreed to accept a plea-bargaining agreement Helms had worked out with U.S. Attorney Earl Silbert. When he fined him the token sum of $2,000, Parker told Helms, "You now stand before this court in disgrace and shame." Helms then left the courtroom and announced to reporters outside, as he held up a copy of Parker's ruling, "I wear this as a badge of honor." In another case involving a United States government plea bargain alleged to protect national security, Parker caused an Egyptian official bribed by the Westinghouse Corporation to be named in court, against the wishes of United States officials.

and their lawyers, Paul Goldberger for Guillermo Novo, Lawrence Dubin for Alvin Ross, and Óscar González Suárez representing Ignacio Novo. To Parker's left, between the defendants and the still-empty jury box, sat the prosecutors: Eugene Propper, E. Lawrence Barcella, and Diane Kelly, a newcomer to the case assigned to draft the many legal memorandums that were expected.

The trial began, and immediately bogged down in the process of selecting a jury. On Friday, January 12, the fourth day of the trial, the twelve members of the jury and six alternates entered the court. All were black. Seven women sat on the jury proper. From their style of dress and carriage they appeared to be working and middle class. Many had government jobs. Judge Parker ordered them sequestered: threats had been received.

"Because of the circumstances of the case, the individual questioning of the jurors has of necessity been long, involved, and detailed," Parker announced. He had screened out anyone with strong opinions about the CIA, Chile, or Cuba, and those who knew about the work of IPS.

The first weekend passed. On Monday, January 15, in a hearing without jury, Parker ruled against a defense motion to suppress evidence found in an apartment rented by Alvin Ross. The evidence included detonating cord, electric fuse igniters, and a receipt for a Fanon-Courier paging device. The ruling that the material was legally obtained by FBI agents was a severe blow to the defendants' case.

Then Parker gave the jury its instructions.

For Eugene Propper, some two and a half years since he had begun his investigation, the time had come to lay out his case to the jury. Straight-backed, nervous as an actor who must walk onto the Broadway stage and say his lines after years of stock-company performances, Propper began his opening statement. He tried to tell a story, to keep the jury from getting lost in a cacophony of Spanish names.

He told them about a man named Salvador Allende, who had been elected to the presidency in a South American country called Chile. The military dictatorship that overthrew that government abolished the Congress, unions, and political parties. Propper explained who Orlando Letelier was and how he came to be considered an enemy of the Chilean military government. He told them about DINA and the CNM, Michael Townley, Manuel Contreras, and the mysterious passports in the names of Juan Williams Rose and Alejandro Romeral Jara.

He spoke of dozens of pieces of evidence he would show them to establish the working relationship between the members of the CNM and the Chilean government, between Guillermo Novo and Alvin Ross and Michael Townley and DINA. Names like Iturriaga, Fernández, and Espinoza became intertwined with remote-control detonators, LAN-Chile, modification of Fanon-Couriers, electric matches, potassium permanganate, clues, letters, fingerprints. It would all become clear as the trial progressed, he assured the jury.

The defense took the floor after lunch. Paul Goldberger, representing Guillermo Novo, promised the jury that he would prove to them that "Michael Townley was a contract agent for the CIA," that since 1974 he had been "a mole in DINA," a double agent. Paul Goldberger, like Propper, had a strong New York accent. He flung the CIA at the jury, shouted its name, insinuated that he had discovered the truth of the case in the mysteries of espionage and spookdom. "This was a monstrous crime committed by monstrous people," Goldberger said, "but we will prove that neither DINA, nor the Cuban Nationalist Movement, nor the Chilean government had any responsibility for it. . . . As hard as it is to believe, the CIA was responsible for a murder in the nation's capital."

His partner, Lawrence Dubin, from the same school of courtroom technique, invoked the name of Vernon Walters, former deputy director of the CIA, as having an ominous connection with the case and with Michael Townley. He and Goldberger tried to leave the jury with the impression that the government had framed their clients and that the Letelier affair related more to the world of spy versus spy than to those idealistic patriots, their clients. The two lawyers promised documents and witnesses to back up their claims that Townley was a CIA agent.

Óscar González Suárez, in his late fifties, spoke for Ignacio Novo, as he had spoken for Cuban exile clients for some eighteen years. His heavily accented English made his presentation difficult to follow at times, but he argued cogently that Ignacio's case should be separated from the murder trial and that in any event Ignacio did nothing more than hear the news of the killings on the radio and drive Townley, "this nefarious character," to the airport.

Late in the day, Propper called Michael Moffitt to the stand. His job was to provide the jury with an account of the horror of the bombing as only a victim who had suffered and survived could relate it. Moffitt's testimony had been rehearsed twice. The rage he had felt at the time of the assassinations and in the aftermath had mostly transformed itself into a general outrage against fascism, the Pinochet government, and the bankers who funded it. But his passion and hate had not entirely dissolved.

"You know, Michael," Propper told him at a rehearsal, "Townley asked me to tell you that he's really sorry about Ronni. And I can tell you that I believe him. Whatever else you may think about him, Mike's a serious guy, and I really believe he feels that way, not about Orlando, but just about Ronni."

"You can tell Mike," Moffitt replied, controlling his voice, "that if I ever have the chance I'll cut his heart out."

On the witness stand, Moffitt did his job.

Other eyewitnesses followed the next morning, January 16. Detective Walter Johnson, the first Metropolitan Police officer who arrived at the bombing site; William Hayden, a motorist driving behind Letelier's car; Danna Peterson, a physician who tried to save Ronni Moffitt's life. Medical examiners Leroy Kiddick and James Luke presented the conclusions of their autopsy examination of the two victims. Judge Parker ruled, however, against admitting in evidence the photographs of the mutilated bodies.

The prosecution then turned to establishing the murder motive and to connecting the defendants with the Chilean government in general and with DINA in particular. Propper and Barcella pulled from their witness bag a man well known to the jury. Senator George McGovern, Democratic presidential candidate in 1972, told the jury in his low-key style how Letelier had effectively "sensitized" him to "the issue of human rights violations" and how discussions between them influenced McGovern to act legislatively to support the cutoff of United States military aid to Chile.

Dutch parliamentarian Relus ter Beck informed the jury about Letelier's anti-junta activities in Holland, especially his efforts to get a Dutch firm to cancel a $63 million investment in Chile. Ter Beck, like McGovern, established Letelier's political importance. The jury could see that the victim had close associations with powerful people in at least two countries.

Late that day the prosecution called Rafael Rivas Vásquez, the Cuban exile who was deputy director of Venezuelan intelligence—DISIP. He testified that Manuel Contreras, as head of DINA, visited Caracas in 1975 to ask for DISIP's help in informing DINA about Chilean exile activities in Venezuela. Rivas Vásquez also remembered meeting Guillermo Novo, who stopped in Caracas on his way to Chile in 1974. But when Propper asked him to identify Guillermo, the witness hesitantly pointed to Ignacio.

Day seven. Isabel Letelier took the stand, wearing a necklace with a carved black stone. The inscription on the stone said "Isa"; Orlando had carved it for her on Dawson Island. She told the jury the story of her husband's life. Her testimony established that Letelier "was in charge of the Chilean resistance in the United States," and that the Pinochet regime imprisoned and mistreated those who disagreed with it. Her softly accented voice evoked suffering, determination, courage. In cross-examination Goldberger and Dubin tried to wrench an admission from her that she believed the CIA responsible for the assassinations. She gave them a pithy lecture on recent Chilean history and on the barbarism and brutality of the junta. "Every minute she stays on the stand," Propper commented during a recess, "she wrings more sympathy from the jury."

Cross-examination of Isabel Letelier by defense lawyers extended until mid-morning the following day, January 18. Michael Townley was next. His entrance into the courtroom was hastily changed to a side door to prevent his meeting Isabel face to face as she left the witness stand. He had gained some thirty pounds since his expulsion from Chile nine months before. He wore a dark blue pin-striped suit; his straight hair was modishly long, his mustache and beard carefully trimmed. As he walked stiffly to the stand, a look of serious detachment on his face, the suspense in the courtroom mounted sharply. Townley was a real-life assassin, a member of a sinister secret police agency about to bear witness against those who had ordered him to kill and those with whom he had worked in his gruesome profession.

The jury, some of whom had appeared perpetually sleepy or bored, began to react to Townley's presence. A tense silence fell over the room. Sitting erect in their chairs, jury members could see, in three-quarter face as he stared straight ahead, the man about whom the prosecutor in his opening statement had spoken so forcefully and upon whose credibility the government's case depended.

Michael Townley had a captive audience waiting eagerly to hear his every word and to observe every expression and move. As he answered the preliminary questions to establish his identity, he gave the impression of a polite young man—respectful, soft-spoken. He looked calm, alert, and intelligent. He often answered questions with a "yes sir" or "no sir." Thirty-six years old; married with two children; never finished high school; active in Patria y Libertad in 1972; hobby, electronics; left Chile; returned after the coup as Kenneth Enyart; recruited as a DINA agent.

Townley's crime dwarfed that of the three defendants, yet as the chief witness for the prosecution, he had become an ally of the United States investigators and prosecutors. Their case had to stand or fall on his ability to portray himself as an assassin whose profession was treachery and brutality, yet convince the jury that he was now telling the truth.

Step by step Townley recounted the story of the first assassination mission he undertook with the aid of the CNM. In short, clear sentences, with no emotion in his voice, he recalled where he had parked his camper in Mexico, and the quantity of explosive and the kind of detonator with which he had planned to murder Carlos Altamirano and Volodia Teitelboim. His voice made no distinction between forging an identity card, ordering a meal, testing a detonator, reading a road map, planning to murder two people, or buying toys for his children.

The judge called a recess for lunch. Townley stepped off the stand and sat down on the witness bench. The morning had yielded Propper's prize witness high credibility, but something else about their relationship had begun to emerge. As soon as Propper finished stuffing paper into his attaché case he walked toward the exit. As he passed Townley, Propper smiled and winked at him, a quick, intimate sign of approval.

Returning for the afternoon session, the three Cuban defendants sat by themselves, the first of the actors to arrive. Soon press and spectators wandered in, sat down, and held subdued conversations in the librarylike atmosphere the marshals had created. Townley was brought in and took his place at the witness bench just inside the railing, about a dozen feet from the defendants. Neither judge, jury, nor lawyers were yet in the courtroom.

Guillermo Novo kept his back to the public and press. To his left sat his brother; next to him, Ross. They kept their eyes on each other or on the papers in front of them. Their loud whispers, in Spanish, at first appeared to pertain to what they read. Townley's neck muscles tightened as the volume grew to stage-whisper proportion: "Faggot." "Traitor." "Watch your step." "Degenerate CIA shit." "Son of a whore." From the spectators' section, a Cuban woman shouted, "Cut out his tongue! Stool pigeons are shot!"

The marshals detected the drama but did not know what the words meant. The defendants didn't look at Townley as they spat their blasphemies at him. Members of the press who understood Spanish translated for their colleagues.

The judge, jury, and attorneys for the defense and prosecution returned to the courtroom minutes later, and Townley resumed the witness stand. Propper guided him to Colonel Espinoza's order to contact the CNM and kill Letelier "in an innocuous form."

Townley recounted the events of the September days after his arrival in New York. He described the meeting at the Chateau Renaissance Motel. "I explained the mission itself, which was to kill —to assassinate—Orlando Letelier, requested persons to assist in this mission, to carry it out." Then he named one by one those present at the meeting. Guillermo Novo, Juan Pulido,* José Dionisio Suárez, Alvin Ross. Had this self-effacing technician decided to speak on other themes the audience might have dozed or departed. But the mundane facts that he recited for each day of the conspiracy

*Pulido died of a heart ailment in summer 1978, before the indictments against the defendants were handed down.

—a meal, a phone call, a hair-splitting definition ("DINA is not government, it is an agency of the government")—transformed the harmless details of everyday life into the substance, texture, and taste of a cold-blooded assassination.

> Q. Tell us whether there came a time that you got a response from anyone in the Cuban Nationalist Movement; if so from whom?
>
> A. The following morning Virgilio Paz came to the Chateau Renaissance where I was and picked me up in his car, and we proceeded to pick up Mr. Guillermo Novo. We had conversations in Virgilio Paz's car, at which time Guillermo Novo told me that the CNM would take on the mission.

Townley described how he received the TNT and C4 explosives and the Fanon-Courier paging device he had modified as a remote-control detonator. He described the route, the highway names and numbers, of the drive to Washington September 16 with Virgilio Paz.

With each detail, he grabbed the interest of the jury, had them leaning forward in suspense over his shopping trips to Sears and Radio Shack for "soldering iron and screwdriver and pliers, things of this type." He took the jury along each minute step taken by the assassins on their way to bomb their victims—to the Holiday Inn and the Congress Regency Motel, to McDonald's and Roy Rogers, and finally, in the early morning of September 19, to Ogden Court where Letelier lived. Then, Townley said, "Paz stated to me that he expected, or that he wanted, desired for me to attach, to affix the device to the car myself."

Townley's matter-of-fact manner of describing murder frustrated any attempt to make moral or metaphysical judgments—he trivialized villainy. As if the literary villain in *Heart of Darkness* had transformed himself from words on paper into real flesh and blood, this polite, obedient young man debunked the very concept of real-life evil. Against the bland setting of the district courtroom, evil dissolved into a farcical image of the inventive bureaucrat, the gadgeteer.

The bomb in place, Townley informed the jury, the trio selected the detonation site. "We had previously spotted a small park that was on the route that Orlando Letelier took in to work and I suggested to them"—Townley, thinking quickly, modified his language to avoid contradiction—"requested of them that this be the place that the device be detonated." Then he explained his humanitarian motives: the park "was highly unpopulated and [it was] highly unlikely that any other person would be injured. I also requested that when detonating the device, Orlando Letelier be in the vehicle by himself." But Townley let himself off the hook. "The final discretion," he told the jury, "as to what and where, was left in their hands."

Townley then took the jury away from Washington. Alvin Ross met him at Newark Airport, listened to his account of the bomb placing, took him to Guillermo Novo's. With the same excruciating attention to trivia Townley told of telephoning, parking a car, buying cigarettes, visiting his sister, and leaving the New York area for Miami on September 19.

Having so far implicated Guillermo Novo and Alvin Ross in the murder conspiracy, Townley, in his account of his three days in Miami, presented the government's case against Ignacio Novo.

"I'm quite sure I called from Audio Intelligence Devices to Mr. Ignacio Novo that same day. I'm not sure whether it was in that phone call or in a subsequent phone call later that afternoon that Ignacio said to me, 'Have you heard the radio? Have you heard the news?' And I said, 'What?' And he said, 'Something big happened in New York—excuse me—in Washington, D.C.'" Townley then told the jury how he had met Ignacio for dinner. "We discussed the operation, what had happened."

Townley continued the tale of conspiracy, replacing the explosives lent for the mission by the CNM, reimbursing them for "their direct expenses that they had incurred in the operation itself." "It was sent to Virgilio Paz and Guillermo Novo," he said, "in the early weeks of October 1976. The sum did not exceed $1,600."

Shortly after 4:00 P.M. Propper concluded his direct examination of Townley. He looked satisfied. Townley's testimony had presented to the jury a coherent, convincing account of the conspiracy. As Townley took his seat at the witness bench, defense lawyer Paul

Goldberger asked to approach the bench. Defense and prosecution crowded in front of Parker and talked animatedly for fifteen minutes out of earshot of spectators and jury. Then Judge Parker dismissed the jury for the day. He and the lawyers adjourned to the judge's chambers to continue their confidential discussion.

Michael Townley, Goldberger contended at these confidential sessions, should be subjected to full interrogation on the stand in the presence of the jury about his participation in the assassination of Carlos Prats in Argentina and the shooting attack against Bernardo Leighton in Rome. Goldberger said he had documentary evidence of Townley's presence in those countries at the time of the attacks, and that furthermore his client, Guillermo Novo, had heard Townley admit to killing Prats in Argentina. The defense attorneys were striking at the soft underbelly of the government case.

Judge Parker listened. It was his task to set the bounds for cross-examination by the defense. Reports of Townley's alleged involvement in other assassinations for DINA had appeared in the press before the trial, and Parker had read them. "I have heard something about an Argentine venture and an Italian venture," he said, and he was inclined to allow the "fullest" cross-examination of Townley.

Propper broke in vehemently to argue that neither case was permissible territory for cross-examination. Townley had a signed agreement with the prosecution that he could only be required to testify on crimes in the United States or against United States citizens; everything else was off limits. That was the deal Propper had worked out with Townley's attorney, and he was determined to hold up his end of the bargain by defending Townley against being questioned about his other DINA activities and crimes. Propper used the argument that Townley had "a Fifth Amendment privilege."

Townley still considered himself a loyal employee of the Chilean government, Propper said, and he only began providing information about the Letelier case after an official of the Chilean government, General Héctor Orozco, had authorized him to do so. Townley, Propper argued, was a "public servant" who had taken a sacred oath: "As a public servant and an agent of DINA, he was released by the government of Chile from his obligation not to talk about the Letelier case, but he can be prosecuted for—and I've got the [Chilean] law here—for fifteen years for everything he talks about other than that, whether that other event is illegal or not."

A bizarre role reversal had occurred. Defense lawyers Goldberger and Dubin, who had opened their case by claiming that neither DINA nor the Cubans had anything to do with the Letelier assassination, now argued that the trial should become a vehicle to expose Townley's crimes for DINA on three continents. Propper and Barcella became staunch defenders of Townley's rights, and their arguments presumed that DINA, far from being the lawless terrorist apparatus Propper had described in his opening statement, was a legitimate government entity whose employees were bound by oaths of secrecy and whose regulations should be respected by the United States court. The wrangling continued until after 6:00 P.M., when Parker ended the conference without ruling on the issues.

The next morning, Judge Parker opened the session by calling the three Cuban defendants to stand before the bench. He reprimanded them for their "threats and invectives" directed against Michael Townley and warned them not to repeat the incident. Ignacio Novo contritely assured the judge that "we did make comments, but there were no threats, if it please the court."

The dispute over permissible areas for cross-examination continued in open court, although in the absence of the jury. Goldberger said he had received a copy of Townley's testimony in Chile before his expulsion to the United States. In that testimony to General Héctor Orozco—the same Chilean officer who had given Townley "permission" to cooperate with the prosecutors—Townley had denied under oath any role in the Letelier assassination. Goldberger argued that the statement should be read to the jury to show that Townley had lied under oath.

Propper jumped to his feet. "That statement is, as I understand it, secret. It was not shown to the United States. It is kept in a sealed book . . . and apparently it is not given out to anyone, and if it were given out to anyone, it would be a violation of Chilean law, with a penalty of up to twenty years." He gestured to copies of the Chilean code on his desk.

Parker snapped, "Are you representing the Chilean government?" He ruled that before cross-examination the statement would have to be shown to Townley to determine if it were actually his testimony.

Goldberger turned the discussion to Prats and Leighton. He argued that the other assassination operations should be examined in order to show Townley's *modus operandi.* Moreover, he said, the United States had "a moral and legal obligation" to inform other governments about the other crimes and Townley's role in them. The prosecution response that the crimes were excluded by Townley's Fifth Amendment right and by the plea-bargaining agreement did not hold water. First, Townley's trip to Europe in 1975, during which he allegedly set up the Leighton attack, began in the United States, where he met Virgilio Paz and persuaded Paz to accompany him on the murder mission. Thus the crime of conspiracy actually began inside the borders of the United States. Secondly, his client's Sixth Amendment right to thorough cross-examination of witnesses should outweigh Townley's Fifth Amendment protection, especially since it involved hypothetical prosecution in a foreign country, Chile, for relatively trivial crimes of violating DINA secrecy rules.

Dubin added that Townley's plea-bargaining agreement included the substantial "benefit" of freedom from prosecution for other crimes, and the jury should know what those other crimes were in order to judge fairly Townley's motives for testifying.

Prosecutor Larry Barcella responded: "He [Townley] was given permission by General Orozco to discuss Letelier in all its ramifications. We didn't have any authority, we still don't have any authority, to order him to go beyond that." He ridiculed the evidence of Townley's role by adding, "Mr. Townley's passport indicates he was in Argentina around the time Prats was killed. There were thirty million other people, I would venture to say, within Argentina at the same time."

Judge Parker cut off the debate and said he was ready to rule. The jury, he said, had seen and heard abundant evidence that Townley was a paid DINA agent and about what kind of organization DINA was. "I think there is enough before the jury right now showing that

Mr. Townley certainly is not the person that you would want to sit next to at a Sunday worship service. I will not allow you to cross-examine the witness with respect to the Argentine and Italian incidents. That is the court ruling."

Parker ordered "the witness Townley" to be brought in. Goldberger showed Townley the statement and asked him whether it was the same as the one he had made in Chile before his expulsion. Townley looked at it, saw it was an unsigned transcription rather than the original statement that he remembered signing in the margin of each page.

"I did not make this statement, no sir," Townley said laconically.

The jury was called back to the courtroom. Propper had led Townley through the story of the plot to kill Letelier, and now asked him to identify exhibits to back up his oral testimony. The array of documents was impressive; most had been brought from Chile by Inés Townley and turned over to the FBI as part of the plea bargain. Propper held up each exhibit, recited its court-assigned number, and asked Townley to describe it.

Passports, drivers' licenses with the Petersen name, Avis Rent-a-Car, motel and gas-station receipts, highway and restaurant tabs, airline tickets and photographs, were entered one by one. Townley identified photos of Guillermo Novo, Ross, and Paz together with Chilean UN Representatives Mario Arnello and Sergio Crespo, tying the CNM to the Chilean government. Then the jury saw wires, plastic cups, electric matches—the stuff of bombs—each piece benign in and of itself. Townley explained how these items, when put together, had served to kill Orlando Letelier and Ronni Moffitt. He gave the jury a brief electronics lesson, complete with "oscillation of a signal," "megahertz," and "VHF," to explain how the Fanon-Courier paging device held in his hand had become a deadly weapon. Then Propper produced the plea-bargaining agreement and read it into the court record.

In mid-afternoon, Paul Goldberger fired the opening volley in the cross-examination of Townley. After two questions, Townley was wounded and looking around for help. Goldberger had simply picked up an electric detonator from among the exhibits on the prosecution table and asked Townley to tell the jury where he had got it. Townley tried to evade the question by saying he "obtained it through my service."

Q. Where, through your service?
A. At this point . . .
MR. PROPPER: May we approach the bench, your honor?

Townley looked imploringly at Propper, then at Judge Parker.

THE COURT: At this point you will answer the question.
TOWNLEY: Your honor, due to the nature of my work and the fact that I might incur legal responsibilities by answering this question, I must respectfully decline to answer the question on the grounds that the answer might tend to incriminate me.

Goldberger, in less than three minutes of questioning, had forced Townley to take the Fifth Amendment to avoid revealing information about DINA.

Parker made no attempt to mask his irritation. He dismissed the jury for the weekend and fumed, "The pace of this case is alarmingly slow at this point; some of the issues [holding us up] should have been solved before this point." After the jury was out of the room, he chided Propper: "You should have alerted the court to this problem long before now."

Goldberger rose from his seat and said solemnly, "I move to strike [Townley's] entire direct testimony on the grounds he cannot selectively invoke the Fifth Amendment privilege." The attorneys approached the bench. Propper asked Parker for permission to interview Townley in secret to persuade him to answer questions about DINA that related directly to the Letelier case. Parker agreed, then adjourned the court until the following Monday.*

On Monday, the tenth day of the trial, Judge Parker opened the

---

*The interview with Townley was conducted in the presence of a court stenographer, but the transcript was kept secret until after the trial was over. A second interview without a stenographer was conducted at Propper's office later that afternoon.

proceedings and immediately called the attorneys to the bench. Again the spectators were cut out of the discussion.

Townley's attorney, Barry Levine,* spoke first. Townley, he said, would answer the question about where he got the electric fuse, but would continue to assert the Fifth Amendment if asked questions "of the scope of the General Prats or the Leighton affairs." The Fifth Amendment question had been resolved through a shaky compromise. Goldberger said that over the weekend he had obtained a copy of Townley's testimony in Chile that was indisputably a copy of the original with Townley's signature on every page. A translation from the Spanish was being prepared.

The day progressed with short periods of cross-examination interspersed with long bench conferences. On the stand, Townley admitted that the statement with his signature on it was authentic. He explained that, in accordance with orders from General Contreras, he had lied in that statement to General Héctor Orozco, telling Orozco the cover story worked out with Captain Armando Fernández. He said that later, after he was expelled to the United States and had agreed to cooperate, he had made a second statement to General Orozco, which contained the truth about his participation in the assassination. Then Townley reverted to his role of assassin as upstanding citizen, clandestine agent as prissy burgher.

"The existence of that document," Townley told Goldberger, "outside or publicly outside of General Orozco's investigation, I know for a fact to be a violation of Chilean law."

"You didn't expect that we would have the statement, did you?"

"No, I didn't, to be quite frank. It's against the law, and whoever broke the law in Chile obtaining the document is going to probably be subject to prosecution," Townley added righteously.

Goldberger and Dubin, barred from questioning Townley about other DINA crimes, were unable to crack his story in cross-examination. But they skillfully chipped away at his credibility by maneuvering him into dialogues to demonstrate his cold-blooded character,

---

*A partner of Seymour Glanzer. Glanzer could not enter the courtroom to represent Townley because defense lawyers had listed him as one of their witnesses.

hoping to convince the jury that a man so despicable would not hesitate to lie.

Goldberger built up to the following dialogue:

Q. Do you have any regrets about killing Letelier?
A. Specifically, Mr. Letelier?
Q. Yes.
A. No, sir. The person accompanying him, yes, very much so, sir.
Q. Letelier was an enemy, as you saw it, is that correct?
A. He was a soldier and I was a soldier. That is correct, sir.
Q. At the same time you killed him, on Massachusetts Avenue, he was a soldier?
A. In his own, within his own party, within his own actions, he was carrying on a battle against the government of Chile.
Q. You saw yourself as a soldier, Mr. Townley?
A. That is correct.
Q. Given an order to carry out a contract, to carry out an assassination?
A. That is correct, sir.
Q. Did the government order you or DINA order you to kill people that you didn't agree with killing?
A. No, sir. I am not saying that I agreed to killing him either. I received an order and I carried it out to the best of my ability.

A soldier, in a war recognized by no one but his commanding officers, had killed a man defined as an enemy soldier. Unfortunately, a civilian had also died. Orders. Following orders. The very words from the Nuremberg Nazi war crimes trials, the words of the American soldiers accused of the My Lai massacre of civilians during the Vietnam War. For a moment the entire two and a half years of investigation into the Letelier-Moffitt murders were frozen in a single frame. The moment had arrived, as in an ancient morality play, for the cast—the spectators, the press, the families, and the protagonists —to stop and reflect. Who had created this monster who called himself a soldier?

But the courtroom scenario did not allow for transcendence. The

Pinochet system, DINA, the Chilean military junta, the crimes of these mini-Nazis of the Third World never became an issue in the U.S. District Court. Instead, the trial, like the investigation itself, narrowed the focus and avoided the historical implications. The "rights" of the government's star witness became the overriding question, as procedure buried the political substance of the crime.

Later the same afternoon, Goldberger and Townley held the following repartee:

Q. When your wife was on the Mexican trip—your wife you said was an agent—she knew what the circumstances were, she knew what you were going for, is that right?

A. She knew we were going to disrupt a meeting, that is correct, sir.

Q. . . . Did she know that you were going to kill some people in Mexico if you could?

A. It was mentioned, yes sir. . . .

Q. Wasn't she part of the plan?

A. . . . She was not involved in the planning itself.

Q. Wasn't she used as a cover, so to speak, for the little camper trip to Mexico?

A. That is part of cover, yes, sir.

Q. And she knew the circumstances of the pla—— and she knew the names of the people . . . Altamirano's name . . . Teitelboim's name?

A. Most Chilean citizens would know those names very well, sir. . . .

Q. Did you plan in the United States to go kill somebody in Mexico?

A. Yes, sir.

Q. Your wife was part of that plan, is that correct?

A. She was to be used within it, that is correct, sir. . . .

Q. So you wanted to not only take yourself into the position you have with your dealing, but you wanted to take your wife out of the possibility of being prosecuted for any crimes in the United States?

A normal husband whose wife accompanied him on business trips. A good father who bought toys for his children after learning that his bomb had killed two people. A family man, a homebody, a man who saw no contradiction between caring for his own loved ones and blowing someone else's to smithereens. The creative assassin chose his courtroom words with precision. Townley's answers carried a faint mocking tone—as if he were answering some incredible hypocrisy on the part of the stagers of the courtroom drama, as if he were laughing at his interrogators' acceptance of his veneer of courtesy and respect, Townley remained on the stand undergoing cross-examination until Thursday, January 25. Throughout his six days of testimony, he remained consistent in his rehashing of the murder plot. But the long and antagonistic cross-examination appeared to have dented his cold composure. During the last day of testimony he kept turning toward the judge as if looking for help, or glancing at Propper as if to ask, "Can't you object?" He complained often of a throat infection, sipped water compulsively between answers, paused frequently. The veneer of confidence had begun to crack, exposing the weak ego of a vulnerable boy.

Meanwhile, *Washington Post* and *New York Times* reporters obtained copies of the confidential bench conferences on January 22 and 23 at which the attorneys and Judge Parker discussed the secret agreement the United States had signed with Chile as a condition for obtaining Townley's expulsion. SILBERT AGREED WITH CHILE TO CURTAIL INFORMATION ran a *Washington Post* headline on January 24. The *New York Times* reported that the agreement signed by U.S. Attorney Earl Silbert and Chilean Deputy Interior Minister Enrique Montero meant that the United States would "restrict the information it would make available to the world" about the Letelier-Moffitt case, specifically information about the Prats and Leighton crimes. Propper's rationale for the agreement, according to the transcript, was that the Chilean government believed "that the United States government was using us as a political prosecution to get rid of the Pinochet government, and they wanted some reassurance that we weren't going to spread the stuff all over the world, and that was the basis of the agreement."

During the bench conference Propper also justified his keeping the agreement secret from the court and the defense. The defense lawyers had been informed of the existence of the agreement by a Chilean lawyer. "For the record, your honor, that was an agreement between the United States and Chile, [in] which Mr. Townley had no part, with respect to turning him over, and it had to do with whether any information we had [had] to be disclosed. We said [it] would be used only in the United States courts or given to the government of Chile. That is, we would not spread it to the press or give it worldwide. And Chile in turn, if it came up with any information in the Letelier case, would give it to the United States."

The discussions at the confidential bench conference, the secret agreement with the Chilean government, and the terms of Townley's plea-bargaining agreement revealed the guidelines the prosecution was following in presenting its case. Taken together, they provided a partial answer to the puzzling question why Chile had turned over Townley in the first place. The answer seemed to be that the United States had worked out in advance with Chile a way to prosecute the Letelier assassination while shielding the Chilean government itself from exposure and blame. DINA, its operations, personnel, and crimes inside and outside Chile, had been declared off limits—with the narrowly defined exception of the Letelier operation. The prosecutors' self-imposed censorship of their evidence became clearer with each new witness, but this did not interfere with their efforts to establish the guilt of three non-Chilean defendants.

After Townley stepped down, a parade of witnesses took the stand to shore up his amazing tale with corroborating evidence. Thursday, January 25, was day thirteen. Townley's brother-in-law, Fred Fukuchi, told the jury about Townley's visit to his home two days before the assassination and showed telephone records of calls to and from Guillermo Novo and CNM hangouts in Union City. An electronics equipment salesman matched a receipt for a Fanon-Courier paging device with a copy found in Alvin Ross's abandoned office.

On Monday, January 29, Special Agent Robert Scherrer took the stand to explain how he obtained a teletype message from "Condor One" to the Paraguayan intelligence service requesting that the Paraguayans help in Townley and Fernández' mission to Washington. It was one of the few pieces of evidence—besides Townley's testimony—linking Chile's DINA to the case. Scherrer was also prepared to tell the jury what he had learned about Operation Condor, the multinational assassination network masterminded by Manuel Contreras and financed by Chile. But he was cut off after describing Operation Condor as an "intelligence network" of South American countries and identifying Manuel Contreras as "Condor One."

José Barral's appearance on the witness stand the same day brought pained expressions to the faces of the three defendants. Guillermo Novo's stage whisper "Carajo!" (literally, "louse") could be heard in the first spectators' row. Barral's face also registered anguish as Propper and Barcella began their interrogation. Barral, a CNM sympathizer who said he had been trained as an explosives expert, described a milieu where people asked each other for parts to make explosives. He pleaded that he was a loyal Cuban Nationalist. "Guillermo Novo is my friend . . . a patriot," he said. "I think he is a man that has suffered a lot for the human cause, and I have a lot of admiration for him."

Barral told the jury that Alvin Ross and José Dionisio Suárez had come to his house in September 1976 and that Suárez "wanted to know if I had a blasting cap, and if I could give it to him." Barral's memory, however, was vague on whether Ross had actually overheard this conversation. Propper showed a blasting cap* to Barral, who identified it as the same as or similar to the one he had given Suárez. He said he took the blasting cap from its hiding place in a flower planter in the back of his house, and gave it to Suárez on the basis of a telephone request from Guillermo Novo. He said he had been interrogated "hundreds of times" by the FBI and had been told he could clear himself by testifying.

Barral was the first of the prosecution's surprise witnesses. His real name had been revealed to the defense only the night before he was to testify. The defense knew there was more to come.

The next afternoon, Ricardo Canete mounted the stand. The

---

*Barral's testimony was delayed because FBI lab men insisted on deactivating the blasting cap before allowing it to be handled in court.

defendants all remembered this former CNM member. Now they were to discover a new Canete: the informer, the man to whom they had bragged about crimes they had committed or wished they had committed.

Canete told the jury how he had approached Ignacio Novo in May 1977. Novo, he said, told him that "the government was trying to lay the Letelier thing on him. I said, 'You don't say?' . . . He said, 'Yeah,' then he said, 'Excuse me. I have to make a phone call. I have to contact some of my friends at DINA—they have been letting me know how things are going.' " Ignacio Novo wanted forged documents from Canete. Canete retold the story of forging two sets of documents in the name of Frederick Pagan and giving one to Ignacio and the other to FBI Agent Larry Wack.

Canete identified a photograph of himself leaving the Szechuan Taste restaurant in New York City with Ignacio Novo and a woman named Martha. He testified that he delivered to Ignacio Novo in Union City a Panamanian passport and still another set of documents under the name of Víctor Triquero, which Guillermo Novo later used when he became a fugitive.

Canete described the crucial meeting with Ross. "While I was typing out the DD214 [false discharge papers] I was bragging about my work. Mr. Ross started to brag about his work. Making bombs . . . Carrying the conversation further . . . Mr. Ross informed me, he said, 'I made the Letelier bomb.' I said, 'So what?' "

Later Canete described a March 1978 meeting with Virgilio Paz at the Bottom of the Barrel bar in Union City. Canete complained that the government was pressuring him to testify before the grand jury about the Letelier case. Alvin Ross joined them at the table.

CANETE: Mr. Paz leaned over the table towards me, looked at me. He said, "Look, we did it. They know it. We know it. But let them prove it." I turned around to look at Mr. Ross for confirmation. Mr. Ross nodded his head indicating "yes." Mr. Ross said . . . "Don't worry about anything. They even have some papers of mine and they're too stupid to even figure out what they have."

Canete then told the jury that he had been working as a paid informant for the FBI since his first meeting with Ignacio Novo. He remained on the stand all of Wednesday, January 31. The next day Special Agent Larry Wack testified about how he had recruited Canete as an informant.

Following Canete's testimony the government presented two criminals, Sherman Kaminsky and Antonio Polytarides, who had been confined with Alvin Ross and Guillermo Novo at New York's Metropolitan Correction Center. Kaminsky, a Zionist who once belonged to Israel's secret army, the Haganah, was serving a term for extortion. He testified that Ross had boasted to him about killing Letelier and about other terrorist acts. He said he volunteered to testify because he believed Ross was dangerous. Polytarides, a convicted arms dealer, testified that Guillermo Novo tried to buy arms and explosives from him. Although the final transaction never came about, Polytarides said, Novo attempted to establish his credentials by bragging about participating in the Letelier assassination.

The trial was often delayed for days at a time while the attorneys argued about what each witness would be allowed to say on the stand in front of the jury. Judge Parker chafed at the delays but took pains to avoid a hasty ruling that might provide grounds for the declaration of a mistrial when the inevitable appeal would be filed. He allowed advance screening of testimony from the four controversial witnesses who had acted as informants: Barral, Canete, Kaminsky, and Polytarides. The press and spectators in the now sparsely populated gallery heard the testimony once at the so-called *voir dire* screening, then listened to an expurgated version of the same testimony when the jury was brought in. The jury was present in the courtroom only small fractions of each day's six-to-seven-hour session.

As the fourth week of the trial began, Propper and Barcella tried to speed things up by paring down their list of witnesses. They worked out stipulations with the defense to read simple statements by minor witnesses to the jury in lieu of having the witnesses appear. FBI explosives and fingerprint experts provided the remaining links in the prosecution's chain of evidence. Having presented 26 witnesses and 125 exhibits, the prosecution rested on the twentieth day, February 6.

Manuel Contreras, confined with his personal entourage to suites in Santiago's Military Hospital, kept track of the proceedings from Chile. The Chilean correspondents covering the trial were portraying it to the Chilean public as a primitive circus of legal disputes and contradictions. As the defense prepared to take the stand, Contreras ordered his lawyer, Sergio Miranda Carrington, a former member of the Chilean Nazi Party, to fly to Washington for the purpose of providing assistance.*

Contreras arranged for tickets and expenses for Miranda and two former DINA agents through a government account. Miranda landed in Washington Saturday, February 3, and checked into the Guest Quarters, a hotel across the street from the Intrigue Hotel, where the defense team had set up their headquarters. During a late-night meeting in Miranda's room, Miranda laid out his bag of tricks for use in the trial: the two former DINA agents would testify that Townley had never been a DINA agent and had himself fabricated his DINA identifications in his home laboratory; they would provide names of "CIA agents" alleged to know of Townley's activities in Chile, stolen letters sent by Townley to his wife in Chile, and the tape of a telephone call from Michael Townley to a DINA agent in Chile.

The meeting went poorly. Miranda railed against the United States case and set forth ways it could be undercut, yet he could not force himself to look at the two defense lawyers, Goldberger and Dubin, both Jewish. They seethed at the indignity of having to deal with such a crass anti-Semite, but were interested in obtaining whatever new evidence might help their clients. They asked Miranda how

---

*Contreras may already have given considerable financial help to the Cuban defendants. After the trial FBI Agents Cornick and Scherrer traced an account in Washington's Riggs Bank to Contreras and discovered that $25,000 had been deposited in the account a few weeks before the trial through a money-laundering procedure. A check signed by Contreras for the same amount was cashed a few days later by a go-between and the money given to LAN-Chile employee Hernán Parada and cashed in Miami, Florida. The FBI agents were unable to trace the money to its final destination, but suspected that it ended up in one of the CNM trial-defense funds in Miami.

the DINA agents would handle cross-examination on DINA. "Easy —they'll just use your wonderful American Fifth Amendment and refuse to say anything," he quipped.

Goldberger examined the "official DINA documents" Miranda had brought, and glowered. "Obvious forgeries! What kind of dopes do they take us for?" he remembered thinking. The letters from Townley seemed genuine, but their content was innocuous. The taped telephone conversation, however, interested the lawyers. They took a copy of the tape with them when they left after midnight, having said "Thanks but no thanks" to Miranda's other offerings.

Tuesday, February 6, the day the prosecution rested, the defense lawyers presented a transcript of the telephone conversation to Judge Parker and to Propper and Barcella. Townley had allegedly made the call from Propper's private office the previous week, dialing direct.

Propper and Barcella returned to their offices to read the transcript. Townley, as had become his custom during the trial, was lounging in the area under light supervision of a marshal. In the transcript—alleged to be Townley's words—they read racial slurs against the judge and jury, insulting remarks about Propper, and suggestions on how to subvert the prosecution's case against the Cubans. They also read what appeared to be a joking suggestion to organize a campaign to intimidate Judge Parker: "I offer right now to ask friends all over the world to call him [Parker] and threaten him and get him to withdraw from the case."

Barcella slammed his fist into the swinging-door gate leading from the reception area of the United States attorneys' offices to the secretaries' desks. The gate swung off its hinges and landed against a desk across the room. Barcella looked at his swelling knuckles. Townley approached him, asking to talk. "Get out of my sight!" Barcella shouted.

The next day in court, Judge Parker treated the tape issue in his usual testy manner, but did not make snap judgments or allow the issue to become a factor in the case. He accepted a hasty FBI lab report citing evidence of different sound ambiences as sufficient proof that the tape of the conversation had been doctored. He ordered Townley to appear on the stand, with the jury absent, to verify that he had actually made the call, and lectured Propper for giving a professional assassin free access to his office and phone.* But he overruled a defense motion to allow the tape to be introduced as evidence to discredit Townley's testimony.

Over the next two days, the defense presented eleven witnesses, all but one of whom had originally been listed as witnesses for the prosecution. They recalled Isabel Letelier and attempted to elicit from her an admission that she suspected the CIA of opening her husband's mail. She said she had indeed told the FBI that her mail from Chile had sometimes been tampered with but that she suspected DINA. "I feared that the Chilean secret police was being let loose in this country to follow Chilean refugees by the United States government. I was concerned that the chief of the Chilean secret police had [once] come to this country and met with the head of the CIA," she said.

In debates in open court but out of hearing of the jury, the defense argued for the admission into evidence of the letters and documents found in Letelier's briefcase. "I want to stand before the jury with the contents of the briefcase and demonstrate what [Letelier] was really doing," Goldberger said. He cited the use of "comrade" in one of Letelier's letters as evidence of Letelier's communist activity and his $1,000 a month stipend from the Chilean Socialist Party as proof that he was a Cuban agent. Barcella argued that letters by a dead man were "classic rank hearsay" and that innuendos by the defense about Letelier's communist connections were "almost like a form of McCarthyism." Judge Parker ruled that the defense could not question Mrs. Letelier about the briefcase papers or place them in evidence.†

Edward Cannell III, a former marine guard at the U.S. Embassy in Santiago, testified that he had gone drinking with Michael Townley many times, but that he had never seen him in the CIA section of the embassy.

---

*In a post-trial letter to U.S. Attorney Earl Silbert, Parker said, "This matter is of grave concern. You are requested to undertake an investigation of this phone call and specifically of Mr. Townley's access to government phones in general."

†In a December 12, 1978 pretrial hearing, Propper said the FBI had "gone over [the briefcase papers] carefully and found no evidence Letelier was working for any government, either Cuban, Chilean, or other."

The next day Ambassador George Landau was called to the witness stand. He had originally been scheduled to testify for the prosecution, but Propper had decided his testimony would be superfluous since the defense had not disputed Townley's story about obtaining the Romeral and Williams passports in Paraguay.

As ambassador to Paraguay at the time of the assassination and ambassador to Chile at the time of Townley's identification and expulsion, Landau had played a continuing and crucial role in the case. The defense lawyers called Laudau because they wanted the jury to hear from his mouth the story of CIA Deputy Director Vernon Walters' connection to the Paraguay incident. Landau, tall, tanned, and dignified, predictably related the chain of events exactly as he had described it in a signed affadavit to Propper months before. He said he had granted visas to two Chilean "army officers" on the request of a Paraguayan official in July 1976 and informed the CIA's Walters that the two men would be arriving in Washington. "I was suspicious right from the beginning," Landau said. "I asked that the passports be given to me after the visas were issued . . . and photographed them, the first to last page, including the photograph of the people."

Landau's testimony differed in only one detail from his earlier affadavit, in which he had said that the request that Paraguay furnish passports for the two Chileans came directly from President Augusto Pinochet to his counterpart General Alfredo Stroessner, president of Paraguay. On the stand, Landau described only a "high-level request from the Chilean government."

Landau painted a portrait of himself as acting forcefully and correctly to efface any appearance of United States government sponsorship for the mission of the two Chileans to the United States. He testified that he told Paraguayan official Conrado Pappalardo to "forget the whole thing. Get me the passports back. They are of no value. Consider the visas revoked. If [the Chileans] try to use them they will obviously be arrested at the port of entry. I informed the Department of State that the visas were revoked."

He said he had got the Romeral and Williams passports back with the pictures of the two men removed several weeks later, in early September 1976, and that in 1978 he had turned them over to the FBI "when this whole thing became active and the names of Williams and Romeral came up."

Landau's photographing of the Romeral and Williams passports in Paraguay had led to the discovery of DINA's assassination team and to the identification and expulsion of Michael Townley. No other event or lead had played such a major role in the investigation of the case. At the trial of the three Cubans, however, its significance was overlooked, and overshadowed by the more spectacular testimony of the assassin himself. Neither defense nor prosecution asked Landau why, if the passport pictures of Romeral and Williams were in his files as well as those of the CIA and State Department weeks before the assassination occurred, it had taken so long for the names and pictures to "come up" in the investigation.

The defense, having failed to elicit from Landau the slightest hint of a CIA connection to the assassination mission, beyond Landau's efforts to hinder it, moved the next day to two witnesses from the CIA itself. Marvin L. Smith, CIA chief of operations, and Robert W. Gambino, CIA security director, had provided affidavits to Propper before the trial stating that Michael Townley had contacted the agency in 1970 and 1973 but had never worked for the agency in any capacity. Out in the hallway during a break, defense attorney Goldberger explained to reporters that in calling them to the stand he didn't expect them to throw up their hands and say, "You got us, he was our agent all the time." The defense tactic, Goldberger said, was to maneuver the CIA officials into exaggerated denials of CIA activities that would convince the jury that a CIA cover-up was at work and that the denials about Townley were lies.

Security Director Gambino, in a brief appearance on the stand, said his office had given "preliminary security approval" to use Mr. Townley "in an operational capacity" in February 1971. The CIA had "some interest" in Townley until December 1971, when security approval was canceled. He said he did not know whether Townley had ever been "used."

But Goldberger and Dubin raised questions to which Gambino offered no answers. Did the CIA have any operations going on in Chile at the time, 1971 to 1973? Gambino had no information as to whether they did or did not. Were there any CIA employees at all in Chile? Not to Gambino's personal knowledge. But somebody at CIA should know that? Gambino had never asked.

Gambino stepped down, and Operations Director Marvin Smith took the oath to tell the whole truth and nothing but the truth. As the official directly responsible for what he called "clandestine operations" abroad, he could be expected to know the answer to some of the questions about Chile and Michael Townley.

In March 1971, he said, "the decision was made to contact [Townley], to assess him for use. . . . It was certainly our intent to pursue it." In August 1971 CIA employees in Chile ("Yes, there were a number of people for the CIA in Chile") tried to reach Townley at an address he had given in Santiago but were told that he had returned to the United States. The CIA then assigned agents to try to find Townley in Miami two weeks later, but were told in Miami that he had returned to Chile.* At that, Smith said, the CIA gave up on Michael Townley.

Goldberger pressed on. "The CIA was also deeply committed to deposing the Allende regime, isn't that right?" Propper jumped to his feet to object to the question. Sustained, Judge Parker said.

Goldberger restated the question: Were there any CIA operations in Chile at that time. Yes. Did the CIA take any role in politics there? No, the files don't reflect that. Was there a section of the U.S. Embassy called Pol/R? I don't know. Do you know where CIA headquarters in Chile was located? No. Goldberger asked about the CIA file on Michael Townley. Yes, there was such a file. No, there are no hidden records at the CIA. No, there was no photo of Michael Townley in CIA files. Did the CIA receive a photo of Michael Townley in 1976? "I can tell you there is no photo of Michael Townley in our files."

Goldberger paused, then said, "Did you ever check under the name Juan Williams Rose?" No, Smith had checked Townley's aliases Andrés Wilson, Hans Petersen Silva, and Kenneth Enyart, but he had never checked for the alias Juan Williams Rose. "Did you know there was an American citizen working for Chile's DINA?" No.

---

*Townley was actually in San Francisco at the time (see Chap. 4, "Condor's Jackal").

Smith fielded the questions and delivered his answers in a total deadpan. Goldberger and Dubin raised their eyebrows and shot sidelong glances at the jury box. The tactic was convoluted and probably lost on the jury members, but the defense questioning scored a point or two against CIA credibility. Moreover, the points had dramatic effect but did not pry loose evidence. Defense questioning failed to budge the basic CIA story that Michael Townley had never worked for the CIA.

The defense's last and best shot was over. The defense rested in early afternoon, Friday, February 9, the twenty-third day of the trial.

Final arguments remained. They began early the following Monday. Exhaustion showed in the faces of the attorneys at both tables. For five weeks they had spent long days in court and long evenings and early mornings preparing witnesses, studying testimony, and elaborating strategy. Defense attorney Goldberger had missed one day because of illness. A virus infection had weakened Propper's voice and sapped his energy during the final days.

Barcella, who had cross-examined most of the defense witnesses, rose to sum up the prosecution's case, to reconstruct the myriad details of the plot to kill Letelier and tie together for the jury each piece of evidence linking Guillermo Novo and Alvin Ross to the murders and Ignacio Novo to the cover-up. Barcella worked to bolster his star witness's credibility and to put to rest any lingering doubts about the propriety of the agreement to obtain Townley's testimony.

"You need an insider. That's how you find out what happens inside a conspiracy," he said. "Without Michael Townley, this monstrous crime never gets fully solved, does it? . . . and without that agreement Michael Townley wouldn't testify . . . and all the co-conspirators would escape."

He offered his interpretations of Chile's seemingly irrational action in giving the FBI the man who could prove that the Letelier assassination was masterminded in Chile. The Chilean government handed Townley over to the FBI, he said, because "Chile doesn't know what Townley knows . . . because Contreras hasn't let anybody know what Townley knows."

The defense attorneys made their arguments. Goldberger attacked Michael Townley as a professional liar and "a man who speaks of eliminating people as if they were bugs," a man who had bartered his testimony against the Cubans in order to avoid spending the rest of his life in jail. "No one should be convicted on the word of Michael Townley, and that's what this case boils down to," said Goldberger. But he tacitly conceded that there was little evidence to back up his opening assertion that Townley was a CIA agent. "We don't have to prove [that] beyond a reasonable doubt," he said. But the jurors should, he suggested, have more than a reasonable doubt about the CIA's disclaimers and about the credibility of Michael Townley.

The trial had taken a strange turn. The government of Chile, charged in the prosecution's opening statement with the responsibility for sending terrorists to the streets of Washington, was barely mentioned in the testimony presented to the jury. Both prosecution and defense chose strategies that eschewed direct criticism of the Pinochet government. It was hardly surprising that the defense should have coordinated its strategy with the Chilean government to fit Contreras' "the CIA did it" theory. But there was little logical explanation for the prosecution's kid-gloves treatment of the Chilean government and even less justification for the chumminess evidenced in the chief prosecutor's relationship with Michael Townley.

Townley had become part of the prosecution team, in effect, and had arrogantly molded the government case to render it harmless to the Pinochet regime. He defined the terms of his own testimony.* He refused to answer questions about the internal workings of DINA and about other crimes he had committed in its service. And his refusal was sanctioned by impassioned prosecution argument, prompting Judge Parker to scold Propper: "It sounds as though you are representing Mr. Townley."

The prosecutors even incorporated into their case Chile's principal argument as to Pinochet's innocence and the noninvolvement of officials outside DINA in the assassination. Prosecutor Barcella repeated Townley's assertion that Contreras had not informed Presi-

*Townley himself formulated point 5 of his plea bargain, which in effect defined crimes outside the United States as off limits in interrogating him.

dent Pinochet about the assassination. Yet Townley knew only what he had been told by Contreras, and had no direct knowledge of whether Contreras and Pinochet had discussed the Letelier assassination at their daily intelligence meetings before and after the fact.

The final argument was the first public acknowledgment that the United States government accepted the fiction that the Letelier assassination had somehow been the act of Manuel Contreras and his DINA followers acting alone—like a kind of rogue elephant out of control of his master, General Pinochet, upon whom the United States generously bestowed the benefit of the doubt.

The next day, after instructions from Judge Parker, the jury retired to do its work. The jurors deliberated for three hours that day, then returned the next. At 3:30 P.M. February 14, exactly eight and a half hours after they began their deliberation, the jurors announced that they had reached a verdict.

In the courtroom more than twenty marshals stood like sentries. More marshals patrolled the corridors. The jury forewoman stood and read the decison without emotion. Guillermo Novo: Count 1— Guilty. Count 2—Guilty. A litany of "Guiltys" followed charge upon charge for Guillermo. Then for Alvin Ross: Guilty, guilty, guilty on all charges. Then the same for Ignacio Novo.

Silvia Novo, Ignacio's wife, and other members of the family began to sob as the first "Guilty" was read. The defendants sat stonefaced. Judge Parker revoked Ignacio's bail and set sentencing and appeal dates. As the defendants rose to be escorted from the courtroom, Ignacio raised a clenched fist and shouted:

"Viva Cuba!"

Then he looked at the reporters and said:

"The dice came up craps."

The trial was over.

EPILOGUE

MARCH 23, 1979. Judge Barrington Parker, commenting "In the ten years I have served on the bench, I've never presided over a trial of a murder as monstrous as this," sentenced Guillermo Novo and Alvin Ross to consecutive terms of life imprisonment in a maximum security institution. They will be eligible for parole in 1999. Ignacio Novo, convicted of perjury and misprision of a felony, was sentenced to eight years imprisonment and will be eligible for parole after serving thirty-two months.

May 11, 1979. Parker sentenced Michael Townley, in accordance with the plea bargain signed over a year before in exchange for his testimony, to ten years with credit for time already served. Townley, under the federal witness protection program, received a new identity and was confined to an undisclosed medium security prison, with parole eligibility as early as October 1981. At the sentencing hearing before Parker, Townley again expressed his lack of remorse for killing Letelier and said he hoped to return to Chile to live after serving his time.

May 31, 1979. Deposed General Manuel Contreras, from confinement in Santiago's Military Hospital, accused Foreign Minister Hernán Cubillos and two other civilian ministers of having "jeopardized the honor of the nation" in their dealings with the United States government on the case. A few days later, after President Pinochet publicly rebuked Contreras for his action, Contreras issued a statement saying: "As a soldier, I am ready, once again, to obey the orders of my general [Pinochet] in spite of the ignominious stance of some of the lackeys that surround him."

In a preliminary ruling on May 16, Chilean Supreme Court President Israel Bórquez had denied extradition of Contreras, Espinoza, and Fernández to the United States to stand trial. The three remained under arrest pending appeal to a panel of the same court. In Washington, Assistant U.S. Attorney Eugene Propper and U.S. Ambassador George Landau lobbied Congressman Tom Harkin to postpone introduction of a resolution signed by fifty-five congressmen calling for the president to suspend private bank loans to Chile under authorization of the International Emergency Economic Powers Act of 1977. Landau and Propper argued that a congressional resolution on the case would be seen in Chile as interference in the judicial process and would provide a pretext for denial of extradition on appeal to the body of the Supreme Court. Propper assured members of Congress that Chile's failure to extradite or at least to conduct a fair trial in Chile would bring forth grave sanctions against the Pinochet regime.

In the nine months following the trial, the Cuban Nationalist Movement's Omega 7 and Zero claimed credit for murdering two Cuban exile leaders who had advocated exile reconciliation with the Cuban government and for six bomb attacks in the New York and Washington areas.

On October 1, the Supreme Court panel upheld Bórquez' ruling that extradition be denied, on the grounds that the United States case rested principally on the word of Michael Townley, whose testimony had been tainted by his plea-bargain agreement with the United States government. Contreras, Espinoza, and Fernández, after just over one year's confinement, were set free, Espinoza and Fernández returning to active duty in the army. The court ruled out any use of the elaborate package of United States evidence against the three in the unlikely event of a future military trial in the case. Ambassador Landau returned to Washington a few days later to discuss possible United States sanctions against Chile. It was the third time since he became ambassador to Chile in November 1977 that he had been recalled to Washington in protest moves in connection with the Letelier case. The *New York Times,* in an editorial, described the Chilean decision as a "kind of judicial pyrotechnics . . . best understood in the context of the current Chilean regime, tightly controlled by persons who might themselves be implicated" in the Letelier assassination.

On November 30, the Carter administration announced a series of measures in retaliation for Chile's actions in the Letelier case. Chile was criticized, not because it had failed to extradite, but because the indicted Chileans were "officials of that government" and because "for over 20 months the Government of Chile has made no serious effort to investigate or prosecute these crimes on its own." The statement said President Carter had ordered the reduction of the U.S. Mission to Chile, termination of the foreign military sales "pipeline," "phasing down" of the U.S. Military Mission, suspension of Export-Import Bank financing, and an end to new activities of the Overseas Private Investment Corporation in Chile. The statement called the assassination an "egregious act of international terrorism" and said Chile's conduct in the matter was "deplorable . . . in particular its refusal to conduct a full and fair investigation of this crime." Chile's military government had, "in effect, condoned this act of international terrorism," the statement said, though it stopped short of holding the Pinochet government responsible for the assassination itself. The measures amounted to "little more than a wrist slap" that "bolstered rather than weakened [Pinochet's] military government," reported the *Washington Post* from Santiago.

Three months after the reprisals were announced not one embassy official had been withdrawn, and Chilean officials were congratulating themselves on having faced down the United States "bluff." By February 1980, United States relations with Chile had returned full circle to the warm support of the early years of the Pinochet dictatorship, but with special United States enthusiasm for Chile's economic model. To control rising labor-union militancy, Pinochet issued new decrees allowing CNI/DINA to arrest dissenters without charge and confine them in remote villages for periods of three months. Although Contreras' removal brought mass arrests and disappearances to an end, CNI/DINA chief Odlanier Mena continued the use of torture and secret interrogation centers. Ambassador George Landau, silent on human rights, approved publication in February of an embassy staff report giving blanket United States endorsement of the Chilean economic program. It said:

> In its reliance on market economics, Chile appears in the vanguard of a world-wide neo-conservative response to the menace of growing inflation. . . . Most U.S. private-sector observers are inclined to believe that the current military regime will be followed within 10 years by a stable, middle-of-the-road government reasonably favorable to free enterprise and foreign investment.

HOW DOES ONE CONCLUDE the story of a complicated historical event, one that involved several nations over a period of years, fundamental issues of ownership of property and wealth, intrigue, assassination, and finally a hunt and capture? In fictional spy stories all the pieces fall into place; the author controls the facts and the characters. In real life, intrigue defies literary controls, and the end of a tale like the one we have just recounted is best served by presenting the reader with a series of questions, partial answers, and deductions from partial evidence. That is the way most judgments are made.

Did the United States government have sufficient foreknowledge to have prevented the murders? The answer depends on who knew what and when and what they did about it. Beginning in July 1976, eight weeks before Orlando Letelier and Ronni Moffitt were killed, a number of high CIA and State Department officials knew that DINA had begun an undercover operation in Washington, D.C. On July 26, 1976, Conrado Pappalardo, Paraguayan President Stroessner's top aide, asked U.S. Ambassador George Landau for United States visas for two Chilean army officers on their way to Washington on an intelligence mission which required them to use Paraguayan rather than Chilean passports. Whatever the normal course of intelligence agency interaction, Landau, according to his

later testimony, considered this an extraordinary request, He nevertheless complied. His decision was apparently based on Pappalardo's
assurances that the request came from President Stroessner himself,
who in turn had been asked by Chilean President Pinochet. He was
also told that CIA Deputy Director General Vernon Walters was
aware of the Chileans' mission and would be in touch with the two
men in Washington.

But, his suspicions aroused, Ambassador Landau took two
precautions: he had the passports of Juan Williams and Alejandro
Romeral photocopied, and he sent a long top-secret cable via the
State Department to General Walters at CIA headquarters. That
cable remains secret, but we learned some of its contents. In it
Landau asked Walters if the Chilean-Paraguayan mission had been
worked out with the CIA.

**Who read Ambassador Landau's cable and how did they act on
it?** Landau's cable and the pictures went, in Walters' absence, to CIA
director George Bush.* At State, the cable reached the office of
Harry Shlaudeman, assistant secretary of state for inter-American
affairs, after first arriving at the office of Secretary of State Henry
Kissinger.

The CIA reaction was peculiar. Landau expected Walters to take
quick action in the event that the Chilean mission did not have CIA
clearance. Yet a week passed during which the assassination team
could well have had time to carry out their original plan to go
directly from Paraguay to Washington to kill Letelier. Walters and
Bush conferred during that week about the matter. We were unable
to learn of any other action by the CIA officials, but Walters cabled
Landau in Paraguay as late as August 4 to inform him that the CIA
wanted nothing to do with the Chilean mission, of which he said he
was "not aware."

Judging from his actions, Ambassador Landau was alarmed. He
revoked the visas and demanded that Paraguayan intelligence retrieve the passports. He considered the affair serious enough to order
lookouts alerting all United States consulates and ports of entry to

*Walters was in the process of retiring from the CIA, and though still on the CIA payroll at
this time, had gone to Florida on vacation to take advantage of accumulated leave time before
officially leaving the agency. Landau sent his cable early July 28; Bush's office acknowledged
receipt that day or the next.

arrest Romeral and Williams if they arrived in the United States. He also made ten telephone calls over the following weeks to insist that the Paraguayans return the unused passports. He has not explained why he was so concerned about the Romeral and Williams matter, but there can be no doubt about the seriousness with which he regarded the incident. He has declined to discuss matters that go beyond his official testimony in the case.

Another important fact became known to United States officials before the assassination. Despite Landau's lookout order, two men using Chilean passports in the names of Juan Williams and Alejandro Romeral obtained United States official A-2 visas at the U.S. Consulate in Santiago and entered the United States on August 22.* United States authorities at Miami International Airport detected their arrival and reported it to the U.S. State Department. Furthermore, when Romeral and Williams arrived in Washington, they alerted the CIA to their presence by having a Chilean Embassy employee call General Walters' office at the CIA's Langley headquarters. It is quite beyond belief that the CIA is so lax in its counterespionage functions that it would simply have ignored a clandestine operation by a foreign intelligence service in Washington, D.C., or anywhere in the United States. It is equally implausible that Bush, Walters, Landau, and other officials were unaware of the chain of international assassinations that had been attributed to DINA. General Walters, head of CIA liaison with foreign intelligence services, certainly had detailed knowledge of DINA assassination activity.

What did they do? We don't know. It would have been logical for those who knew of Chile's ongoing covert operation in Washington to try to find out what Chile was up to. The intelligence services of Chile's DINA and the United States' CIA were not adversaries seeking to subvert each other's systems of government but rather friendly intelligence services in constant touch with each other through normal liaison channels. The Chileans had misrepresented

*According to the official United States investigation, it was not learned until March 1978 that the second Romeral and Williams team was made up of other DINA agents, not the assassins Townley and Fernández.

the mission to Washington as having CIA approval. Did the director and deputy director of the CIA order their representative in Chile to tell his liaison counterpart in DINA and the other Chilean intelligence services, "Hey, we know you're up to something in Washington, so either tell us or stop it"?*

One thing is clear: DINA chief Manuel Contreras would have called off the assassination mission if the CIA or State Department had expressed their displeasure to the Chilean government. An intelligence officer familiar with the case said that any warning would have been sufficient to cause the assassination to be scuttled. Whatever Walters and Bush did—if anything—the DINA mission proceeded. Orlando Letelier and Ronni Moffitt are dead. But the question remains: **Could their murders have been prevented?**

Once the investigation of the murders was under way, why did it take so long? Did Bush, Walters, Landau, and others who by then had become informed of the Chilean undercover activity come forward immediately and disclose what they knew? The assassination occurred September 21, 1976. The indictments were returned August 1, 1978. Yet the evidence that led to the identification of Michael Townley and his expulsion from Chile in April 1978 was already in the hands of high United States officials weeks before the assassination.

The Romeral-Williams information and pictures were obviously pertinent to the FBI investigation of the assassination. Moreover, a week after the assassination, FBI Agent Robert Scherrer reported the existence of Operation Condor. His September 28 cable describing Condor went to the FBI with "lateral distribution" to the State Department and the CIA.

Condor was a network of intelligence services of six South American military dictatorships designed by Contreras to carry out assassinations of exiled dissidents. Condor's procedures called for member countries to provide false documentation for assassination teams made up of agents from other member countries. Paraguay was a

---

*According to an affidavit filed in the case by FBI agent Robert Scherrer, "neither the CIA chief nor any subordinate [in Chile] had communicated in any manner with General Contreras or any other DINA officer in 1976 with regard to travel by any DINA officer to the United States to visit General Walters."

member. Scherrer, even without knowing about the Romeral and Williams affair in Paraguay, concluded that the Letelier assassination fit the specifics of a Condor operation. Those who knew about the Romeral and Williams incident in Paraguay and their subsequent journey to Washington had even more reason to draw the same conclusion. They knew Chile had launched a Condor-type mission via Paraguay in the weeks before the assassination.

What then did Bush, Walters, Landau, and others in State and the CIA do with the Romeral and Williams information and photographs after the assassination? The first week of October, Eugene Propper and several Justice Department officials met CIA Director Bush to discuss procedures for CIA cooperation in the Letelier case investigation. At that meeting, according to one of those present, Bush talked about Operation Condor but did not say a word about the Romeral and Williams pictures and the Paraguay incident. Nor did Bush, Walters, or anyone else from the CIA subsequently volunteer their information about Chile's undercover mission to Propper or the FBI.* Instead of providing the information that pointed the finger of suspicion at DINA and Chile, the CIA seems to have done just the opposite. Stories appeared in *Newsweek,* the *Washington Post,* the *Washington Star,* and the *New York Times* saying the CIA had concluded that DINA had nothing to do with the Letelier assassination. CIA Director Bush was reported to have personally informed Secretary of State Kissinger of his conclusions about DINA's innocence.

At the State Department, some but not all of the pertinent information about Chile's secret mission was turned over to the FBI on October 22, one month after the assassination. The information included the copies of the Paraguayan passports with the photographs of Romeral and Williams, and the fact that two men using those names and official Chilean passports had entered Miami August 22. The State Department has refused to release to us its original memo-

*Nor, apparently, were they asked directly. The FBI did not question Walters about the Paraguay incident until June 14, 1978. Walters said he could "furnish no pertinent information" about the Letelier assassination and had "never discussed with any Paraguayan officials the issuance of false passports or any joint Chilean-Paraguayan intelligence operation." He also offered to take a lie detector test.

randum to the FBI on the matter, so we do not know exactly how it described the Paraguay incident and the source of its knowledge of Romeral and Williams' entry at Miami.

We do know that the Romeral-Williams information and photographs played no active role for the first ten months of the FBI investigation. We have also learned of five cases of withholding, destruction, or concealment of key evidentiary documents in the case. The examples brought to light in our investigation raise the possibility that an attempt was made from within the United States government to sabotage the FBI investigation and divert its focus away from Chile's military government:

1. Assistant U.S. Attorney Propper and the FBI did not receive Ambassador Landau's cable to Vernon Walters explaining the Paraguay incident for more than a year after the assassination.

2. State Department Chile desk officer Robert Driscoll did not inform the FBI of his knowledge that Romeral and Williams were in Washington around the time of the assassination. A memo with that information from Chile desk files reached the FBI more than one year after the assassination.

3. Immigration and Naturalization Service records—I-94 forms —that document entry into the United States of three of the five members of DINA's assassination mission were removed from INS computers. The missing listings were Alejandro Romeral Jara, Juan Williams Rose (the August 22 Miami entry with Chilean passports), and Hans Petersen Silva (the name used by Michael Townley to enter New York September 9, 1976).* Moreover, INS officials conducted

*After Townley's expulsion broke the case in mid-1978, a twenty-four-hour search of INS archives by thirty-five to fifty INS employees at FBI insistence turned up the original I-94 forms for Romeral, Williams, and Petersen.

Propper, who provided a deposition on his conduct of the case for use in the civil suit brought by Isabel Letelier and Michael Moffitt against the Chilean government, was asked about the I-94 forms. His answers:

A. As I recall, the FBI had great difficulty finding them—and I could be wrong about this and the FBI would know—in the INS. But the State Department had pulled them and either put them together with the passport or did something with them, and so they weren't in Immigration files when the FBI went there the first time.

Q. Did you know why those were pulled? Did your investigation ever disclose why that happened?

A. Not that I recall, other than they were eventually given to us. I think the State Department was looking at what was going on in Paraguay.

a file search in 1979 and discovered the disappearance of all paper-work that normally would accompany lookout notices such as those ordered posted by the State Department for Romeral and Williams.

4. Someone with access to United States citizen registration files in the U.S. Consulate in Santiago removed the photograph of Michael Townley on file there.

5. Other evidence in consulate files was destroyed as well. After his expulsion, Townley provided investigators with the names Hans Petersen Silva, Armando Fáundez Lyon, and Liliana Walker Martínez, the names used by himself, Fernández, and the female DINA agent to carry out the surveillance and assassination mission. FBI Agent Scherrer found the official visa application form 257-A for the three names in consulate files when he looked in mid-1978, but discovered that U.S. Consul Josiah Brownell had ordered the shredding of the file of probatory documents which would have included the Foreign Ministry letter requesting visas for the three agents. The letters, signed by a Chilean official, presumably consular section head Guillermo Osorio, may also have contained annotations by United States officials on granting the visas. Consulate officials said the shredding was done according to a routine timetable for the disposal of old files. But Scherrer, in an earlier file search in mid-1977, advised Brownell that additional evidence in the case might still be in the files and they should not be destroyed. We asked Brownell why he had destroyed the files Scherrer had asked him to save. He refused to comment.

A sixth example of misuse of evidence must be added to the list. The entire contents of the briefcase Orlando Letelier was carrying the day he was murdered was copied while in the investigators' vaults and leaked to scores of journalists. Dozens of articles appeared, most of them written by right-wing columnists, portraying Letelier as a paid Cuban agent and by extension a KGB spy. The charges and innuendo were based on the hardly surprising fact that Letelier had been receiving $1,000 a month from the Chilean Socialist Party to offset the expenses incurred in his work in the United States against the Pinochet government. From the fact that the Socialist Party treasurer who wrote to Letelier and mentioned the payments lived in Cuba and was married to a Cuban government official, some of the writers jumped to the conclusion that Letelier was an agent of Castro's DGI. The FBI investigated the briefcase letters and concluded that the charges were baseless. Letelier was exactly who he appeared to be: an exiled political leader who represented the Chilean Popular Unity in the United States.*

Notwithstanding the specious logic of the accusations, their implications for the investigation of the murder were clear: If Letelier was really a spy, then his murder, like a gangland killing, was a settling of accounts among violent men living in a world of assassination and intrigue, an act calling for neither outrage nor prosecution.

What would have happened if the missing information had been provided, or been provided sooner? One FBI agent, after seeing a copy of Driscoll's memo for the first time in late 1977, had this answer: "Considerable investigative effort could have been saved" if the FBI had had earlier knowledge about Romeral and Williams' presence in Washington. He stated that the case could have been "resolved a year earlier."

In our reconstruction of the FBI investigation, two pieces remain missing from the puzzle. One would explain why the FBI, in the weeks after the assassination, did so little with the information it did possess about the Chilean covert mission and instead pursued other less pertinent leads. The other would explain what belatedly spurred the investigators in mid-1977 to resurrect the dormant Romeral-Williams lead and begin showing the photos to their sources.

Although the lack of this information impeded the investigation, it alone does not account for the fact that FBI Agent Carter Cornick and prosecutor Eugene Propper failed for so long to assign a high investigative priority to the Romeral-Williams pictures, the information about the Paraguay incident, and the arrival of the Chilean agents in Miami. Propper and Cornick decline to explain what happened, but maintain that they found no obstacles more serious than "bureaucratic foul-ups" in the course of their investigation. We would ask them to look again.

*However, the FBI did not publicly refute the charges by announcing its own conclusions about the briefcase papers at the time the articles appeared. The refutation finally came in a little-publicized statement by Eugene Propper at a pretrial hearing in December 1978.

It would be naïve for us or those conducting the government investigation to shrug off such examples of withheld and destroyed evidence as the foibles of unthinking bureaucrats, as a case of one part of the government not knowing what another part is doing. Nor is it sufficient explanation that the psychological bent of public officials imbued with anticommunism and susceptible to historically baseless "martyr theories" could somehow have blinded intelligent professional men to the facts before them.

No bureaucratic explanation can account for the detours and obstacles the investigators encountered in solving the case. It was not DINA's cover-ups nor the secretiveness of the Cuban Nationalist Movement that kept the investigation off the right track for almost a year. It was the actions consciously taken or willfully omitted by officials and agencies of the United States government.

Once on the right track, the investigators used the pictures to identify Michael Townley. With his expulsion and confession, the murders were solved, to the credit of the FBI team of Carter Cornick, Robert Scherrer, and Larry Wack, and the U.S. Attorney's Office team of Eugene Propper and Lawrence Barcella. Their investigation and prosecution of the case revealed to the world a terrorist conspiracy masterminded by officials of the Chilean military government. The story of their achievement and the obstacles they overcame fills the latter half of this book. They had all become involved beyond their official duties. In the course of the investigation and trial all worked overtime and often with passion. They took imaginative steps.

At the same time they were bound by the limits of the system in which they worked, and did not challenge the narrow framework established for their investigation and prosecution of the crime. The rules of the Major Crimes Division of the U.S. Attorney's Office dictated that the investigative team track down a political assassination without going to the political source of the murder. As Eugene Propper told a reporter in 1978: "People who are attributing political motivations to the indictment are wrong. There's nothing political about this. It's a straight murder case, a case of blowing someone's legs off."

At key junctures, however, political decisions were required, and at those times the case was removed from the U.S. attorneys' hands. The case was broken because the Carter administration authorized Ambassador Landau to apply pressure to force the Pinochet government to turn Townley over to the FBI.

Yet when the United States set about the even larger task of obtaining Manuel Contreras, the second most powerful man in Chile at his peak, it suddenly reversed its earlier resolve and limited itself to a petition of extradition to the Chilean court system.

Ambassador Landau, who had acted like a lion in forcing the expulsion of Townley, against which the United States had only the bare bones of a case, now became a lamb meekly announcing his trust in the Chilean judiciary.

Why did the United States submit its request—asking in effect to prosecute officials of the Chilean government operating in their official capacity—to the Chilean court system? The United States government asked the Chilean court to turn over for trial the head of the country's most important intelligence service. At the best of times and in the most democratic countries, this would have been an unrealistic request. Chile's courts, in the five years of Pinochet's regime, had never ruled against the military government on any important matter. The fiction of the independence of the Chilean judiciary was transparent. The conclusion must be drawn that the United States government, by accepting that fiction as fact and submitting the case to the court system instead of treating the extradition as a political-diplomatic issue, acquiesced in the failure of the extradition request.

The United States accepted a second fiction, that the DINA assassins were somehow separate from the Chilean government—as if Townley, Fernández, Espinoza, and Contreras had committed the crime as individuals not subject to Pinochet's command. The United States chose not to recognize that the assassination had been committed to serve the political purposes of the Pinochet government, accepting instead the terms suggested by that government for handling the case. Those terms, not surprisingly, included the promise that the United States prosecution of the Letelier case would not implicate the Pinochet regime.

Such shielding was implicit in the secret agreement between U.S.

Attorney Earl Silbert and Chilean official Enrique Montero to obtain Michael Townley's expulsion, and in Townley's plea-bargaining agreement. Both agreements imposed Chile's conditions on the United States' prosecution of the Letelier assassination and curtailed exposure of the crimes of the Pinochet regime.

The United States' decision to shield the Pinochet regime was dictated by foreign policy considerations and was not made to strengthen the prosecutors' ability to obtain convictions against those indicted for the murders. (On the contrary, the exclusion at the trial of evidence about DINA crimes and Pinochet's role provided grounds for appeal of the convictions of the Cuban accomplices.) The decision can be understood as flowing from established policies of the United States government in Latin America. In protecting the Pinochet regime from exposure, the United States was protecting its own relationships, intelligence, and security priorities and large-scale economic stakes.

Pinochet, in getting rid of Allende, had extracted a major thorn from the lion's paw, and Washington was grateful. The thrust of United States policy toward the military government was that of protector to protégé; occasional scolding about Pinochet's human rights image only served to underline the United States' concern for its offspring. The Letelier assassination placed the United States government on the horns of a dilemma: solving the murders carried with it the real threat of discrediting and possibly dethroning Pinochet and his system. The Carter administration was confronted inexorably with the choice between punishing the Chilean government for perpetrating an act of international terrorism and protecting Pinochet.

Just as in the past, when the policymakers invoked national security to justify the support of Latin American dictatorships, the national security argument prevailed. The stability of the Pinochet regime was judged more sacred to United States interests than the prosecution of terrorism on the part of that regime.

The ability of the United States to act in the Letelier case was also limited by the compromising nature of past CIA activity in Chile and the ongoing relationship between the CIA and DINA. The investigation not only threatened to expose Pinochet and his crimes but also raised the specter of a new round of exposures of CIA covert action. The Chilean magazine *Que Pasa* laid bare a vulnerable nerve of the United States intelligence community in a brief commentary in mid-1979: If the United States demands the extradition of Manuel Contreras, the former head of Chilean intelligence, why shouldn't Chile demand the extradition of former CIA director Richard Helms for the CIA's role in plotting the kidnapping-murder of General René Schneider in 1970?

The investigation revealed that the CIA and DINA had a working relationship at the time of the Letelier assassination that allowed DINA operatives routinely to enter the United States. U.S. Embassy officials knowingly issued visas for Chilean intelligence missions. In the Letelier case the members of the DINA assassination team, almost without exception, had past or current ties to the CIA and other United States government agencies. The CIA had spawned Cuban exile terrorism and trained three of the five Cuban accomplices in the murder. The CIA had helped create the propitious conditions for the Chilean military coup; it had encouraged and assisted Manuel Contreras in creating and shaping DINA. United States officials, however, minimized and obfuscated the links between the CIA and Chile's DINA. U.S. Attorney Earl Silbert and Assistant U.S. Attorney Propper, in a letter to defense lawyers a few weeks before the trial, declared that "the relationship, if any, between CIA and DINA is not relevant to this case. If any such relationship is found to exist which is relevant and helpful to the defense, that information will be disclosed." A prosecution memo filed later in court said: "There is absolutely no evidence whatsoever that the Central Intelligence Agency either had advance knowledge of or participated in the Letelier assassination. . . . There is not *the slightest scintilla of evidence to indicate CIA involvement or knowledge in this matter.*" (Italics added)

Finally, it is hard to believe that the CIA's network of agents had not, long before the murders, detected Operation Condor and the joint assassination activities of Latin American police forces.

In the light of the number of complex relationships of United States national security, policy, banking, and business circles to Chile, we must ask why Contreras chose to have Letelier killed in

Washington, D.C. The obvious reasons were that Letelier lived and worked in Washington and therefore would be easier to kill there. By staging the spectacular assassination in the United States capital, Contreras provided the Chilean government with a reverse-psychology argument to reassure those already favorably disposed toward Pinochet of his government's innocence. Chile would not have commited the crime, the rationale went, because Letelier's death could only cast suspicion on and thereby discredit the Pinochet government at precisely the time it had chosen to launch a campaign to improve its human rights image, thus clearing the way for new loans. Contreras was ruthless, and the audacity of an assassination in the United States capital served to intimidate enemies and potential enemies. But besides these obvious explanations, evidence points to a more complex design.

Let us return to Romeral and Williams. Contreras twice invited CIA detection. He knew that the CIA had been informed of the Paraguay attempt, and he had been informed subsequently that the visa revocation meant that the Miami entry would also be detected. On his orders, his agents, traveling as the second Romeral-Williams team, informed CIA headquarters when they arrived in Washington.

Michael Townley, whose credibility we have generally accepted in our account, testified that he was not directly informed about the second Romeral and Williams mission, but that he heard through the DINA grapevine that Contreras ordered the second mission to serve as cover for the real assassination mission. The use of the same names was intended to account for the original Romeral and Williams that had caused so much alarm in Paraguay. Yet it seems illogical for a man plotting an assassination to call attention to the presence of his agents in the place and near the time of the crime he has ordered committed.

We offer the following interpretation of the purpose of the first and second Romeral and Williams missions. Contreras attempted by the mission to Paraguay to implicate the CIA in the operation to kill Letelier without necessarily telling the CIA the real purpose of the mission to Washington. He believed that having had suspicion cast upon it of collaboration in the mission, the CIA would make sure that any subsequent investigation would go nowhere. The purpose of the second so-called cover mission by agents using the Romeral and Williams name may have been to test the water to see if the CIA would act to prevent or control a covert operation in Washington. After informing the CIA of the agents' presence and seeing that nothing happened, Contreras gave the green light for the real assassination operation.

In defense statements that he made in Chile against his extradition Contreras insinuates that the hand of the CIA was present at every step of both Romeral and Williams operations—which he denies had anything to do with Letelier's death. He says the CIA's Chile representative, "whose name [he does] not recall," suggested the use of third-country passports and advised Contreras to postpone the first mission and to use the same names on the second, reactivated mission. Contreras also contends that another CIA official—again his memory for names fails him—carried the Romeral and Williams passports to the U.S. Consulate on August 17, 1976, and personally stamped in the visas.* Contreras says the purpose of both missions was to make contact with his "friend" General Walters of the CIA, who had promised to provide a list of United States congressmen favorable to the Chilean government.

Contreras' tactic seems to be a variation of the "greymail" used successfully in recent years by persons with CIA connections accused of crimes to discourage prosecution by warning that the crime itself was committed as part of a CIA operation or that the prosecution of the crime would bring CIA secrets to light.

How close Contreras' plan came to being accomplished we cannot know. In the final analysis he was wrong to believe that he could carry out an assassination in Washington with impunity. When he decided to murder Letelier in Washington, Contreras did not anticipate that the prosecution could concentrate on the felony of murder

---

*A former DINA officer said he received his visa in this way for a covert DINA operation to the United States in December 1976. A United States official, identified as a CIA officer, took the agent, former Patria y Libertad militant Anthal Lipthay, to the closed consulate on a Saturday afternoon to stamp in his visa so that he could leave the next day. The DINA agent's mission—which later became known to the FBI—involved posing as a leftist in order to elicit not-yet-published information from a *Wilmington News* journalist about a series of articles the journalist was writing on CIA contacts with Chilean rightists before and after the coup.

rather than the crime of political assassination and yet have an impact on a part of the Chilean government without bringing the government itself to fall. He understood neither the flexibility and subtlety of the United States political and legal system, nor the determination of Letelier's and Moffitt's friends and supporters throughout the world. He made a mistake and it cost him—his job and his rank.

As perplexing as Contreras' choice of Washington as the murder site is his selection of the American Michael Townley as the assassin.

The character of Michael Townley has attracted attention and provoked speculation from all those who followed the Letelier case. As if he had sprung from intrigue novels and spy movies, this enigmatic figure not only avoided heavy punishment, but managed to actually charm and impress some of his captors. He and his family received very special consideration and leniency from United States authorities. We have not seen any evidence that shows Townley to be a CIA agent, a mole, or a double agent. But the paradox of a confessed murderer establishing the limits of his own testimony while lounging casually in the courtroom corridors and freely using the prosecutor's telephone for international calls is bizarre. As a government witness, Townley was able to demand and receive immunity from prosecution for his wife and in effect extend his own immunity to crimes committed in foreign countries. Protection from investigative scrutiny extended to his father's activities on behalf of his foreign agent son. In mid-1978, shortly after Michael Townley had begun to cooperate with the FBI, the Miami police served a subpoena for Townley's bank records at his father's place of business, the South East First National Bank. The subpoenaed information would have revealed the joint Jay Vernon Townley–Andrés Wilson account. But within hours, Assistant U.S. Attorney Eugene Propper forced the subpoena to be withdrawn.

A close special relationship with United States officials has been a common thread running through Michael Townley's career as a terrorist, as we have traced it over a decade and a half of contacts with United States diplomats and CIA agents. Yet it was left to a pro-junta Chilean journalist to identify his photograph after it appeared in the press. We are also asked to believe that the CIA did not possess a photograph of Townley in its files.

At this writing neither the CIA, the State Department, nor the FBI has turned over to us any files that we requested under the Freedom of Information Act on the Letelier-Moffitt case. Officials of those agencies have also refused to answer some of our questions on the grounds of "national security."

What interest is served by concealing information about the FBI investigation of the case and CIA cooperation or noncooperation in it? What interest is served by withholding the routine paperwork documenting the handling of the Romeral and Williams visas and lookout notices, for example, and of the original communications between the CIA and State Department when the Chilean under-cover mission was first detected prior to the assassination? What national or security interests are served by hiding the CIA's and State's reasons for routinely allowing foreign secret police from re-pressive regimes to enter the United States? The answers are locked away—but not so that the Pinochets, Stroessners, and Contrerases of the world won't find out. They already know. But the United States public, whose vital interests are affected, are denied access and can learn very little about their own security apparatus.

PINOCHET had perpetrated a terrorist attack on United States soil, but the Carter administration did not see that as sufficiently serious to punish his regime. Pinochet got away with murder.

Orlando Letelier and Ronni Moffitt cannot be brought back to life. To that extent no justice is possible. But their murders did more than simply add two corpses to Pinochet's pile. They produced a qualitative change in the political climate. Owing in part to the publicity and the international political campaign that surrounded the investigation and trial, the Chilean military was forced to weaken its stranglehold and to depose Contreras and dissolve his DINA empire. The Chilean people began again in a limited way to practice politics, to organize opposition, to begin a cautious, determined cam-paign to restore democratic institutions. For the first time since the coup, students and workers demonstrated and organized strikes and women cried out against the disappearance of their husbands, sons, and brothers.

In November 1978, Isabel Letelier returned to Chile to sue for the restoration of her husband's citizenship, to demand that the Chilean court declare that the decree stripping Orlando of his birthright was illegal.

In Chile she repeated what she had said many times since the murders: that Pinochet himself had to have authorized the assassination. CNI/DINA agents openly surveilled her during public appearances and took photos of anyone she spoke with in the street. But she noticed that people didn't seem to be intimidated. They stopped, greeted her, expressed sympathy for her loss, praised her for her continuing battle for justice.

On her last night in Santiago, her legal work done, family visits paid, she attended a folk music concert. After intermission the master of ceremonies greeted the audience for the beginning of the second half of the concert. He introduced dignitaries from the audience. The German and Venezuelan ambassadors stood up to polite applause. "We are also honored tonight," the MC continued, "by the presence of the widow of Orlando Letelier, Isabel—" Thunderous applause broke out. It grew in volume and intensity as Isabel stood. The MC took the microphone and said, "Thank you, ladies and gentlemen. Now, please, let's begin the second part of the show." The applause continued, then assumed a rhythmic beat, *thump, thump, thump.* "Please, ladies and gentleman," the MC pleaded.

In the audience a man with a resonating bass voice chanted: "Compañero Orlando Letelier . . ."

The crowd responded: "¡Presente!"

The bass voice boomed: "Ahora . . ."

The crowd responded: "¡Y siempre!"

Index

About The Authors

JOHN DINGES grew up in Emmetsburg, Iowa. After graduating with a B.A. in English and philosophy from Loras College in Dubuque, he studied theology at the University of Innsbruck in Austria. He taught theology for several years and then changed vocations, starting as a copy editor at the *Des Moines Register and Tribune,* writing book and film reviews, and later becoming a reporter. At Stanford University he took a master's degree in Latin American studies, and subsequently, having been awarded an Inter-American Press Association Scholarship, he went to Chile to cover the Allende Revolution. A projected nine-months stay stretched into five and a half years as correspondent for *Time* magazine, the *Washington Post,* ABC Radio, and the *Latinamerica Press.* He has also published in *People, The Nation,* and *Inquiry* and coedited the volume *Toward a Theology of Christian Faith.*

SAUL LANDAU was born in New York City, graduated from the University of Wisconsin with a B.A. and M.A. in history, and did graduate work at Stanford and the University of California at Berkeley. He is the author, with Paul Jacobs, of *The New Radicals* and *To Serve the Devil.* During the past decade and a half, he has made some three dozen films that include features and documentaries. Among the latter are *Fidel, Brazil: Report on Torture* with Haskell Wexler, and *Paul Jacobs and the Nuclear Gang* with Jack Willis. He has won festival prizes at Ann Arbor, Cannes, Venice, Mannheim, and most recently, for *Paul Jacobs and the Nuclear Gang,* the George F. Polk award for investigative journalism as well as the Emmy. He is a fellow of the Institute for Policy Studies and has served as director of its Transnational Institute.